International Marketing and Management Research

Series Editor
Anshu Saxena Arora
School of Business and Public Administration
University of the District of Columbia
Washington, DC, USA

International Marketing and Management Research (IMMR) Series provides a forum for academics and professionals to share the latest developments and advances in knowledge and practice of global business and international management. The series is a uniquely positioned contribution of interrelated research papers across all business disciplines including: marketing, international business, strategy, digital strategy, organizational behavior and cross-cultural management, international marketing, international finance, global value chains, global supply chain management, sustainable innovations, e-business and e-commerce, social media, new product design and innovation, and business economics. Six volumes have been published under the IMMR series. Each research paper published in this series goes through a double-blind peer review process. Through the series, we examine the impact of cross-cultural issues, characteristics, and challenges with regard to global and sustainable business innovations; institutional and regulatory factors on international marketing and management issues; and the effects of institutional changes on global businesses with regard to both traditional and digital worlds. IMMR series fosters the exchange of ideas on a range of important international subjects, provides stimulus for research, and strengthens the development of international perspectives. The international perspective is further enhanced by the geographical spread of the contributors.

More information about this series at
http://www.palgrave.com/gp/series/14845

George Z. Peng

Toward Behavioral Transaction Cost Economics

Theoretical Extensions and an Application to the Study of MNC Subsidiary Ownership

palgrave
macmillan

George Z. Peng
University of Regina
Regina, SK, Canada

ISSN 2662-8546 ISSN 2662-8554 (electronic)
International Marketing and Management Research
ISBN 978-3-030-46877-4 ISBN 978-3-030-46878-1 (eBook)
https://doi.org/10.1007/978-3-030-46878-1

This Palgrave Macmillan imprint is published by the registered company Springer Nature Switzerland AG
The registered company address is: Gewerbestrasse 11, 6330 Cham, Switzerland

To my wife Alisha H. Zhang
and my daughters Julia Z. Peng & Joanne Z. Peng

Acknowledgments

This book is the outcome of a personal 'eight-year struggle', an academic journey of 'self-enquiry', both in a personal and in an organizational sense. Fortunately, I was not alone on the journey, and I have many people to thank. I begin with my Ph.D. supervisor and mentor, Paul W. Beamish. The book would have been impossible had I not been accorded the access to his expertise as a prestigious scholar. That said, I would stress that all errors, flaws, omissions, contradictions, offenses, and opinions expressed in this book remain the sole responsibility of the author.

The book has gone through a metamorphosis from a faint idea to various versions of a working paper, and then, after significant expansion and restructuring, to its current book form. Valuable inputs and comments on primitive working paper versions from Paul W. Beamish, Christine M. K. Chan, Shih-Fen Chen, Derek Lehmberg, and Alain Verbeke are gratefully acknowledged. The most recent version of the working paper was presented at the 2018 Academy of International Business Southeast Asia Regional (AIBSEAR) Conference in Hong Kong and received a Best Paper Award. I am grateful for the selection committee for having an 'open-minded eye' for new ideas. I would appreciate the helpful comments from Bradley Barnes, Oded Shenkar, and other conference participants.

For the book version, I would first thank Marcus Ballenger, the Commissioning Editor at Palgrave. It was Marcus who made me aware of the Pivot format. Marcus also guided and encouraged me through the publishing process, from initial peer review, through contract signing to final publication. During the pre-publication peer review process, Anshu Arora, the Series Editor, offered constructive feedback that led to significant improvements to the book, and I express my sincere gratitude for her. I should also thank the anonymous reviewer who offered beneficial suggestions during the initial proposal review process. Thanks also go to Sophia Siegler, Susan Westendorf, and Ashwini Elango at Palgrave. I also would like to gratefully acknowledge the spiritual power that I gained from reading many books by or about the Tripitaka Master Xuanzang and Bhagavan Sri Ramana Maharshi. A Dean's Research Grant received from the Paul J. Hill School of Business at University of Regina in 2012 is acknowledged.

Last but not least, I owe so much to my wife, Alisha H. Zhang. She has been a guiding force since I first met her, and I can always feel her strong spirit and determination. A strong woman indeed! I am grateful for my two daughters, Julia Z. Peng and Joanne Z. Peng, for being a source of constant motivation and joy in my life. As the proverb goes, 'the child is the father of the man'. I have learned a lot from them while watching them grow up. To the three women, I dedicate this book.

Contents

Abbreviations

CD	Cultural Distance
CR	Critical Realism
NEA	National Ethical Attitude
OLI	Ownership-Location-Internalization
ROT	Real Options Theory
TCE	Transaction Cost Economics
VAB	Value-Attitude-Behavior

List of Figures

List of Tables

CHAPTER 1

Is Transaction Cost Economics Behavioral?

1.1 Introduction

Williamson's (1975, 1985) transaction cost economics (TCE) has established itself at the center of organizational economics[1] (Groenewegen 1996; Mahoney 2004; Moe 1984) as a dominant lens to view organizational boundary decisions (Parmigiani 2007; Williamson 1981). Contrary to the neoclassical theory of the firm as a production function with zero transaction cost, TCE considers the firm as a governance structure with positive transaction cost (Williamson 1998). Based on three 'behavioral' assumptions (perceived opportunism ***controllability***, bounded rationality, and risk neutrality)[2] and three transaction characteristics (asset specificity, uncertainty, and transaction frequency), TCE advocates that organizations choose governance structures (such as MNC subsidiary ownership) that minimize transaction costs (Williamson 1975, 1985; Zhao et al. 2004). TCE has a broad scope (Rindfleisch and Heide 1997), applicable to any issue that arises as or can be formulated as a contracting problem (Williamson 1998). Thus, TCE has wielded its influence far beyond the pales of economics into strategic management and business research in general and international business in particular (David and Han 2004; Hennart 2010; Williamson 2005; Zhao et al. 2004). Consequently, there exists an awe-inspiring literature (e.g., Macher and Richman 2008; Martins et al. 2010; Masten 2016; Shelanski and Klein 1995), both in theoretical conceptualization and in empirical testing.

G. Z. Peng, *Toward Behavioral Transaction Cost Economics*,
International Marketing and Management Research,
https://doi.org/10.1007/978-3-030-46878-1_1

TCE's achievement has been acknowledged by its proponents and not overlooked by its critics. Williamson (1999b: 1092) deems TCE to be 'an empirical success story', a view echoed by Macher and Richman (2008).

The rise of Williamsonian TCE was a result of continued criticism of the neoclassical economics since the 1950s and 1960s for its unrealistic assumptions such as utility/profit maximization and perfect rationality (perfect information) (Hardt 2009). The same criticism had also been leveled at organization theory (Cyert and March 1963). It was in this context that scholars of the Carnegie School of behavioral research introduced some more realistic psychological and behavioral assumptions which made the development of behavioral economics and behavioral theories of the firm possible[3] (Augier and March 2008a; Hardt 2009; Williamson 1996b). Lying at 'the intersection of economics and organization' (Williamson 1990: 117), TCE's strategy was to combine the behavioral assumptions borrowed from the behavioral organizational theory literature with the quantitative and marginal analysis of neoclassical economics (Allen 1999; Hardt 2009; Williamson 1967). In a sense, what Williamson aspired to achieve is something which can be called a theory of behavioral organizational economics, which applies behavioral economics to organizations and enriches and contextualizes behavioral economics by decision-making and problem-solving processes of managers in organizations (Camerer and Malmendier 2007). The success of such a theory will depend first of all on whether its behavioral assumptions are genuinely applied to organizations.[4] Nevertheless, Williamson provides no firm answer to this question. Despite its borrowed behavioral assumptions, Williamson (2002) admits that TCE is different from the behavioral economics program that flourished at Carnegie in the late 1950s/early 1960s and is 'more neoclassical'. But at the same time, he also seems to suggests that his version of TCE is behavioral by saying that TCE 'nevertheless relates to the Carnegie project in many respects' (Williamson 2002) and can trace its roots in the Carnegie School of behavioral research (Williamson 1996b, 2002).

The ambiguous treatment of behavioral assumptions in TCE has attracted considerable debate and criticism (e.g., Foss 2003a; Foss and Klein 2010; Ghoshal and Moran 1996; Pessali 2006). While such debate and criticism contribute to improving understanding of TCE, they tend to raise rather than answer questions. As such, multiple fundamental questions remain gaping—Can TCE be regarded as a behavioral theory merely based on its invocation of some 'behavioral' assumptions? What causes the serious conflation among opportunism, bounded rationality and uncertainty? Is opportunism a necessary assumption in TCE? Are opportunism and bounded rationality in TCE values, attitudes, or behaviors? How to model bounded rationality? Should managers focus on opportunism or bounded rationality?—While these questions are important for TCE-based research, scholars have been asking these questions in a sporadic way and on an on-and-off basis. Considering the striking contrast between these gaping questions and the self-proclaimed 'success story' (Williamson 1999b: 1092), we deem that a wholesale assessment of these questions would be useful for TCE, particularly at its current mature stage (Bunge 1967), which also is a stage of theoretical stagnation (Furubotn and Richter 2010). While it has long been pointed out that TCE 'needs to be refined and extended...qualified and focused......[and] tested empirically'[5] (Williamson 1992), *fundamental* theoretical extensions to TCE are rare, even though there have been efforts to link it to other theories (e.g., Foss and Foss 2004; Mahoney and Qian 2013; Martinez and Dacin 1999). The current book intends to be such a fundamental undertaking, and the success of which can only be achieved by standing on the shoulders of giants and with the benefit of hindsight.

This book contends that the aforementioned questions arise from TCE's tacit positivist approach, which is inadequate to an innately behavioral process of organizational decision-making. They boil largely down to one overarching objection: while TCE invokes some behavioral assumptions, it is still 'stealthily' committed to the maximization and rationality assumptions in neoclassical economics (Earl 1988; Sent 2004) rather than satisficing and bounded rationality (Williamson 1996b),[6] and is positivist and deductivist in nature (Godfrey and Hill 1995; Ingham 1996; Pratten 1997). It is this tacit positivist approach that prevents TCE from genuinely engaging with its behavioral assumptions and achieving its goal of becoming a behavioral organizational theory. A positivist cart is not capable of carrying much of the weight of explanation in a behavioral theory of the firm which focuses on bounded rationality and evolutionary considerations (Milgrom and Roberts 1988: 450; Foss and Klein 2010). We submit that, in order for TCE to become a truly behavioral theory, it has to be based on ontologically deep philosophical foundations. While TCE claims to be a behavioral theory (Williamson 1996b), its behavioral agenda has not been implemented in a behavioral way due to its shallow ontological depth (see Chapter 2). But before we embark on the shift from the traditional TCE to a behavioral TCE, an evaluation of whether the traditional TCE is behavioral should first be performed. For this purpose, it is necessary to explain the need for behavioral theories and to identify evaluation criteria.

1.2 Why Behavioral Reasoning of the Firm?

Cyert and March's 1963 book, *A Behavioral Theory of the Firm*, has had an extraordinary influence on organizational theory and strategic management. Its concepts and assumptions have become foundational to any behaviorally-oriented scientific inquiry into organizational phenomena (Gavetti et al. 2012). As the title of the book suggests, it is 'a', not 'the', behavioral theory of the firm. Today, there exist a large variety of behavioral theories held together by the ideas which originated from the book.[7] Fundamentally, Cyert and March brought the behavioral reasoning into the study of organizations.

Before the advent of the behavioral thinking, the study of organizations followed the assumptions of traditional economic theory that economic agents are utility maximizers who have perfect information and operate in a realm of full rationality. The conventional organizational analysis had an economy-level focus on price and quantity and tended to prefer aggregate outcome explanations rather than process (Cyert and March 1963). This was not a surprise, though. It was only after World War II that business schools had started to see its development and professionalization (Augier 2013), and thus it was natural to borrow from economics for tools considering that business firms are the major value-creating agents in the economy. Nevertheless, such an approach is beset with contradictions, even though it may still provide some useful macro-level insights (Greve and Argote 2015).

First, there was a level of analysis issue. Theories developed to answer macro-level economic questions are not appropriate for providing micro-level predictions and process explanations (Gavetti et al. 2012): 'there are a number of interesting questions relating specifically to firm behavior that the [conventional theory of the firm] cannot answer and was not developed to answer, especially with regard to the internal allocation of resources and the process of setting prices and outputs' (Cyert and March 1963: 16).

Second, there was a focus issue. The conventional theory of the firm focused externally on 'the economy' rather than internally on 'the economic agent' (Barros 2010). Such a lack of internal focus resulted in insufficient attention to firm strategy and decision-making process. Under rationality and maximization assumptions of traditional economics, the rational behavior depends upon the economic agents only in their goals. Given these goals, the rationality of behavior is determined entirely by the characteristics of the environment in which it takes place (Simon 1976). Decision, however, depends not only on the objective characteristics of the external environment, but also on the decision-maker's cognitive limits (i.e., bound rationality) and the resulting heuristic process that is used to reach the decision (March 1978; Simon 1979). Omission of the decision-maker can lead to underspecified model of firm behavior (Aharoni et al. 2011).

Third, there was a legitimacy issue of business schools. Ever since their birth, they have been under constant pressures for legitimacy (Alajoutsijärvi et al. 2015). They had to conform to the pressure for scientific rigor which was found in some more established fields like economics, and to adopt mimetic practices. However, such practices raised the questions of whether business schools add any value to management practice in addition to economics, and whether the quest for legitimacy have led to 'managerially irrelevant research' (Alajoutsijärvi et al. 2015). Rationalization and scientification have called the legitimacy of business schools into question: 'managerial practice is seldom conducted under the conditions of perfect information that we presume in our theories and classroom' (Spender 2007: 33).

It was against this backdrop that Cyert and March (1963) introduced some more realistic behavioral and psychological assumptions into the economic theory of the firm (Augier and March 2008a). They challenged the rationality and maximization assumptions of traditional economics and sought to 'develop an empirically relevant, process-oriented, general theory of decision making by a business firm' (Cyert and March 1963: 3). In so doing, the black box of organizational decision-making processes can be opened up, observed, and studied (Augier 2013; Gavetti et al. 2012), and certainly yielding empirically relevant insights into how firm behavior are shaped by boundedly rational cognitive processes (Greve and Argote 2015).

1.3 Characteristics of Behavioral Theories of the Firm

The large variety of behavioral theories share a common foundation in ideas of organizational decision-making process and individual bounded rationality (Gavetti et al. 2012). In order for a theory to be considered as behavioral, it should meet the following criteria (Cyert and March 1963; Gavetti et al. 2012; Greve and Argote 2015). While these criteria are not exhaustive, suffice it to say that they are enough for us to use in the evaluation of whether TCE is behavioral in Sect. 1.5.

1. It must focus on the 'psychology of human choice' and be concerned with bounded rationality and how it is affected (Simon 1957, 1961) because 'a realistic account of bounded rationality is pivotal to grasping the behavioral essence of organizations' (Gavetti et al. 2012: 4; Argote and Greve 2007; Cyert and March 1963). Bounded rationality should be the main explanatory variable,[8] although not the only one (Barros 2010), and be explicitly modeled. Relatedly, a behavioral theory should focus not on maximization but on satisficing, which is a concept vis-à-vis external environment. As to be discussed in Sect. 4.5.1 and Chapter 7, bounded rationality, when joined with psychological biases and organizational learning, is an ecological rationality, which emphasizes the fit between the mind's heuristics and the structure of the environment. A behavioral theory becomes behavioral due to the need to adapt, and accordingly, ecological rationality is at its core (Potts 2017). As an extension, a behavioral theory is an evolutionary theory after the introduction of ecological rationality. It is well-known that Nelson and Winter's (1982) evolutionary theory of economic change is constructed atop of Cyert and March's (1963) behavioral theory of the firm, and that the evolutionary theory emphasizes ecological rationality since it regards organizational decision-making process as a set of interdependent routines that are adaptive to performance feedback (Nelson and Winter 1982).
2. It should be built on observation of decision-making processes within firms. Intra-organizational decision-making theories based on human behavior but equilibrium ideas are not behavioral since

they fail the process part of the definition.[9] For example, agency theory is not behavioral (Greve and Argote 2015).

3. Behavior is goal-oriented (but not goal-driven). This is directly related to the two criteria above. While goal definition is the first step in organizational decision-making process (Douma and Schreuder 1992: 66), a behavioral theory should tolerate goal ambiguity (Dew et al. 2008). The 'goal' in Cyert and March (1963) was developed based on a political conception in order to explain the behavior of established firms within well-defined environments (Augier and Sarasvathy 2004; Dew et al. 2008). Behavior based on such a conceptualization of goal is more administrative than 'behavioral', by which we mean behavior affected by human psychology. From a behavioral theory perspective, goals are not necessarily defined a priori but rather they emerge within organizational action processes (Dew et al. 2008; Joas and Beckert 2001). [This is to say goals should be understood in the sense of judgmental rationality of in critical realism (CR) (see Chapter 2)].
4. More accurately speaking, a behavioral theory should focus on effectuation rather than prediction (Dew et al. 2008; Karami 2020), since the former is based on a goal-oriented but means-driven logic (Sarasvathy and Simon 2000; Sarasvathy 2001, 2003).[10,11] Effectuation is an evolutionary approach associated with goal adjustment based on performance feedback and ecological rationality and is particularly relevant to situations with high uncertainty. In effectuation, goal-setting is a process based on initial prereflective aspirations that operate in the action situation in an iterative manner, rather than takes place as a cognitive act prior to action based on prediction (Joas and Beckert 2001: 273). For this, psychological processes have to be moved to the front seat. At the beginning of an action process, organizations have to effectuate based on available means because goals are mostly vaguely understood. Goals become more specific once organizations have a better sense of the possible means to achieve the ends, and even new goals will emerge on the basis of newly available and understood means. The more concrete understanding of goals or their changes will in turn shape new perspective on available means. Because this reflective and iterative process between ends

and means structures action (Joas and Beckert 2001), effectuation renders TCE behavioral[12] (see more in Point 2 in Sect. 1.5, Endnote 12 and Chapters 2–5).

5. Decision-makers use problem frames (gain frame or loss frame) in decision-making and adjust their risk-taking propensity according to performance relative to aspiration levels. Such frames are a form of cognitive heuristics which often bias decision-making. Although this criterion was not part of the original formulation of a behavioral theory of the firm (Greve and Argote 2015), it has since become central in part as a result of cross-fertilization with prospect theory (Argote and Greve 2007; Greve and Argote 2015; March and Shapira 1992). While there is a wide array of behavioral theories based on bounded rationality, prospect theory (Kahneman and Tversky 1979) has probably had more impact than any other on economic research (Shiller 1999). The majority of the recent organizational research that adopts a behavioral approach has been based on prospect theory (Aharoni et al. 2011).
6. A behavioral theory of the firm should see organizational learning as a central and integral part of the decision-making process (Augier and March 2008a; Cyert and March 1963; Gavetti et al. 2012; Greve and Argote 2015; Levitt and March 1988; Selten 2001). Learning is particularly relevant to a behavioral theory since it plays a central role in reducing psychological biases in decision-making (Rabin 1998). As such, a behavioral theory is also a theory of learning, and organizational decision-making process can be viewed as a sequence of adaptive decisions driven by organizational learning.

   In particular, a behavioral theory should treat the firm as a learning organization (Penrose 1959) or explanans (cf. Point 12 below), and Penrosean learning should be at its core. Only when a learning mentality is adopted can bounded rationality be taken seriously vis-à-vis external environment and becomes an ecological rationality. But in order for learning to be genuinely considered, the black box of organizational 'self' has to be opened since Penrosean learning is fundamentally *manas*-centric (see Chapter 4).
7. A behavioral theory of the firm should be committed to the management of uncertainty (Bromiley et al. 2001; Cyert and March 1963). This point is closely related to effectuation. Cyert

and March (1963) first introduced the term 'uncertainty avoidance' to describe how organizations 'avoid' uncertainty in their environments by effectuating (solving immediate problems) rather than predicting (imposing plans and structure and developing long-term strategies) (Mootz 2013). This is because that uncertainty limits economic agents' ability to predict using quantitative analysis (Kang et al. 2018). As such, uncertainty in a behavioral theory should not be aligned with the rationality and maximization assumptions of traditional economics, where analyses are undertaken under the assumptions of complete markets and perfect information. Instead, uncertainty in a behavioral theory should be based on perception, which relates to effectuation process rather than decision outcomes or choices (Alessandri 2008; Alessandri et al. 2004).

8. A behavioral theory of the firm should consider the *fundamental* role of various types of distance, including cultural distance (CD). In addition, the focus should be placed on how they give rise to psychological biases rather than on how they affect information processing and cost in a rational, positivist way. In a sense, a behavioral theory cannot be 'behavioral' in the absence of distance (see Chapters 4 and 7). This is because they are intimately linked to bounded rationality faced by organizations, particularly multinational corporations (MNCs) (Verbeke 2013; Verbeke and Kano 2012). Simon (1959) suggested that distance exacerbates the bounded rationality problem. In international business, these distances are generally considered as 'bounded rationality challenges' (Verbeke and Kano 2012: 142).
9. A behavioral theory of the firm should link models of the firm closely to empirical observations. For this, empirical methods which can accommodate organizational decision processes should be adopted. These may include experiments, case studies, simulations, and regression methods (Gavetti et al. 2012). When regression methods are used, longitudinal and even-history data should be used. A behavioral theory is by definition temporal.
10. Theories that are phrased at very high levels of analysis are not behavior because they fail the process part of the definition of a behavioral theory of the firm (Greve and Argote 2015). A behavioral theory should focus on 'the economic agent' rather than 'the economy' (Barros 2010).

11. A behavioral theory of the firm should be a self-conscious one. In the case of TCE, it was meant to be a behavioral theory for its being more self-conscious. Williamson (1981: 553) suggests that in order for a theory to be considered behavioral, it needs to pay 'more self-conscious attention to "human nature as we know it"', and he believes that TCE's opportunism and bounded rationality assumptions 'add realism and distinguish [TCE] from neoclassical economics'. Williamson (1985: 387) claims that '[a]s compared with other approaches to the study of economic organization, transaction cost economics ... is more ***self-conscious*** about its behavioral assumptions' [italic added]. As such, a behavioral theory of the firm should be a consciousness-based view of organizing (Turunen 2015).
12. To summarize the aforementioned points, a behavioral theory of the firm should treat the firm as an explanans instead of an explanandum (Mäki 2004). Only after the mentality shift from treating the firm as an explanandum to treating the firm as an explanans, can the 'dots' described in the previous points be connected. When the firm is treated as an explanandum, the focus is on the firm itself rather than its relationship to the external world and thus its value creation potential and evolutionary fit based on ecological rationality. Or in other words, a behavioral theory needs to shift from an internal orientation of the explanandum-oriented approach to an external orientation of the explanans-oriented approach (Wright et al. 1991).
13. Related to Point 12 above, Williamson's claim that TCE is a behavioral theory (Williamson 1985, 1991) suffers from a contradiction: if a theory is behavioral, it has to concern itself with transaction value rather than transaction cost and the rationality of interest should be ecological rationality rather than processing bounded rationality (cf. Subsect. 4.5.1 and Sect. 7.2). A theory which is obsessed with transaction cost minimization cannot be behavioral because it requires a closed system wherein firms have no room to 'behave'.

Considering the number of criteria, we summarize them in Table 1.1. In this table, we also include the TCE realities and theoretical obstacles which prevent TCE from being behavioral, as to be discussed in Sects. 1.5 and 1.6.

Table 1.1 Behavioral criteria, TCE realities, and theoretical obstacles

Criteria of behavioral theories...	*Traditional TCE realities*	*Theoretical obstacles*
1. Focus on bounded rationality or the 'psychology of human choice', and how it is affected (Simon 1957, 1961); bounded rationality becomes ecological rationality	• Bounded rationality treated rhetorically as an abstract background condition rather than a variable • TCE was not theoretically and empirically committed to bounded rationality (Foss 2003a, b; Ketokivi and Mahoney 2016) • TCE not explicit about how to model bounded rationality (Foss 2003b) and thus does not explicitly model bounded rationality • TCE considers only processing bounded rationality but ignores psychological bounded rationality (Foss and Weber 2016b) • Ecological rationality not considered	• The conflation of value-attitude-behavior • The conflation of self-mind-brain • Shallow ontology • Bounded rationality treated as a black box rather than a process vis-à-vis external environment; as such, ecological rationality could not be considered
2. Focus on internal decision-making processes of how bounded rationality is affected instead of equilibrium contacting; for this to happen, ecological rationality is fundamental	• TCE is a theory of outcomes based on equilibrium contracting, not decision-making processes (Dow 1987; Foster 2000)	• Rational treatment of bounded rationality (substantive rationality assumption) • Equilibrium analysis • Positivist philosophical position

(continued)

1.4 Opposing Views About Whether TCE Is Behavioral

Williamson claims that TCE was built with an explicit aspiration to bridge economics and organizations using a behavioral approach (Williamson

Table 1.1 (continued)

Criteria of behavioral theories…	*Traditional TCE realities*	*Theoretical obstacles*
3. Behavior is not goal-driven but goal-oriented (focuses on effectuation rather than prediction)	• TCE is goal-driven • The goal in TCE is externally set and deterministic (Simon 1976: 66) • Deterministic determination of rational behavior • goal-setting takes place as a cognitive act prior to action rather than perception in the action process (Joas and Beckert 2001)	• Rational treatment of bounded rationality (substantive rationality assumption) • Equilibrium analysis • Positivist philosophical position
4. Focus NOT on prediction but on effectuation	• TCE is particularly committed to the positivist tradition: It emphasizes 'making predictions and inviting empirical tests' (Williamson 2008: 254)	• Positivist philosophical position
5. Consideration of problem frames based on prospect theory (risk non-neutrality)	• TCE assumes risk neutrality of decision-makers (Chiles and McMackin 1996; Martynov and Schepker 2017) • TCE does not consider problem frames (gain frame or loss frame)	• Risk neutrality goes in tandem with TCE's processing bounded rationality assumption (Martynov and Schepker 2017) • Risk is perceptual and inherently subjective (Martynov and Schepker 2017; Yates and Stone 1992) • Risk perceptions are a product of psychological bounded rationality (Sunstein 2006)

(continued)

Table 1.1 (continued)

Criteria of behavioral theories...	*Traditional TCE realities*	*Theoretical obstacles*
6. Organizational learning as a central and integral part of the decision-making process, which treats the firm as an learning organization (Penrose 1959) or explanans (cf. Point 12)	• TCE makes insufficient link with learning • TCE focuses on an ergodic exogenous environment, learning about which can be regarded as information cost • Learning' in TCE is 'procedural' rather than behavioral • There is no learning about the psychological part of the 'self' in TCE • TCE does not say much about how agents may reduce bounded rationality since bounded rationality is treated as a constraint (or black box)	• The black box of organizational 'self' is not opened; cognition-centric rather than *manas*-centric (Chapter 4) • Penrosean (1959) learning is fundamentally *manas*-centric • The firm is treated as an explanandum rather than explanans (cf. Point 12) • TCE's primary focus on processing bounded rationality (or cognition) and neglect of psychology (or *manas*) • Learning in a behavioral sense should focus on the reduction of psychological biases in decision-making (Rabin 1998) • TCE focuses on the control of opportunism and regards bounded rationality as an abstract constraint (Foss and Weber 2016b; Verbeke and Greidanus 2009; Williamson 1985: 8), or black box

(continued)

1985, 1991). Nevertheless, there exist opposing views about whether TCE is behavioral (Kwon and Silva 2020), even though TCE departs from assumptions of orthodox economics by adopting some 'behavioral' assumptions such as opportunism and bounded rationality (Williamson

Table 1.1 (continued)

Criteria of behavioral theories...	*Traditional TCE realities*	*Theoretical obstacles*
7. Commitment to the management of uncertainty (Bromiley et al. 2001; Cyert and March 1963) through effectuation (Mootz 2013)	• TCE reduces uncertainty into deterministic complexity and focuses on predicting governance structures in a closed system • Uncertainty in TCE relates to decision outcomes or choices rather than decision process • TCE is not committed to the management of uncertainty through effectuation but to the control of opportunism through prediction	• Positivist stance in a closed system • Conflation of uncertainty with opportunism and bounded rationality • Uncertainty is not based on perception due to TCE's rationality and maximization assumptions • Uncertainty is not conceptualized based on controllability • Uncertainty is not compatible with prediction in TCE • Uncertainty limits economic agents' ability to predict and induces them to effectuate
8. Consider the fundamental role of various types of distances in giving rise to psychological biases and thus affecting bounded rationality. A theory cannot be behavioral in the absence of distance	• TCE does not consider distances • While cultural distance and some other types of distance are considered in international business, they are treated rhetorically in a positivist way as 'black boxes' (see Chapter 7). The psychological biases that result from these distances are not considered	• The TCE setting of single closed system • The positivist, rationalist and static stance adopted in MNC theories • The conflation of self-mind-brain (Chapter 4)

(continued)

1975, 1985). Williamson himself claims that his version of TCE is behavioral, and traces its roots back in the Carnegie School of behavioral research (Williamson 1996b). Herbert Simon was not consistent in his

Table 1.1 (continued)

Criteria of behavioral theories...	*Traditional TCE realities*	*Theoretical obstacles*
9. Link models of the firm closely to empirical method which can accommodate organizational decision processes	• Models in TCE empirical literature are largely based on cross-sectional data which cannot closely reflect organizational decision-making processes which are inherently temporal	• Equilibrium contacting mentality
10. Focus on 'the economic agent' rather than 'the economy' (Barros 2010)	• TCE has been applied at three micro-analytic levels of analysis (Williamson 1981) • All the three levels of analysis focus on the economic agent rather than the economy (Williamson 1985)	• (Not applicable)
11. It should be self-conscious	• TCE failed to become a genuinely self-conscious theory of the firm. • The black box of consciousness is not opened up	• The conflation of self-mind-brain • Collapsed ontology of positivism
12. Treat the firm as an explanans rather than an explanandum (Mäki 2004)	• The firm is still largely treated as a black box, at least in a vertical sense (Mäki 2004) • The opening of the neoclassical black box of the firm is accompanied by a switch of the box from that of explanans to that of explanandum (Mäki 2004)	• TCE is not self-conscious due to collapsed ontology and the conflation of self-mind-brain • Vertical de-isolation not taken to its end (Mäki 2004)

(continued)

view, though, and only sometimes counts TCE as belonging to behavioral economics (Simon 1987).

Nevertheless, there are impassioned opponents who are reluctant to count TCE as behavioral (e.g., Earl 1988; Sent 2004). Labeling

Table 1.1 (continued)

Criteria of behavioral theories...	*Traditional TCE realities*	*Theoretical obstacles*
13. Geared toward transaction value	• Obsessed with transaction cost • Transaction costs are indeterminate due to the need for the firm to effectuate • It is desirable to take a transaction value perspective, because transaction value is determinable based on ecological rationality in a process	• See above

(*Source* Author's own creation/summary)

Williamson a pseudo-behavioralist because of his inclinations for maintaining constrained maximization,[6] Earl made an impassioned plea for not counting Williamson among the partisans of behavioral economics (Sent 2004). This is because, while ***nominally*** adopting the bounded rationality assumption, TCE continues to rely on rationality (Furubotn and Richter 2010), albeit a supposedly weaker version (North 1978). In fact, the 'rational' treatment of bounded rationality in TCE has long been pointed out. In a review paper of Cyert and March (1963), Winter noted that Williamson's chapter in it was different from others and focused on 'a model of "rational managerial behavior" that, in terms of method, is much closer to orthodox theory than it is to the decision-process analysis in the rest of the book' (Winter 1964: 147).

Considering the split opinions about whether TCE is behavioral, we think an evaluation should be made against the criteria presented in the previous section. The majority of existing studies tacitly considered TCE as a behavioral theory merely for its so-called behavioral assumptions. We think that this innocent practice contributed to the stagnation of TCE research.

1.5 An Evaluation of Whether TCE Is Behavioral

While TCE claims that it is built on three *behavioral* assumptions (opportunism, bounded rationality, and risk neutrality), it does not necessarily become behavioral merely by invoking these assumptions (Foss 2003a; Pessali 2006). It has to meet the criteria presented in Sect. 1.3. Below, we evaluate TCE against those criteria. Please note that opportunism is not one of the criteria. But since TCE includes it as a necessary or 'essential' assumption, we evaluate how TCE treats it as well at the end of this section. Consistent with the views of many scholars (e.g., Love 1995), we do not think opportunism is a necessary assumption in TCE. We leave the discussion of this point to Sect. 2.4.

1. TCE treats bounded rationality rhetorically as an abstract background condition rather than a variable (let alone a process) and was not theoretically and empirically committed to it (Foss 2003a, b; Ketokivi and Mahoney 2016). Williamson refrains from being explicit about how to model bounded rationality (Foss 2003b) and thus does not explicitly model bounded rationality. In TCE, '[e]conomizing on bounded rationality takes two forms. One concerns decision processes and the other involves governance structures' (Williamson 1985: 46). TCE is not concerned with the former where organizations use problem-solving heuristics in a process manner. Instead, it uses bounded rationality as a rhetorical background assumption (Foss 2003b) in explaining incomplete contracts and thus concerns the choice between governance structures. Under such circumstances, it is not necessary to model bounded rationality itself, even though it is still important to assume its existence as a background condition (Foss 2003b; Williamson 1985).

   Consequently, empirical tests on bounded rationality are lacking (Aharoni et al. 2011; David and Han 2004; John and Reve 2010; Tsang 2006). TCE does not consider the significant variance in bounded rationality across individuals and firms, thus ignoring systematic biases in decision-making due to bounded rationality (Argyres and Mayer 2007; Cyert and March 1963). Relatedly, due to its tangential commitment to bounded rationality, the setup of TCE is in fact based on maximization rather than satisficing (Williamson 1996b).

TCE does not focus on the 'psychology of human choice' and was not concerned with the psychological side of bounded rationality and how it is affected (Simon 1957, 1961). Bounded rationality is defined as 'human behavior [that] is intendedly rational but only limitedly so' (Simon 1961: 24), and there are two types of it. One is processing bounded rationality, which concerns 'processing capacity limitations'; and the other is psychological bounded rationality,[13] which refers to 'cognitive economizing in the form of heuristics and cognitive biases' [and emotional biases][14] which can systematically distort the way information is perceived and processed (Foss and Weber 2016b: 62; Simon 1997a, b). TCE holds that 'the principal ramification of bounded rationality for the study of economic organization is that all complex contracts are unavoidably incomplete' (Williamson 2002: 423). Thus, TCE considers primarily processing bounded rationality to explain incomplete contracting (Foss 2003b; Foss and Weber 2016b; Tsang 2006). To many, bounded rationality in TCE is still rationality since it can simply be considered as positive information costs.[15] While Williamson (2002) believes that considering only processing bounds does not prevent TCE from predicting governance choices, not considering psychological bounds disregards the extensive prospect theory-based literature which suggests that human decision-making is significantly affected by perceptual biases (Kahneman and Tversky 1979; Tversky and Kahneman 1981), thus resulting in a lack of behavioral realism of TCE literature (Augier and March 2008b; Simon 1997a). Because 'a realistic account of bounded rationality is pivotal to grasping the behavioral essence of organizations' (Gavetti et al. 2012: 4), the way in which TCE approaches bounded rationality falls short of that of a behavioral theory.

2. TCE is a theory of efficiency outcomes, not decision-making processes (Dow 1987; Foster 2000). For each transaction cost analysis, it uses 'equilibrium contracting' or 'comparative static equilibration' in its core of theorizing and assumes rationality (Folta 1998; Foss 1994; Foster 2000; Pagano 1992; Williamson 1988, 1991), thus 'making equilibrium appear inevitable under conditions that assure the achievement of minimum transaction costs' (Slater and Spencer 2000: 73). The ongoing 'process' of disequilibrium that arises from external environment may change

transaction costs, but such external shocks are by definition outside the theoretical core for the current transaction cost analysis. Even if environmental changes can be taken into account in the next round of analysis, the analysis again is a static equilibrium-based one. Indeed, the external environmental 'processes' are not real processes because they are random.[16] As such, transaction cost economics is ill-adapted to situations where governance choices are sequentially linked (Barney and Lee 2000). A theory built on observation of decision-making process should be concerned with the internal process of how bounded rationality is affected by learning (Simon 1957, 1961).

3. TCE is goal-driven. TCE aims to establish optimal governance structures which can minimize transaction cost based on some so-called behavioral assumptions and transaction characteristics. Nevertheless, the goal in TCE is deterministic and is not behavioral due to its rational treatment of bounded rationality, equilibrium analysis, and positivist philosophical position. In addition, under TCE's substantive rationality[17] assumption, 'the rationality of behavior depends upon the actor in only a single respect - his goals. Given these goals, the rational behavior is determined entirely by the characteristics of the environment in which it takes place' (Simon 1976: 66).

   Due to this external setting of goals and deterministic determination of rational behavior, goal-setting in TCE takes place as a cognitive act prior to action rather than in the behavioral process itself. TCE does not require the reflective and iterative behavioral process between means and ends, and thus is not inclined for behavioral advances. In contrast, effectuation theory is conducive to a behavioral approach because it focuses on the individual level of analysis and uses a psychological lens (Alvarez et al. 2016; Karami 2020). It is goal-oriented but means-driven, thus allowing goals to emerge in the action process. Such a process is inherently behavioral because it focuses on perception in the action process rather than cognitive act prior to action (Joas and Beckert 2001: 273).

4. Due to its positivist philosophy, TCE focuses on making predictions (Williamson 2008). Williamson (2008) concurs with the positive tradition espoused by Friedman (1953) and supported the view that 'the primary criterion for judging the merit of any

model is its capacity for generating correct and substantively important predictions' (Reder 2003: 528). Thus, effectuation does not even register on the radar of TCE. Even if TCE has difficulties in explaining the initial starting reference point in the determination of governance structure, Williamson avoided any psychological explanations and simply mooted some questions. See Endnote 12 for more information on this.

Nevertheless, the question of whether making predictions in a positivist manner is meaningful can be asked. This is because Friedman (1953) brushed aside questions about the realism of assumptions in favor of the ability to make predictions (Thaler 2016). But such ability is predicated on the existence of '*expert* billiard players' who make predictions '*as if*' they have full rationality (Friedman 1953: 21), and '[u]sing the mere two-word phrase 'as if,' Friedman essentially ended the debate about the realism of assumptions in economics' (Thaler 2016: 1580). If Williamson espouses Friedman's positivist approach, TCE will suffer from a contradiction as a result of its presupposed assumption of bounded rationality. And if the assumptions in the positivist approach are not realistic, then the validity of its predictions is at stake.

5. CE does not consider problem frames (gain frame or loss frame) in decision-making and assumes risk neutrality of decision-makers (Chiles and McMackin 1996; Martynov and Schepker 2017; Rindfleisch and Heide 1997; Williamson 1985). The risk neutrality assumption is unrealistic because it is often violated by decision-makers (Buckley and Strange 2011). Risk is defined as 'the perceived possibility of a loss or damage' (Martynov and Schepker 2017: 126) and is 'an inherently subjective construct' (Yates and Stone 1992: 5). This gap is closely related to point (1) above since risk neutrality goes in tandem with TCE's *processing* bounded rationality assumption (Martynov and Schepker 2017). Since risk perceptions are a product of psychological bounded rationality (Sunstein 2006), the introduction of psychological bounded rationality is necessary in order to study how risk perceptions affect governance structures.
6. TCE makes insufficient link with learning (Foss and Klein 2010; Hodgson 2010; Langlois 1992) and has paid less attention to how organizations dynamically adapt to the environment (Shelanski and

Klein 1995). In TCE, agents possess sufficient prior knowledge or foresight to establish 'efficient' and 'responsive' governance structures based on exhaustive contingencies envisaged at the beginning of time. Such governance structure predates history, and adaptation takes place in a world of a finite set of know scenarios, ensuring responsive preplanning with no need for knowledge acquisition. In this view, there can be 'no surprise, error…or learning' (Slater and Spencer 2000: 74). This is because bounded rationality in TCE follows strict rationality commonly assumed in neoclassical economics rather than bounded rationality in a behavioral sense as TCE claims.[15]

Here, a clarification needs to be made about the statement that 'there is no learning in Williamson's analysis' (Slater and Spencer 2000: 85). Learning has two sides: one about the environment and the other about the 'self', as reflected in the dictum of Sun Tzu, 'know thy enemy and know thyself'. Due to its primary focus on processing bounded rationality (or cognition) and neglect of psychology or the psychological side of the 'self' (see Chapter 4), TCE focuses on an ergodic exogenous environment (see Chapter 2), learning about which can be regarded as information cost, as mentioned in Point (1) above and in Endnote 15. This is to say, 'learning' in TCE is 'procedural' rather than behavioral (see Sect. 2.3.1). As such, whether to call such learning 'learning' is a matter of perspective. However, there is definitely no learning about the psychological part of the 'self' in TCE.

As a result, learning in a Penrosean (1959) sense is not considered in TCE. This is because Penrosean learning is fundamentally a psychology- or *manas*-centric approach (Chapter 4), and the consideration of it requires the opening up of the black box of organizational 'self'. Unfortunately, TCE treats the firm as an explanandum rather than explanans (cf. Point 12 below), and fails to treat the firm as a learning organization (Penrose 1959).

Relatedly, TCE does not say much about how agents may reduce bounded rationality, whether processing or psychological type. As such, TCE made at best a tangential link with learning because the paramount concern in TCE is the control of opportunism, whereas bounded rationality is regarded merely as an *abstract* constraint (Foss and Weber 2016b; Verbeke and Greidanus 2009; Williamson 1985: 8) or black box. This has prevented it from treating organizational learning as a central part of the decision-making process. However, more recent studies suggest that it is more realistic to view the reduction of bounded rationality as the key governance challenge and to treat the control of opportunism as a constraint (Foss and Weber 2016b; Verbeke 2003; Verbeke and Greidanus 2009). This is particularly true when psychological bounds are considered because psychological bounded rationality is closely linked to organizational learning (Cyert and March 1963; Sargent 1993; Simon 1991). While learning is not central to the rational approach to bounded rationality in TCE, it becomes paramount if psychology is moved to the front seat since human behaviors are fallible.

7. While uncertainty is regarded as a transaction characteristic, TCE is not committed to the management of uncertainty through effectuation. As discussed in Sect. 2.2, TCE reduces uncertainty into deterministic complexity and focuses on predicting governance structures in a closed system. Indeed, TCE does not even have a clear conception of uncertainty since there is a serious conflation between uncertainty, opportunism and bounded rationality (see Sect. 2.1). While opportunism can be regarded as an internal uncertainty and the management of it is the 'focus' of TCE, it is relegated to a status of background condition. Uncertainties in TCE, whether internal or external, are not based on perception. Thus, deterministic uncertainty in TCE relates to decision outcomes or choices rather than decision process. In order for TCE to become truly behaviorally realistic, the concept of uncertainty has to be approached differently from the current internal-external distinction, which smacks of a tautology. To render TCE behavioral, we propose the introduction of the concept of 'uncertainty controllability' to facilitate our behavioral agenda (see Sect. 2.3.2).
8. TCE considers neither various types of distance nor locations. This is largely a result of its positivist approach which assumes a single closed system. It cannot even consider distances in dimensions other than those which are correlated with geographic distance, such as technological distance which can arise in a single closed system, because of its rhetorical treatment of bounded rationality as a background condition. While CD and some other types of distance are considered in international business theories such

as the ownership-location-internalization (OLI) paradigm /internalization theory, these distances are treated in a positivist and rationalist way as 'black boxes' (see Chapter 7). The psychological biases that result from these distances are not considered, thus preventing TCE (and the OLI paradigm) from being behavioral.

9. Methodologically, TCE empirical literature is largely based on cross-sectional data (David and Han 2004; Zhao et al. 2004). Models based on cross-sectional data cannot closely reflect organizational decision-making processes which are inherently temporal in nature. In international business research, the inadequacy of cross-sectional data is reflected in the neglect of the decision-making process with regard to MNC ownership adjustment (Zhao et al. 2004).
10. TCE has been applied at three micro-analytic levels of analysis (Williamson 1981). The first is at the overall enterprise level. This level takes the scope of the enterprise as given and asks how its operating parts should be related one to another. The second level focuses on the operating parts and asks which activities should be performed outside the firm, which within it, and why. This level is concerned with firm boundary issue. The third level deals with the way through which human assets are organized. The object here is to match workgroup attributes with internal governance structures in a discriminating way (Williamson 1981). All the three levels of analysis focus on the economic agent rather than the economy (Williamson 1985) since firms are widely viewed as economic agents (Demsetz 1997; Schulz 2016).
11. Despite Williamson's (1981, 1985) insights that a behavioral theory of the firm should be a self-conscious one and his 'self-conscious' attention to the so-called behavioral assumptions of opportunism and bounded rationality, TCE failed to become a genuinely self-conscious theory of the firm. This is because the black box of consciousness is not opened up, and consciousness is not disaggregated and various components of it are not clearly ontologized. The 'who', 'what' and 'how' questions of consciousness, i.e., who is conscious of what and how to be conscious, are not clearly examined. Thus, the goal of becoming a self-conscious behavioral theory failed to be achieved. The lack of attention to the components and 'ontologization' of consciousness is not limited to TCE. It is a widely prevalent deficiency in economics and

management literatures in general. Even though there are recent signs of sporadic attention to a consciousness-based view of organizing (e.g., Turunen 2015), consciousness again is not treated in a disaggregated and ontologically deep manner. We discuss this point in Chapter 4.

12. While TCE opened up the neoclassical black box of the firm which was depicted as a production function devoid of internal structure, the opening of the black box is accompanied by a switch of the box from that of an explanans to that of an explanandum (Mäki 2004). By failing to make the firm as an explaining tool again after breaking the neoclassical black box, the traditional TCE only made a new, albeit larger, black box for itself and spent most of its energy on defining the boundary of the new box rather than on the value creation potential and evolutionary fit of the firm. In so doing, the attention is directed internally without focusing on the firm's relationship with the external world.

    In order for TCE to become behavioral, it has to treat the firm as an explanans, like in neoclassical economics, but with the added understanding of the internal mechanisms of the firm. This point has been suggested by some scholars (Foss 1997; Mäki 2004). For example, Foss (1997) pointed out the similarity between neoclassical economics and the evolutionary theory, which built upon the behavioral theory of the firm. Only after treating the firm as an explanans can the firm serve as 'instruments for adaptation' (Williamson 1999b: 1101; Foss 2003a).

13. TCE has been continuously questioned about its one-sided focus on transaction cost and neglect of transaction value (Child et al. 2019; Peng and Beamish 2014; Zajac and Olsen 1993). When a behavioral element is infused into TCE, it will have to adopt an external orientation and focus on ecological rationality. As a result, it has to focus on transaction value which provides performance feedback. Evolutionary fit is determined based on performance and ecological rationality rather than transaction cost alone, which is only one factor determining performance (see Sect. 7.2, particularly Point 12). Furthermore, transaction costs in TCE are in fact *indeterminate* due to the need for the firm to effectuate. It is desirable to take a transaction value perspective, because transaction value is successively determinable in a process based on ecological rationality.

Compared with the criteria presented in Sect. 1.3, the above assessment suggests that, except for Criteria 10, TCE fails most of the essential criteria for a behavioral theory. In particular, bounded rationality has not been explicitly modeled. The majority of TCE empirical literature neither have treated bounded rationality as a central issue nor adopted longitudinal research method based on longitudinal data. As such, enough attention has not been afforded to MNC decision-making processes. Based on these observations, we can reasonably say that TCE is not behavioral.

Furthermore, TCE also sidestepped dealing with opportunism in a behavioral approach. Even though TCE nominally considers opportunism as an 'essential' behavioral assumption (Williamson 1985: 388), the effect of opportunism has seldom been studied (David and Han 2004; Tsang 2006; Verbeke and Greidanus 2009). Instead of examining whether the concern for opportunism leads to internalization, most studies only invoked opportunism when hypothesizing about the relationships between some typical TCE-related variables (asset specificity, R&D intensity, advertising intensity, country risk, and international experience) and governance structures such as subsidiary ownership (Zhao et al. 2004). Such an approach disregards the variation in propensity for opportunistic behavior between economic agents (Nooteboom 2000) and across nations (Lubatkin et al. 2007).

1.6 What Prevents TCE from Being Behavioral?

Based on above assessment, TCE is deemed not a behavioral theory of the firm. Nevertheless, it has potential to become one if it can refocus on bounded rationality. In order to achieve this goal, we need first to clarify what prevents TCE from being behavioral. We believe there are several factors.

First, the opportunism and bounded rationality assumptions are difficult to measure and model (Verbeke and Greidanus 2009). While TCE does not assume that agents are identically or continuously opportunistic (Williamson 1979: 234, 1993: 98), opportunism is 'essential' to TCE due to agents' supposed inability to differentiate opportunists from non-opportunists ex ante (Foss and Weber 2016a, b; Williamson 1979, 1985), and the fact that even among those less prone to opportunism, most have their price (Williamson 1979). As for bounded rationality, it is even more difficult to measure, and as a result, it was seldom measured in the TCE literature. In fact, as we discuss in Chapter 4, bounded rationality is not even a proper way of expressing the idea that Herbert Simon meant. There is no such thing as bounded rationality as opposed to a '*bounded rationalizing process*', and the proper way of studying bounded rationality is to study the diminishing effect of cognitive bounds on governance structures. As such, it makes sense to measure cognitive bounds rather than bounded rationality. Rationality is only a shifting goal that firms attempt to achieve with increasing learning and decision time.

The measurement difficulty may have resulted from TCE's lack of attention to the differences between value, attitude and behavior with regard to its treatment of opportunism and bounded rationality. According to the value-attitude-behavior (VAB) hierarchy (Fishbein and Ajzen 1975; Homer and Kahle 1988; Rokeach 1973), value, attitude and behavior are separate and distinct concepts. TCE largely treats opportunism and bounded rationality as abstract values rather than behavior-oriented attitudes. Such an approach precludes them from becoming behavioral assumptions since values are difficult to measure and do not directly affect behavior (Dietz et al. 2005; Schwartz 1996).

Second, several key terms in TCE, such as opportunism, bounded rationality and uncertainty, are widely conflated in the literature. For example, TCE posits that bounded rationality and opportunism *jointly* give rise to transaction costs (Williamson 1985). However, TCE is not articulate on how this happens since it conflates the two terms (Dietrich 1994) and uses them rhetorically (Foss 2003a; Pessali 2006). Opportunism is defined both as 'self-interest seeking with guile' and as 'incomplete or distorted disclosure of information' (Williamson 1985: 47). The definition shifts from opportunism to bounded rationality (Dietrich 1994). The rhetorical and conflated treatment of opportunism and bounded rationality allows for neither their separate nor interaction effects (Foss 2004). Furthermore, TCE distinguish between external uncertainty and internal uncertainty. The former is defined as environmental unpredictability, which is further divided into primary uncertainty and secondary uncertainty. The former arises from random acts of nature and unpredictable changes in the environment (Williamson 1985). The latter arises from 'lack of communication, that is from one decision maker having no way of finding out the concurrent decisions and plans made by others' (Williamson 1985: 57) and from 'computational inability to ascertain the structure of the environment' (Williamson 1975: 23). Here secondary uncertainty is conflated with bounded rationality. TCE defines internal uncertainty as that which is attributable to the potential opportunistic behavior of partners (Williamson 1985: 57–58, 1996a: 48). Here internal uncertainty is conflated with opportunism. In order for TCE to become behavioral, a clarification of key terms is urgently needed.

Third, and relatedly, numerous terms have been used in the literature for internal and external uncertainty, creating a conceptual mire (Ahsan and Musteen 2011; De Weck et al. 2007; van Asselt and Rotmans 2002). Despite their multitude, these terms are not conducive for TCE to become a behavioral theory of the firm because they do not reflect the subjective or perceptual nature of uncertainty. The adjectives 'internal' and 'external' are misleading and confusing because the question of 'internal or external to whom' has seldom been asked and answered. In addition, 'internal' and 'external' implies outcome rather than independent variables since TCE is concerned with what to internalize and what to externalize. The current use of 'internal uncertainty' and 'external uncertainty' smacks of a tautology.

Fourth, the existing literature is not clear about how to model organizational decision-making process, particularly with regard to bounded rationality, and thus fails to link models of the firm closely to empirical observations. Behaviorists hold that falsifiability is a crucial requirement for scientific propositions (Popper 1959). For TCE to be regarded as 'scientific', at least with regard to its opportunism and bounded rationality assumptions, their 'definitions must be operational. No matter how concrete or abstract conceptually, they must be relevant empirically' (Eulau 1963: 6). The potential of TCE as a scientific theory lies in its ability in generating falsifiable hypotheses, which hinges on the extent that transaction costs can be measured a priori (Aldrich 2015; Shelanski and Klein 1995). Opportunism and bounded rationality, when treated as abstract values, become non-falsifiable and therefore have limited the empirical success of TCE (Bachmann and Zaheer 2008). This lack of understanding about how to model bounded rationality not only prevent TCE from being behavioral, but also detract somewhat from its being scientific and 'an empirical success story' (Williamson 1999b: 1092; Macher and Richman 2008).

Fifth, lack of attention to contexts was also a significant impediment for TCE to become behavioral. Despite an extensive literature, the majority of it is constrained within one context. As a result, TCE has to focus on the comparison of alternative governance structures instead of on contextual factors, thus 'disallow[ing]...any impact of social structure and social relations' (Granovetter 1985: 483).[18] Consequently, traditional TCE could not systematically account for variation in social contexts and structures in which organizations establish their boundaries, and paid insufficient attention to the possibility that contextual factors could independently influence organizational boundaries (Huitink 2017). As discussed in Chapter 2, the ignoring of the 'environmental context' strips traditional TCE of a domain wherein it can operate in a behavioral way by considering variations in psychological biases.

Six, TCE did not pay due attention to the fundamental role that various types of distances play in affecting bounded rationality because it conflates cognitive bounds with the 'bounded rationalizing process' in its rhetoric treatment of bounded rationality. This occurs because TCE has not achieved its goal as a self-conscious theory, and the black box of consciousness has not been opened up. As a result, consciousness is not disaggregated and various components of it are not clearly disaggregated and ontologized. To genuinely incorporate distances into TCE theorizing, they have to be treated as reflecting cognitive bounds after the conceptual separation of cognitive bounds and 'bounded rationalizing'. And for this to happened, the concepts of the self, the mind and the brain should not be conflated (see Chapter 4).

Seventh, the aforementioned factors arise from a positivist and deductivist position that TCE adopts (Pratten 1997; Williamson 2008). Such a philosophical stance is ontologically flat, static, and incapable of analyzing the interplay between structure and agency and hence the dynamics of social processes (Kitching and Rouse 2020; Pratten 1997).[19] It assumes a closed system by imposing 'closure' on economic system (Pratten 1997; Slater and Spencer 2000) and adopts a positivist epistemology which reduce ontology into what can be empirically known and thus commit 'the epistemic fallacy' (Bhaskar 1998: 27). For TCE to become behavioral, a more sound philosophical foundation and a more general methodological framework need to be adopted, and we claim that the adoption of CR (Fletcher 2017) would provide the philosophical buttressing necessary for a behavioral theory of organizational decision-making.

Eighth, and most fundamentally, TCE treats the firm as an explanandum rather than an explanans. This literally closes the system and prevents TCE from being an explaining tool after breaking the neoclassical black box (cf. Point 12 in Sect. 1.5), and thus becoming a behavioral theory (Foss 1997; Mäki 2004). Instead, it switched to a bigger black box of that of explanandum (Mäki 2004). In order for TCE to become an explanans-oriented behavioral theory, a deeper ontology is necessary for the firm to come out of the positivist black box of being an explanandum.

1.7 A Roadmap of Chapters Ahead

This book aspires to contribute to the TCE literature by make it behavioral. It proceeds as follows. In Chapter 2, we first clarify key terms of TCE with the goal of dispelling several major conceptual conflations which become roadblocks to the pursuit of our behavioral agenda of TCE. We propose ways to increase the definitional precision of these terms. In particular, we propose that uncertainties should be conceptualized based on their perceived controllability for its conceptual consistency with a behavioral theory. We conclude the chapter with a philosophical discussion about TCE's uncertain philosophical foundations (Slater and Spencer 2000) and propose that the CR perspective can help reduce confusion and render TCE behavioral in multiple ways. In Chapter 3, we explain how the VAB hierarchy can help us understand why TCE has not treated opportunism and bounded rationality in a more engaging way. We propose that these two assumptions should be dealt with at an attitude level, and that an institutional approach should be taken to measure them as attitudes. We also suggest measures for them. Next, we proceed to an important chapter in the book, Chapter 4, where we discuss in detail how to model bounded rationality (or more accurately, bounded rationalizing process). Subsequently, we discuss how to make the conversion from traditional TCE toward a behavioral theory of the firm in Chapter 5, based on the foundations we laid in the previous chapters. In Chapter 6, we demonstrate the fruitfulness of the proposed behavioral TCE approach with an empirical application to MNC subsidiary ownership. Finally, we conclude this book in Chapter 7, where we discuss the many theoretical and practical implications of our behavioral TCE and empirical findings, and point out some fundamental future research directions.

To conclude this chapter, we would further point out two things. First, while at the beginning of this chapter we invoked Williamson's (1992) call for the need to extend TCE, and accordingly give the book its current title, we did so because the conventional TCE is the site where most scholars are currently domiciled (Williamson 2008). As the book shows, it is difficult to use a light vehicle to pull a heavy load, and the content of the book quickly outgrows its title. Our approach to TCE can be better described as its theoretical subsumption into a fuller two-sided, assumption-symmetrical behavioral framework of organizational decision-making which adopts CR as its philosophical foundations. In addition, as discussed in Chapter 7, even the TCE side of the symmetrical framework should be more fittingly called '*transaction value economics*'. Nevertheless, we choose to keep the current title considering that scholars are currently still at the shore of positivism. This book aspires to show that, by abandoning the dryness of the positivist shore and crossing the river of pragmatism, we can reach the other fertile shore of CR. And only by the time when we are at the other shore, can we realize that CR is not the antithesis of positivism since it still needs positivism: CR is a behavioral process, where positivism is still useful in the empirical domain since judgmental rationality in CR depends on 'positivist' falsification.

Second, since internalization theory (or the international business version of TCE)[20] is one of the dominant paradigm in international business (Rugman 1986; Verbeke and Greidanus 2009), particularly in the study of multinational corporation (MNC) subsidiary ownership and entry mode (Zhao et al. 2004), and since the author's background is in international business, some contents of the book will be contextualized in international business literature. This book suggests that international business is a particularly rich ground for behavioral TCE because CD has significant implications to TCE's bounded rationality assumption, as discussed in Chapter 4. In addition, our CR-based behavioral TCE serves to ontologize and contextualize the *hegemonic* (Dörrenbächer and Geppert 2017) OLI paradigm, an important stream of internalization theory (Narula et al. 2019),[21] and thus holds important implications for international business. Nevertheless, such implications cannot be fully appreciated until the behavioral TCE itself is fully developed. As such, we leave the link between our behavioral TCE and internalization theory to Chapter 7.

Third, this book aims to radically revise and overhaul the traditional TCE into a behavioral theory of the firm. For this, a multitude of terms and concepts will be involved. In order to focus on our main pursuit, it is often necessary to slightly sacrifice detail on the definitions of some commonly used and well-accepted terms, and to adopt a descriptive approach using figures and tables. For readers who are interested in fuller treatment of such terms and concepts, we provide detailed bibliographical information of cited references.

Notes

1. Organizational economicsis a term used to refer to several theories that use economic logic and methods to understand the existence, nature, design, and performance of organizations (Gibbons and Roberts 2013). These theories include TCE, property rights theory and agency theory, among others (Mahoney 2004; Mahoney and Qian 2013).
2. As we discuss in Sects. 2.3 and 2.4, opportunism is not a necessary assumption of TCE. Instead, perceived opportunism *controllability* (or more accurately perceived uncertainty controllability; see Sect. 2.3.2) is what TCE actually assumes. In a Coasean (1937) world, global rationality means that opportunism and other manifestations of inefficiencies (such as information asymmetry) can be eliminated using governance structures based on rational expectations (Galanis 2011). Nevertheless, it is not necessary to eliminate opportunism in full: Williamson's (1996a) 'principle of remediable efficiency, according to which governance remedies are limited to a feasible set of imperfect options, and the fact that safeguarding carries a cost which increases at the margin, both suggest that equilibrium levels of safeguards will be reached before the effects of opportunism are entirely eliminated' (Carson and John 2013: 1073). If so, opportunism is not a necessary behavioral assumption of TCE because it only reflects a safeguarding cost. We will touch upon this topic passim. While risk neutrality is an assumption of TCE (Williamson 1985), it has gone virtually unnoticed in comparison with opportunism and bounded rationality (Chiles and McMackin 1996). So it is not uncommon that only opportunism and bounded rationality are mentioned as the behavioral assumptions of TCE. This book shows that the assumption of risk neutrality is unrealistic and unconducive to a behavioral theory of the firm. Instead, variable risk preferences should be the assumption appropriate for a behavioral theory (Chiles and McMackin 1996; Martynov and Schepker 2017).
3. Behavioral economics is an umbrella term for a broad array of approaches that seek to extend the explanatory power of economics by providing it with more realistic psychological foundations (Camerer and Loewenstein 2003).
4. Only after this is achieved can behavioral theories of the firm be considered as belonging to organizational economics and can behavioral economics be linked to organizational economics, as suggested by some prestigious scholars (Barney and Ouchi 1986; Mahoney 2004). Mahoney (2004) pointed out that Simon's (1982) work in the area of behavioral economics is worthy of careful attention by students studying organizational economics. We believe that Williamsonian TCE fails to fulfill its aim, and this book aspires to genuinely link behavioral economics to organizational economics.

5. While there exists a huge empirical TCE literature, the most needed empirical testing of TCE's opportunism and bounded rationality assumptions is lacking, as subsequently discussed.
6. Williamson (1996b: 150) admits that '...although the objective function of the firm was reformulated in favor of realism in motivation, I worked out of a maximization rather than a satisficing setup'.
7. In a recent review, Kwon and Silva (2020) identified sixty-two behavioral theories, and even this list is not exhaustive. Behavioral theories of the firm often start by taking a bounded rationality view of organizational behavior and decision-making. However, bounded rationality, like rationality, is not unlike ancient Rome—all roads lead to it, so various bounded rationality -based theories can look strikingly different from the original (Argote and Greve 2007).
8. As discussed in Chapter 4, bounded rationality should be modeled as a process rather than be treated as a variable (cf. Simon 1976, 1978). Here, nevertheless, we tentatively use this expression because the majority of scholars still fail to conceptualize bounded rationality as a process.
9. 'Behavioral' was not part of Cyert and March's (1963) guidelines for theory construction; but in order for a theory to be oriented toward decision-making process and to be empirically relevant, it had to focus on actual decision-making behavior (Greve and Argote 2015). In this sense, 'a process theory of the firm' may be a better term than 'a behavioral theory of the firm'. However, the former may lead to a neglect of internal cognitive bounds by focusing on administrative processes external to economic agents. In balance, 'behavioral' is still a better choice of word.
10. The main proponent of effectuation theory, Saras D. Sarasvathy, was a student of Herbert Simon at Carnegie Mellon University (Stoiko et al. 2019). In fact, effectuation theory was developed in close collaboration with Simon (Sarasvathy and Simon 2000; Sarasvathy 2003). It is related to and extends Simon's work on the satisficing principle (Chandra 2007: 64).
11. While effectuation is one of the dominant theories in entrepreneurship literature, it is 'a theory of action' (Dew and Sarasvathy 2002) and can be applied to human action in general (Watson 2013).
12. Please note here that there is a fundamental difference between effectuation and TCE' remediability or remediableness criterion (Williamson 1993, 1996a, 1999a, b), which argues that there is no optimal governance structure and that all feasible governance structures are flawed. Thus, the 'optimal' governance structure in TCE is only a temporarily *presumed* 'efficient' solution in the absence of feasible better alternatives based on 'comparative static equilibration' (see Sect. 1.5). For initial comparison, a reference point is necessary, but Williamson (1993: 131) said that '[i]f all

feasible forms of organization are flawed......then references......are operationally *irrelevant*. That does not deny that hypothetical ideals can be useful as a reference standard, but standards are often *arbitrary*' (italic added). Thus, he avoided to provide a starting reference point in the determination of governance structure. Instead, he mooted some questions: 'Is unbounded rationality the relevant standard? How about perfect stewardship, in which event opportunism vanishes?' It seems that he is still struggling with his own assumptions of bounded rationality and opportunism, and that the governance structure is in fact still based on the assumption of unbounded rationality and equilibrium contracting (see Point 2 in Sect. 1.5). If the reference standard can be arbitrary, then psychological biases are not considered. Effectuation theory and prospect theory are more developed with regard to the initial governance structure by using initial prereflective aspiration level as a reference point. More on this point can be found in various parts of the book.

13. Here we use the two terms 'processing bounded rationality' and 'psychological bounded rationality' for consistency with the mentioned literature. As we explain in Chapter 4, these terms are inaccurate for their intended meanings and should be more accurately referred to as 'cognitive bounds' and '(bounded) rationalizing', respectively.
14. We added 'emotional biases' here, to be more accurate and consistent with the term 'psychological bounded rationality'. Cognitive biases and emotional biases are interrelated and affect each other (Hertel and Mathews 2011). Nevertheless, the former are information processing biases resulting from quantitative or statistical *errors* of judgment, which are relatively easy to reduce with additional information or through education about the flaws in one's decision-making process. In this sense, cognitive biases belong more to 'processing capacity limitations'. In contrast, emotional biases are much deeper and are based on feelings and attitudes, consciously and unconsciously. It is emotional biases that cause systematical distortions in information perception and processing. More information on this can be found in Chapter 4. For convenience and to be consistent with terms used in the existing literature, we use 'cognitive biases' to refer to both in this chapter.
15. While we refer to these two bounds as processing bounded rationality and psychological bounded rationality (cf. Endnote 13 above), respectively, to be consistent with recent terminology (e.g. Foss and Weber 2016b), these two bounds are also often respectively referred to as rationality and bounded rationality in some literatures (e.g. Jones 1999). This is because, to quite many scholars, TCE's 'bounded' rationality is but another way of expressing positive information costs (e.g. Posner 1993: 80; Simon 1997b: 38; Scott 1994: 316), and thus is still rational. TCE use bounded

rationality in the sense of incomplete information (Williamson 1985), but 'rationality is not omniscience' (Posner 1993: 80).

16. As we discuss in Chapter 2, TCE is not well suited to the study of external environmental uncertainties, which are the realm of real options theory.
17. Simon distinguishes between two types of rationality, substantive and procedural. The former refers to rationality that grew up within economics, while the latter developed within psychology (Simon 1976). Substantive rationality is not affinitive to a behavioral approach because, given certain goals, rational behavior is determined entirely by the external task environment (Simon 1976). Even though Simon's procedural rationality is a step further toward a behavioral theory direction, it refers to 'computational procedures' rather than procedures in a real behavioral sense which considers psychological biases. Refer to Sect. 4.5.1.
18. The aforementioned difficulty in measuring opportunism and bounded rationality assumptions is related to the current point. That TCE focuses on one context implies that it is not even necessary to measure them due to lack of variance, given a particular context. See Sect. 3.5.
19. Van de Ven (2007: 46), citing Hanson (1958), notes: 'a major defect of logic positivism was that it confines attention only to the finished product of scientific reasoning and gives no attention to the process of reasoning whereby laws, hypotheses, and theories receive their tentative first proposal'.
20. Rugman (1986: 112) suggests that 'underlying logic and analysis of the two approaches is characterized more by their similarity than any substantial differences'. Verbeke and Greidanus (2009: 1471–1472) regard internalization theory as TCE thinking applied in the international business context, which relies heavily on Coase's (1937) original analysis of relative costs of internal vs external markets, and parallels to a large extent Williamson's (1975, 1985) development of TCE as a general theory of the firm (Safarian 2003). Maybe the more apparent difference lies in that internalization theorists are predominantly British-based whereas TCE theorists are American-based (Rugman 1986).
21. The relationship between the OLI paradigm and internalization theory is debatable. The literature is not conclusive whether the former should subsume latter or the other way around. See Subsection 7.3.2.1 for our new insights into this issue.

References

Aharoni, Y., Tihanyi, L., & Connelly, B. L. (2011). Managerial decision-making in international business. *Journal of World Business, 46*(2), 135–142.

Ahsan, M., & Musteen, M. (2011). Multinational enterprises' entry mode strategies and uncertainty. *International Journal of Management Reviews, 13*(4), 376–392.

Alajoutsijärvi, K., Juusola, K., & Siltaoja, M. (2015). The legitimacy paradox of business schools. *Academy of Management Learning & Education, 14*(2), 277–291.

Aldrich, H. E. (2015). Dimly through a fog. In A. Fayolle & P. Riot (Eds.), *Rethinking entrepreneurship* (pp. 12–27). London: Routledge.

Alessandri, T. M. (2008). Risk and procedural rationality: A behavioral theory perspective. *Journal of Strategy and Management, 1*(2), 198–217.

Alessandri, T. M., Ford, D. N., Lander, D. M., Leggio, K. B., & Taylor, M. (2004). Managing risk and uncertainty in complex capital projects. *Quarterly Review of Economics and Finance, 44*(5), 751–767.

Allen, D. W. (1999). Transaction costs. In B. Bouckaert & G. de Geest (Eds.), *Encyclopedia of law and economics* (pp. 893–926). Cheltenham: Edward Elgar.

Alvarez, S. A., Audretsch, D., & Link, A. N. (2016). Advancing our understanding of theory in entrepreneurship. *Strategic Entrepreneurship Journal, 10*(1), 3–4.

Argote, L., & Greve, H. R. (2007). A behavioral theory of the firm—40 years and counting. *Organization Science, 18*(3), 337–349.

Argyres, N. S., & Mayer, K. J. (2007). Contract design as a firm capability. *Academy of Management Review, 32*(4), 1060–1077.

Augier, M. (2013). Behavioral theory of the firm. *M@n@gement, 16*(5), 636–652.

Augier, M., & March, J. G. (2008a). A retrospective look at a behavioral theory of the firm. *Journal of Economic Behavior & Organization, 66*(1), 1–6.

Augier, M., & March, J. G. (2008b). Realism and comprehension in economics. *Journal of Economic Behavior & Organization, 66*(1), 95–105.

Augier, M., & Sarasvathy, S. D. (2004). Integrating evolution, cognition and design. *Strategic Organization, 2*(2), 169–204.

Bachmann, R., & Zaheer, A. (2008). Trust in inter-organizational relations. In S. Cropper, M. Beers, C. Huham, & P. S. Ring (Eds.), *Oxford handbook of inter-organizational relations* (pp. 553–554). Oxford: Oxford University Press.

Barney, J. B., & Lee, W. (2000). Multiple considerations in making governance choices. In N. J. Foss & V. Mahnke (Eds.), *Competence, governance, and entrepreneurship* (pp. 304–317). Oxford: Oxford University Press.

Barney, J., & Ouchi, W. G. (1986). *Organizational economics*. San Francisco, CA: Jossey-Bass.

Barros G. (2010). Herbert A. Simon and the concept of rationality. *Brazilian Journal of Political Economy, 30*(3), 455–472.

Bhaskar, R. (1998). Philosophy and scientific realism. In M. Archer, R. Bhaskar, A. Collier, T. Lawson, & A. Norrie (Eds.), *Critical realism: Essential readings* (pp. 16–47). London: Routledge.

Bromiley, P., Miller, K., & Rau, D. (2001). Risk in strategic management research. In M. A. Hitt, R. E. Freeman, & J. S. Harrison (Eds.), *Handbook of strategic management* (pp. 259–288). Oxford: Blackwell.

Buckley, P. J., & Strange, R. (2011). The governance of the multinational enterprise. *Journal of Management Studies, 48*(2), 460–470.

Bunge, M. (1967). The maturation of science. In I. Lakatos & A. Musgrave (Eds.), *Problems in the philosophy of science* (pp. 120–137). Amsterdam: North-Holland.

Camerer, C. F., & Loewenstein, G. (2003). Behavioral economics. In C. F. Camerer, G. Loewenstein, & M. Rabin (Eds.), *Advances in behavioral economics* (pp. 3–51). Princeton NJ: Princeton University Press.

Camerer, C. F., & Malmendier, U. (2007). Behavioral economics of organizations. In P. Diamond & H. Vartiainen (Eds.), *Behavioral economics and its applications* (pp. 235–290). Princeton NJ: Princeton University Press.

Carson, S. J., & John, G. (2013). A theoretical and empirical investigation of property rights sharing in outsourced research, development, and engineering relationships. *Strategic Management Journal, 34*(9), 1065–1085.

Chandra, Y. (2007). *Internationalization as an entrepreneurial process* (Doctoral dissertation). Australia: University of New South Wales.

Child, J., Faulkner, D., Tallman, S., & Hsieh, L. (2019). *Cooperative strategy: Managing alliances and networks*. Oxford: Oxford University Press.

Chiles, T. H., & McMackin, J. F. (1996). Integrating variable risk preferences, trust, and transaction cost economics. *Academy of Management Review, 21*(1), 73–99.

Coase, R. H. (1937). The nature of the firm. *Economica, 4*(16), 386–405.

Cyert, R. M., & March, J. G. (1963). *A behavioral theory of the firm*. Oxford: Blackwell.

David, R. J., & Han, S. (2004). A systematic assessment of the empirical support for transaction cost economics. *Strategic Management Journal, 25*(1), 39–58.

De Weck, O., Eckert, C. M., & Clarkson, P. J. (2007). A classification of uncertainty for early product and system design. In *Proceedings of ICED 2007*.

Demsetz, H. (1997). *The economics of the business firm*. Cambridge: Cambridge University Press.

Dew, N., Read, S., Sarasvathy, S. D., & Wiltbank, R. (2008). Outlines of a behavioral theory of the entrepreneurial firm. *Journal of Economic Behavior & Organization, 66*(1), 37–59.

Dew, N., & Sarasvathy, S. D. (2002). *What effectuation is not*. Paper presented at the Annual Meeting of the Academy of Management.

Dietrich, M. (1994). *Transaction cost economics and beyond*. London: Routledge.

Dietz, T., Fitzgerald, A., & Shwom, R. (2005). Environmental values. *Annual Review of Environment and Resources, 30*, 335–372.

Dörrenbächer, C., & Geppert, M. (2017). Multinational corporations and organization theory: An introduction to post-millennium perspectives. In C. Dörrenbächer & M. Geppert (Eds.), *Multinational corporations and organization theory* (pp. 3–42). Emerald: Bingley.

Douma, S., & Schreuder, H. (1992). *Economic approaches to organizations*. New York: Prentice-Hall.

Dow, G. K. (1987). The function of authority in transaction cost economics. *Journal of Economic Behavior & Organization, 8*(1), 13–38.

Earl, P. E. (1988). *Behavioral economics*. Aldershot, UK: Edward Elgar.

Eulau, H. (1963). *The behavioral persuasion in politics*. New York: Random House.

Fishbein, M., & Ajzen, I. (1975). *Belief, attitude, intention, and behavior*. Reading, MA: Addison-Wesley.

Fletcher, A. J. (2017). Applying critical realism in qualitative research. *International Journal of Social Research Methodology, 20*(2), 181–194.

Folta, T. B. (1998). Governance and uncertainty. *Strategic Management Journal, 19*(11), 1007–1028.

Foss, K., & Foss, N. J. (2004). The next step in the evolution of the RBV: Integration with transaction cost economics. *Management Revue, 15*(1), 107–121.

Foss, N. J. (1994). The two Coasian traditions. *Review of Political Economy, 6*(1), 37–61.

Foss, N. J. (1997). Evolutionary and contractual theories of the firm: How do they relate? *Rivista Internazionale Di Scienze Sociali, 105*(3), 309–337.

Foss, N. J. (2003a). The rhetorical dimensions of bounded rationality. In S. Rizzello (Ed.), *Cognitive developments in economics* (pp. 158–176). London: Routledge.

Foss, N. J. (2003b). Bounded rationality in the economics of organization. *Journal of Economic Psychology, 24*(2), 245–264.

Foss, N. J. (2004). Cognition and motivation in the theory of the firm. *Journal Des Economistes et Des Etudes Humaines, 14*(1), 79–100.

Foss, N. J., & Klein, P. G. (2010). Critiques of transaction cost economics. In P. G. Klein & M. Sykuta (Eds.), *The Elgar companion to transaction cost economics* (pp. 263–272). Northampton, MA: Edward Elgar.

Foss, N. J., & Weber, L. (2016a). Expand bounded rationality. *Academy of Management Review, 41*(4), 741–744.

Foss, N. J., & Weber, L. (2016b). Moving opportunism to the back seat. *Academy of Management Review, 41*(1), 61–79.

Foster, J. (2000). Is there a role for transaction cost economics if we view firms as complex adaptive systems? *Contemporary Economic Policy, 18*(4), 369–385.

Furubotn, E. G., & Richter, R. (2010). *Institutions and economic theory*. Ann Arbor, MI: University of Michigan Press.

Galanis, M. (2011). Vicious spirals in corporate governance. *Oxford Journal of Legal Studies, 31*(2), 327–363.

Gavetti, G., Greve, H. R., Levinthal, D. A., & Ocasio, W. (2012). The behavioral theory of the firm. *Academy of Management Annals, 6*(1), 1–40.

Ghoshal, S., & Moran, P. (1996). Bad for practice. *Academy of Management Review, 21*(1), 13–47.

Gibbons, R., & Roberts, J. (2013). Introduction. In R. Gibbons & J. Roberts (Eds.), *The handbook of organizational economics* (pp. 1–8). Princeton, NJ: Princeton University Press.

Godfrey, P. C., & Hill, C. W. L. (1995). The problem of unobservables in strategic management research. *Strategic Management Journal, 16*(7), 519–533.

Granovetter, M. (1985). Economic action and social structure. *American Journal of Sociology, 91*(3), 481–510.

Greve, H. R., & Argote, L. (2015). Behavioral theories of organization. In J. D. Wright (Ed.), *International encyclopedia of the social & behavioral sciences* (pp. 481–486). Amsterdam: Elsevier.

Groenewegen, J. (1996). Transaction cost economics and beyond. In J. Groenewegen (Ed.), *Transaction cost economics and beyond* (pp. 1–9). Dordrecht: Springer.

Hanson, N. R. (1958). *Patterns of discovery*. Cambridge: Cambridge University Press.

Hardt, Ł. (2009). The history of transaction cost economics and its recent developments. *Erasmus Journal for Economics and Philosophy, 2*(1), 29–51.

Hennart, J. F. (2010). Transaction cost theory and international business. *Journal of Retailing, 86*(3), 257–269.

Hertel, P. T., & Mathews, A. (2011). Cognitive bias modification. *Perspectives on Psychological Science, 6*(6), 521–536.

Hodgson, G. M. (2010). Limits of transaction cost analysis. In P. G. Klein & M. Sykuta (Eds.), *The Elgar companion to transaction cost economics* (pp. 297–306). Northampton, MA: Edward Elgar.

Homer, P. M., & Kahle, L. R. (1988). A structural equation test of the value-attitude-behavior hierarchy. *Journal of Personality and Social Psychology, 54*(4), 638–646.

Huitink, Z. S. (2017). *Three essays on public procurement*. Dissertations - ALL. 698. https://surface.syr.edu/etd/698.

Ingham, G. (1996). Some recent changes in the relationship between economics and sociology. *Cambridge Journal of Economics, 20*(2), 243–275.

Joas, H., & Beckert, J. (2001). Action theory. In J. H. Turner (Ed.), *Handbook of sociological theory* (pp. 269–285). New York: Springer.

John, G., & Reve, T. (2010). Transaction cost analysis in marketing. *Journal of Retailing, 86*(3), 248–256.

Jones, B. D. (1999). Bounded rationality. *Annual Review of Political Science, 2*(1), 297–321.

Kahneman, D., & Tversky, A. (1979). Prospect theory. *Econometrica, 47*(2), 263–291.

Kang, H.-G., Woo, W., Burton, R. M., & Mitchell, W. (2018). Constructing M&A valuation. *Journal of Organization Design, 7*, Article 2.

Karami, M. (2020). Effectual versus causal international opportunity discovery and creation. In V. Ratten (Ed.), *Entrepreneurship and the community* (pp. 29–48). Cham: Springer.

Ketokivi, M., & Mahoney, J. T. (2016). Transaction cost economics as a constructive stakeholder theory. *Academy of Management Learning & Education, 15*(1), 123–138.

Kitching, J., & Rouse, J. (2020). Contesting effectuation theory. *International Small Business Journal, 38*(6), 515–535.

Kwon, H. R., & Silva, E. A. (2020). Mapping the landscape of behavioral theories. *Journal of Planning Literature, 35*(2), 161–179.

Langlois, R. N. (1992). Transaction cost economics in real time. *Industrial and Corporate Change, 1*(1), 99–127.

Levitt, B., & March, J. G. (1988). Organizational learning. *Annual Review of Sociology, 14*(1), 319–338.

Love, J. H. (1995). Knowledge, market failure and the multinational enterprise. *Journal of International Business Studies, 26*(2), 399–407.

Lubatkin, M., Lane, P., Collin, S., & Very, P. (2007). An embeddedness framing of governance and opportunism. *Journal of Organization Behavior, 28*(1), 43–58.

Macher, J. T., & Richman, B. D. (2008). Transaction cost economics. *Business and Politics, 10*(1), Article 1.

Mahoney, J. T. (2004). *Economic foundations of strategy*. London: Sage.

Mahoney, J. T., & Qian, L. (2013). Market frictions as building blocks of an organizational economics approach to strategic management. *Strategic Management Journal, 34*(9), 1019–1041.

Mäki, U. (2004). Theoretical isolation and explanatory progress: Transaction cost economics and the dynamics of dispute. *Cambridge Journal of Economics, 28*(3), 319–346.

March, J. G. (1978). The 1978 Nobel Prize in economics. *Science, 202*(4370), 858–861.

March, J. G., & Shapira, Z. (1992). Variable risk preferences and the focus of attention. *Psychological Review, 99*(1), 172–183.

Martinez, R. J., & Dacin, M. T. (1999). Efficiency motives and normative forces: Combining transactions costs and institutional logic. *Journal of Management, 25*(1), 75–96.

Martins, R., Serra, F. R., Leite, A. L. D. S., Ferreira, M. M. P., & Li, D. (2010). Transactions cost theory influence in strategy research. *Journal of Strategic Management Education, 6*(3), 177–197.
Martynov, A., & Schepker, D. J. (2017). Risk preferences and asset ownership. *Managerial and Decision Economics, 38*(2), 125–143.
Masten, S. E. (2016). Transaction cost economics. In *Elgar research reviews in economics* (pp. xxx–xxx). Cheltenham: Edward Elgar.
Milgrom, P., & Roberts, J. (1988). Economic theories of the firm. *Canadian Journal of Economics, 21*(3), 444–458.
Moe, T. M. (1984). The new economics of organization. *American Journal of Political Science, 28*(4), 739–777.
Mootz, J. (2013). Dimensions of culture (Geert H. Hofstede)—Uncertainty avoidance. In *The Encyclopedia of Cross-Cultural Psychology* (pp. 407–409. Hoboken: Wiley.
Narula, R., Asmussen, C. G., Chi, T., & Kundu, S. K. (2019). Applying and advancing internalization theory. *Journal of International Business Studies, 50*(8), 1231–1252.
Nelson, R. R., & Winter, S. G. (1982). *An evolutionary theory of economic change*. Cambridge, MA: Belknap Press of Harvard University Press.
Nooteboom, B. (2000). Trust as a governance device. In M. Casson & A. Godley (Eds.), *Cultural factors in economic growth* (pp. 44–68). Berlin: Springer.
North, D. C. (1978). Structure and performance. *Journal of Economic Literature, 16*(3), 963–978.
Pagano, U. (1992). Authority, co-ordination and disequilibrium. *Structural Change and Economic Dynamics, 3*(1), 53–77.
Parmigiani, A. (2007). Why do firms both make and buy? *Strategic Management Journal, 28*(3), 285–311.
Peng, G. Z., & Beamish, P. W. (2014). The effect of host country long term orientation on subsidiary ownership and survival. *Asia Pacific Journal of Management, 31*(2), 423–453.
Penrose, E. T. (1959). *The theory of the growth of the firm*. Oxford: Oxford University Press.
Pessali, H. F. (2006). The rhetoric of Oliver Williamson's transaction cost economics. *Journal of Institutional Economics, 2*(1), 45–65.
Popper, K. R. (1959). *The logic of scientific discovery*. New York: Harper Zorch.
Posner, R. A. (1993). The new institutional economics meets law and economics. *Journal of Institutional and Theoretical Economics, 149*(1), 73–87.
Potts, J. (2017). Behavioral innovation economics. In R. Frantz, S. H. Chen, K. Dopfer, F. Heukelom, & S. Mousavi (Eds.), *Routledge handbook of behavioral economics* (pp. 392–404). Abingdon: Routledge.
Pratten, S. (1997). The nature of transaction cost economics. *Journal of Economic Issues, 31*(3), 781–803.

Rabin, M. (1998). Psychology and economics. *Journal of Economic Literature, 36*(1), 11–46.
Reder, M. W. (2003). Remarks on 'The methodology of positive economics'. *Journal of Economic Methodology, 10*(4), 527–530.
Rindfleisch, A., & Heide, J. B. (1997). Transaction cost analysis. *Journal of Marketing, 61*(4), 30–54.
Rokeach, M. (1973). *The nature of human values*. New York: Free Press.
Rugman, A. M. (1986). New theories of the multinational enterprise: An assessment of internalization theory. *Bulletin of Economic Research, 38*(2), 101–118.
Safarian, A. E. (2003). Internalization and the MNE: A note on the spread of ideas. *Journal of International Business Studies, 34*(2), 116–124.
Sarasvathy, S. D. (2001). Causation and effectuation. *Academy of Management Review, 26*(2), 243–263.
Sarasvathy, S. D. (2003). Entrepreneurship as a science of the artificial. *Journal of Economic Psychology, 24*(2), 203–220.
Sarasvathy, S. D., & Simon, H. A. (2000). *Effectuation, near-decomposability, and the creation and growth of entrepreneurial firms*. Paper presented at the first annual research policy technology entrepreneurship conference, University of Maryland.
Sargent, T. J. (1993). *Bounded rationality in macroeconomics*. Oxford: Oxford University Press.
Schulz, A. W. (2016). Firms, agency, and evolution. *Journal of Economic Methodology, 23*(1), 57–76.
Schwartz, S. H. (1996). Value priorities and behavior. In C. Seligman, J. M. Olson, & M. P. Zanna (Eds.), *The psychology of values, the Ontario symposium* (Vol. 8, pp. 1–24). Mahwah, NJ: Lawrence Erlbaum.
Scott, K. E. (1994). Bounded rationality and social norms. *Journal of Institutional and Theoretical Economics, 150*(1), 315–319.
Selten, R. (2001). What is bounded rationality? In G. Gigerenzer & R. Selten (Eds.), *Bounded rationality* (pp. 13–36). Cambridge, MA: MIT Press.
Sent, E. M. (2004). Behavioral economics. *History of Political Economy, 36*(4), 735–760.
Shelanski, H. A., & Klein, P. G. (1995). Empirical research in transaction cost economics. *Journal of Law Economics and Organization, 11*(2), 335–361.
Shiller, R. J. (1999). Human behavior and the efficiency of the financial system. In J. B. Taylor & M. Woodford (Eds.), *Handbook of macroeconomics* (Vol. 1, pp. 1305–1340). Amsterdam: Elsevier.
Simon, H. A. (1957). *Models of man*. New York: Wiley.
Simon, H. A. (1959). Theories of decision making in economics and behavioural science. *American Economic Review, 49*(3), 253–283.
Simon, H. A. (1961). *Administrative behavior*. New York: Macmillan.

Simon, H. A. (1976). From substantive to procedural rationality. In T. J. Kastelein, S. K. Kuipers, W. A. Nijenhuis, & G. R. Wagenaar (Eds.), *25 years of economic theory* (pp. 65–86). Boston, MA: Springer.
Simon, H. A. (1978). Rationality as process and as product of thought. *American Economic Review, 68*(2), 1–16.
Simon, H. A. (1979). Rational decision making in business organizations. *American Economic Review, 69*(4), 493–513.
Simon, H. A. (1982). *Models of bounded rationality: Behavioral economics and business organization*. Cambridge, MA: MIT Press.
Simon, H. A. (1987). Behavioral economics. In J. Eatwell, M. Milgate, & P. Newman (Eds.), *The new Palgrave: A dictionary of economics* (Vol. 1, pp. 221–225). London: Macmillan.
Simon, H. A. (1991). Bounded rationality and organizational learning. *Organization Science, 2*(1), 125–134.
Simon, H. A. (1997a). *An empirically based microeconomics*. Cambridge: Cambridge University Press.
Simon, H. A. (1997b). *Models of bounded rationality* (Vol. 3). Cambridge, MA: MIT Press.
Slater, G., & Spencer, D. A. (2000). The uncertain foundations of transaction costs economics. *Journal of Economic Issues, 34*(1), 61–87.
Spender, J. C. (2007). Management as a regulated profession. *Journal of Management Inquiry, 16*(1), 32–42.
Stoiko, M., Egan, T., & Duane, A. (2019). Entrepreneurial internationalization takes the effectuation turn. *SSRN* 3453813.
Sunstein, C. R. (2006). Misfearing. *Harvard Law Review, 119*(4), 1110–1125.
Thaler, R. H. (2016). Behavioral economics: Past, present, and future. *American Economic Review, 106*(7), 1577–1600.
Tsang, E. W. K. (2006). Behavioral assumptions and theory development. *Strategic Management Journal, 27*(11), 999–1011.
Turunen, M. (2015). *Toward a consciousness-based view of organizing* (Doctoral Dissertations 203/2015). Espoo, Finland: Aalto University.
Tversky, A., & Kahneman, D. (1981). The framing of decisions and the psychology of choice. *Science, 211*(4481), 453–458.
van Asselt, M. B. A., & Rotmans, J. (2002). Uncertainty in integrated assessment modelling. *Climatic Change, 54*(1/2), 75–105.
Van de Ven, A. H. (2007). *Engaged scholarship*. Oxford: Oxford University Press.
Verbeke, A. (2003). The evolutionary view of the MNE and the future of internalization theory. *Journal of International Business Studies, 34*(6), 498–504.
Verbeke, A. (2013). *International business strategy*. Cambridge: Cambridge University Press.

Verbeke, A., & Greidanus, N. S. 2009. The end of the opportunism vs. trust debate. *Journal of International Business Studies, 40*(9), 1471–1495.
Verbeke, A., & Kano, L. (2012). An internalization theory rationale for MNE regional strategy. *Multinational Business Review, 20*(2), 135–152.
Watson, T. J. (2013). Entrepreneurial action and the Euro-American social science tradition. *Entrepreneurship & Regional Development, 25*(1–2), 16–33.
Williamson, O. E. (1967). Hierarchical control and optimum firm size. *Journal of Political Economy, 75*(2), 123–138.
Williamson, O. E. (1975). *Markets and hierarchies*. New York: Free Press.
Williamson, O. E. (1979). Transaction-cost economics. *Journal of Law and Economics, 22*(2), 233–261.
Williamson, O. E. (1981). The economics of organization. *American Journal of Sociology, 87*(3), 548–577.
Williamson, O. E. (1985). *The economic institutions of capitalism.* New York: Free Press.
Williamson, O. E. (1988). Technology and transaction cost economics. *Journal of Economic Behavior & Organization, 10*(3), 355–363.
Williamson, O. E. (1990). Interview. In R. Swedberg (Ed.), *Economics and sociology* (pp. 115–129). Princeton, NJ: Princeton University Press.
Williamson, O. E. (1991). Comparative economic organization. *Administrative Science Quarterly, 36*(4), 269–296.
Williamson, O. E. (1992). Markets, hierarchies and the modern corporation. *Journal of Economic Behavior & Organization, 17*(3), 335–352.
Williamson, O. E. (1993). Transaction cost economics and organization theory. *Industrial and Corporate Change, 2*(2), 107–156.
Williamson, O. E. (1996a). *The mechanisms of governance.* Oxford: Oxford University Press.
Williamson, O. E. (1996b). Transaction cost economics and the Carnegie connection. *Journal of Economic Behavior & Organization, 31*(2), 149–155.
Williamson, O. E. (1998). Transaction cost economics. *De Economist, 146*(1), 23–58.
Williamson, O. E. (1999a). Public and private bureaucracies. *Journal of Law Economics and Organization, 15*(1), 306–342.
Williamson, O. E. (1999b). Strategy research: Governance and competence perspectives. *Strategic Management Journal, 20*(12), 1087–1108.
Williamson, O. E. (2002). Empirical microeconomics. In M. Augier & J. G. March (Eds.), *The economics of choice, change and organization* (pp. 419–441). Cheltenham: Edward Elgar.
Williamson, O. E. (2005). Transaction cost economics and business administration. *Scandinavian Journal of Management, 21*(1), 19–40.

Williamson, O. E. (2008). Friedman (1953) and the theory of the firm. In U. Mäki (Ed.), *The methodology of positive economics* (pp. 241–256). Cambridge: Cambridge University Press.
Winter, S. G. (1964). Review of 'a behavioral theory of the firm'. *American Economic Review, 54*(2), 144–148.
Wright, P., Kroll, M., Chan, P., & Hamel, K. (1991). Strategic profiles and performance. *Journal of the Academy of Marketing Science, 19*(3), 245–254.
Yates, J. F., & Stone, E. R. (1992). The risk construct. In J. F. Yates (Ed.), *Risk taking behavior* (pp. 1–25). New York: Wiley.
Zajac, E. J., & Olsen, C. P. (1993). From transaction cost to transactional value analysis. *Journal of Management Studies, 30*(1), 131–145.
Zhao, H., Luo, Y., & Suh, T. (2004). Transaction cost determinants and ownership-based entry mode choice. *Journal of International Business Studies, 35*(6), 524–544.

CHAPTER 2

Clarifying Key Terms and Philosophical Foundations of Transaction Cost Economics

The advance of any good theory starts from a set of clearly-defined concepts (Bruyat and Julien 2001), and clear definitions cannot be achieved without a solid philosophical foundation about the ontology and epistemology of the concepts to be defined (Fetzer et al. 1991; Poulis and Poulis 2018). The key concepts of TCE were first presented by Williamson (1979), in which he suggests that comparative institutional assessments should be based on the interplay among two[1] behavioral assumptions about economic actors (i.e., opportunism and bounded rationality) and three key transaction attributes (i.e., asset specificity, uncertainty, and transaction frequency). These five concepts form the foundation of TCE and have been continuously used by Williamson (1985, 1992, 1996) and other TCE scholars in general (Rindfleisch 2019; Shelanski and Klein 1995).

However, these concepts lack definitional precision and there exists serious confusion about opportunism, bounded rationality, and uncertainty (Macher and Richman 2008). Scholars often either conflate them or use multiple and sometimes competing definitions for the same concepts (Dunn 2000). We consider this situation a significant theoretical impediment and offer to clarify them in order to facilitate theory-building of a behavioral TCE. Since the definitions of asset specificity and transaction frequency are straightforward and are less prone to such conceptual

G. Z. Peng, *Toward Behavioral Transaction Cost Economics*,
International Marketing and Management Research,
https://doi.org/10.1007/978-3-030-46878-1_2

confusion, we focus on disentangling the concepts of opportunism, bounded rationality, and uncertainty.[2]

2.1 The Serious Conflation Among Opportunism, Bounded Rationality and Uncertainty

In TCE, opportunism refers to 'the incomplete or distorted disclosure of information, especially to calculated efforts to mislead, distort, disguise, obfuscate, or otherwise confuse'; or in short, 'self-interest seeking with guile' (Williamson 1985: 47). This definition can be divided into two parts: The 'incomplete or distorted disclosure of information' part is referred to as subtle 'passive opportunism', while the 'calculated efforts to mislead, distort, disguise, obfuscate, or otherwise confuse' part is referred to as blatant 'active opportunism' (Williamson 1985: 47; Wathne and Heide 2000: 38). Opportunism also includes both ex ante and ex post types (Williamson 1985).

Bounded rationality is defined as 'human behavior [that] is intendedly rational but only limitedly so' (Simon 1961: 24), and there are two types of it. One is processing bounded rationality, which concerns 'processing capacity limitations', and the other is psychological bounded rationality, which refers to 'cognitive economizing in the form of heuristics and cognitive biases' and emotional biases[3] which can systematically distort the way information is perceived and processed (Foss and Weber 2016b: 62; Simon 1997a, b). TCE holds that 'the principal ramification of bounded rationality for the study of economic organization is that all complex contracts are unavoidably incomplete' (Williamson 2002: 423). Thus, TCE considers primarily processing bounded rationality to explain incomplete contracting (Foss 2003; Foss and Weber 2016b; Tsang 2006).

When it comes to uncertainty, TCE distinguishes between 'external uncertainty' and 'internal uncertainty'. The former is defined as environmental unpredictability, which is further divided into primary uncertainty and secondary uncertainty. The former arises from random acts of nature and unpredictable changes in the environment (Williamson 1985). It is a macro-level uncertainty to the focal economic agent. The latter arises from 'lack of communication, that is from one decision maker having no way of finding out the concurrent decisions and plans made by others' (Williamson 1985: 57) and from 'computational inability to ascertain the structure of the environment' (Williamson 1975: 23). Here, secondary uncertainty is conflated with bounded rationality. TCE defines internal uncertainty as uncertainty that is attributable to the potential opportunistic behavior of partners (Williamson 1985: 57–58; 1996: 48). Here, internal uncertainty is conflated with opportunism.

In the above definition of opportunism, the subtle 'passive opportunism' part is conflated with bounded rationality; while the blatant 'active opportunism' is conflated with uncertainty: 'opportunism is a troublesome source of 'behavioral' uncertainty in economic transactions' (Williamson 1985: 49), and 'uncertainty of a strategic kind is attributable to opportunism and will be referred to as behavioral uncertainty' (Williamson 1985: 58). If so, why use an additional term 'opportunism'? Opportunism is simply a micro-level partner uncertainty (variability)[4] which is *external* to the focal economic agent since he/she is uncertain about whether his/her business partner will behave opportunistically or not (Foss and Weber 2016a, b; Williamson 1985).

2.2 Confusion About Uncertainty

To make the situation even worse, there is great confusion about uncertainty. TCE is not clear about whether uncertainty is a behavioral assumption or a transaction attribute. While it mentioned uncertainty as a transaction attribute, a large chunk of TCE literature focused on 'behavioral uncertainty', or 'opportunism', which is also regarded as a behavioral assumption. In addition, a huge variety of terms have been used about uncertainty, creating a conceptual mire (Ahsan and Musteen 2011; De Weck et al. 2007; Magnani and Zucchella 2018; van Asselt and Rotmans 2002). For example, Williamson himself used 'internal uncertainty' (Williamson 1985: 57–58; 1996: 48), 'behavioral uncertainty', and 'opportunism' (Williamson 1985: 49, 58) interchangeably. Such 'internal uncertainty' is also variously referred to as 'endogenous uncertainty' (e.g., Folta 1998), 'endogenously resolved uncertainty' (Cuypers and Martin 2010), 'subjective uncertainty' (Chawla et al. 2012), 'epistemological uncertainty', and 'informative uncertainty', among others (Ahsan and Musteen 2011; van Asselt and Rotmans 2002). These terms conflate, to differing degrees, the ontology and epistemology of 'internal uncertainty' or opportunism. 'External uncertainty' has also been referred to as 'environmental uncertainty', 'exogenous uncertainty', 'exogenously resolved uncertainty', and 'macroeconomic uncertainty', among others. Gatignon and Anderson (1988: 315) suggest that external uncertainties are 'generally understood to mean the extent to which a country's political, legal, and economic environment threatens the stability of a business operation'.

Further, Williamson's (1975, 1985) version of TCE in fact focused on deterministic complexity and information asymmetry rather than uncertainty (Alvarez et al. 2018; Slater and Spencer 2000; Spender 2018). According to Duncan (1972), external environment can be characterized by two dimensions: the simple-complex dimension (complexity) and the static-dynamic dimension (change). The former is defined as the number of environmental factors that the decision-makers take into consideration, whereas the latter refers to the degree to which these factors change over time. While both contribute to uncertainty experienced by decision-makers, the latter is more important. In a static or closed environment, uncertainty is reduced to complexity which is deterministic and objectively fixed (Slater and Spencer 2000). TCE's inability to consider genuine uncertainty arises from its positivist philosophical position, and we will discuss this point further in this chapter passim.

In TCE-based international business literature, scholars largely adopted the use of 'internal uncertainty' and 'external uncertainty', following Williamson (1985), even though sometimes other terms are also used. However, these terms are confusing because the question of 'internal or external to whom' has seldom been answered. This is particularly true for 'internal uncertainty'. The so-called internal uncertainty, or opportunism (Williamson 1985: 57–58; 1996: 48), is apparently an 'external uncertainty' since it refers to the unpredictability of the other side of the transaction, which is external to the focal economic agent. If it is considered 'internal' because it is internalized, then such use implies outcome rather than explanatory variables since TCE is concerned with what to internalize and what to externalize. In this sense, the use of the terms 'internal uncertainty' and 'external uncertainty' smacks of a tautology. In addition, the internal-external distinction is a categorical variable, and such distinction is ill-suited to the reality of uncertainties which exhibit a continuum according to the degree of influence or control that firms have in being able to mitigate uncertainties (De Weck et al. 2007; Miller and Lessard 2001).

Internal uncertainty is also referred to as 'behavioral uncertainty' and 'opportunism' (Williamson 1985: 49, 58). The term 'behavioral uncertainty' causes additional confusion in the context of a behavioral theory approach to which TCE belongs [as Williamson claims]. While the focus of a behavioral theory of the firm is supposed to be the behavior of the focal economic agent in a decision environment, as discussed in Chapter 1, the 'behavior' implied in the term 'behavioral uncertainty' is that of the transaction partner of the focal agent. In addition, if we use 'behavioral uncertainty' for micro-level uncertainty (e.g., potential partner opportunism), it may create yet another confusion: Macro-level uncertainty (or 'external uncertainty') is also behavioral since macroeconomics is concerned with the investigation of aggregate behavior.[5] As such, the term 'behavioral uncertainty' should be avoided since we would reserve the word 'behavioral' for the focal transaction partner in the sense of a behavioral theory of the firm.

2.3 A Proposition to Increase Definitional Precision

Considering the above serious conflation and confusion permeating the TCE literature, it is apparent that the precision of these key terms in TCE needs to be improved. We make multiple suggestions in the following subsections for the sake of conceptual clarity. Please note that while we suggest the discontinued use of the term 'external uncertainty' as previously discussed, we temporarily use it in Sect. 2.3.1 and propose better terminology in Sect. 2.3.2.

2.3.1 Conceptual Separation of Bounded Rationality, Uncertainty, and Opportunism

First, we propose that bounded rationality and uncertainty should be clearly distinguished since bounded rationality is not uncertainty.[6] Bounded rationality is related to the behavior of the focal economic agent, whereas uncertainty is related to the unknowability and unpredictability of the future states of the world (Dunn 2000; Knight 1921). Uncertainty is an ontological concept, while bounded rationality is an epistemological one. The former is about 'being' and the latter about 'knowing'. We discuss further this point in Sects. 2.6 and 2.7.

Second, external uncertainty should be narrowed to the primary external uncertainty of Williamson (1985), which refers to the unpredictability of the external environment, and bounded rationality should be used instead of his secondary external uncertainty. Furthermore, external uncertainty should be understood in an *ergodic*[7] (statistical) sense as TCE implicitly assumes that transactions are surrounded by immutable (ergodic) processes (Dunn 2000; Sanderson 2012; Slater and Spencer 2000).[8,9] This point can be substantiated by Williamson's insistence that unbounded rationality would allow for complete contracting, which presupposes that future events are preconstituted[10] and follow a knowable probability distribution. It is bounded rationality that makes economic agents uncertain about the future and prevents complete market contracting in that it is difficult to assign probability values to preconstituted future events due to complexity and limited human intellect (Slater and Spencer 2000: 73). In this sense, external uncertainty in TCE should be clearly understood as procedural uncertainty rather than fundamental uncertainty (Dequech 2006).[11] The former assumes an immutable (ergodic) environment and can be significantly reduced (but not eliminated)[12] through information acquisition and learning, whereas the latter assumes a transmutable (nonergodic, non-statistical) environment and can never be learned[13] (Davidson 1996; Dequech 2006). While in normal situations markets exhibit both ergodic and nonergodic uncertainties and firms confront both (Alessandri et al. 2004; Dunn 2000), TCE gradually loses its applicability with increasing levels of nonergodic uncertainties. Williamson (1975: 20) famously proposed that 'in the beginning there were markets'. When nonergodic fundamental uncertainties dominate, there will be no markets in the end (cf. Dew et al. 2008), and the boundary conditions of TCE will be invalidated (e.g., Rese and Roemer 2004). Under such nonergodic uncertainty, it is more difficult to defend the positivist, artificially closed system assumed in TCE (Pratten 1997; Slater and Spencer 2000) and to compare transaction costs of using alternative governance structures.

Ergodic uncertainty is actually risk in the sense of Knight (1921), who distinguishes between uncertainty and risk. Uncertainty is defined as the unknowability and unpredictability of the future states, whereas risk is considered measurable in terms of a probability distribution. Nevertheless, we follow the convention in TCE and real options theory (ROT) in referring to it as external uncertainty instead of risk (Cuypers and Martin 2010). We use external uncertainty in an ergodic sense for several reasons: (a) It is what TCE essentially assumes (Dunn 2000; Langlois and Robertson 1995; Slater and Spencer 2000: 73). (b) It is also used in ROT (Cuypers and Martin 2010; Leiblein 2003), which assumes that it is possible to develop, a priori, potential value estimates of various options associated with an investment (Leiblein 2003). Thus, the use of it will facilitate theory extension and integration in Chapter 5. (c) As we subsequently discuss in Sect. 2.7, this book adopts critical realism, and the use of external uncertainty in an ergodic sense in the traditional TCE framework can be integrated into the broader behavioral TCE framework based on CR [see Sect. 2.11].

Third, we propose that the term '*partner uncertainty*' be used instead of 'opportunism' and 'behavioral uncertainty'. The term 'opportunism' is not desirable for several reasons: (a) It is vague because it does not specify whose opportunism it is. Both sides of a transaction can be opportunistic and it is unfair to just blame transaction partner for being so. (b) The term 'opportunism' tends to give the impression that opportunism always plays a role in any transaction. But TCE does not assume that agents are identically or continuously opportunistic (Williamson 1979: 234; 1993: 98).[14] In addition, TCE suggests that partner opportunism itself does not constitute a governance problem if every economic actor always behaves opportunistically with certainty. Such certain opportunism can be factored into governance mechanisms (Slater and Spencer 2000; Williamson 1985). It is economic actors' supposed inability to differentiate opportunists from non-opportunists ex ante that poses governance challenges (Foss and Weber 2016a, b; Williamson 1985). Such inability to predict something accurately is commonly referred to as uncertainty (Milliken 1987).[15] (c) The use of the term 'partner uncertainty' helps to parry criticisms that TCE overemphasizes opportunism (Donaldson 1990; Ghoshal and Moran 1996; Granovetter 1985; Hill 1990; Kogut and Zander 1992, 1993). Since the focal transaction partner is only uncertain about its partner's behavior, no offense is committed to the majority of businesspeople. While Slater and Spencer (2000) suggest a term called 'opportunistic uncertainty', this term is still not as neutral as 'partner uncertainty'.

2.3.2 *Uncertainties Should Be Classified According to Controllability*

Considering the confusion and conflation surrounding the three key TCE terms, we propose that uncertainties be classified according to their perceived controllability rather than the internal-external distinction which smacks of a tautology.[16] Our proposition follows the view that the explanation of governance structures relies on perceived, rather than objective, transaction costs (Chiles and McMackin 1996; Miller and

Tsang 2011), and is consistent with a large body of 'risk perception' literature (e.g., Boholm 1998; Ricciardi and Rice 2014; Slovic 1987) in many other disciplines including behavioral finance and economics. [Please note that from this point on, we use risk and uncertainty interchangeably, based on our detailed discussion in the previous subsection.] The various existing conceptions of uncertainty in TCE prevent it from being behavioral because the psychology of uncertainty is not considered. The risk perception literature suggests that risk perception is a subjective concept about its perceived controllability (Hendrickx and Vlek 1991; Sitkin and Pablo 1992; Slovic 1987) and risk controllability is one of the most important factors[17] which affect managerial decision-making (Aaker and Jacobson 1990; Johnson and Tversky 1984; Sitkin and Weingart 1995). Miller and Lessard (2001) and De Weck et al. (2007) suggested that uncertainties can be classified into five levels according to controllability, i.e., the degree to which decision-makers can influence the outcomes, often through relationships (Francolini 2010; van de Vrande et al. 2009). These five levels include technical/project level, industry/competitive level, country/fiscal level, market level, and natural level, from the highest to the lowest controllability. Technical/project uncertainties are related to factors such as operations, partner/ally, project management, and technicalities. Uncertainties at industry/competitive level include those related to industry evolution, demand and growth rate, supply conditions, infrastructure, and competition. Country/fiscal uncertainties include financial, economic and political stability, inflation, regulatory stability or intervention, contract enforcement, legal stability, etc. At the market level, uncertainties are reflected in variations in exchange rates, commodity prices, interest rates, and risk premiums. And at the highest level, natural uncertainties are concerned with the unpredictability caused by weather and geology. According to the above five-level framework, the dominant concern of TCE, opportunism or 'partner uncertainty', is only one potential uncertainty at the highest level of controllability. Too much focus on opportunism may have caused scholars to fail to see the forest.

In Table 2.1, we compare controllable uncertainty with uncontrollable uncertainty and put various terms used in the literature under these two types. Please note that risk controllability is a continuous variable, and controllability is a relative term (cf. 7.7.6). Such risk perception also varies according to the firm's own resources and capabilities and its position in the broader industrial organization, or firm heterogeneity in the context of emic-etic distinction (see Sect. 3.3 and Chapter 7).

Table 2.1 Comparing uncertainties based on controllability

Term proposed	*Controllable uncertainty*	*Uncontrollable uncertainty*
Origin	• Ontological and epistemological	• Ontological and epistemological
Level	• Micro-level	• Macro-level
Resolvability	• Internally resolvable—by the firm (Cuypers and Martin 2010) • 'Can be decreased by actions of the firm' (Folta 1998) • Often relationship specific (van de Vrande et al. 2009) • Relations uncertainty (Francolini 2010)	• Externally resolvable—by the environment over time • 'Largely unaffected by firm actions' (Folta 1998) • Not firm or industry dependent (Li 2007; Cuypers and Martin 2010) • Object uncertainty (Francolini 2010)
Avoid using these terms	• Opportunism (negative connotation; just one of many controllable uncertainties) • Internal uncertainty (Internal to whom? Internal implies the decision to internalize, which is an outcome) • Behavioral uncertainty (Whose behavior?) • Endogenous uncertainty (not endogenous; cf. Slater and Spencer 2000)	• External uncertainty (External to whom?)
Examples	• Partner uncertainty ('opportunism') (Haunschild and Miner 1997) • Supplier uncertainty (Sutcliffe and Zaheer 1998) • Cultural uncertainty • Capability development uncertainty • Activity scope-related uncertainty • Task uncertainty (Santoro and McGill 2005).	• Technological uncertainty (Haunschild and Miner 1997; Rese and Roemer 2004; Santoro and McGill 2005; van de Vrande et al. 2009) • Social and economic uncertainty • Institutional uncertainty • Environmental turbulence • Price and demand uncertainty • Host government opportunism
Ways of reducing uncertainty	• Learning by reacting	• Learning by waiting

(continued)

Table 2.1 (continued)

Term proposed	*Controllable uncertainty*	*Uncontrollable uncertainty*
Subject to what biases?[1]	• Assimilation bias • Contrast bias	• Overconfidence bias (over-optimism) • Discounting bias (over-pessimism)
Benefits of using the term	• Enables study of other uncertainties in addition to partner uncertainty ('opportunism') • Allows link to perception and thus cognitive bias and psychological bounded rationalizing process • Not tautological • Link with prospect theory	• Enables connection with risk perception literature • External is a neutral term, and uncontrollable is an emotional term, thus enabling connection with cognitive bias literature • Allows link to perception and thus cognitive bias and psychological bounded rationalizing process • Link with prospect theory
Fit with behavioral TCE?[2]	• Yes (van de Vrande et al. 2009)	• No (but fit with behavioral real options theory) (van de Vrande et al. 2009)
Fit with effectuation?[3]	• Yes	• Yes

Notes (1) Refer to Sect. 4.11. (2) Refer to Sect. 5.3. (3) See Sect. 2.10
Source Author's own creation/summary

2.3.3 Benefits of Classifying Uncertainties Based on Controllability

Classifying uncertainties according to their perceived controllability has the following advantages for TCE research:

1. The risk perception approach redresses the traditional TCE assumption of risk neutrality of decision-makers (Chiles and McMackin 1996; Martynov and Schepker 2017; Rindfleisch and Heide 1997; Williamson 1985), which prevent TCE from being a behavioral theory. By considering uncertainty from a psychological risk perception perspective, problem frames (gain frame or loss frame) in decision-making can be considered since risk perceptions have

long been regarded as having a natural link with prospect theory (Kahneman and Tversky 1979; Tversky and Kahneman 1981).

2. It allows for firm boundary adjustment as uncertainty is reduced as a result of both knowledge collection and the reduction of perceptual biases through learning. TCE is a theory about firm boundaries but its conceptualization of uncertainty does not consider inaccurate boundary decisions due to psychological factors and the reduction thereof. TCE views uncertainty as arising from lack of information and therefore knowledge collection is seen as the antidote to uncertainty (Buckley 2016).
3. It is not tautological. Some uncertainties like 'behavioral uncertainty' ('opportunism' or 'partner uncertainty') are internalized for their perceived controllability.[18] This is consistent with the 'locus of control' literature which suggests that events are considered either under internal control or external control due to their perceived controllability (e.g., Rotter 1966).
4. It does not force uncertainties into a categorical variable (i.e., internal-external), thus allowing for the consideration of varying degree of influence or control that firms have in mitigating uncertainties (De Weck et al. 2007; Miller and Lessard 2001). The continuous nature of risk controllability also opens up future research avenues for it to become an additional important explanatory variable in TCE research.
5. It broadens the scope of focus of TCE with regard to TCE's 'internal uncertainty'. While Williamson (1985) considers demand or technological uncertainty and uncertainty associated with information asymmetry to be 'nonstrategic' or 'innocent' and focused instead on 'opportunism' or 'internal uncertainty', such a focus had the unintended effect of constraining TCE research and giving rise to the impression that opportunism is a necessary assumption in TCE [we discuss this in Sect. 2.4]. Recent studies have started to broaden the focus to include uncertainties related to capability development and scope of activities (e.g., Cuypers and Martin 2010), which apparently belong to the high controllability uncertainties of Miller and Lessard (2001), i.e., technical/project uncertainties.
6. It facilitates theory integration. In order to render TCE behavioral, it has to be integrated with prospect theory because decision-makers

use problem frames which often bias decision-making. TCE conception of uncertainty arises only from lack of knowledge and thus does not consider the psychology of uncertainty. Perceived controllability of uncertainty has to be considered in order to link TCE with prospect theory. We leave further discussion on the distinction between controllable uncertainty and uncontrollable uncertainty to Chapter 5, where we will discuss the significance of this distinction because it will affect how organizations frame different uncertainty according to prospect theory.

7. Relatedly, uncertainty controllability facilitates the integration of TCE with effectuation theory, which is conducive to behavioral TCE. Effectuation focuses 'on the controllable aspects of an unpredictable future' (Sarasvathy 2001: 251), or controllable aspects of uncertainties, of both controllable and uncontrollable types. Furthermore, uncertainty controllability serves to make effectuation theory consistent. We discuss this point in Sect. 2.10.
8. Uncertainty controllability facilitates the integration of behavioral TCE with behavioral ROT in a full two-sided, symmetrical theoretical framework that we propose in Chapter 5. Real options are also affected by heuristics and biases (Miller and Shapira 2004).

2.4 Is Opportunism a Necessary Assumption in TCE?

According to Sect. 2.3, opportunism or 'partner uncertainty' is only one of many controllable uncertainties at the technical/project level. If so, the question about whether opportunism is a necessary *assumption* to TCE arises again. Whether opportunism is a necessary assumption to TCE has been debated for several decades (e.g., Alchian and Woodward 1988; Love 1995; Williamson 1993). While Williamson insists that opportunism is a necessary assumption (Williamson 1993), many other disagree and suggest that opportunism is a sufficient but not necessary condition to explain ownership of assets (Coase 1988; Foss 1996a, b; Foss and Weber 2016a, b; Hodgson 2004; Martynov and Schepker 2017; Weber and Mayer 2014), and that a theory of the firm can be developed independent of opportunism (Love 1995, 2005; Madhok 1996). Demsetz (1997: 20) points out that it is clear from Coase's later writings (e.g., 1988) that

Coase 'does not believe opportunism offers a *special* [italic original] justification for vertical integration'. Verbeke and Greidanus (2009) suggest that a focus on opportunism does not fit the business reality where long-term collaborative relationships are the norm rather than exception.

Put in the large context of the wide array of uncertainties with different degree of controllability, we agree with scholars who suggest that partner opportunism is only one out of many uncertainties which are perceived to be controllable by the firm. As such, opportunism is not a necessary, but a sufficient, transaction characteristic (not assumption) which calls for internalization. In a sense, 'opportunism is arbitrarily selected as the only disposition of relevance' (Moran and Ghoshal 1996: 60). Opportunism leads to hierarchy because such uncertainty is relation specific and only 'doing' can reveal additional information to reduce such uncertainty (Folta 1998). In the absence of opportunism, transaction cost can be caused by other uncertainties and these uncertainties should also be studied. Unfortunately, due to TCE's narrow focus on opportunism, the effect of other controllable uncertainties is under-studied, with few exceptions (e.g., Cuypers and Martin 2010). Specifically, opportunism is not a necessary assumption in TCE for the following (non-exhaustive) reasons:

1. TCE only invokes it (Tsang 2006) and has not been seriously engaged with it. Due to the conflation of opportunism and bounded rationality, opportunism in TCE is a value judgment about the other party's potential behavior, which can be more accurately considered as an propositional attitude *ascribed* to the other economic agent (the partner) from the epistemological angle of the focal economic agent (Tollefsen 2015), or a 'subjective opportunism judgments' (Arikan 2020), which is subject to bounded rationality. In this sense, it should be more accurately stated that bounded rationality is a necessary assumption in TCE, rather than opportunism.
2. If opportunism is indeed necessary, TCE will have to consider how partners' propositional opportunism affects governance structures (de Bruin and Moore 2005; Jones 2001). If opportunism is treated as a disposition, then it gives rise to the 'TCE schizophrenia', whereby opportunism is dispositional and static, yet safeguard against opportunism is situational and dynamic (Moran and Ghoshal 1996: 60; Verbeke and Greidanus 2009: 1473). Since TCE treated opportunism in the former way, its relevance is subject to challenge. We discuss this point further in Sects. 3.4 and 3.5.

3. In a Coasean (1937) world, global rationality means that opportunism and other manifestations of inefficiencies (such as information asymmetry) can be eliminated using governance structures based on rational expectations (Galanis 2011). Thus, the threat of opportunism is treated as something that can be bought off (Buckley and Chapman 1997). If so, opportunism is not a necessary behavioral assumption of TCE because it only reflects a safeguarding cost. If opportunism is admitted as a behavioral property of transaction partners, then the production and use of information may be the object of misrepresentation for strategic purpose and safeguarding becomes impossible. Furthermore, TCE is not even committed to the elimination of opportunism because of Williamson's (1996) 'principle of remediable efficiency, according to which governance remedies are limited to a feasible set of imperfect options, and the fact that safeguarding carries a cost which increases at the margin, both suggest that equilibrium levels of safeguards will be reached before the effects of opportunism are entirely eliminated' (Carson and John 2013: 1073).
4. In addition, what matters in the relationship between opportunism and internalization is not even about partner opportunism, but about whether this type of uncertainty is perceived to be controllable or not. This uncertainty *controllability* is what TCE assumes. Opportunism does not necessarily lead to internalization if it is not controllable. For example, opportunism can arise at higher levels such as host government opportunism (Combe and Mucchielli 1998). Under uncontrollable opportunism, it is advisable for firms not to use hierarchy, but instead to treat such opportunism as another uncontrollable uncertainty.
5. When TCE is applied in international business in the form of internalization theory, opportunism does not play a strong role (Lundan 2010; Verbeke and Greidanus 2009). It is believed that the lack of such a role of opportunism even has made internalization theory more empirically relevant, and thus an attractive alternative approach to TCE (Lundan 2010). Verbeke and Greidanus (2009) suggest that a focus on opportunism does not sit well with business reality where long-term collaborative relationships are the norm rather than exception.

In sum, opportunism is not a necessary condition for the existence of the firm and should be treated as one of many uncertainties that the firm faces. What matters is not whether a partner is opportunistic or not, but whether such uncertainty is perceived to be controllable or not. Putting opportunism in the broad picture of the wide array of uncertainties that organizations have to cope with will not only obviate the many complications arising from using such a negative term but also set TCE research free from the trap of a narrow focus.

2.5 TCE Is not Well Suited to the Study of Uncontrollable Uncertainty

TCE's approach to transaction cost analysis is claimed to be micro- or even nano-analytic (Williamson 1990). As such, its insights into the potential effects of controllable uncertainties, which are largely micro-level uncertainties, have been largely consistent, even though these uncertainties are often only invoked but not empirically tested directly. It is generally accepted that when controllable uncertainty is high, firms are better off assuming higher levels of internalization to resolve such uncertainty within firm boundaries. However, the situation for uncontrollable uncertainties is different. TCE's prescription runs counter to insights from other perspectives such as ROT and strategic management.

TCE posits that when uncontrollable uncertainties are high (but not too high[19]), governance structures with a high degree of control or integration are more desirable because such governance structures can reduce adaptation problems and lower transaction cost (David and Han 2004; Rindfleisch and Heide 1997; Williamson 1991). Nevertheless, here TCE conflates two different types of adaptations: internal adaptation to unanticipated changes at micro-level due, for example, to potential partner opportunism, and external adaptation to unforeseen macro-level uncontrollable environmental change (Peng 2012). More recent TCE-based studies suggest that low integration should be preferred under conditions of high uncontrollable uncertainties in order to increase strategic flexibility (Peng 2012; Peng and Beamish 2019; Zhao et al. 2004). However, such arguments are in fact ROT arguments (Brouthers et al. 2008; Chi et al. 2019; Cuypers and Martin 2010). Being fundamentally an internalization theory (Alpers 2019), TCE does not have a well-developed notion of externally resolvable uncertainty (Kulkarni and Heriot 1999) and, as a result, cannot offer insights into how firms should cope with such uncertainty. By treating opportunism (which is only one of many controllable uncertainties) as a theoretical assumption, TCE focuses on the impact that partner uncertainty has on governance choices (Williamson 1975, 1985), and has thus been ill-equipped to deal with uncontrollable uncertainties. ROT is needed to account for externally resolvable uncertainties (Kulatilaka 1995; Santoro and McGill 2005). Empirical TCE literature to date has yet to fully discern the effects of these two types of uncertainties on organizational governance (Macher and Richman 2008).

Similarly, while TCE can accommodate sequential decision-making under micro-level uncertainty, it is ill-equipped to address sequential decision-making under macro-level uncertainty. This is because TCE focuses on how firms resolve micro-level uncertainty with a transaction cost minimization focus within firm boundaries (Williamson 1985). With such a focus, it fails to sufficiently account for environmental uncertainty which is externally resolvable outside firm boundaries. Pure TCE should thus be applied to situations where environmental uncertainty is expected to be low (Rese and Roemer 2004). The resolution of macro-level uncertainties outside firm boundaries needs a value maximization focus by considering sequential decisions as real options (Trigeorgis and Mason 1987). Other behavioral theories which can address how firms respond to macro-level uncertainties need to be integrated with TCE to provide a fuller account of how firms simultaneously respond to uncertainties at various levels of controllability (Greve and Argote 2015). ROT is apparently one of such theories considering its value maximization focus. We leave this topic to Chapter 5.

In fact, the various symptoms of confusion about uncertainty, as discussed in Sect. 2.2, arise in part from TCE's ill-compatibility with uncontrollable external uncertainty. The difficulty of TCE in addressing uncontrollable external uncertainty is actually a consequence of its unclear philosophical position and weak philosophical foundations. Due to its tacit adoption of positivism and consequently a collapsed ontology, TCE did not have a clear idea about its 'generative mechanism(s)' in the real domain of CR; thus it is difficult for TCE to consider multiple 'generative mechanisms'. We discuss this in depth shortly.

2.6 The Philosophical Roots of Confusion About Uncertainty in TCE

The previously mentioned conflation and confusion may have resulted from a lack of attention to the philosophical foundation of uncertainty.

As noted by some scholars (e.g., Slater and Spencer 2000), TCE has not offered an explanation of the nature and origins of uncertainty (both 'behavioral' and 'external' types), and it has not been engaged with uncertainty at a philosophical level (Foss 1994). The aforementioned terminological mire may have resulted from the fact that uncertainty (ontological uncertainty) and bounded rationality (epistemological uncertainty) in TCE are the two faces of the same uncertainty 'coin'. The same concepts are sometimes defined from the epistemological perspective, and other times from the ontological perspective, resulting in conceptual confusion that thwarts theoretical advances.

Uncertainty can be seen as having both an ontological ('being') and an epistemological ('knowing') aspect, and these two aspects are strongly entwined (Dequech 2004; Dewey 1929). Bounded rationality in TCE is actually an epistemological uncertainty which arises from limitation on human ability which prevents economic agents from obtaining relevant knowledge about ontological uncertainty (Davidson 1996; Milliken 1987; Walker et al. 2003), while opportunism (or 'internal uncertainty') and 'external uncertainty' are ontological uncertainty which arises from variability in the external world (Dequech 2004; Kahneman and Tversky 1982).

The origin of uncertainty is more complicated than a dualistic separation of epistemology from ontology, and its attribution depends on what philosophical position is adopted. While Milliken (1987) suggests that the origin of uncertainty lies in the environment external to the focal firm, such a view reflects the orthodox positivist approach which presupposes some kind of ontology or reality in a closed system (Pratten 1997). More recent anti-positivist movements, notably post-modernism and social constructivism, question the existence of an objective ontology and submit that 'ontological uncertainty' is not purely value-free and objective (van Asselt and Rotmans 2002). According to this view, uncertainty is ultimately epistemological.

2.7 A Call for Critical Realism

There have been 'paradigm wars' between positivists and constructivists in the 1980s, and CR emerged as a scientific alternative to both (Denzin and Lincoln 2011). CR was introduced through the work of Bhaskar (e.g., 1979, 2008) and was further elaborated by critical realists such as Archer (1995), Collier (1994), Sayer (1992), and Lawson (1997). CR draws elements from both approaches in its account of ontology and epistemology, and its ontological stance is placed between the two extremes of positivists and constructivists/interpretists. Thus, CR is considered a comprehensive philosophy of science and a general methodological framework for research (Fletcher 2017).

TCE has not broken away from positivism and emphasizes the objective approach to uncertainty (Gazendam and Jorna 2002; Pratten 1997).[20] This can largely be attributed to its superficial treatment of bounded rationality in a rational way. A behavioral theory approach should be concerned with the epistemological interpretation of uncertainty as well (Gazendam and Jorna 2002) since psychology plays a vital role in epistemology (Goldman 1985). While a positivist position is regarded as 'fundamentally inappropriate as well as intellectually impoverishing' for behavioral theories (Jessor 2019: 8), and there has been an increased rejection of positivism in behavioral research (Smith 2019), we concur with Kurki (2007) that the relationship between positivism and CR is complementary rather than acrimonious, and CR is only more holistic than positivism. Ontologically, CR maintains realist assumptions about the existence of reality. Epistemologically, CR adopts epistemological relativism and judgmental rationality which does not reject either positivist statistical analysis or interpretivism. Instead, judgmental rationality depends on 'positivist' falsification (Sayer 1992). Without getting too entangled into the debate between various philosophical perspectives, suffice it to say that ontological realism, epistemological relativism, and judgmental rationality constitute the 'holy trinity' of CR (Bhaskar 2010) and CR is preferred in this study for its neat fit with our behavioral approach.[21] Since the debate between positivism and CR has been dominating the philosophical literature and waged continuously (Boyd et al. 1991), this section focuses on CR in its contrast with positivism (Godfrey and Hill 1995). We believe that the adoption of the more holistic CR perspective has the following advantages over positivism in our behavioral agenda.

1. CR posits a realist ontology (ontological realism) and a fallibilist epistemology (epistemological relativism), or as Bhaskar (2008: 43) puts it, 'to be a fallibilist about knowledge, it is necessary to be a realist about things'. A realist ontology relates to the existence of an external world independent of an organization's knowledge of it (Miller and Tsang 2011), while a fallibilist epistemology holds that

organization's knowledge of the external world is socially and historically produced (Bhaskar 2008; Miller and Tsang 2011; Popper 1972). A realist ontology is consistent with the current TCE ontological stance toward uncertainty, but is richer and deeper in its domain (see Point 3 below). Please note that 'independent of' does not imply 'exhausted by', and the concept of reality can be *real* but *fallible*[22] (Gorski 2013).

2. The fallibilist epistemology relates to bounded rationality (Banai 1995; Bhaskar 2011; Johnston 1989) and thus is consistent with TCE's bounded rationality assumption. Fallibility of epistemology is reflected in both processing bounded rationality and cognitive bias, thus facilitating the broadening of the scope of bounded rationality in TCE. TCE treats bounded rationality in a rational way and focuses on the ontological side and neglects the epistemological side of uncertainty. A rational treatment of bounded rationality implies 'deterministic uncertainty' (Liesch et al. 2011) and ultimately reduces human epistemology into a non-necessity, and as a result, 'the individual becomes a "zero"' (Foss 1994: 53). Hence, TCE fails to become a behavioral theory. CR sets out to join both ontology and epistemology (Miller and Tsang 2011), and to bridge the divides created, ontologically and epistemologically, by other one-sided philosophies (Banai 1995), and the joining of both a real but fallible ontology and a fallibilist epistemology will necessitate a serious consideration of epistemology. The fallibility of epistemology potentially brings all sorts of human biases into account and thus has the potential to make TCE behavioral.

   CR is consistent with the view that bounded rationality 'signifies a type of theory, not outcomes' (Gigerenzer and Selten 2001: 6). CR fits with Simon's conceptualization of bounded rationality as scissors whose two blades are cognitive limitation of an economic agent and the structure of task environments (Simon 1990: 7). The CR perspective redresses the tendency to focus on the cognitive side in theories of human inference, which equates the notion of bounded rationality with human cognitive limitation and thus, paradoxically, reassures classical rationality as the normative standard for bounded rationality (Gigerenzer and Goldstein 1996). A CR perspective, by enabling bounded rationality as a theory, is conducive to making TCE a behavioral theory based on bounded rationality.

3. CR distinguishes between three overlapping but ontologically distinct domains of reality: the real, the actual, and the empirical (Bhaskar 2008). The real domain is the realm of generative mechanisms or causal tendencies,[23] which are 'the ways of acting of things' (Bhaskar 2008: 3). These mechanisms are the intransitive causal tendencies which give rise to events in the actual domain under contingent conditions by simultaneously enhancing or counteracting each other. The empirical domain is the realm of empirically measurable events as we experience them directly or indirectly. This is the transitive level of reality, where meanings, social ideas, decisions, and actions occur. At the actual level, events are not mediated by human experience; they occur whether or not we experience them, and are often different from what is observed at the empirical level (Fletcher 2017; Miller and Tsang 2011). The three domains provide a hierarchical view of reality and thus give CR a particular ontological depth. CR holds that these domains are often unsynchronized, or out of phase with each other, and that the causal mechanisms of the real domain are non-empirical and can only be partially experienced through events in the empirical domain as 'partial event regularities'. The purpose of science is to identify and explain the generative mechanisms in the real domain rather than to make empirical predictions about event regularities in the empirical domain (Downward et al. 2002: 495), which reduces ontology into epistemology and commits 'the epistemic fallacy' (Bhaskar 1998: 27).

TCE adopts a positivist and deductivist approach and has not ventured to break out of the empirical domain (Pratten 1997).[24] At this level, TCE is not able to explore the richer generative mechanisms in the real domain since empirical reality cannot be regarded as prime indicator of such mechanisms, which often countervail each other. TCE has contented itself with prediction as the test of a theory, which does not require any meaningful understanding of generative mechanisms (Bromiley and Harris 2006; Pratten 1997). By imbuing TCE with a realist spirit, it is hoped that TCE can embrace multiple perspectives in arriving at meaningful explanations about deeper generative mechanisms instead of predictions.[25] Such an understanding of deep mechanisms will shed more light on managerial decision-making process, thus making TCE behavioral [see Sects. 2.8 and 2.9, and Chapter 5].

4. Based on the three-domain conception of reality, CR adopts an open system view and does not impose 'closure' on economic system wherein the future is already predetermined (Pratten 1997; Slater and Spencer 2000).[26] CR adopts a dynamic view toward the interplay between social structures[27] (social contexts) and agency: Agency presupposes the existence of social structures and social structures can be dynamically affected by agency (Bhaskar 1986). Social structures or contexts are comprised of historically constituted set of social norms, values, rules, and interrelationships (Pawson and Tilley 1997; Slater and Spencer 2000) in which human agency has played and will keep playing a role. In comparison, the positivist stance tacitly assumed in TCE implies at most a diminutive consideration of human agency,[28] preventing TCE to pursue a behavioral agenda since the intrinsically dynamic nature of social processes of time and history appears to be ignored (Pratten 1997). By raising the scientific inquiry to the real domain and link ontology and epistemology more closely, the role of human agency is moved to the center stage, and this is conducive to a behavioral approach to TCE.
5. Relatedly, the consideration of causally complex social context in the actual domain of CR can also remedy behavioral theories' lack of focus on organizational environments and social contexts (Baum and Ingram 2002; Gavetti et al. 2007). While behavioral theories should be commended for their commitment to a decision-centered view of organizations, by concentrating on decision-making, they tend to focus predominantly on the impact of cognitive characteristics of the decision-makers which are largely uninfluenced by social structures (Baum and Ingram 2002). Adopting CR contributes to the much needed linking of behavioral theories with an open system view of organizations embedded in their social contexts (Gavetti et al. 2007).
6. Despite a fallibilist epistemology, CR rejects judgmental relativism (the inability to judge the merits of theories) and holds that the possibility of judgmental rationality (judgments of inferiority and superiority of competing theoretical explanations about the real domain) remains (Sayer 1992: 206; Miller and Tsang 2011; Porpora 2015). As such, it does not preclude falsification used in positivism since judgmental rationality depends on falsification. Rather, CR encourages falsification efforts in order to advance theory development and scientific knowledge. However, CR views falsifications

as a process, and they are never definitive and may be revised (Sayer 1992). As such, theories are provisionally accepted so long as they have not been falsified (Popper 1990; Runde 1996). In this sense, CR is by definition not refutable. Nevertheless, this does not prevent scientific endeavors from making advances based on a fallible ontology. As Popper[29] once noted, we believe that 'while realism is neither demonstrable nor refutable … it is arguable, and the weight of the argument is overwhelmingly in its favor … Common sense is clearly on the side of realism' (1972: 38). A behavioral approach does not dismiss the positive aspects of positivism such as concern with evidence, verifiability, and causality (Smith 2019).

7. It is consistent with our overall context in this book, particularly Chapter 4, where we adopt some ideas from the Yogācāra school of Buddhism, which are consistent with CR (Kochumuttom 1982). It is also consistent with Chapter 3, where we discuss whether opportunism and bounded rationality in TCE are treated as values, attitudes, or behavior. The VAB hierarchy corresponds respectively to the real, actual, and empirical domains in CR, and we suggest that TCE's confusing treatment of opportunism and bounded rationality arises from its unclear philosophical position.
8. It does not conflict with TCE and effectuation. Instead, it deepens the ontological depths of both and integrates them into a generalized behavioral theory of organizational decision-making (Fletcher 2017). Absent CR as a solid philosophical foundation, TCE can only lower its aspiration level to the explanation of firm behavior using '(partial) ***mechanisms*** rather than……(general) theories' (Williamson 1998: 23; italic in original). [Please note here Williamson means partial event regularities by partial mechanism]. In fact, TCE is not clear about its generative mechanism(s)[30] in the real domain and diverts it attention to the governance of opportunism. One of the symptoms of this lack of attention to generative mechanisms is exactly the difficulty that TCE faces to account for the relationship between external uncertainty and governance structures, as we mentioned in Sect. 2.5. Through ontology deepening, TCE can find its generative mechanism(s) in the real domain.

2.8 Critical Realism Can Inform Effectuation Theory

As mentioned in Sect. 1.3, a behavioral approach should focus on effectuation, which refers to a logic that 'is non-predictive in the sense that it does not require clear goals, accurate predictions, or an adaptive stance toward a largely exogenous environment' (Dew et al. 2008: 43). It entails 'molding and enhancing initiatives, formulating new goals and creating new opportunities rather than positioning oneself within environments largely outside one's control or taking opportunities as exogenously given' (Wiltbank et al. 2009: 129). As such, 'effectuation implies a specific stance toward the world' (Dew et al. 2008: 43) and is closely akin to CR (Kitching and Rouse 2020). It is also consistent with the behavioral tradition in its strong emphasis on being empirically based (Dew et al. 2008: 43).

As mentioned in Point 3 in Sect. 2.7, TCE adopts a positivist stance and focuses on prediction or causation (Sarasvathy 2001). Such a stance prevents it from being behavioral. In order to render TCE behavioral, an effectual approach should be adopted. Sarasvathy (2001, Table 1) and Dew et al. (2008, Table 2) compared prediction/causation with effectuation in detail. We refrain from repeating the comparisons for space limitations, but will include such comparisons in Table 5.4 when we compare behavioral TCE with traditional TCE. Suffice it to say here, temporarily,[31] that effectuation is the straight inversion of prediction/causation in terms of fundamental philosophical position, overall logic, problem space, and decision-making process (Read and Sarasvathy 2005; Sarasvathy 2001). Since effectuation is means-driven, rests on non-predictive logic, considers the environment endogenous to the action of effectuators, and therefore seeks to effectuate environment through pre-commitment, the effectuation perspective is conducive to a behavioral theory of the firm (Read and Sarasvathy 2005). While effectuation theory is seldom used in the context of TCE research, such use has been hinted at (e.g., Sarasvathy 2008).[32]

Despite the affinity of effectuation to CR, the potential of CR to advance effectuation theory has seldom been attempted, and effectuation theory has suffered from a flat ontology (Kitching and Rouse 2020). This can be told from several symptoms. First, effectuation is characterized by four dimensions: pre-commitment, experimentation, affordable loss, and flexibility (Chandler et al. 2011; Deligianni et al. 2017; Harms and Schiele

2012). However, due to the flat theorization in effectuation theory, there exist some confusions about these concepts and their interrelationships. A deeper ontology which can incorporate uncertainty controllability can greatly harmonize these concepts in effectuation theory by hierarchizing them into different domains of CR. We discuss this in detail shortly in Sect. 2.10.

Second, due to its lack of ontological depth, effectuation theory pays inadequate attention to social and cultural contexts, or social structures in the actual domain of CR. As a result, the potential contribution of effectuation theory is limited because the insights it can offer are ahistorical and under-socialized (Kitching and Rouse 2020). In addition, while effectuation itself is a heuristic (Sarasvathy 2001), the biases in effectuation process have been given short shrift in the literature (Zhang et al. 2018). CR can inform effectuation theory by considering social structures, such as cultures and cultural distance (CD), and the biases arising from CD. We leave further discussion on this point to Sect. 4.8, where we discuss how CD contextualizes effectuation.

Third, related to the previous point, effectuation theory flattens the different domains of CR and reduces the process of venture creation to a decision-making logic (Kitching and Rouse 2020) at the level of the individual (Karami 2020; Reuber et al 2016; Sarasvathy and Ventakaraman 2011). While it does acknowledge the generative logics in the real domain of CR, due to its flat ontology, it pays insufficient attention to the various contingent conditions in the actual domain of CR, which are embedded in the social and cultural structures. Effectuation theory conceptualizes the influence of social context in terms of a generic, abstract context of uncertainty (Kitching and Rouse 2020). Thus, it fails to differentiate between different types of uncertainties according to controllability in the actual domain, and how such contingent conditions may activate different generative mechanisms in the real domain. By relegating uncertainties into a status of a vague background, the conditioning effects of social structure, which generate mechanism-expressing events (whether experienced or unexperienced by human agents), are neglected. As a result, organizations are granted excessive powers of agency (Kitching and Rouse 2020). We will discuss how the concept of uncertainty controllability harmonizes effectuation theory in Sect. 2.10.

Fourth, effectuation theory acknowledges its roots in Peirce's (1960) pragmatism (Reuber et al. 2016; Sarasvathy 2001), which implies a flat ontology (Pratt 2016). While pragmatism and CR share a realist, tentative ontology and a critical, subjectivist epistemology, they have a different focus. Pragmatism tends to background ontological considerations in favor of epistemology and experiences, whereas CR tends to foreground ontology and focuses on generative mechanisms in the real domain (DeForge and Shaw 2012), while not ignoring epistemology (Fletcher 2017). The pragmatism-rooted effectuation literature tends to emphasize epistemology, reinforce the tendency for organizations to be insensitive to 'social contexts' (Watson 2013), and conduct research primarily at the level of the individual (Reuber et al. 2016), thus resulting in the aforementioned symptoms. An explicit adoption of CR and the foregrounding of ontology will not only raise the level of analysis to the actual domain level which is capable of considering socio-institutional contexts but also enable the consideration and harmonization of various mechanisms in the real domain (Gross 2009) [see Sect. 2.10].

In addition, CR and pragmatism differ distinctly in their positions vis-à-vis ontological relativism. CR is marked by a rejection of ontological relativism, whereas pragmatism involves more of an agnostic stance, in which the so-called problem of ontological relativism is not a serious issue (Proctor 1998). Thus, pragmatism is not theoretically committed to ontological reality in the sense of CR, and this lack of commitment tends to give rise to a constructionist ontology, the relativist logic of which leads to insensitivity to social contexts (Üsdiken 2010; Watson 2013). The combination of a subjectivist epistemology and a constructionist ontology flirts dangerously with relativism (Phelan 2016). Even though this accusation has provoked a sharp response from Sarasvathy and Dew (2008), who argue that the existence of an intersubjective process through which people can share knowledge suggests an underlying ontological reality (Phelan 2016), such subject-dependent reality is at most in the domain of actual in CR (Mingers 2006). Intersubjectivity, or 'intersubjective consensus' (Sarasvathy and Ventakaraman 2011), belongs to a domain of 'arbitrary and contextual' (Maturana 1978: 48; Mingers 2006: 61) interlocked behaviors. While organizations 'live' and 'experience' within the actual domain based on intersubjective consensus, they may not share and experience the same 'consensus'. What organizations are likely to experience are various 'local' consensuses in the actual domain, such as various forms of social networks or mental models (Porac and Rosa 1996), which reflect 'locally viable market-specific agreements between firms' decision-makers' (Baum et al. 2003: 702). Such mental models can be interpreted as firms' attempts to impose stability on markets and control potentially destabilizing competitive situations (Baum and Ingram 2002; Fligstein 1996). Thus, invocation to intersubjectivity (Sarasvathy and Dew 2008) cannot rid effectuation theory of relativism since intersubjective consensuses are socially-constructed 'realities', albeit generated intersubjectively rather than individually. While such 'realities' enable new channels of knowledge sharing and communication, they are no more than objectivized social construction. The overall tendency of effectuation is still to subjectivize the discourse on reality (Ramoglou and Tsang 2016), even though such subjectivization may be 'constrained' (Dew and Sarasvathy 2002). To make the situation even worse, effectuation research 'has not even scratched the surface of intersubjective interactions' (Sarasvathy and Ventakaraman 2011: 126) and has treated intersubjectivity in a egocentric manner, in which the effectuator single-handedly manages uncertainty while other 'stakeholders' (Sarasvathy and Ventakaraman 2011) assume a rather passive role (Jansen 2016).

Fifth, relatedly, pragmatism suffers from 'epistemic fallacy' (Bhaskar 1998: 27) because it collapses ontology (what is real) into epistemology (what we know) and views ontological reality as entirely constructed through and within human discourse or knowledge (Fletcher 2017; Watson 2013). It does not conceive of a deeper ontology in terms of generative mechanisms as that in the real domain of CR, which is external to human interpretation and can be 'revealed' (Watson 2013) or activated (Ramoglou and Tsang 2016). To suggest that human cognitive activity creates ontological reality is to commit 'ontological exaggeration' (Fleetwood 2005), a mistake which gives non-existent power to epistemology. The mistake does not disappear even after 'making the intersubjective a key unit of analysis' (Sarasvathy and Ventakaraman 2011) because intersubjectivity is also socially constructed. It is the focus on epistemology and the neglect of an objective ontology that cause effectuation to lapse into relativism. In order to legitimately refute the accusation that effectuation suffers from relativism, the focus needs to be turned to an objective ontology (while not ignoring epistemology),[33] and CR can exactly serve this purpose. CR foregrounds ontology and aims for 'revealing the mechanisms which connect things and events in causal sequences' (Ackroyd and Fleetwood 2000: 15). Attention to the existence of such mechanisms in the real domain rids effectuation of the suspicions of relativism and epistemic fallacy. It also provides effectuation theory with an ontological depth, into which key effectuation concepts can be mapped coherently [see Sect. 2.10].

Sixth, CR helps effectuation theory to fend off criticisms regarding its treatment of opportunity and value creation. Some scholars are concerned that effectuation theory lacks a core theoretical explanation about the creation of value or the origin of opportunity,[34] and that it appears to tacitly assume that any 'opportunity' imagined by the effectuator in an uncertain environment will add value (Arend et al. 2015). CR assumes that opportunities are propensities which exist objectively in the form of possible or unmet market demand that can be subjectively *actualized* by effectuators into profits (Ramoglou and Tsang 2016). Thus, the objective propensity mode of opportunity existence does not contradict the subjective process of opportunity actualization. Such actualization happens in a social context where effectuation takes place.

In order to address the above-mentioned lacunas and deepen the ontological depth of effectuation theory, we propose that effectuation theory be closely coupled with CR, as summarized in Table 2.2. Instead of approaching the underlying ontological reality from a subjectivist epistemology using pragmatism as the base camp, effectuation theory can benefit from clearer reasoning and reduced confusion by adopting CR as its philosophical foundations.

Table 2.2 Critical realism informs effectuation theory with a deep ontology

Domain	*Real*	*Actual*	*Empirical*
Mechanisms (Pre-commitment, affordable loss)	✓		
Events Contingent conditions: uncertainty[1] controllability[2]	✓	✓	
Experiences	✓	✓	✓

Notes (1) Uncertainties are social contexts (Horst and Grabska 2015; Kitching and Rouse 2020). (2) See Sect. 2.10 and Table 2.5
Source Author's creation based on Bhaskar (2008: 2)

2.9 Critical Realism 'Integrates' TCE and Effectuation

While effectuation theory is conducive to a behavioral theory of decision-making and uncertainty management, it may have gone too far by asserting that 'effectuation is a straight inversion of rational choice theory (also referred to as causal or predictive rationality)' (Read and Sarasvathy 2005: 50). Sarasvathy (2001: 251) suggests that the underlying logic for prediction (or causation) processes, which TCE adopts, can be described as 'to the extent we can predict future, we can control it', and that for effectuation processes as 'to the extent we can control future, we do not need to predict it'. The former focuses on 'control as outcome', whereas the latter on 'control as strategy' (Read et al. 2016).

However, this dichotomous distinction between prediction and effectuation is deemed unduly simplistic (Kitching and Rouse 2020). Arend et al. (2015: 641, italics in original) pointed out that '*control requires prediction*', and experimentation to generate possible effects with given means is '*tests of prediction*'. Effectuation scholars also occasionally accept that effectuators sometimes make 'highly speculative *guesstimates*' of expected returns (Sarasvathy and Dew 2005: 554, italics in original). Effectuation is a weaker or uncertain form of prediction and prediction is a firmer or certain type of effectuation. As such, prediction/causation and effectuation should be integrated. While uncertainty may constrain firms' ability to predict, explain, and diagnose, it does not destroy it. On the contrary, it is uncertainty that forms the foundation of the behavioral analysis of economic agents even though they themselves are unable to ascertain their decisions (Alchian 1950). In the presence of fallibilist epistemology and judgmental rationality, an inaccurate use of conventional prediction tools can be effectively used in the effectuation process to continuously validate the *improving* hypothesis, given natural selection[35] (Alchian 1950; Friedman 1953).

In the context of this book, TCE and effectuation should be integrated since traditional TCE is based on the logic of prediction (Sarasvathy 2008). We suggest that the adoption of CR can greatly facilitate such integration, as suggested in the previous sections. Before we proceed further, however, it is a good idea to briefly describe and clarify some terms related to reasoning based on Peirce (1960) and more recent literature. This is because of the central role of the 'abduction' mode of reasoning in effectuation theory (Sarasvathy 2001), which was developed by the logician

Charles Sander Peirce as a third kind of reasoning in contrast to induction and deduction, on which TCE is based.[36] Another reason that we need to clarify these terms is that we disagree with Peirce's treating abduction as a third kind of reasoning as opposed to induction and deduction since he was actually comparing apples and oranges. The terms we are going to clarify include *(positivist) deduction*, *(positivist) induction*, *abduction*, *retroduction*, *abductive/retroductive deduction*, and *abductive/retroductive induction*.

2.9.1 Deduction, Abduction, and Retroduction

There exists considerable confusion about these terms (Chiasson 2005; Heeks and Wall 2018). In particular, the terms abduction[37] and retroduction cause the most confusion. Some scholars (e.g., Mingers et al. 2013) treat retroduction and abduction as synonymous. This can in part be attributed to the conflation of these two terms by Peirce himself since there is some slippage in the way he used these terms over time (Chiasson 2005). In addition, the difference between the terms deduction/induction and abductive (retroductive) deduction/abductive (retroductive) induction has seldom been clearly explained, with few exceptions (Fletcher 2017; Taylor et al. 2018). We suggest that CR can make an important contribution in clarifying these terms by providing an ontological depth to the reasoning process. We first present how these terms can fit into the CR framework in Tables 2.3 and 2.4, and provide a brief explanation following the tables.

When talking about induction and deduction, it is first of all necessary to be aware of whether the context is a closed system or an open one. This is because, as Tables 2.3 and 2.4 shows, the correct terms to be used in open systems should be abductive (retroductive) deduction and abductive (retroductive) induction depending on ontological depths of the assumed reasoning processes, i.e., whether it is in the actual domain or in the real domain. In this sense, deduction and induction should be properly considered as directional reasoning logics which can be applied to different ontological depths.[38] In a closed system, deduction is defined as the top-down reasoning process that leads to true conclusions as a result of its assumed true premise. It is used to evaluate a theory-driven hypothesis and should be more accurately referred to as 'positivist deduction'. In contrast, induction refers to the bottom-up reasoning, whereby a conclusion is reached via generalization (validation or falsification) from

Table 2.3 Deduction and induction in closed system vs open system

Direction of inference	*Closed system (Collapsed ontology)*	*Open system (Stratified ontology)*	*Open system (Stratified ontology)*
Top-down	(Positivist) deduction[1]	Abductive deduction	Retroductive deduction[2] (Retrodiction)
Bottom-up	(Positivist) induction[1]	Abductive induction	Retroductive induction[2] (Retroduction)[3]
Reasoning mode and domain(s) of concern	Deduction[4] Empirical	Abduction (Abductive cycle): Empirical↔Actual	Retroduction[3] (Retroductive cycle): Empirical↔Actual↔Real

Notes (1) While the literature generally defines deduction and induction within the context of positivist closed system, they should be more accurately considered as directional reasoning logics applicable to different ontological depths (see Table 2.4). (2) Heeks and Wall (2018). (3) In the literature, retroduction can refer to two things: One is the retroductive cycle as a whole, and the other is retroductive induction. (4) In a closed system, positivist induction is relegated to the status of a way to test hypotheses derived from positivist deduction. As such, there is not much reasoning involved in positivist induction
Source Author's creation

observed data with the understanding of the already formed hypothesis, and it is used to justify a hypothesis with empirical data[39] (Blagden 2016; Deutscher 2002; Sarasvathy 2001; Taylor et al. 2018), and it should be more accurately referred to as 'positivist induction'. As such, positivist deduction and positivist induction are related in a positivist closed system, and they complement each other to form a reasoning cycle in the empirical domain. However, the so-called true premises in a closed system are not necessarily true and do not come from 'nowhere'. They are derived from the tacit and unconscious abduction or retroduction processes in open systems from a CR perspective. A major deficiency of positivism is that it is confined to tentatively finished product of scientific reasoning and pays no attention to the reasoning process whereby the so-called true premises receive their tentative first proposal (Van de Ven 2007). Such premises are in fact partial event regularities or '(partial) *mechanisms*' in Williamson (1998: 23), which is collapsed into the empirical domain from the real domain due to the flat ontology of TCE. In addition, positivist deduction, by definition, cannot accommodate multiple mechanisms because it starts from a true premise or axiom (Sarasvathy 2001). As such, positivist deduction and positivist induction are merely phases of testing

Table 2.4 Critical realism integrates TCE and effectuation

Domain	TCE	Eff.	CR	Closed system	Open system	Open system
Real			✓	Mechanism	Mechanism objectification	Mechanisms
Actual		✓	✓	Mechanism and social context collapsed into empirical domain	Single 'foreign' 'context'/ culture Abductive induction	Multiple contexts/ cultures Retroductive induction
Empirical	✓	✓	✓	Home Context/ Culture Positivist induction Positivist deduction Emic	Abductive deduction Dialectic	Retroductive deduction Etic
Notes:				• Causation comes first • Cognition prior to action • Deterministic induction: cannot lead to the discovery of new knowledge (Taylor et al. 2018) • Rationality • Single context • No ontological depth • No temporal depth • Assumptional asymmetry • Cultural distance as black box • Derivational unification	• Psychological processes come first since the initiation of abduction is inherently emotional (Blagden 2016; Thagard 2007). • Perception in the action process • Creative induction: learning is essential; knowledge discovery is grounded on abduction (Bamberger and Ang 2016) • 'Assumed rationality' (Bhaskar 2008) • Single constrained context (Dew and Sarasvathy 2002) • Ontologically deeper and wider • Temporally deep • Assumptional symmetry • Cultural distance give rise to biases	• Psychological processes come first. Retroduction is an intuitive process rather than a logical one. • Perception in the action process • Creative induction • Learning is essential • 'Assumed rationality' (Bhaskar 2008) • Transfactual, transcontextual and trans-disciplinary (e.g. Price and Martin 2018) • Ontologically the deepest and the widest • Temporally deep • Assumptional symmetry • Ontological unification

Source Author's creation based on Bhaskar (2008: 2). Eff. = Effectuation theory. The emic/dialectic/etic distinction is discussed in Sect. 3.3 and Chapter 7. Assumptional (a)symmetry and ontological unification are discussed in Sects. 2.12, 5.5 and 7.5.4.

an already formed tentative hypothesis (Deutscher 2002) in the closed system of the empirical domain.

In open systems, the actual and the real domains of CR become relevant, and the reasoning modes are retroduction and abduction, depending on aspired ontological depth. CR adopts retroduction as its main methodology for scientific inquiry, which is a 'mode of inference in which events are explained by postulating (and identifying) mechanisms which are capable of producing them' (Sayer 1992: 107; Mukumbang et al. 2019). As such, CR is particularly conducive to the consideration of the possibility of multiple mechanisms (Wynn and Williams 2012). In addition, while retroduction emphasizes generative mechanisms as the basis of explanation, it also allows researchers to 'identify the necessary contextual conditions for a particular causal mechanism to take effect and to result in the empirical trends observed' (Fletcher 2017: 189) and to understand that mechanisms are context dependent and thus may or may not be activated or experienced (Wynn and Williams 2012). This is natural considering its ontological depth, or more figuratively speaking, its ontological 'commanding heights'. In the literature, retroduction can refer to two things, one is the retroductive cycle as a whole, and the other is retroductive induction. Retroductive induction moves across the domains from the empirical via the actual to the real and represents the way by which the domains are connected within active research (Heeks and Wall 2018). Retroductive cycle is a reflective iteration in which (1) mechanisms are postulated by working backward from data in the empirical domain via the consideration of contextual conditions and then to causal mechanism (retroductive induction) (Fletcher 2017; Heeks and Wall 2018), and (2) previously identified mechanisms are applied to the explanation of an outcome in a new setting (retrodiction or retroductive deduction) (Wynn and Williams 2012). As such, retroduction is a transfactual and transcontextual reasoning mode which focuses on the identifications of generative mechanisms, and has its ontological base in CR (Blaikie and Priest 2019; Chamberlain 2006).

While abduction and retroduction are often treated as synonymous (Chiasson 2005; Mingers et al. 2013), abduction has its ontological base in interpretivism (Blaikie and Priest 2019; Chamberlain 2006: 295) at the actual domain level and is less concerned with ontological reality in the real domain. Abduction works backward from empirical domain to the actual domain (Fletcher 2017) in order to infer the best explanation for a given set of data (Fischer et al. 1991). This apparently parallels effectuation, which focuses on choosing the best achievable effects within a given set of means (Sarasvathy 2001). The so-called 'best' here is obviously highly speculative guesstimates (Sarasvathy and Dew 2005) based on perception since abduction reflects how much perceptual inference is conducted (Blagden 2016). Peirce indicated that guessing is a creative and deliberate part of abduction (Tschaepe 2014). As such, abduction is a reasoning of a psychological kind (Brogaard 1999).

Similar to the case of retroduction, abduction is also an iterative cycle, which involves abductive induction and abductive deduction. The former focuses on the role of creative 'flash of insight' (Blagden 2016; Waltz 1979: 4), whereas the latter involves a type of reasoning which has a logic form (Brogaard 1999). Abductive deduction is just a weak counterpart of positivist deduction. Since effectuation theory asserts that 'effectuation is a straight inversion of rational choice theory (also referred to as causal or predictive rationality)' (Read and Sarasvathy 2005: 50), and 'abduction involves creating new hypotheses purely from imagination' (Sarasvathy 2001: 257), effectuation theory leans too much on abductive induction (e.g., Arend et al. 2015). This is not a surprise since they share the same reasoning philosophy. This type of inference is a process of forming tentative creative hypotheses based on new facts or phenomena (Deutscher 2002). When information is limited or when some surprises are encountered, it is often a relevant strategy to start from little details or from surprising facts, and try with what is known or available to find a tentative hypothesis (Åsvoll 2014: 291), which, if confirmed, would explain the observed facts/phenomena (Deutscher 2002). Nevertheless, according to CR, the open systems in the actual domain imply that events and their magnitude are often the outcomes of multiple influences which simultaneously enhance or counteract each other. Because initial abduction takes place in one context and because of the overall tendency of effectuation to subjectivize the discourse on reality (Ramoglou and Tsang 2016), effectuation based on abduction is contingent on context, and explanation that works in one context does not guarantee its practical utility in another. Consequently, effectuation is not transfactual or transcontextual. In addition, the interpretivist approach used in effectuation[40] (Packard 2017; Sarasvathy 2001) and abduction (Shanahan 1989) also implies that effectuators need to become immersed in the interpretivist reality of the situation (Chamberlain 2006). As a result, the potential of effectuation theory is constrained (Dew and Sarasvathy 2002) at the actual domain since it is difficult to understand potentially multiple real mechanisms in one effectuation context. Effectuation theory has to get freed out of the actual domain in order to make further theoretical contributions.

Due to its ontological depth and behavioral theory-friendly assumptions, CR can apparently do a better job in bringing about a behavioral theory by 'integrating' TCE and effectuation theory. Here, we need to be more accurate about the word 'integrate'. Because TCE, effectuation theory, and CR are operative at the empirical, the actual, and the real levels, respectively, CR, or our proposed behavioral TCE, is a wholesale replacement for traditional TCE rather than a parallel.[41] What CR integrates are the inductive and deductive reasonings which can be used in all the three domains of CR, as shown in Tables 2.3 and 2.4. However, because TCE adopts a deductivist approach in the empirical domain (Pratten 1997) and effectuation leans on abductive induction (Arend et al. 2015), and because TCE and effectuation arguments are used in this book to build a behavioral TCE, we give Sect. 2.9 the current title for convenience.

2.9.2 *Critical Realism Facilitates a Better Understanding of Generative Mechanisms*

We also would like to suggest the benefits of the proposed integration in Sect. 2.9.1, particularly with regard to generative mechanisms. For TCE, the first benefit is the potential of getting a clear idea about the generative mechanisms behind its partial event regularities. As mentioned in the previous sections, TCE is not clear about its generative mechanism(s) in the real domain and incapable of accounting for uncontrollable external uncertainties. This is a symptom of its shallow positivist ontology. This careless attitude toward deep-domain generative mechanisms is further compounded by its inattention to social contexts, a concomitant symptom of its shallow ontology (Pratten 1997). The proposed integration will prompt TCE to give serious thought to its deep-lying generative mechanisms in the real domain and how they manifest in the actual domain. In so doing, it is hoped that it can reclaim its status as a genuine science by focusing on the identification and explanation of generative mechanisms in the real domain and how they manifest themselves in various social contexts in the actual domain rather than on event regularities in the empirical domain (Downward et al. 2002: 495).

Second, the adoption of a CR position will enable the consideration of more mechanisms which may either simultaneously enhance or counteract each other or be out of phase with each other. The deductivism in TCE forces it to subscribe to a dictum that 'explanations in the social sciences should […] be organized around (partial) *mechanisms* rather than around (general) *theories*' (Williamson 1998: 23; italic in original). As a result, it is constrained to consider only one mechanism, as discussed in Sect. 2.5 and Chapter 5.

Third, the integration opens up possibility for TCE to embrace learning once it is freed from the deductive trap and its ontological depth is deepened in an open system. The positivist deduction in a closed system, given its presupposition of an axiomatic premise, cannot lead to the discovery of new knowledge since the conclusion, as a logical necessity, has already been embedded in the premise (Blagden 2016; Taylor et al. 2018). TCE-based governance structures may give rise to the 'anti-innovation bias' (Williamson 1975; Teece 1996), which results in lower incentives to learn and innovate and slower response to technological opportunities in the external environment. In order for it to become a behavioral theory and benefit from creative inductive inferences at deeper ontological depths, psychological processes have to be moved to the front seat while deductive reasoning be relegated to the back seat since the initiation of abductive induction is inherently emotional (Thagard 2007).

Fourth, the deductivism in TCE constrains its potential to develop more compelling treatments of social institutions and human agency (Pratten 1997: 786). By broadening its domain into the actual domain, it is possible to consider social structure and firm behavior in a more coherent and convincing manner. Doing so is conducive to heightened awareness of generative mechanisms in the real domain.

For effectuation theory, the CR-based integration provides a clearly stratified ontology, which will lead effectuation to pay more attention to the contexts in the actual domain and generative mechanisms in the real domain. While effectuation is absorbed in '"*abducting*" a theory of effectual reasoning' (Sarasvathy 2001: 257), effectuation cannot happen in a vacuum; it has to be contextualized in the actual domain and anchored to generative mechanisms in the real domain. Effectuation theory suffers from the same problems as that with TCE: It has a much confused conceptualization of its generative mechanisms. The existing effectuation literature focuses on the actual domain that is conceptualized as a generic, abstract context of uncertainty (Kitching and Rouse 2020), without differentiating different types of uncertainties, and neglects the correct location of generative mechanisms by collapsing them into the actual domain. By adopting a CR position and by deepening the ontology of effectuation theory, the generative mechanisms can be correctly located in the real domain, and different types of uncertainties can be regarded as contingent contexts in the actual domain which actuate various mechanisms, consistent with recent advances in entrepreneurship literature (Ramoglou and Tsang 2016). Furthermore, the deepened ontology of both TCE and effectuation and their integration may provide TCE with the much needed mechanisms in the real domain. We discuss this point in Sect. 2.10.

Furthermore, for both TCE and effectuation theory, the CR-based integration adds temporal depth to each. In contrast to the deterministic deduction and induction in TCE due to its positivist stance, both abduction in effectuation theory and retroduction in CR involve dynamic iteration of an inductive (effectuation) process and a deductive (causation) process. For such iteration to take place, a temporal depth is needed. Since CR assumes an open system, it also opens up possibilities of organizations temporally interweaving causation and effectuation over time and thus learning (Chetty et al. 2015). The way the two reasoning processes interact parallels that between psychological 'rationalizing' and cognition, which is to be covered in Chapter 4.

In a longer span of firm life cycle, inductive and deductive reasonings can be considered as responses to different circumstances at different stages of firm development. Experienced firms are capable of using both modes well. Effectuation is preferred to causal reasoning in the early stages of a new investment, while causal reasoning becomes more relevant at later stages (Sarasvathy 2008). This is largely an outcome of organizational learning. With increasing learning, effectuation will give way to prediction, and causation models such as traditional TCE gain more dominance (Sarasvathy et al. 2014; Karami 2020). This is because learning enables firms to accumulate more pre-existing knowledge and make the future more predictable. As suggested by Sarasvathy (2001), the use of causation models depends on whether firms believe they are coping with a *perceptually* predictable situation. In this sense, effectuation theory converges with a behavioral TCE.

2.10 Uncertainty Controllability Makes Effectuation Theory Coherent

Effectuation is characterized by four dimensions: *pre-commitment*, *experimentation*, *affordable loss*, and *flexibility* (Chandler et al. 2011; Deligianni et al. 2017; Harms and Schiele 2012). Sarasvathy (2001: 251) suggests that effectuation focuses 'on the controllable aspects of an unpredictable future' using the underlying logic that 'to the extent we can control future, we do not need to predict it'. Considering the multitude of concepts adopted, some scholars (e.g., Arend et al. 2015) point out that effectuation defies easy explanation. [Thus, we leave the descriptions of these terms to Chapter 5 in Table 5.4.] These four dimensions and the logic of control are not stringed together in a consistent and coherent manner, and effectuation theory has been criticized for not having been critically analyzed and being counterintuitive (Arend et al. 2015; Kitching and Rouse 2020). Chandler et al. (2011) suggested that effectuation is a formative, multidimensional construct: While experimentation, affordable loss, and flexibility are associated and consistent with each other, the pre-commitment dimension is shared with the causation logic used in traditional TCE. Chandler et al. (2011) and Sarasvathy (2001) also suggest that experimentation is positively correlated with uncertainty, while causation is negatively associated with uncertainty.

We suggest that the confusion and lack of coherence in effectuation theory arise from an unclear understanding of the above-mentioned concept in effectuation theory, particularly with regard to uncertainty and experimentation. Such confusion can be attributed to the flat ontology that effectuation theory adopts, as pointed out in Sect. 2.8. While effectuation is the process of organizations experimenting, improvising, and adjusting in response to uncertainty, or the management of uncertainty (Galkina and Lundgren-Henriksson 2017; Sarasvathy 2001), effectuation theory has not clearly distinguished between controllable and uncontrollable uncertainty, and how different uncertainties, acting as contingent conditions in the actual domain of CR (cf. Kitching and Rouse 2020), may activate different generative mechanisms in the real domain which simultaneously enhance or counteract each other. The effectuation literature seems to have focused on uncontrollable uncertainty. Consistent with this focus, experimentation in effectuation theory seems to refer only to that based on affordable loss logic in order to adapt flexibly to uncontrollable environmental uncertainty. However, effectuation theory defines experimentation as competence-building through trial-and-error learning (Chandler et al. 2011). Experimentation so-defined can and should accommodate a different type of experimentation, one which is based on the logic of pre-commitment in order to adapt to controllable uncertainties through behavioral control based on relational interactions. Such effectuation logic will facilitate the transformation of business partners from dividing an existing pie to co-creating a new pie, and this co-creation allows for more flexibility in innovating outcomes (Galkina and Lundgren-Henriksson 2017; Peng and Beamish 2014; Read et al. 2015, 2016). Such flexibility is an internal type of flexibility based on organizational creativity enabled by aligning business partners. The ideas in this paragraph are summarized in Table 2.5.

Table 2.5 suggests that uncertainty controllability makes effectuation theory coherent by dispelling the confusion in the literature. While Sarasvathy (2001: 251) suggests that effectuation focuses 'on the controllable aspects of an unpredictable future' using the underlying logic that 'to the extent we can control future, we do not need to predict it', the distinction between relation/behavior and exposure, the two fundamentally different types of 'controllable aspects' of uncertainty according to controllability, has not been brought out. In addition, the distinction between capabilities and resources, which are required respectively for the control of relation/behavior and exposure, has not been articulated. Since effectuation theory is said to be one of the managements of uncertainty (Sarasvathy 2001; Sarasvathy and Ventakaraman 2011), it apparently can benefit from a more clear understanding about different types of uncertainties according to controllability.

Table 2.5 Uncertainty controllability makes effectuation theory coherent by activating different generative mechanisms[1]

Uncertainty controllability	*Controllable uncertainties*	*Uncontrollable uncertainties*
• Experimentation logic (Generative mechanism)	Pre-commitment	Affordable loss
• Flexibility (Adaptation logic)	Internal flexibility	External flexibility
• Control logic (Control as strategy rather than outcome)[2]	Through co-creation (Capabilities within control)[2]	Through setting loss limit (Resources within control)[2]
• Controllable aspects[3]	Relation/Behavior	Exposure

Notes (1) Table 5.4 contextualizes and expounds the ideas in this table in fuller detail. (2) Read et al. (2015, 2016). While organizations are control focused and prefer to select and exploit 'things' within their control (Read et al. 2015), the differences between resources and capabilities in effectuation have received scant attention. (3) Effectuation focuses 'on the controllable aspects of an unpredictable future' (Sarasvathy 2001: 251), or controllable aspects of uncertainties, which should consider both controllable and uncontrollable types. (4) Underlined are the four variables which characterize effectuation (Chandler et al. 2011; Deligianni et al. 2017; Harms and Schiele 2012)
Source Author's creation based on the introduction of uncertainty controllability

2.11 Ergodic/Nonergodic Uncertainties: A False Distinction According to Critical Realism

In Sect. 2.3.1, we mentioned that external uncertainty in the traditional non-behavioral version of TCE should be understood in an ergodic sense, since TCE adopts a tacit positivist philosophical position. We also said that traditional TCE gradually loses its applicability with increasing levels of nonergodic uncertainties, and suggested that behavioral TCE should be used to consider both ergodic and nonergodic uncertainties in a process manner. After the introduction of CR in the preceding sections, we can now discuss the distinction between ergodic and nonergodic uncertainty, point out the falsity of the distinction, and integrate them in a holistic view using CR in order to be consistent with a behavioral TCE.

2.11.1 The Ontological Confusion in the Ergodic/Nonergodic Distinction

The distinction between ergodic and nonergodic systems is a hallmark of post-Keynesianism, and there has been passionate debate about it (O'Donell 2014; Davidson 2015). According to post-Keynesianism, ergodic uncertainty is 'ontological' *certainty*, and nonergodic uncertainty is 'ontological' uncertainty (Downward et al. 2002; O'Donell 2014). The former is considered as risk with a probability distribution, and the latter generates 'intractable' *unknown* uncertainty. However, such distinction, even though it touches the concept of ontology, is ontologically confusing and questionable (Foldes 1958; O'Donell 2014),[42] as we discuss below.

First, the ergodic/nonergodic distinction suggests the existence of two mutually exclusive and independent ontologies or generative mechanisms: an ergodic mechanism that generates probabilistic uncertainty and a nonergodic mechanism that generates irreducible uncertainty (Davidson 1993: 425; 1996: 499; 2011: 99–100; Foldes 1958; O'Donell 2014). But as argued by O'Donell (2014), the former mechanism is epistemologically impossible pre-infinity, and at infinity, the latter becomes certainty. As such, nonergodic uncertainty should be the norm in the real world and there can be only one mechanism for uncertainty in the real domain. Ergodic uncertainty can only be conceptualized in a falsely closed system wherein 'closure' on economic system is imposed and the future is already predetermined. In this sense, the ergodic/nonergodic dichotomization corresponds closely to the distinction between closed and open systems in CR. To say that ergodic uncertainty can be 'completely' characterized by a probability distribution is just another way of saying that a falsely closed system exhibits partial event regularities, albeit stochastic ones (Lewis 2003). Since stochastic process theory is just a probabilistic manifestation of orthodox economics commitment to positivist deductivism (Lawson 1997; Lewis 2003), ergodic uncertainty is committed to positivism.

Second, nevertheless, the philosophical underpinnings of nonergodic uncertainty are a moot issue. Post-Keynesianism interprets probabilities as inherent in objects or events, and separates probabilities from their contexts or situations (Popper 1990; Runde 1996). Consequently, nonergodic uncertainty, due to its not taking the form of stochastic event regularities, cannot be adequately conceptualized. The ergodic/nonergodic distinction underlies an epistemological dichotomy between probabilistic knowledge of the future on the one hand and total ignorance of the future on the other (Lewis 2003). This dualistic stance toward knowledge implies that total ignorance reigns in situations where knowledge of event regularities cannot be obtained. This is a nihilistic view indeed (Lewis 2003) and raises the question of where the probabilistic distribution for the ergodic system comes from in the first place. The separation of probability distribution from its context implies that context is ignored and probability distribution is treated as objectified knowledge (Willet 1951). Such knowledge also exists prior to organizational actions rather than in the action process. This precludes the possibility of knowledge about social structures, which may well be the foundations of future probability distributions since probabilities are not inherent in events or objects but are properties of the whole social contexts (Popper 1990; Runde 1996). Even when knowledge about event regularities is insufficient or impossible, knowledge about social structure, which can facilitate socio-economic activities, is still attainable (Lewis 2003), especially thorough effectuation. The ergodic/nonergodic distinction presupposes the a priori existence of the probability distribution of ergodic systems, thus ruling out human agency in deriving the distribution. As such, nonergodic uncertainty in post-Keynesianism can be regarded as serving only a rhetorical role.[43] But without a clear treatment of nonergodic uncertainty, the foundations of ergodic uncertainty become shaky.

Third, the ergodic/nonergodic dichotomization is questionable for yet another reason. Since the dichotomization is made based on statistical

Table 2.6 Stratified ontology of uncertainties based on critical realism

Domain	*Real*	*Actual*	*Empirical*
Mechanisms	✓		
Ontological uncertainty			
Events (Nonergodic uncertainty)	✓	✓	
Perceived/interpretive uncertainty			
Complexity and change[1]			
Experiences (Ergodic uncertainty)	✓	✓	✓
Objectified uncertainty			
Complexity (deterministic)[1]			
Event regularities (Lewis 2003)			

Note (1) Duncan (1972)
Source Author's creation based on Bhaskar (2008: 2)

measurability, the dichotomization breaks down if we think of measurability as a matter of degree because all gradations exist and there is no clear dividing line (Foldes 1958). In fact, the confusion about the ergodic/nonergodic distinction arises from the word 'measurability' since it suggests a yes/no answer. We think that statistical *measuredness*[44] may be a better word for the intended meaning in line with CR.

In sum, the problems with the ergodic/nonergodic distinction can be attributed to the fact that 'the post-Keynesian school of thought represents a positive statement of methodology, ideology and content' (Arestis 1990: 223; Lawson 1994). As a result, confusion arises from the flat ontology of the positivist deductive approach (Lawson 1997; Lewis 2003). We submit that the above confusions about ergodic/nonergodic uncertainties can be resolved by resorting to the ontological depth of CR and locating them into different domains of CR, as shown in Table 2.6. In so doing, the stance toward uncertainty can be raised from positivism to CR, and such a change in philosophical stance will be conducive to the introduction of a behavioral TCE. We explain this point below.

2.11.2 Ontological Depth of Critical Realism Integrates Ergodic/Nonergodic Uncertainties

According to CR, post-Keynesianism conflates various CR domains and collapses uncertainties in the actual domain into the empirical domain, thus imposing artificial 'closure' on economic systems and precluding the analysis of the *relationship* between uncertainties at different ontological depths. CR can integrate ergodic and nonergodic uncertainties for its ontological depth which can harmonize uncertainties in different domains. Ergodic and nonergodic uncertainties reflect the same ontological uncertainty manifested in the empirical and actual domains of CR, respectively. What the post-Keynesianist ergodic/nonergodic distinction was intended to mean is that between objective and subjective *interpretations* of probabilities (Foldes 1958; Popper 1990; Runde 1996). CR can perfectly integrate these two views of probabilities.

Ergodic uncertainty should be regarded as an empirical uncertainty in the empirical domain which falsely imposes artificial closure on an open system and reduces ontological uncertainty to 'certainty' within the shallow epistemology of the empirical domain. Such uncertainty is in fact falsely objectified[45] uncertainty which is separated from organizational actions. Contrary to the post-Keynesian view that ergodic uncertainty is not uncertainty because such uncertainty can be reduced to certainty through objectified knowledge of a probability statement (Davidson 1972, 1991), CR suggests that probability is inseparable from uncertainty and is thus still uncertainty (O'Donell 2014), albeit in the empirical domain. Probabilities are still relevant to uncertainty since their distributions are empirically derived from observing relative frequencies, thus only reflecting the statistical measurability of uncertainty rather than uncertainty itself (O'Donell 2014). According to CR, probabilities are propensities,[46] and both are situationally dependent since propensities are properties of the whole ontological situations (Popper 1990; Runde 1996). Probability distribution in the empirical domain is only *a deductive tool* (Barnett 1999), reflecting, accurately or inaccurately, the ontological generative mechanism in the real domain (Downward et al. 2002; Popper 1990). In addition, with bounded human cognition and 'information asymmetry', ergodic uncertainty can cause market inefficiency or even market failure (Williamson 1975, 1985).

Nonergodic uncertainty should be properly considered as an uncertainty in the actual domain which has not been experienced by human actors. While Knight (1921) considered such uncertainty as something unmeasurable, uncertainty measurability should be considered as a process rather than a dichotomy between measurable and unmeasurable uncertainties. The process view allows for one underlying generative mechanism in the real domain while the dichotomy view suggests two different ontologies. It is nonergodic uncertainty that opens up possibilities for making TCE behavioral because nonergodic uncertainty is subjective (Foldes 1958; Knight 1921) and relates to a state of the mind (Pfeffer 1956). It is in the actual domain that organizational effectuators can immerse in the context of nonergodic uncertainties, do sense-making, and effectuate actions (Horst and Grabska 2015), and it is nonergodic uncertainty that necessitates the shift from positivism to CR in order to consider human fallibility and the accompanying shift toward a behavioral TCE.[47] In contrast, ergodic uncertainty in traditional TCE is only a procedural uncertainty (Dequech 2006), which requires only substantive rationality, thus not conducive to a behavioral TCE approach (see Sect. 4.5.1 and Table 4.4).

2.11.3 Critical Realism and the Long-Run Applicability of Transaction Cost Economics

To conclude this chapter, we would also mention that the behavioral shift from positivism to CR can help resolve the debate about the long-run applicability of the traditional version of TCE. Some scholars are concerned that traditional TCE might lose its applicability under ergodic uncertainties since such uncertainties can be mitigated through learning and, as a result, markets will eventually supersede firms (e.g., Dunn 2000; Slater and Spencer 2000: 80). They suggest that nonergodic uncertainty can be used to explain the existence of firms in the long run. Nevertheless, such a suggestion reveals that they embrace two mutually exclusive and independent generative mechanisms and are committed to something close to 'nihilistic positivism' (cf. Lewis 2003).

From a CR perspective, however, the debate can be readily resolved: TCE is applicable in the long run if it is rendered behavioral by adopting a CR framework. Under a behavioral TCE, the distinction between ergodic and nonergodic uncertainties is regarded as a false one since they both reflect the same ontological reality. The 'ergodic' uncertainty in the empirical domain is not certainty since probability distributions reflect causal mechanisms which generate only 'tendencies' (Popper 1990). Hence, such 'ergodic' uncertainty does not necessarily cause a problem to the theory of the firm, particularly under bounded rationality. As for 'nonergodic' uncertainties, they exist in actual domain and have not been experienced by economic actors. They do not cause a problem either, whether experienced or not. If experienced, they serve to update the probability distribution in the empirical domain based on judgmental rationality in CR. Here, we assume that in normal market 'ergodic' uncertainties dominate, and this is not a strong assumption considering the firms mainly experience in the empirical domain. If by any chance nonergodic uncertainties become dominant, the boundary conditions of TCE will be invalidated, as discussed previously. The existence of firms has to be justified based on other theories, such as the effectuation theory and competence-based perspectives (Dahle et al. 2020). This is because firms will be more focused on effectuation than prediction when nonergodic uncertainties dominate. Since effectuation takes a set of means as given and focuses on choosing between alternative effects that can be achieved within the set of means (Sarasvathy 2001), theories which have a bearing on means (resources and capabilities) should be backing up the effectuation process. Scholars have also pointed out the potential synergies between the resource-based view and the concept of nonergodicity in post-Keynesianism (Dunn 2000). CR integrates TCE and effectuation into a behavioral theory of decision-making, as we will discuss more about this in Chapter 5.

2.12 Assumptional Symmetry and Ontological Unification

Based on the previous sections, it can be said that the assumptions of TCE are not clearly articulated by Williamson and not well understood by scholars who use it. We can conclude that TCE in fact fundamentally assumes only bounded rationality and *controllable* uncertainty. By equivocating about *uncontrollable* uncertainty, TCE theoretically suffers from 'assumptional asymmetry' and lacks 'ontological unification'[48] (Foss and Hallberg 2014), which hinders theoretical advancement since the effects of uncontrollable uncertainty is treated as indeterminate and peripheral to governance structures. Empirically, the asymmetrical treatment of its assumptions leads TCE empirical research to rely on the use of assumption-omitted, reduced models, which are capable only of predicting event regularities rather than of 'mechanismic explanations' (Bunge 1997; Tsang 2006). We discuss this point passim in this book.

While Foss and Hallberg (2014: 903) have made an extremely insightful contribution in stating that 'assumptional symmetry leads to theoretical advancement by promoting the development of theory with greater falsifiability and stronger ontological grounding', the potential of CR to contextualize and facilitate ontological grounding was not spelled out. Based on foregoing presentations of CR and its link with various theoretical aspects, we suggest that, in order for theoretical scholars to 'discover' symmetrical assumptions, they will need to theorize at the real domain level from the outset. This book contributes to what Foss and Hallberg (2014) have proposed by achieving both assumptional symmetry and ontological unification in the setting of the development of a behavioral TCE. Chapter 5 demonstrates the points in this section in fuller detail.

Notes

1. As mentioned in Chapter 1, Williamson (1985) used risk neutrality as another assumption of TCE. However, risk neutrality has gone virtually unnoticed in comparison with opportunism and bounded rationality (Chiles and McMackin 1996). In this book, we show that the assumption of risk neutrality is unrealistic and suggest that variable risk preferences should be the assumption appropriate for a behavioral theory (Chiles and McMackin 1996; Martynov and Schepker 2017).
2. Among the five concepts mentioned in this sentence, only asset specificity is usually numerically measured (Buckley and Chapman 2002). While transaction frequency is mentioned as a transaction attribute, it is not dealt with directly in the model by Williamson. It is largely considered to be a less important factor in TCE (Mahoney 1992; Rindfleisch and Heide 1997). In fact, the difficulty in incorporating transaction frequency arises from equilibrium contracting at the core of TCE, which cannot adequately consider frequency. Transaction frequency loses its relevance in a behavioral theory of the firm. As we discuss in Chapter 7, even the empirical findings about the relationship between asset specificity and governance structures are subject to challenge.
3. See Endnote 14 in Chapter 1.
4. Parker (1978) notes that 'behavioral variability was...related to the opportunist/specialist distinction: the opportunists or generalists were more behaviorally diverse'.
5. This argument is in line with the concept of near-decomposability (Simon 1996) to which TCE subscribes (Williamson 1999, 2002): In a nearly decomposable system, the short-run behavior of each of the subcomponent is approximately independent of the short-run behavior of the other subcomponents, and the long-run behavior of any one of the subcomponents depends in only an aggregative way on the behavior of the other subcomponents (Simon 1996). Additionally, the concept of decomposability is in fact another way of saying methodological individualism, which TCE and other mainstream economics exhibit (Ingham 1996).

6. This distinction can only be made based on an assumption about the separation of ontology and epistemology and the presupposition of an ontology. We discuss this further in Sect. 2.6.
7. In an ergodic world, events are governed by probability distributions: '[t]he future is merely the statistical reflection of the past and economic actions are in some sense timeless', and '[i]n the ergodic circumstances of objective probability distributions, probability is knowledge, not uncertainty!' (Davidson 1991: 132). This idea can be easily understood using a quote from the Bible: 'what has been will be again, what has been done will be done again; there is nothing new under the sun' (NIV Ecclesiastes 1: 9). More information on the distinctions between ergodic and nonergodic processes can be found in Dunn (2000, 2001).
8. Nevertheless, whether this point is clear in TCE is debatable. This can be explained in the context of MNC subsidiary ownership literature wherein there are conflicting views about the relationship between external uncertainty and subsidiary ownership levels. On the one hand, Williamson (1975, 1985, 1991) proposes that external uncertainty will lead firms to internalize their control. This seems to suggest that external uncertainty in TCE is nonergodic 'fundamental uncertainty' which precludes economic agents from comprehensive ex ante contracting *even in the long run* (Dunn 2000). On the other hand, other scholars (e.g., Anderson and Gatignon 1986) propose that external uncertainty will result in forms assuming low ownership levels in order to retain strategic flexibility in adapting to environmental changes. This seems to suggest that external uncertainty is ergodic. The fact that the latter view has generally been taken in the international business literature (Slangen and van Tulder 2009) seems to agree with the view that TCE implicitly assumes ergodic processes surrounding transactions (Dunn 2000).
9. Please note that the discussion in this and the following paragraph is based on the traditional, non-behavioral version of TCE that adopts a tacit positivist philosophical position. We will return to provide a behavioral view about the distinction between ergodic and nonergodic uncertainties in Sect. 2.11 after the introduction of CR in Sect. 2.7.
10. As subsequently discussed in Sect. 2.7, from a CR view, it is more accurate to say that the causal mechanisms in producing future events are 'preconstituted'.
11. We refrain from a detailed discussion on this, considering the multitude of terms and classifications about uncertainty in numerous articles and books (Magnani and Zucchella 2018). Refer to Dequech (2006: 112–117) for a short summary of different conceptions of uncertainty.
12. Two points are worth noting here. (1) The words 'reduced' and 'eliminated' are used for convenience since many people use such expressions as 'to reduce uncertainty'. But as Slater and Spencer (2000) pointed out,

uncertainty in TCE is entirely exogenous and objectively fixed and as such cannot be reduced. What can be reduced is bounded rationality through learning. (2) Such uncertainty cannot be eliminated for an epistemological reason arising from bounded rationality. There is a difference between information and knowledge: The former is just 'data organized into a meaningful pattern' whereas the latter is 'information with a layer of intellectual analysis' (Hislop 2005: 16), which can be obtained only via processes of cognition and interpretation (Hodgson 1998). Bounded rationality can lead to imperfect knowledge even in the presence of perfect information (Hardt 2009). See Chapter 4.

13. The distinction between ergodic and nonergodic systems is a hallmark of post Keynesianism (O'Donell 2014). Even though some scholars think that Williamson 'misinterprets the concept of statistically predictable risk for nonergodic uncertainty' (Davidson and Davidson 1984), Williamson was aware of the distinction and claimed that 'the distinction is not one with which I will be concerned – if indeed it is a truly useful one to employ in any context whatsoever' (1975: 23). Other scholars argue that the distinction is vague and applying probabilistic calculus to uncertainty causes no problem (e.g., LeRoy and Singell 1987). Nevertheless, as discussed in Sect. 2.11, ergodic and nonergodic uncertainties can be integrated in CR.
14. If so, how can opportunism be considered as a behavioral *assumption*? Here, Williamson contradicts himself.
15. Here, uncertainty refers to 'epistemological uncertainty' or bounded rationality (Dunn 2001). Refer to Sect. 2.6.
16. The tautology can also be resolved by considering whether the uncertainty of concern is 'internalizable' or not. 'Internalizable' and 'internal' (or internalized) relate to the senses of independent variable and dependent variable, respectively. Because controllability leads to internalizability, and because the former term is more widely used in the risk perception literature, we use the former term as well.
17. The other factor is 'familiarity' or knowledge about risk (Slovic 1987), which actually refers to the epistemological side of risk. Risk researchers in the psychometric paradigm have consistently found a factor space for risks with two main dimensions, controllability and familiarity (Johnson and Tversky 1984; Slovic 1987; Slovic et al. 1982; Vlek and Stallen 1981). In the context of this book, this familiarity factor belongs to bounded rationality. Some other scholars define risk perception as an economic agent's evaluation of how risky or uncertain a situation is in terms of probabilistic estimates of the degree of consequence uncertainty and how confident the agent is in those estimates, in addition to controllability (Sitkin and Weingart 1995).

18. Howell and Burnett (1978) applied the terms 'internal uncertainty' and 'external uncertainty', respectively, to uncertainties that organization can or cannot control. We think they should have simply used 'controllable uncertainty' and 'uncontrollable uncertainty' for conceptual clarity.
19. This raises the question of how to define 'not too high'. See subsequent explanation that TCE should be applied to situations where uncontrollable uncertainties are low (Rese and Roemer 2004).
20. Foss (1994: 56) pointed out that 'while an ontology that recognizes the open-endedness of the economic universe is necessary to Williamson's theorizing, he has not gone very far down that road of process that would be implied by such an ontology'.
21. For the interested reader, a succinct introduction to CR can be found in Gorski (2013). Miller and Tsang (2011: 144) provide some references which compare critical realism with various other philosophical perspectives.
22. A fallible ontology implies the existence of a real ontology. While Cruickshank (2004) argues that CR has two definitions of ontology, i.e., a definition of a reality beyond our knowledge claims and a fallible concept or interpretation of reality. These two definitions do not contradict each other. Fallible ontology reaffirms a realist ontology since 'fallible' implies something 'real'. It also suggests a fallibilist epistemology and such an epistemological stance distances CR from other perspectives such as interpretivism (Satsangi 2013).
23. Generative mechanisms are more than 'powers' but 'tendencies', which are not just potentialities but potentialities that may be exercised without being manifested (Bhaskar 2008: 40; Steinmetz 1998: 177). This definition of generative mechanism is consistent with the eight-consciousness model that we will discuss in Chapter 4, according to which the eighth consciousness is a storehouse consciousness that contains the tendencies from all past experiences and actions and their continuing influence upon present processes of mind (Waldron 2003).
24. Bhaskar (1986: 193) points out that positivism is content to 'stick to appearances in opposition to the law which regulates, and explains, them'.
25. This is because multiple generative mechanisms governing different theories can operate simultaneously in the actual domain.
26. Note that closed system and open system operate in different domains. The positivist approach is tied to the empirical domain and adopts a deductivist approach for predicting empirical regularities, and as such, it treats systems as closed and adopts the conception of laws as regularity laws. When the three-domain concept of ontology is introduced, the actual domain is treated as open systems since actual events may happen outside closed systems under open-ended contingent conditions and the influence of various mechanisms. In open systems, event regularities may

not occur but events are still governed by 'something', or the tendencies of causal mechanisms. Open systems at the actual level arise as a result of the endless potential eventualizations of causal mechanism. At the real domain, CR seeks to identify what 'governs phenomena in open systems' (Bhaskar 2011: 16). For more information, see Fleetwood (2017).

27. While the CR literature sometimes uses generative mechanisms and social structure interchangeably, this study uses these two terms to mean different things. We use social structure to mean contingent conditions under which mechanism-expressing events (whether experienced or unexperienced by human agents) are generated. Such social structures include institutions, which may be unexperienced (Leca and Naccache 2006), and social phenomena, which are experienced (Steele 2005), etc.
28. Slater and Spencer (2000: 77–78) note that 'there can be neither agency nor socially constituted behavior' in Williamson's 'one-shot equilibrium in which efficient organization is achieved at the outset'.
29. Runde (1996) points out that Popper's final thinking is at one with CR.
30. Generative mechanisms should not be confused with governance mechanisms in the sense of Williamson (1996), which refer to governance structures (contracts) against potential opportunism.
31. This is because we disagree with the antithesis of prediction and effectuation, as discussed in Sect. 2.9.
32. Effectuation theory is widely used in the entrepreneurship literature. Nevertheless, effectuation can be readily applied to other areas since Sarasvathy (2001) uses the term 'entrepreneurship' to refer to the process by which new business ventures are created and 'entrepreneur' to people creating new ventures. Sarasvathy (2001) has also suggested that effectuation theory might be relevant to non-new business settings (Kitching and Rouse 2020).
33. A neglect of the epistemology side will lead to a justification for the status quo.
34. In entrepreneurship literature, value is often stated in terms of what constitutes an opportunity (Arend et al. 2015; Shane and Venkataraman 2000).
35. Natural selection favors rational strategies: 'given natural selection, acceptance of the hypothesis can be based largely on the *judgment* that it summarizes appropriately the conditions for survival' (Friedman 1953: 22; italic added).
36. Prediction is deduction (Shanahan 1989).
37. While the term abduction may have been used for its common suffix ('duction', from the Latin *ducere*, to lead) with deduction and induction, the original term used, 'presumption', or guessing, may be easier to

understand. Peirce (1902) explained that '[R]easoning is of three elementary kinds; but mixed reasonings are more common. These three kinds are induction, deduction, and presumption'.

38. They can also be applied to both etic and emic studies (Douglass and Lindauer 1988). See Sect. 3.3.
39. '[T]he narrow empiricism traditionally associated with the term positivism would actually be more in keeping with induction than the deduction' (Blagden 2016: 199).
40. Sarasvathy (2001: 257) even mentioned that 'abduction involves creating new hypotheses purely from imagination'. Since effectuation theory emphasizes '"*abducting*" a theory of effectual reasoning' (Sarasvathy 2001: 257), effectuation is presumption according to Endnote 37 above.
41. While Dew and Sarasvathy (2002) regarded effectuation as a parallel of predictive rationality, they conflated empirical and actual domains of CR.
42. Some scholars argue that the distinction is vague and applying probabilistic calculus to uncertainty causes no problem (e.g., LeRoy and Singell 1987).
43. This is also a general criticism about the 'method' in conventional economics which offers no methodology in reality but only a rhetorical trick (Schumacher 1973; Voss 2016).
44. In fact '[t]he orthodox conception of 'scientific' economic knowledge about the future relationship among observable economic variables [...] essentially involves projecting statistical averages based on past and/or current realisations to forthcoming events' (Davidson 1989: 477–478).
45. Knight (1921) refers to risk or ergodic uncertainty as 'objective' and to nonergodic uncertainty as 'subjective' probability (Foldes 1958).
46. This is because probability becomes a measure of unobservable but ontologically real propensity (Runde 1996).
47. Some scholars suggest that ergodic uncertainty is consistent with CR, while nonergodic uncertainty is not since it precludes the existence of real governing mechanisms behind events (Downward et al. 2002). This is a misunderstanding. Ergodic uncertainty and nonergodic uncertainty do not contradict each other since CR assumes fallible ontology. The ergodic-nonergodic distinction is not concerned with causal mechanisms but is only a comment on the heterogeneity of economic behavior over time (Walters and Young 1999) in the actual domain. Such distinction can be readily reconciled based on the assumption of fallible ontology, fallibilist epistemology, and judgmental rationality of CR.
48. Foss and Hallberg (2014: 907) stated that '[a]ssumptional symmetry is closely related to the idea of "ontological unification," that is, to the extent that phenomena share basic characteristics, science should be aimed at "redescribing apparently independent and diverse phenomena as manifestations (outcomes, phases, forms, aspects) of one and the same small

number of entities, powers, and processes" (Mäki 2001: 498)'. Mäki (2001) distinguished between 'ontological unification' and 'derivational unification' as two variants of 'explanatory unification', and we will return to this distinction in Chapter 7.

References

Aaker, D. A., & Jacobson, R. (1990). The risk of marketing. In R. A. Bettis & H. Thomas (Eds.), *Risk, strategy and management* (pp. 137–160). Greenwich, CT: JAI Press.

Ackroyd, S., & Fleetwood, F. (2000). Realism in contemporary organization and management studies. In S. Ackroyd & F. Fleetwood (Eds.), *Realist perspectives on management and organisations* (pp. 3–25). London: Routledge.

Ahsan, M., & Musteen, M. (2011). Multinational enterprises' entry mode strategies and uncertainty. *International Journal of Management Reviews, 13*(4), 376–392.

Alchian, A. A. (1950). Uncertainty, evolution, and economic theory. *Journal of Political Economy, 58*(3), 211–221.

Alchian, A. A., & Woodward, S. (1988). The firm is dead. *Journal of Economic Literature, 26*(1), 65–79.

Alessandri, T. M., Ford, D. N., Lander, D. M., Leggio, K. B., & Taylor, M. (2004). Managing risk and uncertainty in complex capital projects. *Quarterly Review of Economics and Finance, 44*(50), 751–767.

Alpers, I. (2019). *Managing the 'unknowns'*. Doctoral dissertation. University of St. Gallen.

Alvarez, S. A., Afuah, A., & Gibson, C. (2018). Should management theories take uncertainty seriously? *Academy of Management Review, 43*(2), 69–72.

Anderson, E., & Gatignon, H. (1986). Modes of foreign entry: A transaction cost analysis and propositions. *Journal of International Business Studies, 17*(3), 1–26.

Archer, M. S. (1995). *Realist social theory*. Cambridge: Cambridge University Press.

Arend, R. J., Sarooghi, H., & Burkemper, A. (2015). Effectuation as ineffectual? *Academy of Management Review, 40*(4), 630–651.

Arestis, P. (1990). Post-Keynesianism: A new approach to economics. *Review of Social Economy, 48*(3), 222–246.

Arıkan, A. T. (2020). Opportunism is in the eye of the beholder. *Journal of Business Ethics, 161*, 573–589.

Åsvoll, H. (2014). Abduction, deduction and induction. *International Journal of Qualitative Studies in Education, 27*(3), 289–307.

Bamberger, P., & Ang, S. (2016). The quantitative discovery. *Academy of Management Discoveries, 2*(1), 1–6.

Banai, R. (1995). Critical realism, and urban and regional studies. *Environment and Planning B, 22*(5), 563–580.
Barnett, V. (1999). *Comparative statistical inference*. New York: John Wiley & Sons.
Baum, J. A. C., & Ingram, P. (2002). Interorganizational learning and network organizations. In M. Augier & J. March (Eds.), *The economics of choice, change, and organization* (pp. 191–218). Cheltenham: Edward Elgar.
Baum, J. A. C., Shipilov, A. V., & Rowley, T. J. (2003). Where do small worlds come from? *Industrial and Corporate Change, 12*(4), 697–725.
Bhaskar, R. (1979). *The possibility of naturalism*. Atlantic Highlands, NJ: Humanities Press.
Bhaskar, R. (1986). *Scientific realism and human emancipation*. London: Routledge.
Bhaskar, R. (1998). Philosophy and scientific realism. In M. Archer, R. Bhaskar, A. Collier, T. Lawson, & A. Norrie (Eds.), *Critical realism* (pp. 16–47). London: Routledge.
Bhaskar, R. (2008). *A realist theory of science*. London: Routledge.
Bhaskar, R. (2010). Contexts of interdisciplinarity. In R. Bhaskar, C. Frank, K. G. Høyer, P. Naess, & J. Parker (Eds.), *Interdisciplinarity and climate change* (pp. 15–38). London: Routledge.
Bhaskar, R. (2011). *Reclaiming Reality*. London: Routledge.
Blagden, D. (2016). Induction and deduction in international relations. *International Studies Review, 18*(2), 195–213.
Blaikie, N. W. H., & Priest, J. (2019). *Designing social research: The logic of anticipation*. Medford, MA: Polity.
Boholm, A. (1998). Comparative studies of risk perception. *Journal of Risk Research, 1*(2), 135–163.
Boyd, R., Gasper, P., & Trout, J. D. (1991). *The philosophy of science*. Cambridge: MIT Press.
Brogaard, B. O. (1999). Peirce on abduction and rational control. *Transactions of the Charles S. Peirce Society, 35*(1), 129–155.
Bromiley, P., & Harris, J. (2006). Trust, transaction cost economics, and mechanisms. In R. Bachmann & A. Zaheer (Eds.), *Handbook of trust research* (pp. 124–143). Northampton, MA: Edward Elgar.
Brouthers, K. D., Brouthers, L. E., & Werner, S. (2008). Real options, international entry mode choice and performance. *Journal of Management Studies, 45*(5), 936–960.
Bruyat, C., & Julien, P. A. (2001). Defining the field of research in entrepreneurship. *Journal of Business Venturing, 16*(2), 165–180.
Buckley, P. J. (2016). The contribution of internalization theory to international business. *Journal of World Business, 51*(1), 74–82.

Buckley, P. J., & Chapman, M. (1997). The use of native categories in management research. *British Journal of Management, 8*(4), 283–299.

Buckley, P. J., & Chapman, M. (2002). Transactions costs and uncertainty: Theory and practice. In S. C. Dow & J. Hillard (Eds.), *Post Keynesian Econometrics, Microeconomics and the Theory of the Firm* (pp. 44–59). Cheltenham, UK: Edward Elgar.

Bunge, M. (1997). Mechanism and explanation. *Philosophy of the Social Sciences, 27*(4), 410–465.

Carson, S. J., & John, G. (2013). A theoretical and empirical investigation of property rights sharing in outsourced research, development, and engineering relationships. *Strategic Management Journal, 34*(9), 1065–1085.

Chamberlain, G. P. (2006). Researching strategy formation process. *Quality & Quantity, 40*(2), 289–301.

Chandler, G. N., DeTienne, D. R., McKelvie, A., & Mumford, T. V. (2011). Causation and effectuation processes. *Journal of Business Venturing, 26*(3), 375–390.

Chawla, C., Mangaliso, M., Knipes, B., & Gauthier, J. (2012). Antecedents and implications of uncertainty in management. *Journal of Management History, 18*(2), 200–218.

Chetty, S., Ojala, A., & Leppaaho, T. (2015). Effectuation and foreign market entry of entrepreneurial firms. *European Journal of Marketing, 49*(9), 1436–1459.

Chi, T., Li, J., Trigeorgis, L. G., & Tsekrekos, A. E. (2019). Real options theory in international business. *Journal of International Business Studies, 50*(4), 525–553.

Chiasson, P. (2005). Abduction as an aspect of retroduction. *Semiotica, 153*(1/4), 223–242.

Chiles, T. H., & McMackin, J. F. (1996). Integrating variable risk preferences, trust, and transaction cost economics. *Academy of Management Review, 21*(1), 73–99.

Coase, R. H. (1937). The nature of the firm. *Economica, 4*(16), 386–405.

Coase, R. H. (1988). The nature of the firm: Influence. *Journal of Law Economics and Organization, 4*(1), 33–47.

Collier, A. (1994). *Critical realism*. London: Verso.

Combe, E., & Mucchielli, J. L. (1998). The multinational firm versus the host country. In A. M. Rugman & J. Mucchielli (Eds.), *Multinational location strategy* (pp. 185–210). Emerald: Bingley.

Cruickshank, J. (2004). A tale of two ontologies. *Sociological Review, 52*(4), 567–585.

Cuypers, I. R. P., & Martin, X. (2010). What makes and what does not make a real option? *Journal of International Business Studies, 41*(1), 47–69.

Dahle, Y., Nguyen-Duc, A., Steinert, M., & Reuther, K. (2020). Six pillars of modern entrepreneurial theory and how to use them. In A. Nguyen-Duc, J. Münch, R. Prikladnicki, X. Wang, & P. Abrahamsson (Eds.), *Fundamentals of Software Startups* (pp. 3–25). Cham: Springer.
David, R. J., & Han, S. (2004). A systematic assessment of the empirical support for transaction cost economics. *Strategic Management Journal, 25*(1), 39–58.
Davidson, P. (1972). *Money and the real world*. London: Macmillan.
Davidson, P. (1989). The economics of ignorance or ignorance of economics? *Critical Review, 3*(3/4), 467–487.
Davidson, P. (1991). Is probability theory relevant for uncertainty? *Journal of Economic Perspectives, 5*(1), 129–143.
Davidson, P. (1993). Austrians and Post Keynesians on economic reality. *Critical Review, 7*(2/3), 423–444.
Davidson, P. (1996). Reality and economic theory. *Journal of Post Keynesian Economics, 18*(4), 479–508.
Davidson, P. (2011). *Post Keynesian macroeconomic theory*. Cheltenham, UK: Edward Elgar.
Davidson, P. (2015). A rejoinder to O'Donnell's critique of the ergodic/nonergodic explanation of Keynes's concept of uncertainty. *Journal of Post Keynesian Economics, 38*(1), 1–18.
Davidson, P., & Davidson, G. S. (1984). Financial markets and Williamson's theory of governance. *Quarterly Review of Economics and Business, 24*(4), 50–63.
de Bruin, A., & Moore, C. (2005). Incorporating ethical and trust-based behaviour into economics. *Journal of Interdisciplinary Economics, 16*(3), 289–306.
De Weck, O., Eckert, C. M., & Clarkson, P. J. (2007). A classification of uncertainty for early product and system design. In *Proceedings of ICED 2007*.
DeForge, R., & Shaw, J. (2012). Back- and fore-grounding ontology. *Nursing Inquiry, 19*(1), 83–95.
Deligianni, I., Voudouris, I., & Lioukas, S. (2017). Do effectuation processes shape the relationship between product diversification and performance in new ventures? *Entrepreneurship Theory and Practice, 41*(3), 349–377.
Demsetz, H. (1997). *The economics of the business firm*. Cambridge: Cambridge University Press.
Denzin, N. K., & Lincoln, Y. S. (2011). *The Sage handbook of qualitative research*. Thousand Oaks, CA: Sage.
Dequech, D. (2004). Uncertainty. *Cambridge Journal of Economics, 28*(3), 365–378.
Dequech, D. (2006). The new institutional economics and the theory of behavior under uncertainty. *Journal of Economic Behavior & Organization, 59*(1), 109–131.

Deutscher, G. (2002). On the misuse of the notion of 'abduction' in linguistics. *Journal of Linguistics, 38*(3), 469–485.
Dew, N., Read, S., Sarasvathy, S. D., & Wiltbank, R. (2008). Outlines of a behavioral theory of the entrepreneurial firm. *Journal of Economic Behavior & Organization, 66*(1), 37–59.
Dew, N., & Sarasvathy, S. D. (2002). *What effectuation is not*. Paper presented at the Annual Meeting of the Academy of Management.
Dewey, J. (1929). *The quest for certainty*. New York: Perigee.
Donaldson, L. (1990). The ethereal hand. *Academy of Management Review, 15*(3), 369–381.
Douglass, A. A., & Lindauer, O. (1988). Hierarchical and nonhierarchical approaches to ceramic design analysis. *American Antiquity, 53*(3), 620–626.
Downward, P., Finch, J. H., & Ramsay, J. (2002). Critical realism, empirical methods and inference. *Cambridge Journal of Economics, 26*(4), 481–500.
Duncan, R. B. (1972). Characteristics of organizational environments and perceived environmental uncertainty. *Administrative Science Quarterly, 17*(3), 313–327.
Dunn, S. P. (2000). Fundamental uncertainty and the firm in the long run. *Review of Political Economy, 12*(4), 419–433.
Dunn, S. P. (2001). Bounded rationality is not fundamental uncertainty. *Journal of Post Keynesian Economics, 23*(4), 567–587.
Fetzer, J. H., Shatz, D., & Schlesinger, G. N. (1991). *Definitions and definability*. Dordrecht: Springer.
Fischer, O., Goel, A., Svirbely, J. R., & Smith, J. W. (1991). The role of essential explanation in abduction. *Artificial Intelligence in Medicine, 3*(4), 181–191.
Fleetwood, S. (2005). Ontology in organization and management studies. *Organization, 12*(2), 197–222.
Fleetwood, S. (2017). The critical realist conception of open and closed systems. *Journal of Economic Methodology, 24*(1), 41–68.
Fletcher, A. J. (2017). Applying critical realism in qualitative research. *International Journal of Social Research Methodology, 20*(2), 181–194.
Fligstein, N. (1996). Markets as politics. *American Sociological Review, 61*(4), 656–673.
Foldes, L. (1958). Uncertainty, probability and potential surprise. *Economica, 25*(99), 246–254.
Folta, T. B. (1998). Governance and uncertainty. *Strategic Management Journal, 19*(11), 1007–1028.
Foss, N. J. (1994). The two Coasian traditions. *Review of Political Economy, 6*(1), 37–61.
Foss, N. J. (1996a). Knowledge-based approaches to the theory of the firm. *Organization Science, 7*(5), 470–476.

Foss, N. J. (1996b). More critical comments on knowledge-based theories of the firm. *Organization Science, 7*(5), 519–523.
Foss, N. J. (2003). Bounded rationality in the economics of organization. *Journal of Economic Psychology, 24*(2), 245–264.
Foss, N. J., & Hallberg, N. L. (2014). How symmetrical assumptions advance strategic management research. *Strategic Management Journal, 35*(6), 903–913.
Foss, N. J., & Weber, L. (2016a). Expand bounded rationality. *Academy of Management Review, 41*(4), 741–744.
Foss, N. J., & Weber, L. (2016b). Moving opportunism to the back seat. *Academy of Management Review, 41*(1), 61–79.
Francolini, A. (2010). *Object and relations uncertainty*. London: University of Western Ontario.
Friedman, M. (1953). The methodology of positive economics. In M. Friedman (Ed.), *Essays in positive economics* (pp. 3–43). Chicago, IL: University Chicago Press.
Galanis, M. (2011). Vicious spirals in corporate governance. *Oxford Journal of Legal Studies, 31*(2), 327–363.
Galkina, T., & Lundgren-Henriksson, E. L. (2017). Coopetition as an entrepreneurial process. *Industrial Marketing Management, 67,* 158–173.
Gatignon, H., & Anderson, E. (1988). The multinational corporation's degree of control over foreign subsidiaries. *Journal of Law Economics and Organization, 4*(2), 305–336.
Gavetti, G., Levinthal, D., & Ocasio, W. (2007). Neo-Carnegie. *Organization Science, 18*(3), 523–536.
Gazendam, L., & Jorna, R. J. (2002). *Transaction cost economics and plausible actors* (Internal Report). University of Groningen.
Ghoshal, S., & Moran, P. (1996). Bad for practice. *Academy of Management Review, 21*(1), 13–47.
Gigerenzer, G., & Goldstein, D. G. (1996). Reasoning the fast and frugal way. *Psychological Review, 103*(4), 650–669.
Gigerenzer, G., & Selten, R. (2001). *Bounded rationality*. Cambridge: MIT Press.
Godfrey, P. C., & Hill, C. W. L. (1995). The problem of unobservables in strategic management research. *Strategic Management Journal, 16*(7), 519–533.
Goldman, A. I. (1985). The relation between epistemology and psychology. *Synthese, 64*(1), 29–68.
Gorski, P. S. (2013). What is critical realism? And why should you care? *Contemporary Sociology, 42*(5), 658–670.
Granovetter, M. (1985). Economic action and social structure. *American Journal of Sociology, 91*(3), 481–510.

Greve, H. R., & Argote, L. (2015). Behavioral theories of organization. In J. D. Wright (Ed.), *International encyclopedia of the social & behavioral sciences* (pp. 481–486). Amsterdam: Elsevier.

Gross, N. (2009). A pragmatist theory of social mechanisms. *American Sociological Review, 74*(3), 358–379.

Hardt, Ł. (2009). The history of transaction cost economics and its recent developments. *Erasmus Journal for Economics and Philosophy, 2*(1), 29–51.

Harms, R., & Schiele, H. (2012). Antecedents and consequences of effectuation and causation in the international new venture creation process. *Journal of International Entrepreneurship, 10*(2), 95–116.

Haunschild, P. R., & Miner, A. S. (1997). Modes of interorganizational imitation. *Administrative Science Quarterly, 42*(3), 472–500.

Heeks, R., & Wall, P. J. (2018). Critical realism and ICT4D research. *Electronic Journal of Information Systems in Developing Countries, 84*(6), e12051.

Hendrickx, L., & Vlek, C. (1991). Perceived control, nature of risk information and risk taking. *Journal of Behavioral Decision Making, 4*(4), 235–247.

Hill, C. W. L. (1990). Cooperation, opportunism, and the invisible hand. *Academy of Management Review, 15*(3), 500–513.

Hislop, D. (2005). *Knowledge management in organizations*. Oxford: Oxford University Press.

Hodgson, G. M. (1998). Evolutionary and competence-based theories of the firm. *Journal of Economic Studies, 25*(1), 25–56.

Hodgson, G. M. (2004). Opportunism is not the only reason why firms exist. *Industrial and Corporate Change, 13*(2), 401–418.

Horst, C., & Grabska, K. (2015). Flight and exile—Uncertainty in the context of conflict-induced displacement. *Social Analysis, 59*(1), 1–18.

Howell, W. C., & Burnett, S. A. (1978). Uncertainty measurement. *Organizational Behavior and Human Performance, 22*(1), 45–68.

Ingham, G. (1996). Some recent changes in the relationship between economics and sociology. *Cambridge Journal of Economics, 20*(2), 243–275.

Jansen, J. W. (2016). *An intersubjective perspective on entrepreneurial decision making*. Aachen, Germany: RWTH Aachen.

Jessor, R. (2019). Perspectives on behavioral science. In R. Jessor (Ed.), *Perspectives on behavioral science* (pp. 3–18). New York: Routledge.

Johnson, E. J., & Tversky, A. (1984). Representations of perceptions of risks. *Journal of Experimental Psychology: General, 113*(1), 55–70.

Johnston, R. J. (1989). Philosophy, ideology and geography. In D. Gregory & R. Walford (Eds.), *Horizons in human geography* (pp. 48–66). New York: Barnes and Noble.

Jones, G. R. (2001). Towards a positive interpretation of transaction cost theory. In M. A. Hitt, R. E. Freeman, & J. S. Harrison (Eds.), *Handbook of strategic management* (pp. 208–228). Oxford: Blackwell.

Kahneman, D., & Tversky, A. (1979). Prospect theory. *Econometrica, 47*(2), 263–291.

Kahneman, D., & Tversky, A. (1982). Variants of uncertainty. *Cognition, 11*(2), 143–157.

Karami, M. (2020). Effectual versus causal international opportunity discovery and creation. In V. Ratten (Ed.), *Entrepreneurship and the community* (pp. 29–48). Cham: Springer.

Kitching, J., & Rouse, J. (2020). Contesting effectuation theory. *International Small Business Journal, 38*(6), 515–535.

Knight, F. H. (1921). *Risk, uncertainty and profit*. Boston, MA: Houghton Mifflin.

Kochumuttom, T. A. (1982). *A Buddhist doctrine of experience*. New Delhi: Motilal Banarsidass.

Kogut, B., & Zander, U. (1992). Knowledge of the firm, combinative capabilities, and the replication of technology. *Organization Science, 3*(3), 383–397.

Kogut, B., & Zander, U. (1993). Knowledge of the firm and the evolutionary theory of the multinational corporation. *Journal of International Business Studies, 24*(4), 625–645.

Kulatilaka, N. (1995). The value of flexibility. In L. Trigeorgis (Ed.), *Real options in capital investment* (pp. 89–108). Westport, CT: Praeger.

Kulkarni, S. P., & Heriot, K. C. (1999). Transaction costs and information costs as determinants of the organizational form. *American Business Review, 17*(2), 43–52.

Kurki, M. (2007). Critical realism and causal analysis in international relations. *Millennium, 35*(2), 361–378.

Langlois, R. N., & Robertson, P. (1995). *Firms, markets and economic change*. London: Routledge.

Lawson, T. (1994). The nature of Post Keynesianism and its links to other traditions. *Journal of Post Keynesian Economics, 16*(4), 503–538.

Lawson, T. (1997). *Economics and reality*. London: Routledge.

Leca, B., & Naccache, P. (2006). A critical realist approach to institutional entrepreneurship. *Organization, 13*(5), 627–651.

Leiblein, M. J. (2003). The choice of organizational governance form and performance. *Journal of Management, 29*(6), 937–961.

LeRoy, S. F., & Singell, L. D. (1987). Knight on risk and uncertainty. *Journal of Political Economy, 95*(2), 394–406.

Lewis, P. (2003). Naturalism and economics. In J. Cruickshank (Ed.), *Critical realism: The difference it makes* (pp. 181–196). London: Routledge.

Li, J. (2007). Real options theory and international strategy. In J. J. Reuer & T. W. Tong (Eds.), *Advances in strategic management* (Vol. 24, pp. 67–101). Amsterdam: Elsevier.

Liesch, P. W., Welch, L. S., & Buckley, P. J. (2011). Risk and uncertainty in internationalization and international entrepreneurship studies. *Management International Review, 51*(6), 851–873.
Love, J. H. (1995). Knowledge, market failure and the multinational enterprise. *Journal of International Business Studies, 26*(2), 399–407.
Love, J. H. (2005). On the opportunism-independent theory of the firm. *Cambridge Journal of Economics, 29*(3), 381–397.
Lundan, S. M. (2010). What are ownership advantages? *Multinational Business Review, 18*(2), 51–69.
Macher, J. T., & Richman, B. D. (2008). Transaction cost economics. *Business and Politics, 10*(1), 1.
Madhok, A. (1996). The organization of economic activity. *Organization Science, 7*(5), 577–590.
Magnani, G., & Zucchella, A. (2018). Uncertainty in entrepreneurship and management studies. *International Journal of Business and Management, 13*(3), 98–133.
Mahoney, J. T. (1992). The choice of organizational form. *Strategic Management Journal, 13*(8), 559–584.
Mäki, U. (2001). Explanatory unification: Double and doubtful. *Philosophy of the Social Sciences, 31*(4), 488–506.
Martynov, A., & Schepker, D. J. (2017). Risk preferences and asset ownership. *Managerial and Decision Economics, 38*(2), 125–143.
Maturana, H. (1978). Biology of language: The epistemology of reality. In G. Millar & E. Lenneberg (Eds.), *Psychology and biology of language and thought* (pp. 27–63). New York: Academic Press.
Miller, K. D., & Shapira, Z. (2004). An empirical test of heuristics and biases affecting real option valuation. *Strategic Management Journal, 25*(3), 269–284.
Miller, K. D., & Tsang, E. W. (2011). Testing management theories. *Strategic Management Journal, 32*(2), 139–158.
Miller, R., & Lessard, D. R. (2001). *The strategic management of large engineering projects*. Cambridge: MIT Press.
Milliken, F. J. (1987). Three types of perceived uncertainty about the environment. *Academy of Management Review, 12*(1), 133–143.
Mingers, J. (2006). *Realising systems thinking*. New York: Springer.
Mingers, J., Mutch, A., & Willcocks, L. (2013). Critical realism in information systems research. *MIS Quarterly, 37*(3), 795–802.
Moran, P., & Ghoshal, S. (1996). Theories of economic organization. *Academy of Management Review, 21*(1), 58–72.
Mukumbang, F. C., Marchal, B., Van Belle, S., & van Wyk, B. (2019). Using the realist interview approach to maintain theoretical awareness in realist studies. *Qualitative Research, 20*(4), 485–515.

O'Donell, R. (2014). A critique of the ergodic/nonergodic approach to uncertainty. *Journal of Post Keynesian Economics, 37*(2), 187–209.

Packard, M. D. (2017). Where did interpretivism go in the theory of entrepreneurship? *Journal of Business Venturing, 32*(5), 536–549.

Parker, C. E. (1978). Opportunism and the rise of intelligence. *Journal of Human Evolution, 7*(7), 597–608.

Pawson, R., & Tilley, N. (1997). *Realistic evaluation*. London: Sage.

Peirce, C. S. (1902). Reasoning. In J. M. Baldwin (Ed.), *Dictionary of philosophy and psychology* (Vol. 2, pp. 426–428). London: Macmillan.

Peirce, C. S. (1960). *Collected papers of Charles Sanders Peirce* (Vol. 8). Cambridge, MA: Harvard University Press.

Peng, G. Z. (2012). FDI legitimacy and MNC subsidiary control. *Journal of International Management, 18*(2), 115–131.

Peng, G. Z., & Beamish, P. W. (2014). The effect of host country long term orientation on subsidiary ownership and survival. *Asia Pacific Journal of Management, 31*(2), 423–453.

Peng, G. Z., & Beamish, P. W. (2019). Subnational FDI legitimacy and foreign subsidiary survival. *Journal of International Management, 25*(3), 100662.

Pfeffer, I. (1956). *Insurance and economic theory*. Homewood, IL: Richard D. Irwin.

Phelan, S. E. (2016). Austrian theories of entrepreneurship. *Review of Austrian Economics, 29*(3), 277–297.

Popper, K. R. (1972). *Objective knowledge*. Oxford: Clarendon.

Popper, K. R. (1990). *A world of propensities*. Bristol: Thoemmes.

Porac, J. F., & Rosa, J. A. (1996). Rivalry, industry models, and the cognitive embeddedness of the comparable firm. In J. A. C. Baum & J. E. Dutton (Eds.), *Advances in strategic management* (Vol. 13, pp. 363–388). Bingley: JAI Press.

Porpora, D. V. (2015). *Reconstructing sociology*. Cambridge: Cambridge University Press.

Poulis, K., & Poulis, E. (2018). International business as disciplinary tautology: An ontological perspective. *Academy of Management Perspectives, 32*(4), 517–531.

Pratt, S. F. (2016). Pragmatism as ontology, not (just) epistemology. *International Studies Review, 18*(3), 508–527.

Pratten, S. (1997). The nature of transaction cost economics. *Journal of Economic Issues, 31*(3), 781–803.

Price, L., & Martin, L. (2018). Applied critical realism in the social sciences. *Journal of Critical Realism, 17*(2), 89–96.

Proctor, J. D. (1998). The social construction of nature. *Annals of the Association of American Geographers, 88*(3), 352–376.

Ramoglou, S., & Tsang, E. W. K. (2016). A realist perspective of entrepreneurship. *Academy of Management Review, 41*(3), 410–434.

Read, S., & Sarasvathy, S. D. (2005). Knowing what to do and doing what you know. *Journal of Private Equity, 9*(1), 45–62.

Read, S., Sarasvathy, S. D., Dew, N., & Wiltbank, R. (2015). *Unreasonable assumptions in ASB*. www.effectuation.org.

Read, S., Sarasvathy, S. D., Dew, N., & Wiltbank, R. (2016). Response to Arend, Sarooghi, and Burkemper (2015). *Academy of Management Review, 41*(3), 528–536.

Rese, M., & Roemer, E. (2004). Managing commitments and flexibility by real options. *Industrial Marketing Management, 33*(6), 501–512.

Reuber, A. R., Fischer, E., & Coviello, N. (2016). Deepening the dialogue: New directions for the evolution of effectuation theory. *Academy of Management Review, 41*(3), 536–540.

Ricciardi, V., & Rice, D. (2014). Risk perception and risk tolerance. In H. K. Baker & V. Ricciardi (Eds.), *Investor behavior* (pp. 325–345). Hoboken, NJ: Wiley.

Rindfleisch, A. (2019). Transaction cost theory: Past, present and future. *AMS Review*. https://doi.org/10.1007/s13162-019-00151-x.

Rindfleisch, A., & Heide, J. B. (1997). Transaction cost analysis. *Journal of Marketing, 61*(4), 30–54.

Roemer E. (2004). *Real options and the theory of the firm* (Working Paper). University of Bradford.

Rotter, J. B. (1966). Generalized expectancies for internal versus external control of reinforcement. *Psychological Monographs: General and Applied, 80*(1), 1–28.

Runde, J. (1996). On Popper, probabilities, and propensities. *Review of Social Economy, 54*(4), 465–485.

Sanderson, J. (2012). Risk, uncertainty and governance in megaprojects. *International Journal of Project Management, 30*(4), 432–443.

Santoro, M. D., & McGill, J. P. (2005). The effect of uncertainty and asset co-specialization on governance in biotechnology alliances. *Strategic Management Journal, 26*(13), 1261–1269.

Sarasvathy, S. D. (2001). Causation and effectuation. *Academy of Management Review, 26*(2), 243–263.

Sarasvathy, S. D. (2008). *Effectuation: Elements of entrepreneurial expertise*. Cheltenham: Edward Elgar.

Sarasvathy, S. D., & Dew, N. (2005). New market creation through transformation. *Journal of Evolutionary Economics, 15*(5), 533–565.

Sarasvathy, S. D., & Dew, N. (2008). Is effectuation Lachmannian? *Organization Studies, 29*(3), 423–429.

Sarasvathy, S. D., Kumar, K., York, J. G., & Bhagavatula, S. (2014). An effectual approach to international entrepreneurship. *Entrepreneurship Theory and Practice, 38*(1), 71–93.
Sarasvathy, S. D., & Ventakaraman, S. (2011). Entrepreneurship as method. *Entrepreneurship Theory and Practice, 35*(1), 113–135.
Satsangi, M. (2013). Synthesizing feminist and critical realist approaches to housing studies. *Housing, Theory and Society, 30*(2), 193–207.
Sayer, A. (1992). *Methods in social science*. London: Routledge.
Schumacher, E. F. (1973). Does economics help? In J. Robinson (Ed.), *After Keynes* (pp. 26–36). Oxford: Blackwell.
Shanahan, M. (1989). Prediction is deduction but explanation is abduction. In *Proceedings of the 11th International Joint Conference on Artificial Intelligence (IJCAI 89)* (pp. 1055–1060). San Francisco, CA: Morgan Kaufmann.
Shane, S., & Venkataraman, S. (2000). The promise of entrepreneurship as a field of research. *Academy of Management Review, 25*(1), 217–226.
Shelanski, H. A., & Klein, P. G. (1995). Empirical research in transaction cost economics. *Journal of Law Economics and Organization, 11*(2), 335–361.
Simon, H. A. (1961). *Administrative behavior*. New York: Macmillan.
Simon, H. A. (1990). Invariants of human behavior. *Annual Review of Psychology, 41*(1), 1–19.
Simon, H. A. (1996). *The sciences of the artificial*. Cambridge: MIT Press.
Simon, H. A. (1997a). *An empirically based microeconomics*. Cambridge: Cambridge University Press.
Simon, H. A. (1997b). *Models of bounded rationality* (Vol. 3). Cambridge: MIT Press.
Sitkin, S. B., & Pablo, A. L. (1992). Reconceptualizing the determinants of risk behavior. *Academy of Management Review, 17*(1), 9–38.
Sitkin, S. B., & Weingart, L. R. (1995). Determinants of risky decision-making behavior. *Academy of Management Journal, 38*(6), 1573–1592.
Slangen, A. H. L., & van Tulder, R. J. M. (2009). Cultural distance, political risk, or governance quality? *International Business Review, 18*(3), 276–291.
Slater, G., & Spencer, D. A. (2000). The uncertain foundations of transaction costs economics. *Journal of Economic Issues, 34*(1), 61–87.
Slovic, P. (1987). Perception of risk. *Science, 236*(4799), 280–285.
Slovic, P., Fischhoff, B., & Lichtenstein, S. (1982). Why study risk perceptions? *Risk Analysis, 2*(2), 83–93.
Smith, M. B. (2019). Psychology and the decline of positivism. In R. Jessor (Ed.), *Perspectives on behavioral science* (pp. 53–69). New York: Routledge.
Spender, J. C. (2018). Managing—According to Williamson, or to Coase? *Kindai Management Review, 6,* 13–34.
Steele, G. R. (2005). Critical thoughts about critical realism. *Critical Review, 17*(1–2), 133–154.

Steinmetz, G. (1998). Critical realism and historical sociology. *Comparative Studies in Society and History, 40*(1), 170–186.
Sutcliffe, K. M., & Zaheer, A. (1998). Uncertainty in the transaction environment. *Strategic Management Journal, 19*(1), 1–23.
Taylor, R., Torugsa, N. A., & Arundel, A. (2018). Leaping into real-world relevance. *Nonprofit and Voluntary Sector Quarterly, 47*(1), 206–227.
Teece, D. J. (1996). Firm organization, industrial structure, and technological innovation. *Journal of Economic Behavior & Organization, 31*(2), 193–224.
Thagard, P. (2007). Abductive inference. In A. Feeney & E. Heit (Eds.), *Inductive reasoning* (pp. 226–247). Cambridge: Cambridge University Press.
Tollefsen, D. P. (2015). *Groups as agents*. Cambridge: Polity.
Trigeorgis, L., & Mason, S. P. (1987). Valuing managerial flexibility. *Midland Corporate Finance Journal, 5*(1), 14–21.
Tsang, E. W. K. (2006). Behavioral assumptions and theory development. *Strategic Management Journal, 27*(11), 999–1011.
Tschaepe, M. (2014). Guessing and abduction. *Transactions of the Charles S. Peirce Society, 50*(1), 115–138.
Tversky, A., & Kahneman, D. (1981). The framing of decisions and the psychology of choice. *Science, 211*(4481), 453–458.
Üsdiken, B. (2010). Between contending perspectives and logics. *Organization Studies, 31*(6), 715–735.
Van Asselt, M. B. A., & Rotmans, J. (2002). Uncertainty in integrated assessment modelling. *Climatic Change, 54*(1/2), 75–105.
Van de Ven, A. H. (2007). *Engaged scholarship*. Oxford: Oxford University Press.
Van de Vrande, V., Vanhaverbeke, W., & Duysters, G. (2009). External technology sourcing. *Journal of Business Venturing, 24*(1), 62–80.
Verbeke, A., & Greidanus, N. S. (2009). The end of the opportunism vs. trust debate. *Journal of International Business Studies, 40*(9), 1471–1495.
Vlek, C., & Stallen, P. J. (1981). Judging risks and benefits in the small and in the large. *Organizational Behavior and Human Performance, 28*(2), 235–271.
Voss, S. (2016). *How should the Post Keynesian School define 'uncertainty'?* Lecture held at the 40 Years of the Cambridge Journal of Economics Conference.
Waldron, W. S. (2003). *The Buddhist unconscious*. New York: Routledge-Curzon.
Walker, W. E., Harremoës, P., Rotmans, J., Van Der Sluijs, J. P., Van Asselt, M. B., Janssen, P., et al. (2003). Defining uncertainty. *Integrated Assessment, 4*(1), 5–17.
Walters, B., & Young, D. (1999). Is critical realism the appropriate basis for Post Keynesianism? *Journal of Post Keynesian Economics, 22*(1), 105–123.
Waltz, K. N. (1979). *Theory of international politics*. New York: McGraw Hill.
Wathne, K. H., & Heide, J. B. (2000). Opportunism in interfirm relationships. *Journal of Marketing, 64*(4), 36–51.

Watson, T. J. (2013). Entrepreneurial action and the Euro-American social science tradition. *Entrepreneurship & Regional Development, 25*(1–2), 16–33.
Weber, L., & Mayer, K. (2014). Transaction cost economics and the cognitive perspective. *Academy of Management Review, 39*(3), 344–363.
Willet, A. H. (1951). *The economic theory of risk insurance*. Philadelphia: University of Pennsylvania Press.
Williamson, O. E. (1975). *Markets and hierarchies*. New York: Free Press.
Williamson, O. E. (1979). Transaction-cost economics. *Journal of Law and Economics, 22*(2), 233–261.
Williamson, O. E. (1985). *The economic institutions of capitalism*. New York: Free Press.
Williamson, O. E. (1990). The firm as a nexus of treaties. In M. Aoki, B. Gustafsson, & O. E. Williamson (Eds.), *The firm as a nexus of treaties* (pp. 1–25). Newbury Park, CA: Sage.
Williamson, O. E. (1991). Comparative economic organization. *Administrative Science Quarterly, 36*(4), 269–296.
Williamson, O. E. (1992). Markets, hierarchies and the modern corporation. *Journal of Economic Behavior & Organization, 17*(3), 335–352.
Williamson, O. E. (1993). Opportunism and its critics. *Managerial and Decision Economics, 14*(2), 97–107.
Williamson, O. E. (1996). *The mechanisms of governance*. Oxford: Oxford University Press.
Williamson, O. E. (1998). Transaction cost economics. *De Economist, 146*(1), 23–58.
Williamson, O. E. (1999). Strategy research. *Strategic Management Journal, 20*(12), 1087–1108.
Williamson, O. E. (2002). Empirical microeconomics. In M. Augier & J. G. March (Eds.), *The economics of choice, change and organization* (pp. 419–441). Cheltenham, UK: Edward Elgar.
Wiltbank, R., Read, S., Dew, N., & Sarasvathy, S. D. (2009). Prediction and control under uncertainty. *Journal of Business Venturing, 24*(2), 116–133.
Wynn, D., & Williams, C. K. (2012). Principles for conducting critical realist case study research in information systems. *MIS Quarterly, 36*(3), 787–810.
Zhang, S. X., Foo, M. D., & Vassolo, R. (2018). *Effectuation is a heuristic, then how about its biases?* https://ssrn.com/abstract=3271633 or http://dx.doi.org/10.2139/ssrn.3271633.
Zhao, H., Luo, Y., & Suh, T. (2004). Transaction cost determinants and ownership-based entry mode choice. *Journal of International Business Studies, 35*(6), 524–544.

CHAPTER 3

Opportunism and Bounded Rationality in Transaction Cost Economics: Values, Attitudes, or Behaviors?

There has been a long-standing debate in international business about whether TCE treats opportunism as an attitude or a behavior, and it is believed that TCE conflates the two (Ghoshal and Moran 1996; Lubatkin et al. 2007; Verbeke and Greidanus 2009). Such debate can apparently benefit from a good understanding of the VAB hierarchy (Homer and Kahle 1988; Rokeach 1973), a widely used framework to study behavior grounded in various theories, including TCE (e.g., John 1984). While some scholars have pointed out that TCE does not theoretically distinguish between 'opportunism as an attitude' and 'opportunism as a behavior' (Ghoshal and Moran 1996; Lubatkin et al. 2007; Verbeke and Greidanus 2009), we contend that, from a CR perspective, TCE actually conflates '*opportunism as an attitude*' with '*opportunism as a value*' in its theorization. We propose that a clear understanding of what opportunism and bounded rationality refer to is important for TCE, and that opportunism and bounded rationality be approached at the attitude level to make the two 'assumptions'[1] behavioral. In addition, we contend that the said conflations in TCE can be attributed to its lack of ontological depth due to its insufficient attention to its philosophical foundation. We submit that the CR perspective can help reduce such confusions and render TCE behavioral since value, attitude, and behavior in the VAB hierarchy correspond respectively to the real, the actual, and the empirical domains in CR.

G. Z. Peng, *Toward Behavioral Transaction Cost Economics*,
International Marketing and Management Research,
https://doi.org/10.1007/978-3-030-46878-1_3

3.1 The Value-Attitude-Behavior Hierarchy

The VAB hierarchy suggests that value, attitude, and behavior are different and hierarchically ordered concepts (Dietz et al. 2005; Hitlin and Piliavin 2004; Hofstede 1998; Homer and Kahle 1988; Rokeach 1973). Values are defined as trans-situational ideals and are used to evaluate people and events and to justify actions (Schwartz 1992). They represent volitions (Weinberg 1927) and trans-situational social cognition that facilitates environmental adaptation (Kahle 1983; Vaske and Donnelly 1999). Opportunism and bounded rationality are considered as values since they are relevant to environmental selection and adaptation (Aldrich 1999; Genewein et al. 2015; Parker 1978). Attitudes refer to situational evaluations whether to act favorably or unfavorably toward situations or objects (Ajzen 2005; Eagly and Chaiken 1993; Fishbein and Ajzen 1975; Kotler 1997). They 'are for the most part acquired behavior patterns having been built up out of our experiences in characteristic situations' (Bernard 1926). Thus, attitudes are emotions that do not come with birth (Deonna and Teroni 2015). Attitude is action oriented and is 'potential action' toward objects or situations (Thurstone 1931), and emotions are the proximate causes of most behavior (Frank 1990). Values and attitudes are both related and different. They are related because of the well-known bandwidth-fidelity tradeoff (Ajzen 2012; Cronbach and Gleser 1957). Broad bandwidth values apply to a wide range of behaviors but they predict behaviors with low precision, whereas narrow bandwidth situation-specific attitudes can predict the corresponding behaviors with great accuracy but are unlikely to relate strongly to other specific situations even in the same behavioral domain (Ajzen 2012). Values are latent dispositions or propensities underlying attitudes.

Values and attitudes are different in several ways because they lie at different positions in the bandwidth-fidelity tradeoff. First, values are abstract and trans-situational; attitudes are specific and situational (Dietz et al. 2005; Rokeach 1973; Hitlin and Piliavin 2004). Second, value is not directly implicated in behavior (Dietz et al. 2005; Schwartz 1996), and attitude is 'potential behavior' (Thurstone 1931) and implies action intention and can thus be used to predict behavior (Ajzen and Fishbein 1980; Triandis 1979). Attitudes are behavior patterns or repertoires and can even be viewed as the 'beginnings of acts' (Mead 1934: 43). Third, values focus on ideals; attitudes are applied to more concrete social objects (Hitlin and Piliavin 2004). Fourth, attitudes are more propositional (attitudes with objects), whereas values are more dispositional ('attitudes[2] without objects') (Hepler and Albarracín 2013). Fifth, while the number of values tends to be limited (dozens), attitudes can be numerous (thousands) (Vaske and Donnelly 1999).

3.2 The Link Between Value-Attitude-Behavior Hierarchy and Critical Realism

The conflation in TCE about whether opportunism is a value, attitude, or behavior arises largely from its unclear philosophical foundations, as discussed in Chapter 2. Due to TCE's positivist and deductivist position (Pratten 1997), opportunism in TCE is deterministic and the value-attitude-behavior distinction is not important since in a deterministic world value determines attitudes, which in turn will necessarily lead to behaviors. As a result of the 'closed' system and collapsed ontology adopted in TCE, the debate about whether TCE conflates opportunism as an attitude and opportunism as a behavior will not be productive.

We contend that CR should be adopted to resolve the above-mentioned debate. As can be seen from Table 3.1, the VAB hierarchy can be regarded as a positivist parallel (Eagly and Chaiken 1993; Ho 2015; Miller 2017) to CR, and a partial understanding of the complicated hierarchical relationship between values, attitudes, and behaviors based on a positivist and reductionist approach. While the VAB hierarchy has been widely used in a positivist direction, it can be integrated into a CR framework for its affinity with CR, as shown in Table 3.1. From a CR perspective, opportunism (Archer 1995) and bounded rationality (Aldrich 1999) as values are generative mechanisms. These mechanisms may or may not be activated or may be activated to different degrees depending on the prevailing social structures in the actual domain, thus forming different attitudes or behavior patterns toward potential behaviors (Table 3.2). In this sense, CR provides VAB with the much needed ontological depth for human behaviors.

Table 3.1 Contrasting the value-attitude-behavior hierarchy with critical realism

Critical realism	*Value-attitude-behavior hierarchy*
Reality as 'stratified' and 'differentiated' into real, actual, and empirical domains, all of them are part of the same reality	Behavior as 'hierarchical' (behavior is the end state of value)
Generative mechanisms (real domain) • Mechanisms are transfactual (Bhaskar 2008; Popper 1990), transempirical, and real (Blom and Morén 2011) causal tendencies • Mechanisms are used to explain why observable events occur (Blom and Morén 2011) • Mechanisms are mostly possible to grasp only indirectly (Blom and Morén 2011) • Mechanisms may or may not be exercised (Bhaskar 2008) • Mechanisms 'exist independently of and are often out of phase with the actual pattern of events' (Bhaskar 2008: 2) • Mechanisms exist in the real domain (Bhaskar 1979)	*Values* • Values are trans-situational ideals and tendencies (Rokeach 1973; Schwartz 1992) • Values are used to evaluate events and to justify actions (Schwartz 1992) • Value is not directly implicated in behavior (Dietz et al. 2005; Schwartz 1996), • Values may or may not be activated (Dreezens et al. 2008) • Values and behaviors may not be consistent since a value may be something that one prefers or desires, but does not have yet (Peng et al. 1997)
Events (actual domain) • Patterns of events; multiple generative mechanism may co-act (Bhaskar 2008) • Events are generated under contingent conditions (Bhaskar 2008) • Events express generative mechanisms, which may exist without being expressed (Bhaskar 2008; Steinmetz 1998) • Events may or may not be experienced; if experienced, they constitute social phenomena (Steele 2005)	*Attitudes* • Behavior patterns built up out of our experiences in characteristic situations (Bernard 1926; Park and Burgess 2019) • Attitudes are situational and specific, and are applied to concrete social objects or entities (Hitlin and Piliavin 2004) • Attitudes are value-expressing (Maio and Olson 2000) • Attitudes emerge from and are embedded in social phenomena (Wood 2000)
Experiences (empirical domain) • Concerned with events embedded in human activities that humans can empirically experience, perceive, and interpret (Fletcher 2017; Leca and Naccache 2006) • Humans are not able to be aware of all the existing events in the wider actual domain	*Behavior* • Behavior is predicted by specific behavioral intentions, which is determined by attitudes

(continued)

Table 3.1 (continued)

Critical realism	*Value-attitude-behavior hierarchy*
Assumptions and approaches • Bounded rationality/fallibilist epistemology (Bhaskar 2008) • Post-positivist and retroductionist approach (Jennings 2004)	*Assumptions and approaches* • Rational decision-making (a major limitation) (Eagly and Chaiken 1993; Miller 2017) • Positivist and reductionist approach (Ho 2015)

Source Author's own summary

Table 3.2 Opportunism/bounded rationality based on critical realism

Domain	*Real*	*Actual*	*Empirical*
(Mechanisms) Opportunism/bounded rationality as value [Institutional logics] Dispositional	✓		
(Events) Opportunism/bounded rationality as attitude [Institutions] Situational/Propositional	✓	✓	
(Experiences) Opportunism/bounded rationality as behavior [Experiences] Situational/Propositional(1)	✓	✓	✓

Note (1) Cf. Table 4.2
Source Author's creation based on Bhaskar (2008: 2) and Leca and Naccache (2006). Contents in '[ ]' are related to Sect. 3.5

3.3 The Link Between Critical Realism and the Emic-Etic Distinction

After linking CR to the VAB hierarchy, we also would further like to link CR to the emic-etic distinction which is frequently made in the literatures of cross-cultural studies, psychology, and international business in order to understand culture and behavior (e.g., Harris 1976; Pike 1967; Stahl and Tung 2015). We will explain the reasons for the need for the link shortly, but would first like to point out that this link is a natural one considering that (1) the etic approach focuses on identifying abstract cross-cultural value universals in the real domain, which underlie analytic (Stoltz 2018) social structures (Berry 1990; Morris et al. 1999; Schwartz 1992); (2) the emic perspective is experience based, focusing on what the cultural insiders actually experience and how they *normatively* behave; (3) we have linked positivist induction/deduction, abduction and retroduction to the three domains of CR in Sect. 2.9; and (4) as we explain later, it is in the actual domain of CR that the proposed dialectic perspective (e.g., Berry 1990; Morris et al. 1999; Polsa 2013) can take place in an ontologically-deeper way. The etic, emic, and dialectic (combined emic/etic) approaches in international business research also parallel the retroduction, positive deduction, and abduction approaches in general management (cf. Polsa 2013).[3] We first illustrate the link in Table 3.3 and Table 2.4, and then provide some brief explanations below.

The emic perspective refers to cultural insiders' shared *normative*[4] view of cultural knowledge from within a specific culture, which offers insight into cultural complexities and nuances (Pike 1967; Zhu and Bargiela-Chiappini 2013). The emic research is often done in a positivist way based on 'native categories' or the native classifications and shared frames of references in a particular culture, which are embodied in native viewpoints about cultural phenomena of concern (Buckley and Chapman 1997; Buckley et al. 2014). This is because a culture could be regarded as a system of classifications (Buckley et al. 2014). It has been noted that much of the data used in international business research is emic and grounded in the categories and classifications of the cultures under research (Buckley et al. 2014). The etic perspective, on the other hand, refers to research that studies cross-culturally comparable issues or categories (Berry 1990). As such, it is a comparative perspective, which resorts to 'universals' or all-purpose analytical tools (Jorion 1983). The bandwidth-fidelity tradeoff mentioned in Sect. 3.1 is similarly applicable to the relationship between emic and etic approaches. Broad bandwidth etic universals apply to a wide range of cultural setting but they describe cross-cultural issues with low precision, whereas narrow bandwidth cultural-specific emic viewpoints from within a specific culture can offer accurate insight into cultural complexities and nuances of the said culture but are unlikely to relate strongly to cultural peculiarities in other cultures even in the same category. Additionally, an emic frame of reference may even not exist across cultures (Ronen and Shenkar 1988).

The link is necessary for a few reasons. First, we are going to propose the use of CD and NEA as the respective measure of cognitive bounds (bounded rationality) and opportunism in Sect. 3.5, which are culturally derived. The inconclusiveness of some relationships involving CD oftentimes leads scholars to oscillate between emic and etic perspectives (e.g.,

Table 3.3 Ontologizing etic/dialectic/emic perspectives in critical realism

Domain	*Real*	*Actual*	*Empirical*
(Mechanisms) Etic (cultural universals) • Trans-cultural: the outside perspective of comparativist researchers, who attempt to describe differences across cultures in terms of a general, external standard (Morris et al. 1999) • Identification and assessment of universal behavioral and attitudinal concepts (Sinkovics and Holzmüller 2001) • Based on a set of common analytical categories (Lees 2016) • Uncovering systemic cultural practices and relationships that cultural insiders may be unaware of (Harris 1980: 33) • Often using quantitative method (Sinkovics and Holzmüller 2001).(1) Surveys across many cultures (Hofstede 1980) • Lengthwise focus: etic perspective tends to isolate particular cultural components and hypothesize about their distinct antecedents and consequences • Meta-rationality	✓		
(Events) Dialectic (cultural contexts)/emic x etic • Culturally contextualized • The three-stage sequence of imposed etics-emics-derived etics can take place (Berry 1989, 1990; Morris et al. 1999) • Applicable in culturally diverse environments (Polsa 2013) • Cultural biases of imposed etics can be considered (Berry 1990) • Psychological biases arising from cultural distance can be considered • Organizational learning is possible • Cultural distance as asset and opportunity: the 'upside of cultural distance' can be considered (Stahl and Tung 2015) • 'Cross-sectional x lengthwise' interaction • Bounded rationality	✓	✓	

(continued)

Harzing and Pudelko 2016). Second, traditionally, TCE research is done in an emic approach and in a positivist way based on 'native categories' or shared frames of references in a particular culture, often Western (Buckley and Chapman 1997; Buckley et al. 2014). When applied in international business, TCE is used in an imposed etic way wherein native categories are simply exported from the researchers' home culture (Berry 1990;

Table 3.3 (continued)

Domain	*Real*	*Actual*	*Empirical*
(Experiences) Emic (cultural specifics) • Culturally bound: the inside perspective to the study of shared frame of reference within a particular culture in its own terms (Lees 2016; Morris et al. 1999); 'the native's point of view' (Malinowski 1922) • Based on 'native categories' (Buckley and Chapman 1997; Buckley et al. 2014) • Often using qualitative method (Sinkovics and Holzmüller 2001). Fieldwork in a single culture (Morris et al. 1999) • Concerned with whether a cultural account is recognized by cultural insiders as 'real, meaningful, or appropriate' (Harris 1980: 32) • Cultural distance as liability (when applied in an imposed etic manner) • Cross-sectional focus: Emic view tends to assume that a culture is best understood as an interconnected system or whole • Rational treatment of bounded rationality (e.g., Lockie 2016)	✓	✓	✓

Notes (1) The association between emic-etic perspectives and qualitative-quantitative methods is not absolute (Morris et al. 1999)
Source Author's creation based on Bhaskar (2008: 2). A detailed comparison between etic and emic views can be found in Table 1 in Morris et al. (1999)

Morris et al. 1999), and the relationship between market and hierarchy is defined in terms of an imposed etic relation (Stoltz 2018). Transaction is largely treated as given and unproblematic (Buckley and Chapman 1997; Martin 1993). Nevertheless, in international business settings, transaction itself can often become 'relativized' (Buckley and Chapman 1997) and even Williamson himself once acknowledged that 'it may be more accurate, and sometimes even essential, to regard the exchange process itself as an object of value' (1975: 38). Third, the emic-etic distinction has implications to organizational learning, particularly with regard to the view that cultural difference has inverse effect on two types of learning: It hinders exploitation (of existing routines) and enables exploration (adapting existing routines or developing new ones) (Morosini et al. 1998; Stahl and Tung 2015). But in order for learning to happen, the emic and etic perspectives need to interact with each other in a process in the actual domain of CR. We will return to this point in Chapter 7 when we discuss the practical implications of this book. Fourth, the emic-etic distinction should not be understood as a dichotomy; instead, the emic and etic approaches should be integrated into a process in the forms of the so-called combined (Polsa 2013) or dialectic (Hymes 1990; Lockie 2016) approach to the emic-etic distinction. Nevertheless, the integration has been done in an ontologically shallow way, and we suggest that the link to CR should be clearly articulated to rid the emic-etic literature of many confusions (cf. Modell 2020). We suggest that the emic, dialectic, and etic perspectives can be mapped into the CR framework as shown in Table 3.3 and Table 2.4.

Although the emic-etic contrast can be considered as 'a continuum' (we differ on this, see the paragraph after next), a common tendency scholars taking each perspective is to dismiss insights from the other perspective, and as a result, the divide between these two approaches persists in contemporary scholarship on culture (Lee 1991; Morris et al. 1999: 782). However, each of these perspectives has its own limits, in addition to the aforementioned bandwidth-fidelity tradeoff. On the one hand, while etic research is often criticized for its inherent 'scientific' Western ethnocentrism[5] and emic research is called for since the majority of research conducted in the field has been (imposed) etic (e.g., Buckley et al. 2014; Stahl and Tung 2015), the etic perspective enables scholars to move beyond the subjective and intersubjective worldviews of cultural insiders and search for regularities, patterns, and structural relationships that may be outside cultural insiders' individual and/or collective awareness (Harris 1980; Lees 2016). Purely emic approach also makes it difficult for researchers to distill the universals because cross-cultural contrasts are often needed for spotting the abstraction that unites cultures (Morris et al. 1999). On the other hand, emic can often add value beyond the etic, and emic matters in some cases more than etic (Buckley et al. 2014). The cross-national data that international business researchers use is also emic in nature (Buckley et al. 2014).

As such, emic and etic perspectives should be integrated (Buckley et al. 2014; Morris et al. 1999). While most of the researchers have treated them as dichotomous, treating them as complementary approaches can have added value (Buckley et al. 2014). In a sense, the emit-etic distinction is only for convenience because they cannot be separated. All outsiders are locals in their own cultures and their own cultural backgrounds affect the way they move from emic to universal generalizations, and studies which begin as etic have to be translated into local categories in order to work, thus becoming emic (New 2001). Among the tools used in an etic approach are the elementary units for emic analysis, associated heuristic principles, and a general catalog of emic systematics (Jorion 1983). Because etic perspective can often provide surprising insights outside cultural insiders' individual and/or collective awareness (Harris 1980; Lees 2016), a great deal of emic research, with its goal to unveil and demystify the gap between reality and representation, might be more accurately categorized as substantially etic in nature (Lees 2016).

Nevertheless, there are obstacles to the emic-etic integration. We suggest that one of such obstacles is the inattention to ontological depth. For example, Morris et al. (1999) considered the emic-etic contrast as 'a continuum'. If a construct is so conceptualized, then scholars will tend to take an either-or approach because they lack ontological depth and width to conduct an integrative analysis of social phenomena across space and time. Instead of treating emic-etic distinction as a continuum, we suggest that emic-etic research can benefit from a hierarchization of the emic, the dialectic, and the etic perspectives in an ontologically deep CR framework. We show this in Tables 2.4 and 3.3. Considering the extensive literature on the emic-etic distinction, we refrain from providing further general discussion, but would like to highlight the importance of the dialectic perspective in the actual domain of CR with regard to the psychological process that organizations are involved across cultures. Only through the dialectic interaction in the actual domain can a theory become genuinely behavioral. We concur with Modell (2020) that it is important 'to combine emic and etic perspectives to delve into the complex causal relationships that give rise to context-specific events as well as more generally occurring tendencies'.

The etic perspective aims to find the common denominators of the variables involved in the psychological process across cultures, and identifying cultural components with equivalent meanings across cultures is easier to do if they are conceptualized abstractly (Berry 1990; Morris et al. 1999). Such abstraction leads to an abstract *objectivist* approach (Voloshinov 1929), which focuses on cultural universals and the underlying social structures (Schwartz 1992) which are analytical in nature (Stoltz 2018). As to be discussed in Chapter 4, the etic approach unveils the cognitive structure and its bounds, but it is essentially a cognition-centric approach which is not only partial but devoid of a subject of human behavior, thus incapable of accounting for human behavior and unconducive to a behavioral theory. As a result, the etic approach leaves scholars with a highly abstract and incomplete view of the psychological process and fails to offer predictions about any particular case (Morris et al. 1999). Because it is an objective approach, psychological biases and other human defects cannot be taken into account.

It is in the actual domain and through a dialectic approach that the individual subjectivist (Voloshinov 1929) emic view can interact with the etic view and the three-stage sequence of imposed etics-emics-derived etics can take place in culturally diverse settings (Berry 1990; Morris et al. 1999; Polsa 2013). The emic-etic interaction in a dialectic way in the actual domain of CR is conducive to a behavioral approach for several reasons. First, cultural biases of imposed etics can be exposed, considered, and corrected in the process of reaching cultural-general 'derived-etic' constructs (Berry 1990). Please note here that such biases arise in the process of exporting native categories from the researchers' home culture to other cultures, and they are cognitive in nature. Such biases are details that cannot be measured with equivalence across cultures and need to be filtered and eliminated in the translation process (Morris et al. 1999). Thus, they are not psychological biases related to perception and emotion. Second, psychological biases arising from CD can be considered. This is an important insight the CR framework can offer to the emic-etic research since bounded rationality and the psychological biases which accompany bounded rationality are seldom considered. This gap is striking considering that cross-cultural research is not solely about cultural profiles in individual emic settings and their cross-cultural comparison in a positivist way, but also about the way emic cultural differences at the two ends of CD can create uneven psychological perceptions about the same objective CD (cf. Azar and Drogendijk 2019). Third, it is in the actual domain where bounded rationality and psychological biases can be considered that organizational learning can play a genuine role in an organizational theory and the 'upside of cultural distance' (Stahl and Tung 2015) can be accommodated and considered. In the etic approach mentioned previously, the discovery of etic constructs is objective and cognition-centric, capturing only partial influences on the psychological process of internationalization by ignoring the behavioral side of the process. While CD is etic (universal), psychological biases are emic or cultural specific (e.g., Rieger et al. 2015). In the case of imposed etics, the exported home country mental models are not necessarily consistent with cognition attributes and frames of reference in host countries. In both etic and imposed etic processes, it is human agents with various home country backgrounds who apply these approaches, and as a result, a great deal of etic research might be more emic in nature. This complements the view of Lees (2016) about the possibility that a great deal of emic research might be etic in nature. Thus, the integration of both etic and emic perspective is indispensable to capture the full influences on the psychological process of internationalization (Morris et al. 1999). And this can only happen in the actual domain of CR, where organizations form new mental models by combining perspectives of both cultural insiders and outsiders (Edman 2016). It is in the process of forming new mental models that the positive aspects of CD can be appreciated, such as increased problem-solving quality, adaptability, learning, and innovation and creativity (Adler 1997; Maseland et al. 2018; Stahl and Tung 2015; Stahl et al. 2017). Because sense-making in such processes is not solely etic (dependent on outsiders' view) but also has to be emic (dependent on insiders' view), organizations tend to promote a more positive perspective on CD as a result of the need to make sense of a host culture's internal logic (Stahl and Tung 2015). Etic sense-making often sees more anarchy while emic sense-making often reports more rationality and structure in the host cultures (Woodside et al. 2005). Such an intimate understanding of host cultures will ultimately lead to improved learning and organizational performance. The etic-dialectic-emic distinction of CD parallels the value-attitude-behavior distinction of bounded rationality.

To conclude this section, we would like to point out that the link between CR and the emic-etic distinction can even be borne out by the similar confusions that they are subjected to. A common confusion in the emic-etic distinction literature is the tendency to equate etic with deductive and emic with inductive research (e.g., Onwuegbuzie et al. 2010). But as discussed in Subsect. 2.9.1 and shown in Tables 2.3 and 2.4, deduction and induction should be properly considered as directional reasoning logics which can be applied to different ontological depths. As such, the terms etic and emic are not interchangeable with deductive and inductive, since both emic and etic research can be done inductively or deductively (Douglass and Lindauer 1988).

3.4 Opportunism and Bounded Rationality Should Be Treated as Attitudes

3.4.1 *Opportunism as Attitude*

TCE is concerned with opportunism as an attitude or potential behavior (Thurstone 1931) rather than as a behavior which is a purely ex post phenomenon and cannot be observed until it has happened since it is 'state unobservable'[6] (Godfrey and Hill 1995). The dominant concern of TCE is to make provisions for and mitigate against potential ex post opportunistic behavior in the ex ante organizational design (David and Han 2004; Geyskens et al. 2006; Godfrey and Hill 1995; Richter 2005; Rindfleisch and Heide 1997; Williamson 1998). Thus, it is the perceived threat of opportunism that TCE considers in the calculation of ex post transaction cost (Godfrey and Hill 1995), and such perception is largely based on attitude.

Hofstede (1998: 479) illustrated the difference between values and attitudes using the following example: 'in an employee survey, "how satisfied are you with your career opportunities?" is an attitude question, but "how important is it to you to have career opportunities?" is a value question'. Using an example similar to Hofstede's, a question like 'how important is it for you to be opportunistic in your business relationships?',[7] addressed to the business partner, is a value question; but 'how likely will you behave opportunistically?' addressed to the business partner, is an attitude question.

TCE apparently conflates 'opportunism as a value' with 'opportunism as an attitude'. This can be shown by using several quotes from Williamson. For one, he pointed out that 'it is not necessary that all agents be regarded as opportunistic in identical degree. It suffices that those who are less opportunistic than others are difficult to ascertain ex ante' (Williamson 1979: 234). In another work, he rejected a belief 'that most economic agents are engaged in opportunistic practices most of the time. Rather, most economic agents are engaged in business-as-usual, with little or no thought to opportunism, most of the time. That opportunism does not continuously intrude is partly because many economic agents are well-socialized' (Williamson 1993: 98). In his acceptance speech for the Nobel Prize in 2009, Williamson added that 'while accurate descriptions of what is going on 'most of the time' are plainly essential, much of what is interesting about human behavior in general and organizations in particular has reference not to routines but to exceptions'.

In the above quotes, the distinction between 'opportunism as a value' and 'opportunism as an attitude' has not been clearly appreciated. In most cases, economic agents are less likely to behave opportunistically because they are well socialized; nevertheless, it is important to consider opportunism in business relationships because there are opportunistic agents which are the exception rather than the rule. The former refers to attitude and the latter to value. As a theoretical premise (though not a necessary one), opportunism in TCE refers to 'opportunism as a value', but as an empirical phenomenon, opportunism in TCE refers to 'opportunism as an attitude'. Because values do not directly affect behavior (Dietz et al. 2005; Schwartz 1996), opportunism has to be considered differently from an abstract value in order to make TCE behavioral. We suggest that opportunism be treated as an attitude due to attitude's high relevance to behavior.

There are existing arguments which support our distinguishing between 'opportunism as a value' and 'opportunism as an attitude', even though these arguments were originally used to argue for the distinction between the so-called 'opportunism as an attitude' and 'opportunism as a behavior' (Moran and Ghoshal 1996; Verbeke and Greidanus 2009). It was suggested that Williamson's opportunism is dispositional and non-contextual, thus wanting in how opportunism develops or how it can be reduced in various contexts (Verbeke and Greidanus 2009). Moran and Ghoshal (1996) have referred to a schizophrenic view in TCE toward opportunism, whereby opportunism is dispositional and static, yet safeguards against opportunism have to take place in various contexts and thus are situational and dynamic. Traditional TCE cannot rid itself of this schizophrenia because of its collapsed ontology into the empirical domain and the concomitant inability to consider social contexts and human agency (Pratten 1997), as discussed in Chapter 2.

Treating opportunism as an attitude also has an additional benefit. TCE distinguishes between ex ante and ex post opportunism. The former is associated with the costs of writing contingent-claims contracts in order to curb ex post opportunistic behaviors, while the latter relates to the costs of monitoring, modifying, and enforcing contract terms (Williamson 1985). It generally believed that ex ante opportunism can be dealt with in relative ease when compared to ex post opportunism, and the research focus has been on the latter. Nevertheless, considering that high ex ante opportunism can often lead to high ex post opportunism (Barney and Lee 2000; Williamson 1975, 1985), it is essential that ex ante opportunism be given its due attention. Transaction costs that occur in relationship initiation and partner selection stages can provide valuable cues about future transaction success (Al-Khatib et al. 2005). Since both ex ante and ex post opportunistic behaviors can be predicted by opportunism as an attitude, an attitude-based approach helps to consider both types of opportunism.

3.4.2 Bounded Rationality as Attitude

Similarly, a distinction can be made between bounded rationality as an attitude and bounded rationality as a value. This distinction is not something new as the difference between rationality as an attitude and rationality as a value (principle) has long been discussed by some scholars (Popper 1967: 149; the translation of this discussion can be found in Langlois 1989: 233). What we do is simply extend this argument into the discussion with regard to bounded rationality. Bounded rationality (epistemological uncertainty), as an attitude, can be construed as an attitudinal, situation-specific construct toward uncertainty (Braithwaite et al. 2002; Wolff et al. 2011). It is a fundamental human attitude to use partial information by making abstractions (Bergson 1946; Gigerenzer and Todd 1999; Novarese 2009), which may be a consequence of bounded rationality (Genewein et al. 2015).

TCE treats bounded rationality as a value rather than an attitude. Using an analogous example to Hofstede's (1998: 479), a question like 'how important is it for you to consider your bounded rationality when making decisions?' is a value question, but 'how boundedly rational do you think you are with regard to your business (such as an overseas subsidiary)?' is an attitude question. Scholars have pointed out that bounded rationality in TCE is treated as 'a fixed background condition' or a value, which ignores the drastic difference of economic agents' bounded rationality (as an attitude) and the systematic biases in decision-making due to bounded rationality (Argyres and Mayer 2007; Cyert and March 1963). It has been suggested to the effect that turning 'bounded rationality as a value' into 'bounded rationality as an attitude' can effectively elaborate TCE (Ketokivi and Mahoney 2016: 132).

In a sense, the value-attitude distinction of bounded rationality is related to Bergson's (1946) distinguishing between two kinds of abstraction: one which arising from a reduced capacity to see differences due to human cognitive limits and the other which represents an ability to find elements of unity among different situations (Novarese 2009). The former is also referred to as 'the law of abstraction' and the latter to 'the law of constancy' (Zeki 2001). Bounded rationality as a value, which is trans-situational, will lead to the former type of abstraction not because some stimuli are more similar than others but because of human incapacity to treat different inputs differently due to bounded rationality (Genewein et al. 2015; Zeki 2001). Such abstraction is a process in which the particular is subordinated to the general so that what is represented can be applied to many particulars (Zeki 2001). This is consistent with the definition of values (Kahle 1983; Schwartz 1992; Vaske and Donnelly 1999). Nevertheless, bounded rationality as a value will lead the economic agent to shut down his mental processes and learning. Bounded rationality as a value is thus a limitation (Novarese 2009).

Bounded rationality as an attitude, on the other hand, is situational and focuses on the 'constant and essential characteristics of objects' (Zeki 2001: 51). The essence of an object is what enables its identification under various circumstances. As such, bounded rationality as an attitude has to be contextualized or subject to varied or changing situations in order for it to be manifested, identified, and understood. As such, it is a prerequisite for learning since context recognition is a tool or a step of procedural rationality which activates learning (Novarese 2009). Bounded rationality as an attitude is thus a potential capability or a mentality which opens up doors for capability development. Treating bounded rationality as a value implies that TCE ignores the learning-enabling and capability-enhancing aspect of bounded rationality.

As such, the difference between bounded rationality as a value and bounded rationality as an attitude is clearly a result of the difference between the real domain and the actual domain in CR. TCE, as a positivist theory, is stuck in the empirical domain and thus incapable of making the shift from treating bounded rationality as a limitation to treating bounded rationality as an opportunity due to its ontological shallowness. As a result, its link to competence-based theories has been made difficult. We suggest that the adoption of CR can provide the much needed ontological depth and facilitate treating bounded rationality as an attitude. We propose that CD can play a role in contextualized bounded rationality and will discuss this point in Sect. 3.5.2 in brief and in Chapter 4 in detail. To conclude this subsection, we would also point out that, interestingly, the difference between 'the law of abstraction' and 'the law of constancy' (Zeki 2001) is a recurring theme in various streams of literature, even though differently manifested. Refer to Tables 7.3 and 7.4 for similar distinctions.

3.5 An Institutional Approach to Opportunism and Bounded Rationality as Attitudes

We propose that the value-to-attitude shift can be achieved by adopting an institutional approach which is particularly germane due to its focus on the centrality of attitudes, routines, and habits in economic life. This point has long been pointed out by the founding fathers of the original institutional theory (Hodgson 1998). For example, Veblen (1909: 626) defines institutions as 'settled habits of thought common to the generality of men', and Cooley (1909: 314) suggests that 'in the individual the institutions exist as habit of mind and of action'. Since attitudes are habits of thought (Eiser 1994), institutions have direct bearing on attitudes (Crespi 1977; Scott and Davis 2016). Institutional theory thus provides a theoretical foundation to explain how attitudes and institutions are linked (Larsen 2006; Naumann 2014).

Indeed, attitudes per se are not internal to individuals (Shove 2010). They are reproduced and sustained by the ongoing social practices through which individual attitudes and social institutions coevolve. As such, attitudes and institutions are intertwined and cannot be separated (Shove 2010), and the propositional attitudes of economic actors are not their internal states but the 'dispositional' states of the whole systems in that groups are the bearers of mental states (Tollefsen 2006, 2015). An institutional approach is also consistent with our CR approach, according to which institutional analysis can be done within the three levels of CR (see Table 3.2). Leca and Naccache (2006) have developed detailed theorizing about this and we do not repeat, but suffice it to say that institutions and attitudes must be considered in the domain of actual and they are at the same level (Leca and Naccache 2006: 632; Table 3.1). Attitudes are themselves institutions[8] (Busemeyer et al. 2020; North 1990). In this light, we suggest that the national ethical attitude index developed by Franke and Nadler (2008) and the widely used CD measure developed by Kogut and Singh (1988) can be used as measures for opportunism as an attitude and bounded rationality as an attitude, respectively.[9]

3.5.1 National Ethical Attitude as a Measure of 'Opportunism as an Attitude'

Opportunistic attitude has been shown to be largely constrained by institutions and social relationships (Chen et al. 2002). One such institution is the national ethical environment which affects economic agents' opportunistic behavior. Franke and Nadler (2008: 259) constructed a measure, national ethical attitude (NEA), to proxy national ethical environment, and this measure can be used as a measure of 'opportunism as an attitude'. The NEA measure was constructed based on four items from the World Values Survey (Inglehart et al. 2004): (1) claiming government benefits to which you are not entitled; (2) avoiding a fare on public transport; (3) cheating on taxes if you have a chance; and (4) someone accepting a bribe in the course of their duties. The four items are clearly in line with the definition of opportunism as 'self-interest seeking with guile' (Williamson 1985: 47). Higher NEA values indicate higher ethical standards. This measure has seen increasing usage (Beamish et al. 2019; Foss 2012; Muralidharan and Pathak 2017; Peng 2008; Peng and Beamish 2012).

3.5.2 Cultural Distance as a Measure of 'Bounded Rationality as an Attitude'[10]

From an institutional perspective, bounded rationality does not merely arise from inherent mental limitations of any individual but is culturally acquired and shared (Zukin and DiMaggio 1990; Dequech 2003; Sunstein 2006). Institutions include culture (North 1990), which is a set of shared attitudes, and studies involving CD are considered part of the institutional literature focusing on the informal aspects of institutional constraints (Meyer and Peng 2005).

CD can be regarded as a measure of bounded rationality for the following related reasons, among others. First, information asymmetry and information costs increase with CD (Bergh et al. 2019; Erramilli and Rao 1993; Morschett et al. 2010). Because one source of bounded rationality is the availability and reliability of information, CD gives rise to bounded rationality (Rosanas 2004). Second, 'culture' is information shared among individuals. It can be seen as a 'fast and frugal' (Gigerenzer and Selten 2001: 10) behavioral mechanism which speeds up information processing and facilitates fast decision-making through 'cultural transmission mechanism' in which costly individual data processing can be skipped (Henrich et al. 2001). Such mechanism gradually loses its efficacy with increasing CD (Weber and Mayer 2014). Third, bounded rationality arises vis-à-vis 'structure of task environments' (Simon 1956). Because the most important type of environment structure is created by culture (Todd and Gigerenzer 2007) and institutions (Simon 1990), the structures of host country environments become increasingly different from the structure of environment at home with increasing CD, and economic agents' cognitive abilities become more limited with diminishing common ground (Weber and Mayer 2014), which 'set bounds on rationality by restricting the opportunities and alternatives [economic agents] perceive' (Barley and Tolbert 1997: 94). The greater CD is, the more difficult it is for MNCs to process and interpret host country information (Morschett et al. 2010).

In fact, the deeper reasons for using CD as a measure for bounded rationality lie in the fact that human cognition is conditioned and affected by cultural context (Scott 1995; Knight 1997), which serves as cognitive structures that are taken for granted and shared by the people in a culture (Scott 1995). CD thus reflects cognitive bounds which are fundamental to bounded rationality. This cannot be fully understood without an understanding of the distinction between the brain, the mind, and the self. We provide fuller presentation of this topic in Chapter 4.

Notes

1. As discussed in the previous chapter, we do not think opportunism is a necessary assumption for TCE. We do not even consider it as an assumption. As for bounded rationality, we tend to agree with Gigerenzer and Selten's (2001: 6) view that bounded rationality 'signifies a type of theory', not an assumption.
2. Hepler and Albarracín (2013) used terms 'dispositional attitudes' and 'attitudes without objects'. They measured such attitudes by 'having individuals evaluate a wide range of stimuli and then averaging across all evaluations for each individual' (2013: 1063). Since what they measure is trans-situational, their dispositional attitudes are in fact values, or something in between values and attitudes considering the aforementioned bandwidth-fidelity tradeoff.
3. As discussed in Subsect. 2.9.1 and stated at the last paragraph of this section, deduction and induction should be correctly considered as directional reasoning logics which can be applied to both emic and etic research at different ontological depths.

4. Emic accounts aim to uncover the concepts that are meaningful to the members of a given culture, i.e., their concepts of the rational norm (Lockie 2016).
5. Ethnocentrism refers to the practice of applying emic constructs derived in one (often Western) culture to other cultural settings in an etic way, resulting in an 'imposed etic' (Berry 1990).
6. Opportunism is state unobservable because the observation of the behavior of an economic agent causes a change of state in the agent.
7. As mentioned in Sect. 3.1, opportunism is an important value since it is relevant to environmental selection and adaptation (e.g., Parker 1978).
8. They also have similar definitions. For example, institutions are defined as recurrent and self-reproducing patterns of behavior (Leca and Naccache 2006).
9. Both measures are derived based on data from cross-cultural surveys. Such attitude measures are supposed to have high explanatory powers in predicting firm behavior. This is because studies on national cultures have shown that national cultural principles are usually acquired early in life and have lasting influence on individual and organizational behavior (Abdi and Aulakh 2012). Hofstede (1991) shows that national cultures explain 50% of the variations in managers' values, beliefs, and attitudes.
10. CD is one of the most widely used constructs in international business (Zaheer et al. 2012) and the subsidiary ownership literature in particular (Zhao et al. 2004). However, there is much confusion about what it measures. It has been widely used as a proxy for both external uncertainty and opportunism. Nevertheless, CD is clearly not a measure of external uncertainty because it does not cause the unpredictability of the external environment (Slangen and van Tulder 2009) and managers view them as distinct constructs (Tihanyi et al. 2005). CD is not a measure for opportunism either, because it does not cause partner opportunism. While firms may attribute greater opportunism to partners that are culturally distant (Luo 2007), CD in this case reflects cognitive biases as a result of bounded rationality. This study uses CD as a measure for bounded rationality, or, more accurately, cognitive bounds. Detailed theorizing can be found in Chapter 4, in addition to what offered here in this subsection.

References

Abdi, M., & Aulakh, P. S. (2012). Do country-level institutional frameworks and interfirm governance arrangements substitute or complement in international business relationships? *Journal of International Business Studies, 43*(5), 477–497.

Adler, N. J. (1997). *International dimensions of organizational behavior*. Cincinnati, OH: South-Western College Publishing.

Ajzen, I. (2012). Values, attitudes, and behavior. In S. Salzborn, E. Davidov, & J. Reinecke (Eds.), *Methods, theories, and empirical applications in the social sciences* (pp. 33–38). Wiesbaden: VS Verlag für Sozialwissenschaften.

Ajzen, I. (2005). *Attitudes, personality and behavior*. Milton Keynes: Open University Press.

Ajzen, I., & Fishbein, M. (1980). *Understanding attitudes and predicting social behavior*. Englewood Cliffs, NJ: Prentice-Hall.

Aldrich, H. E. (1999). *Organizations evolving*. Newbury Park, CA: Sage.

Al-Khatib, J., Rawwas, M. Y., Swaidan, Z., & Rexeisen, R. J. (2005). The ethical challenges of global business-to-business negotiations. *Journal of Marketing Theory and Practice, 13*(4), 46–60.

Archer, M. S. (1995). *Realist social theory*. Cambridge: Cambridge University Press.

Argyres, N. S., & Mayer, K. J. (2007). Contract design as a firm capability. *Academy of Management Review, 32*(4), 1060–1077.

Azar, G., & Drogendijk, R. (2019). Ex-post performance implications of divergence of managers' perceptions of 'distance' from 'reality' in international business. *Management International Review, 59*(1), 67–92.

Barley, S. R., & Tolbert, P. S. (1997). Institutionalization and structuration. *Organization Studies, 18*(1), 93–117.

Barney, J. B., & Lee, W. (2000). Multiple considerations in making governance choices. In N. J. Foss & V. Mahnke (Eds.), *Competence, governance, and entrepreneurship* (pp. 304–317). Oxford: Oxford University Press.

Beamish, P. W., Peng, G. Z., & Nkongolo-Bakenda, J. M. (2019). Ethical issues in Japanese foreign direct investment in developed versus developing countries. In L. C. Leonidou, C. S. Katsikeas, S. Samiee, & C. N. Leonidou (Eds.), *Socially-responsible international business* (pp. 284–312). Cheltenham: Edgar Elgar.

Bergh, D. D., Ketchen, D. J., Orlandi, I., Heugens, P. P., & Boyd, B. K. (2019). Information asymmetry in management research. *Journal of Management, 45*(1), 122–158.

Bergson, H. (1946). *The creative mind: An introduction to Metaphysics*. New York: Philosophical Library.

Bernard, L. L. (1926). *An introduction to social psychology*. New York: Henry Holt and Company.

Berry, J. W. (1989). Imposed etics-emics-derived etics: The operationalization of a compelling idea. *International Journal of Psychology, 24*(6), 721–735.

Berry, J. W. (1990). Imposed etics, emics, derived etics: Their conceptual and operational status in cross-cultural psychology. In T. N. Headland, K. L. Pike, & M. Harris (Eds.), *Emics and etics: The insider/outsider debate* (pp. 28–47). Newbury Park, CA: Sage.

Bhaskar, R. (1979). *The possibility of naturalism*. Atlantic Highlands, NJ: Humanities Press.

Bhaskar, R. (2008). *A realist theory of science*. London: Routledge.

Blom, B., & Morén, S. (2011). Analysis of generative mechanisms. *Journal of Critical Realism, 10*(1), 60–79.

Braithwaite, D., Sutton, S., & Steggles, N. (2002). Intention to participate in predictive genetic testing for hereditary cancer. *Psychology and Health, 17*(6), 761–772.

Buckley, P. J., & Chapman, M. (1997). The use of native categories in management research. *British Journal of Management, 8*(4), 283–299.

Buckley, P. J., Chapman, M., Clegg, J., & Gajewska-De, Mattos H. (2014). A linguistic and philosophical analysis of emic and etic and their use in international business research. *Management International Review, 54*(3), 307–324.

Busemeyer, M. R., Abrassart, A., Nezi, S., & Nezi, R. (2020). Beyond positive and negative. *British Journal of Political Science*, 1–26.

Chen, C. C., Peng, M. W., & Saparito, P. A. (2002). Individualism, collectivism, and opportunism. *Journal of Management, 28*(4), 567–583.

Cooley, C. H. (1909). *Social organization*. New York: Charles Scribner's Sons.

Crespi, I. (1977). Attitude measurement, theory, and prediction. *Public Opinion Quarterly, 41*(3), 285–294.

Cronbach, L. J., & Gleser, G. C. (1957). *Psychological tests and personnel decisions*. Urbana, IL: University of Illinois Press.

Cyert, R. M., & March, J. G. (1963). *A behavioral theory of the firm*. Oxford: Blackwell.

David, R. J., & Han, S. (2004). A systematic assessment of the empirical support for transaction cost economics. *Strategic Management Journal, 25*(1), 39–58.

Deonna, J. A., & Teroni, F. (2015). Emotions as attitudes. *Dialectica, 69*(3), 293–311.

Dequech, D. (2003). Cognitive and cultural embeddedness. *Journal of Economic Issues, 37*(2), 461–470.

Dietz, T., Fitzgerald, A., & Shwom, R. (2005). Environmental values. *Annual Review of Environment and Resources, 30*, 335–372.

Douglass, A. A., & Lindauer, O. (1988). Hierarchical and nonhierarchical approaches to ceramic design analysis. *American Antiquity, 53*(3), 620–626.

Dreezens, E., Martijn, C., Tenbült, P., Kok, G., & de Vries, N. K. (2008). The missing link. *Basic and Applied Social Psychology, 30*(2), 142–152.

Eagly, A. H., & Chaiken, S. (1993). *The psychology of attitudes*. Forth Worth, TX: Harcourt Brace Jovanovich.

Edman, J. (2016). Reconciling the advantages and liabilities of foreignness: Towards an identity-based framework. *Journal of International Business Studies, 47*(6), 674–694.

Eiser, J. R. (1994). *Attitudes, chaos and the connectionist mind*. Oxford, UK: Blackwell.
Erramilli, M. K., & Rao, C. P. (1993). Service firms' international entry-mode choice. *Journal of Marketing, 57*(3), 19–38.
Fishbein, M., & Ajzen, I. (1975). *Belief, attitude, intention, and behavior*. Reading, MA: Addison-Wesley.
Fletcher, A. J. (2017). Applying critical realism in qualitative research. *International Journal of Social Research Methodology, 20*(2), 181–194.
Foss, N. J. (2012). Linking ethics and economic growth. *Contemporary Economics, 6*(3), 4–9.
Frank, R. H. (1990). A theory of moral sentiments. In J. J. Mansbridge (Ed.), *Beyond self-interest* (pp. 71–96). Chicago: University of Chicago Press.
Franke, G. R., & Nadler, S. S. (2008). Culture, economic development, and national ethical attitudes. *Journal of Business Research, 61*(3), 254–264.
Genewein, T., Leibfried, F., Grau-Moya, J., & Braun, D. A. (2015). Bounded rationality, abstraction, and hierarchical decision-making. *Frontiers in Robotics and AI, 2*, Article 27.
Geyskens, I., Steenkamp, J. B. E. M., & Kumar, N. (2006). Make, buy, or ally. *Academy of Management Journal, 49*(3), 519–543.
Ghoshal, S., & Moran, P. (1996). Bad for practice. *Academy of Management Review, 21*(1), 13–47.
Gigerenzer, G., & Selten, R. (2001). *Bounded rationality*. Cambridge, MA: MIT Press.
Gigerenzer, G., & Todd, P. M. (1999). *Simple heuristics that make us smart*. Oxford: Oxford University Press.
Godfrey, P. C., & Hill, C. W. L. (1995). The problem of unobservables in strategic management research. *Strategic Management Journal, 16*(7), 519–533.
Harris, M. (1976). History and significance of the emic/etic distinction. *Annual Review of Anthropology, 5*, 329–350.
Harris, M. (1980). *Cultural materialism: The struggle for a science of culture*. New York: Vintage Books.
Harris, M. (2001). *The rise of anthropological theory: A history of theories of culture*. London: AltaMira.
Harzing, A. W., & Pudelko, M. (2016). Do we need to distance ourselves from the distance concept? *Management International Review, 56*(1), 1–34.
Hepler, J., & Albarracín, D. (2013). Attitudes without objects: Evidence for a dispositional attitude. *Journal of Personality and Social Psychology, 104*(6), 1060–1076.
Henrich, J., Albers, W., Boyd, R., Gigerenzer, G., McCabe, K. A., Ockenfels, A., & Young, P. H. (2001). Group report. In G. Gigerenzer & R. Selten (Eds.), *Bounded rationality* (pp. 343–359). Cambridge, MA: MIT Press.

Hitlin, S., & Piliavin, J. A. (2004). Values. *Annual Review of Sociology, 30,* 359–393.

Ho, E. (2015). Bound by ethical complexities and socio-material histories. *Energy Research & Social Science, 10,* 150–164.

Hodgson, G. M. (1998). Evolutionary and competence-based theories of the firm. *Journal of Economic Studies, 25*(1), 25–56.

Hofstede, G. (1991). *Cultures and organizations: Software of the mind.* London: McGraw-Hill.

Hofstede, G. (1998). Attitudes, values and organizational culture. *Organization Studies, 19*(3), 477–493.

Homer, P. M., & Kahle, L. R. (1988). A structural equation test of the value-attitude-behavior hierarchy. *Journal of Personality and Social Psychology, 54*(4), 638–646.

Hymes, D. H. (1990). Emics, etics, and openness: An ecumenical approach. In T. N. Headland, K. L. Pike, & M. Harris (Eds.), *Emics and etics: The insider/outsider debate* (pp. 120–126). Newbury Park, CA: Sage.

Inglehart, R., Halman, L., & Welzel, C. (2004). Introduction. In R. Inglehart, M. Basanez, J. Diez-Medrano, L. Halman, & R. Luijkx (Eds.), *Human beliefs and values* (pp. 1–20). Mexico: Siglo Veintiuno Editors.

Jennings, G. R. (2004). Business research, examples of theoretical paradigms that inform. In K. Kempf-Leonard (Ed.), *Encyclopedia of social measurement* (pp. 211–217). San Diego, CA: Academic Press.

John, G. (1984). An empirical investigation of some antecedents of opportunism in a marketing channel. *Journal of Marketing Research, 21*(3), 278–289.

Jorion, P. (1983). Emic and etic: Two anthropological ways of spilling ink. *Cambridge Journal of Anthropology, 8*(3), 41–68.

Kahle, L. R. (1983). *Social values and social change.* New York: Praeger.

Ketokivi, M., & Mahoney, J. T. (2016). Transaction cost economics as a constructive stakeholder theory. *Academy of Management Learning & Education, 15*(1), 123–138.

Knight, J. (1997). Social institutions and human cognition. *Journal of Institutional and Theoretical Economics, 153*(4), 693–699.

Kogut, B., & Singh, H. (1988). The effect of national culture on the choice of entry mode. *Journal of International Business Studies, 19*(3), 411–432.

Kotler, P. (1997). *Marketing management.* Upper Saddle River, NJ: Prentice-Hall.

Langlois, R. N. (1989). Rationality, institutions, and explanation. In R. N. Langlois (Ed.), *Economics as a process* (pp. 225–255). Cambridge: Cambridge University Press.

Larsen, C. A. (2006). *The institutional logic of welfare attitudes.* Aldershot: Ashgate.

Leca, B., & Naccache, P. (2006). A critical realist approach to institutional entrepreneurship. *Organization, 13*(5), 627–651.

Lee, A. S. (1991). Integrating positivist and interpretive approaches to organizational research. *Organization Science, 2*(4), 342–365.

Lees, N. (2016). International society is to international system as world society is to...? *Journal of International Relations and Development, 19*(3), 285–311.

Lockie, R. (2016). Perspectivism, deontologism and epistemic poverty. *Social Epistemology, 30*(2), 133–149.

Lubatkin, M., Lane, P., Collin, S., & Very, P. (2007). An embeddedness framing of governance and opportunism. *Journal of Organization Behavior, 28*(1), 43–58.

Luo, Y. (2007). An integrated anti-opportunism system in international exchange. *Journal of International Business Studies, 38*(6), 855–877.

Maio, G. R., & Olson, J. M. (2000). What is a 'value-expressive' attitude? In G. R. Maio & J. M. Olson (Eds.), *Why we evaluate* (pp. 249–269). Mahwah, NJ: Lawrence Erlbaum.

Malinowski, B. (1922). *Argonauts of the Western Pacific*. London: Routledge.

Martin, R. (1993). The new behaviorism: A critique of economics and organization. *Human Relations, 46*(9), 1085–1101.

Maseland, R., Dow, D., & Steel, P. (2018). The Kogut and Singh national cultural distance index: Time to start using it as a springboard rather than a crutch. *Journal of International Business Studies, 49*(9), 1154–1166.

Mead, G. H. (1934). *Mind, self, and society*. Chicago: University of Chicago Press.

Meyer, K. E., & Peng, M. W. (2005). Probing theoretically into Central and Eastern Europe. *Journal of International Business Studies, 36*(6), 600–621.

Miller, Z. D. (2017). The enduring use of the theory of planned behavior. *Human Dimensions of Wildlife, 22*(6), 583–590.

Modell, S. (2020). Across the great divide: Bridging the gap between economics- and sociology-based research on management accounting. *Journal of Management Accounting Research, 32*(2), 1–15.

Moran, P., & Ghoshal, S. (1996). Theories of economic organization. *Academy of Management Review, 21*(1), 58–72.

Morosini, P., Shane, S., & Singh, H. (1998). National cultural distance and cross-border acquisition performance. *Journal of International Business Studies, 29*(1), 137–158.

Morris, M. W., Leung, K., Ames, D., & Lickel, B. (1999). Views from inside and outside: Integrating emic and etic insights about culture and justice judgment. *Academy of Management Review, 24*(4), 781–796.

Morschett, D., Schramm-Klein, H., & Swoboda, B. (2010). Decades of research on market entry modes. *Journal of International Management, 16*(1), 60–77.

Muralidharan, E., & Pathak, S. (2017). National ethical institutions and social entrepreneurship. In B. Christiansen & H. Chandan (Eds.), *Handbook of research on human factors in contemporary workforce development* (pp. 379–402). Hershey, PA: IGI Global.
Naumann, E. (2014). *The dynamics of welfare attitudes in times of welfare state retrenchment* (Dissertation). University of Mannheim, Mannheim.
New, C. (2001). Realising the potential: The ESRC seminar series on social realism and empirical research. *Alethia, 4*(1), 43–47.
North, D. C. (1990). *Institutions, institutional change, and economic performance*. New York: Cambridge University Press.
Novarese, M. (2009). *Is bounded rationality a capacity, enabling learning?* (EERI Research Paper Series No. 12/2009).
Onwuegbuzie, A. J., Bustamante, R. M., & Nelson, J. A. (2010). Mixed research as a tool for developing quantitative instruments. *Journal of Mixed Methods Research, 4*(1), 56–78.
Park, R. E., & Burgess, E. W. (2019). *Introduction to the science of sociology*. Glasgow: Good Press.
Parker, C. E. (1978). Opportunism and the rise of intelligence. *Journal of Human Evolution, 7*(7), 597–608.
Peng, G. Z. (2008). The effect of national corporate responsibility environment on Japanese MNCs' location choice. *Academy of Management Proceedings, 2008*(1), 1–6.
Peng, G. Z., & Beamish, P. W. (2012). *The effect of national ethical environment on subsidiary ownership: Transaction cost and learning perspectives*. Boston, MA: Academy of Management Annual Meeting.
Peng, K., Nisbett, R. E., & Wong, N. Y. (1997). Validity problems comparing values across cultures and possible solutions. *Psychological Methods, 2*(4), 329–344.
Pike, K. L. (1967). *Language in relation to a unified theory of the structure of human behavior*. The Haque: Mouton.
Polsa, P. (2013). The crossover-dialog approach. *Journal of Business Research, 66*(3), 288–297.
Popper, K. R. (1967). La rationalité et le statut du principe de rationalité. In E. Classen (Ed.), *Les fondements philosophiques des doctrines économiques* (pp. 142–150). Paris: Payot.
Popper, K. R. (1990). *A world of propensities*. Bristol: Thoemmes.
Pratten, S. (1997). The nature of transaction cost economics. *Journal of Economic Issues, 31*(3), 781–803.
Rieger, M. O., Wang, M., & Hens, T. (2015). Risk preferences around the world. *Management Science, 61*(3), 637–648.
Rindfleisch, A., & Heide, J. B. (1997). Transaction cost analysis. *Journal of Marketing, 61*(4), 30–54.

Richter, R. (2005). The new institutional economics. *European Business Organization Law Review, 6*(2), 161–200.

Rokeach, M. (1973). *The nature of human values*. New York: Free Press.

Ronen, S., & Shenkar, O. (1988). Clustering variables: The application of nonmetric multivariate analysis techniques in comparative management research. *International Studies of Management & Organization, 18*(3), 72–87.

Rosanas, J. A. (2004). *Bounded rationality, value systems and time-inconsistency of preferences as rational foundations for the concept of trust* (IESE Business School Working Paper No. 567).

Schwartz, S. H. (1992). Universals in the content and structure of values. In M. P. Zanna (Ed.), *Advances in experimental social psychology (Vol. 25)* (pp. 1–65). Orlando, FL: Academic Press.

Schwartz, S. H. (1996). Value priorities and behavior. In C. Seligman, J. M. Olson, & M. P. Zanna (Eds.), *The psychology of values, the Ontario symposium (Vol. 8)* (pp. 1–24). Mahwah, NJ: Lawrence Erlbaum.

Scott, W. R. (1995). *Institutions and organizations*. Thousand Oaks, CA: Sage.

Scott, W. R., & Davis, G. F. (2016). *Organizations and organizing*. New York: Routledge.

Shove, E. (2010). Beyond the ABC. *Environment and Planning A, 42*(6), 1273–1285.

Simon, H. A. (1956). Rational choice and the structure of the environment. *Psychological Review, 63*(2), 129–138.

Simon, H. A. (1990). Invariants of human behavior. *Annual Review of Psychology, 41*(1), 1–19.

Sinkovics, R. R., & Holzmüller, H. H. (2001). National differences in materialism. *Journal of International Consumer Marketing, 13*(2), 103–134.

Slangen, A. H. L., & van Tulder, R. J. M. (2009). Cultural distance, political risk, or governance quality? *International Business Review, 18*(3), 276–291.

Stahl, G. K., Miska, C., Lee, H.-J., & De Luque, M. S. (2017). The upside of cultural differences. *Cross Cultural and Strategic Management, 24*(1), 2–12.

Stahl, G. K., & Tung, R. L. (2015). Towards a more balanced treatment of culture in international business studies. *Journal of International Business Studies, 46*(4), 391–414.

Steele, G. R. (2005). Critical thoughts about critical realism. *Critical Review, 17*(1–2), 133–154.

Steinmetz, G. (1998). Critical realism and historical sociology. *Comparative Studies in Society and History, 40*(1), 170–186.

Stoltz, D. S. (2018). Relations and relationships. *American Sociologist, 49*(1), 64–79.

Sunstein, C. R. (2006). Misfearing. *Harvard Law Review, 119*(4), 1110–1125.

Thurstone, L. L. (1931). The measurement of social attitudes. *Journal of Abnormal and Social Psychology, 26*(3), 249–269.

Tihanyi, L., Griffith, D. A., & Russell, C. J. (2005). The effect of cultural distance on entry mode choice, international diversification, and MNE performance. *Journal of International Business Studies, 36*(3), 270–283.

Todd, P. M., & Gigerenzer, G. (2007). Environments that make us smart. *Current Directions in Psychological Science, 16*(3), 167–171.

Tollefsen, D. P. (2006). From extended mind to collective mind. *Cognitive Systems Research, 7*(2/3), 140–150.

Tollefsen, D. P. (2015). *Groups as agents*. Cambridge: Polity.

Triandis, H. C. (1979). Values, attitudes, and interpersonal behavior. *Nebraska Symposium on Motivation, 27*(1), 195–259.

Vaske, J. J., & Donnelly, M. P. (1999). A value-attitude-behavior model predicting wildland preservation voting intentions. *Society & Natural Resources, 12*(6), 523–537.

Veblen, T. B. (1909). The limitations of marginal utility. *Journal of Political Economy, 17*(9), 620–636.

Verbeke, A., & Greidanus, N. S. (2009). The end of the opportunism vs. trust debate. *Journal of International Business Studies, 40*(9), 1471–1495.

Voloshinov, V. N. (1929). *Marxism and the philosophy of language* (L. Matejka & I. R. Titunik, Trans.). Cambridge, MA: Harvard University Press.

Vora, D., & Kostova, T. (2007). A model of dual organizational identification in the context of the multinational enterprise. *Journal of Organizational Behavior, 28*(3), 327–350.

Weber, L., & Mayer, K. (2014). Transaction cost economics and the cognitive perspective. *Academy of Management Review, 39*(3), 344–363.

Weinberg, A. (1927). Value-interpretation. *International Journal of Ethics, 38*(1), 44–56.

Williamson, O. E. (1975). *Markets and hierarchies*. New York: Free Press.

Williamson, O. E. (1979). Transaction-cost economics. *Journal of Law and Economics, 22*(2), 233–261.

Williamson, O. E. (1985). *The economic institutions of capitalism*. New York: Free Press.

Williamson, O. E. (1993). Opportunism and its critics. *Managerial and Decision Economics, 14*(2), 97–107.

Williamson, O. E. (1998). *Human actors and economic organization*. Paris: ISNIE conference.

Wolff, K., Nordin, K., Brun, W., Berglund, G., & Kvale, G. (2011). Affective and cognitive attitudes, uncertainty avoidance and intention to obtain genetic testing. *Psychology & Health, 26*(9), 1143–1155.

Wood, W. (2000). Attitude change. *Annual Review of Psychology, 51*(1), 539–570.

Woodside, A. G., Pattinson, H. M., & Miller, K. E. (2005). Advancing hermeneutic research for interpreting interfirm new product development. *Journal of Business & Industrial Marketing, 20*(7), 364–379.

Zaheer, S., Schomaker, M. S., & Nachum, L. (2012). Distance without direction. *Journal of International Business Studies, 43*(1), 18–27.

Zeki, S. (2001). Artistic creativity and the brain. *Science, 293*(5527), 51–52.

Zhao, H., Luo, Y., & Suh, T. (2004). Transaction cost determinants and ownership-based entry mode choice. *Journal of International Business Studies, 35*(6), 524–544.

Zhu, Y., & Bargiela-Chiappini, F. (2013). Balancing emic and etic. *Academy of Management Learning & Education, 12*(3), 380–395.

Zukin, S., & DiMaggio, P. (1990). Introduction. In S. Zukin & P. DiMaggio (Eds.), *Structures of capital* (pp. 1–36). Cambridge: Cambridge University Press.

CHAPTER 4

Modeling Bounded Rationality: Mediation or Moderation—Or Bounded Rationalizing?

Williamson (1985: 387) made an important statement that '[a]s compared with other approaches to the study of economic organization, transaction cost economics ... is more *self-conscious* about its behavioral assumptions' [italic added]. Herbert Simon once pointed out that the most fundamental understanding that 'could lead us to an understanding of economic processes and to empirically sound theories of them reside inside human *minds*. Accordingly, we must seek to discover what went on in the *heads* of those who made the relevant decision' (Simon 1997a: 70–71) [italic added]. Both of the prestigious scholars hit on some important ideas, but they seemed not to distinguish between the self, the mind and the brain.

In this chapter, we submit that it is exactly because the conflation of the three concepts that thwarts theoretical and empirical advances in TCE. Absent a clear understanding of them, it is difficult for TCE to become self-conscious and thus behavioral due to the absence of the subject of behaviors. Without a clear understanding of this point, the so-called behavioral assumptions tend to be treated as something external and prior to firm behavior rather than as an integral part of the behavioral process. While Williamson intended to make TCE more self-conscious and thus behavioral, the positivist approach he adopted prevented him from reaching his behavioral goal.

G. Z. Peng, *Toward Behavioral Transaction Cost Economics*,
International Marketing and Management Research,
https://doi.org/10.1007/978-3-030-46878-1_4

As we discussed in Chapter 2, bounded rationality, as epistemological uncertainty, is unavoidably intertwined with other ontological uncertainty in a CR framework. We also submitted that, for practical purposes, the classification of uncertainty into ontological and epistemological types makes common sense, provided that a clear classification as suggested in Chapter 2 is used. We also briefly discussed why CD can be regarded as a measure for bounded rationality in Chapter 3. However, there are still some deeper confusions about bounded rationality which cannot be realized until the time of modeling it. Verbeke et al. (2017: 41) suggest that bounded rationality likely functions 'as mediators (and in some cases as moderators) with respect to the link between perceptions of distance and preferences for a particular alternative or course of action'. Here they said 'likely', thus they were not specific about when bounded rationality acts as a mediator and when as a moderator. Nevertheless, no matter bounded rationality functions as a mediator or moderator, the hidden assumption in Verbeke et al. (2017) is that bounded rationality first needs to stand alone on its own. This suggests that the authors treated bounded rationality as something external and prior to organizational process rather than an integral part thereof. They also do not differentiate between cognitive bounds (see Note in Table 4.3 for disambiguation of the term) and psychological 'bounded rationalizing' (see Sect. 4.5). For TCE to become behavioral, bounded rationality has to be treated neither as mediation nor moderation, but as a process of psychological bounded rationality 'economizing' cognitive bounds over time (see Sect. 4.9).

To treat bounded rationality as something standing alone on its own is contradictory to its definition since both rationality and bounded rationality are defined with respect to human behavior. Rationality is 'broadly conceived as behavior that is...sensible or logical in pursuing one's goals' (Dean and Sharfman 1993: 1070) and is generally identified with the maximization of expected utility or profit (Bell et al. 1988; Simon 2000). Bounded rationality is defined as 'human behavior [that] is intendedly rational but only limitedly so' (Simon 1961: 24). Bounded rationality, as a feature of the mental process, is not accessible for direct observation and only manifests through behavior (Toomela 2008). In fact, 'all knowledge about mind...is based on interpretation of behavior' (Toomela 2008: 260). If so, how can bounded rationality be studied using mediation or moderation, which necessitates direct measurement of a metal phenomenon?

In the following, we make the distinction between the brain, the mind and the self. Such distinction requires theories of the brain and the mind in the first place. We then highlight the need to separate cognitive bounds from psychological 'bounded rationalizing' in order to model bounded rationality. We also suggest that a CR approach matches neatly with our endeavor. This chapter draws to a close by highlighting the need for an ontologically deep psychoanalytic understanding of the self in order for TCE to become a truly self-conscious behavioral theory.

4.1 The Distinction Between the Brain, the Mind and the Self

For many, these three concepts are conflated and mean largely the same thing. However, these terms have different meanings and connotations to psychologists, thus to behavioral TCE which necessitates a psychological turn. Among these terms, the definition of the brain has minimal controversy. Oxford Learner's Dictionaries define it as 'the organ inside the head that controls movement, thought, memory and feeling'. Other dictionaries provide very similar definitions. Modern neuroscience literature provides a basic fact about the human brain: it consists not of a homogeneous mass of nerve cells but of many specialized components, many of which have been found to be linked with particular functions and behaviors. Behaviors are the observable manifestation of interactions among different components of the brain (Lo 2005).

However, the definition of the mind becomes more challenging. The Cambridge Dictionary defines it as 'the part of a person that makes it possible for him or her to think, feel emotions, and understand things', but did not specify which part and where it is. Does it imply the brain? If so, what is the relationship between the mind and the brain? The Collins' definition is the 'ability to think and reason'. Oxford Learner's Dictionaries define it as 'the part of a person that makes them able to be aware of things, to think and to feel' and the 'ability to think and reason; [the] intelligence; the particular way that somebody thinks'. Pinker (2009: 24) was more specific: 'the mind is not the brain, but what the brain does, and not even everything it does, such as metabolizing fat and giving off heat.... The brain's special status comes from a special thing the brain does, which makes us see, think, feel, choose, and act. That special thing is information processing, or computation'. This is to say, mind is a faculty of the brain. However, treating mind as a faculty and an extension of the brain is putting the cart before the horse[1] since it is brain-centric or cognition-centric and deductivist (see this chapter, passim). From a CR perspective, this also leads to 'the epistemic fallacy' (Bhaskar 1998: 27), which reduce ontology into what can be empirically known by the brain. Some commonly asked questions in Buddhism, such as 'who/where was I before I was born?', intend exactly to expose the limits of the brain. As such, the brain has to be viewed as an organ used by the mind (Maharshi 1985), since the mind is higher than the brain (cf. Endnote 5). In CR terms, the mind extends beyond the brain and the brain can only partially experience events that the mind is capable of producing (Sheldrake 2012).

In the above definitions of the brain and the mind, various pronouns, as the subject in those definitions, are referred to or implied. This actually is deeply misleading. Where are we, and who are we? If the brain, the most important thing for 'us' is an organ, then what else is not an organ? Indeed, the body itself in whole is an organ. But whose organ? The answer is that of the 'self' (Maharshi 1985).

Both Buddhism and modern psychology suggest that the self is nonlocal, and 'the search for the self will not result in a location' in our human body, but 'the absence of evidence is not the evidence of absence' (Goldberg 2015: 9). The relationship among the triad of brain/mind/self is a complicated one, and it takes numerous births and rebirths for people to understand this. Since most of us in the world are not enlightened like the Buddha or Bhagavan Sri Ramana Maharshi, let's just take what they teach as is. Suffice it to say that the three are different but related concepts. Considering the striking parallels between the Yogācāra School of Mahayana Buddhism (Xuanzang and Wei 1973) and CR (Kochumuttom 1982), the relationship among the self, the mind and the brain can be understood in a CR framework as shown in Table 4.1.[2]

Table 4.1 The stratified ontology of the self based on critical realism

Domain	*Real*	*Actual*	*Empirical*
Self (generative mechanisms/tendencies)	✓		
Mind (events)	✓	✓	
Brain (experiences)	✓	✓	✓

Source Author's creation based on Bhaskar (2008: 2)

4.2 The Theory of the Human Brain

To understand the brain, multiple models have been proposed, including the triune brain model (MacLean 1990), the left brain/right brain model (Sperry 1975), the four-quadrant model (Herrmann 1996), and the system 1/system 2 model (Kahneman 2011). While these models are not the same, they overlap considerably. The system 1/system 2 model can be subsumed into the triune model, and the four-quadrant model is a combination of the triune brain model and the left brain/right brain model. The left brain/right brain model, while appealing to general public, directed attention to the physical laterality of brain functions rather than to the functions themselves. The triune model has been accepted as the most influential view of human brain in post-war neuroscience (McKinney 1998; Pogliano 2017). We adopt this model for its affinity with both CR and the eight-consciousness model of the mind that we adopt in the next section.

The triune model proposes that the human brain consists of three phylogenetic layers or systems which were developed successively in response to evolutionary pressures during different phases of evolution: the reptilian (inner core), the paleomammalian (limbic), and the neomammalian (neocortex). These layers can be understood as three nested brains, with each successively higher level brain wrapping around its lower level brain. The reptilian part is the oldest, located in the inner core of the brain consisted of basal ganglia and thalamus. The reptilian brain is focused on the governing of unconscious vital functions such as digestion, respiration, heartbeat, blood pressure and circulation. It is active even during deep sleep. The paleomammalian brain corresponds to the limbic brain regions, including amygdala, hippocampus, and parahippocampal gyrus. It functions as the primary center of emotions and instincts. Particularly, the amygdala regulates the fight-or-flight response when under threat. The neomammalian brain is the outmost layer of the brain and is the center of higher-order mental functions such as planning, reasoning, complex analysis, problem-solving and conscious inhibition of action. While each of the three layers is geared toward its separate functions, they respond to and interact with each other. Neuroscientists also suggest that although the systems in the entire brain are relevant to the production of emotions, it is the limbic system that plays a dominant role in mediating emotions and behaviors (Mascolo and Fischer 2010). We return to this point shortly.

In business and management literature, much attention has been focused on an interesting phenomenon called 'amygdala hijack' (Goleman 1996). In a fight-or-flight situation, the quick and emotional amygdala response can take over, often resulting in irrational and biased behaviors before the slower higher-order logical reasoning can mediate this reaction. This is because 'the architecture of the brain gives the amygdala a privileged position as an emotional sentinel, able to hijack the brain' (Goleman 1996: 17).[3] The fast and slow modes of response are also referred to as system 1 and system 2 thinking, respectively (Kahneman 2011). An understanding of the different response pathways provides deeper insights into the causes of and remedies for some common behavioral biases that affect business decision-making.

A very important but less researched topic in management literature is the so-called *Hebbian learning* (Hebb 1949; Sejnowski 1999; Yuste 2015). Hebb (1949) proposed that learning might exist at the level of synapses, the connections between nerve cells, in a way described as '[neurons] that fire together wire together' (Shatz 1992). The connections between neurons that interact with each other would be strengthened by a particular pattern of stimulus activation and the repetition thereof, resulting in 'Hebbian synapse'. Neurons connected with Hebbian synapses would develop into spontaneous neuronal assemblies, which would exhibit recursive and recurrent patterns of neuronal activation and generate spontaneous functional states in the brain, such as specific behaviors and memories (Yuste 2015). Such spontaneous functions are emergent, meaning they arise from interaction among elements but are not present in the individual elements (Churchland and Sejnowski 1992; Yuste 2015). Hebb also proposed that the synaptic connections could be altered by a learning rule, or a local change in synaptic strength due to correlated patterns of activities (Yuste 2015). Due to this 'synaptic plasticity', the assemblies have 'learned' patterns of activities, storing them into their altered repertoire of synaptic connections.[4] In short, learning is the process of formation and subsequent modification of synapses. As we discuss in Sect. 4.4, this conceptualization of learning in modern neuro-science is consistent with the eight-consciousness model of the mind.

While the modern neuroscience has made dramatic advance, there still remain many fundamental questions. These include: Where does the brain comes from? Who reacts to external stimuli? Who learns? Where does 'learning' or 'knowledge' reside? How does learning happen? Where does knowledge go when the brain dies? These are fundamental questions that science cannot answer, at least for the time being. The answers to these questions will directly affect how we understand the concept of bounded rationality and how we model it. We tend to think that the current stagnation in modeling bounded rationality and lack of a standardized research method can in part be attributed to a lack of interest in or understating of philosophy and metaphysics (Liao and Chien 2017). We propose that our understanding about human rationality and decision-making can be informed by the eight-consciousness model developed in the tradition of the Yogācāra School of Mahayana Buddhism (Xuanzang and Wei 1973).

4.3 The Eight-Consciousness Model of the Mind

According to Xuanzang and Epstein (1986), our consciousness involves eight interrelated and interacting types of consciousness: (1) eye-consciousness (seeing), (2) ear-consciousness (hearing), (3) nose-consciousness (smelling), (4) tongue-consciousness (tasting), (5) body-consciousness (tactile feeling), (6) mind-consciousness (cognition, namely, mental consciousness), (7) *manas* (the defiling mind-consciousness), and (8) *alaya* (storehouse consciousness, storehouse of tendencies). [This study prefers to use the term 'cognitive consciousness' and 'emotional/affective consciousness' for the sixth and seventh consciousnesses, respectively, in order to reduce confusion and match new development in modern neurosciences (e.g., LeDoux and Brown 2017; Panksepp 2003a, b, 2004). The sixth and seventh consciousnesses were called the 'mind-consciousness' and the 'defiling mind-consciousness' probably because of lack of words to describe them]. While the first five physical senses are relatively easy to understand, the remaining three and their interrelationships among themselves and relationships with the other five require some explanation.

Xuanzang and Epstein (1986) note that the term 'consciousness' is used 'exclusively in the sense of distinction-making activities of the mind, which include both the making of the distinctions and the distinctions made. Conscious awareness and what is normally unconscious are both considered aspects of consciousness in the Buddhist sense of the word'. Such distinctions are made by mental consciousnesses *consciously* (in the common English sense of the word) and by *manas unconsciously* (in the common English sense of the word). Since the first five senses cannot make distinctions themselves, the mental consciousness and *manas* always accompanies the first five consciousnesses. This is to say, the first five senses are not consciousnesses on their own but only capable of representations. Only the sixth consciousness and *manas* are capable of making distinctions, but the distinction-making by the former is not continuous even though conscious, as opposed to that by the latter which is unconscious but continuous (see more explanation shortly). The five senses only feed sensory data to the sixth consciousness and *manas* where distinctions are made and/or interpreted consciously and unconsciously, respectively. As such, the first five consciousnesses are the base consciousnesses of the sixth consciousness and *manas*. The making of the distinctions and all of the distinctions that mental consciousness made based on sensory data are also fed into *manas* (Harvey 2013). *Manas* is regarded as an 'organ' for the sixth consciousness, or mind-organ (Harvey 2013). This is to say, the relationship between mind-consciousness to *manas* is similar to that between seeing to the eye. *Manas* uses the mind-consciousness to conceptualize distinctions in a conscious way, but it also capable of distinction-making in a unconscious way without using the sixth consciousness for routinized distinction-making. *Manas* is emotional while mind-consciousness is cognitive.[5]

Manas is the 'I' that we refer to in a common sense, or the Ego awareness, since 'the Ego exists constantly with manas' (Cook 1999; Ni 2004; Tola and Dragonetti 2005; Xuanzang and Wei 1973). The *alaya* consciousness is the karmic 'storehouse' consciousness that forms the basis of the other seven consciousnesses. It stores karma, or impressions (*vasana*) fed from *manas*, which collects 'mental states' or images generated by its 'volitions' accompanying the first six consciousness in action (Harvey 2013: 131). Thus, karma is the consequence of past 'willed action' or action based on volition. However, such stored karma is only a state of the karmic circle since it in turn leads to future action with the accompanying volition. In this sense, karma so stored is the source of future action, and is figuratively referred to as karmic 'seeds'. In sum, karma is a concept used to account for the karmic circle of cause and consequences of willed action. Since volition is behind all actions that produce karma, karma is volition and volition is at the center of the karmic circle (Rao and Paranjpe 2016). Because volition implies the capacity to choose a course of action among possible alternatives (Rao and Paranjpe 2016), karmic seeds are in fact habitual tendencies which can be viewed as generative mechanisms in the real domain of CR. In addition, karma stored in *alaya* can also be considered as judgmental rationality, which is

Table 4.2 The stratified ontology of consciousness based on critical realism

Domain	*Real*	*Actual*	*Empirical*
Generative mechanisms/tendencies	✓		
Alaya/Volition			
Dispositional (Coseru 2017)			
Events	✓	✓	
Manas/Emotion			
Propositional (Deigh 1994)			
Experiences	✓	✓	✓
Cognitive consciousness/Cognition			
Propositional (Blanco 2018)			

Note '[A]ll cognition is propositional activity but not all propositional activity is cognition' (Blanco 2018)
Source Author's creation based on Bhaskar (2008: 2)

ontologizable in the real domain of CR as well (see Table 4.4). Thus, we can summarize the previous paragraphs into Table 4.2.

Among the eight consciousnesses, the main 'protagonist' in this drama of human experience is *manas*. The Yogācāra School proposes that this drama starts from beginningless eternity when *manas* 'grasps' the *alaya* for its 'self' and the *apparently* real external world for reality. But in fact the only reality is the *alaya* consciousness (the view of Maharshi [1985] is consistent with the Yogācāra School), which appears spontaneously in the form of a seeing aspect and a seen aspect: 'the seeming reality of an inner self perceiving external events is nothing more than one aspect of [the alaya] consciousness perceiving itself in the form of images' (Cook 1999: 3). *Manas* is 'born' of the *alaya* (Suzuki 1978: 293). While *manas* falsely grasps or interprets the two aspects as a self and an external world, the seemingly real external world is nothing but the internal images of *alaya* itself perceived by itself, which is grasped by *manas* as a source of attachment (Cook 1999). The reality is but one alaya consciousness: what *manas* perceived as 'me' or a 'subjective self' is in fact only the perceiving aspect of the *alaya*; and what *manas* perceived as the external world is the perceived aspect of the *alaya*. In this false grasping, the new 'seeds' from previous experience enters *alaya* and updates it, which becomes the target of *manas*' grasping in the next phase of consciousness. As such, a recursive situation is 'created', opening up opportunity for learning and spiritual enlightenment. In this sense, what *manas* does is very similar to the emergent functions of neural networks mentioned previously. The process of learning by *manas* is also consistent with the mechanism of learning mentioned in Sect. 4.2, and *manas* reflects fallibilist epistemology in CR. While *manas* arises from the interactions between the perceiving and the perceived aspects of *alaya*, it is by definition an emergent function, which is not present in either 'separate' aspect of *alaya*, but is paradoxically in *alaya*.

As such, the sense of 'I' is fundamentally false and reflects only an illusion which obscures one's true nature with its 'grasping' tendency. This ego is but a false idea and 'perishable element of the equally perishable act of cognition' (Tola and Dragonetti 2005: 463). The Yogācāra School sees *manas* as a subliminal process of consciousness, which processes information fed from the sixth consciousness, but often in a way biased by the 'I am' conceit due to its being a fundamental fallacy (Harvey 2013). Because of its tendency for misperception, it is also referred to as 'defiled' or 'afflicted' *manas* (Harvey 2013). As such, *manas* is a 'defiled' consciousness which has 'defiling' effects on perception.

The Yogācāra School also divides the consciousness according to its structure into four parts. Kern (1988) translated this quadruple differentiation, using the phenomenological terms of Husserl, as an objectivating act, an objective phenomenon, self-consciousness, and consciousness of self-consciousness. The Yogācāra School also suggests that the consciousness does not directly involve the objective phenomenon itself but perceive it by extracting images thereof, a concept very similar to that of 'qualia' in philosophy and psychology (Peters 2014). As such, the Yogācāra School has been clearly aware of the difference between consciousness and qualia.

Only mental (cognitive) consciousness has all the four parts, while other consciousnesses lack the latter two parts. As such, mental consciousness is the genuinely recursive and reflexive consciousness (cf. Panksepp [2003a] for similar view from modern neuroscience[6]) which give rise to self-perceiving, self-recognizing and self-knowing (Peters 2014). While *manas* is the protagonist or master in human experience, the mental consciousness is its powerful servant.

The eight-consciousness model can be characterized by two dimensions: continuity and distinction-making (Xuanzang and Epstein 1986). The first five consciousnesses are neither continuous nor distinction-making. The mind consciousness is capable of distinction-making but is not continuous. The *alaya* functions continuously but does not make distinctions. Only *manas* has both characteristics. It constantly making judgments, often biased, based on distinctions in the process of selecting what is best for the false 'self' or ego.

The eight-consciousness model also distinguishes between three types of knowledge: veridical perception, inference and fallacy. Only veridical perceptions function within the fields of the first five consciousnesses. The mind consciousness can generate all three types of knowledge, and all that *manas* can do is to generate fallacy because it is fallacy itself. Because this fallacious mind-organ uses cognitive consciousness as an instrument, and the mind consciousness is capable of all three types of knowledge; and because *manas*' 'volition' accompanies the first six consciousnesses (Harvey 2013), the seeds stored in *alaya* can be of various qualities. The fundamental fallacy of *manas* also implies that our thoughts and perceptions are largely fabrications of *manas*, which are often biased. Nevertheless, due to the aforementioned recursive loop between mind consciousness, *manas* and *alaya*, and the inferential capability of the cognitive consciousness, learning is possible.

4.4 The Eight-Consciousness Model Can Inform the Theory of Bounded Rationality

Scholars have noticed that there exist remarkable parallels between modern neuroscience and Buddhism with regard to how our cognitive and perceptual worlds are shaped by our mind and experience (e.g., Sharp 2011).[7] Parallels between neuroscience and CR (Healey and Hodgkinson 2014) and that between Buddhism and CR (Kochumuttom 1982) have also been suggested. As such, neuroscience, CR and Yogācāra Buddhism can cross-fertilize each other, and the theory of the firm stands to benefit from this cross-fertilization. Camerer et al. (2004: 555) once commented that 'neuroeconomics uses knowledge about brain mechanisms to inform economic theory. It opens up the 'black box' of the brain, much as organizational economics opened up the theory of the firm'. We can similarly say that the eight-consciousness model can potentially inform TCE since it serves to open up the 'black box' of bounded rationality by explicating the fundamental mechanisms underpinning managerial decision-making, much as it has opened up the theory of the mind. This is particularly true in the case of bounded rationality modeling from a CR perspective. Among the eight consciousnesses, mind-consciousness (cognitive consciousness) and *manas* (emotional consciousness) and their interrelationship are particularly important in providing insights into bounded rationality.

Indeed, TCE treats bounded rationality as a black box: By treating bounded rationality as a background condition, it fails to focus on the psychological side of bounded rationality and how it is affected (Simon 1957, 1961). It focuses only on processing capacity limitations (cognitive consciousness or processing bounded rationality) but ignores the implications of psychological bounded rationality (Foss and Weber 2016b: 62; Simon 1997a, b), or emotional consciousness. This can be attributed to TCE's tacit positivist philosophical position and the accompanying de facto full rationality assumption, despite its frequent invocation of bounded rationality. But as Table 4.3 shows, and as we previously discussed, psychological bounded rationality may be more vital in opening up the black box of bounded rationality. Cognitive consciousness is only a servant of emotional consciousness and reflects only a 'snowball' on top of the consciousness 'iceberg'[8] (Wilson 2002). Thus, focusing on processing bounded rationality without considering psychological bounded rationality implies the absence of epistemology, which stripped TCE of the possibility of becoming a behavioral theory. The discrete and incontinuous nature of processing bounded rationality also suggests that a fuller behavioral theory need to be based on something more continuous and constant. As such, psychological bounded rationality needs to be brought to the center stage. In order to do so, we propose that processing bounded rationality and psychological bounded rationality be more accurately referred to as '***cognitive bounds***' and '***bounded rationalizing***', considering that nouns denote states or qualities (and suggest of being 'material' [Habermas 1992]), and gerunds processes. The use of a noun phrase such 'bounded rationality' reflects an attempt to objectify an otherwise dynamic process, which is not conducive to a behavioral thinking. Viewed from a CR perspective, to use a noun to denote a process is to collapse bounded rationality in the actual domain into pseudo-'bounded' rationality in the empirical domain, thus imposing artificial 'closure' on an open process along the ontological depth of CR.

The definition of psychological bounded rationality as 'bounded rationalizing' is consistent with the description of *manas* as continuously distinction-making in Yogācāra Buddhism. We also propose that cognitive bounds and psychological 'bounded rationalizing' should be conceptually separated to enable the social extension of cognitive bounds, which

Table 4.3 Contrasting psychological bounded rationality and processing bounded rationality

Psychological bounded rationality (Emotional consciousness) [Rationalizing]	*Processing bounded rationality (Cognitive consciousness) [Cognitive bounds]*
Based on modern neuroscience	
Paleomammalian	Neomammalian
Limbic (amygdala, hippocampus and parahippocampal gyrus)	Neocortex
Amygdala hijack	Cognitive control
Emotions and instincts	Cognition (problem solving, and conscious inhibition of action)
State functions • (Global control of brain activities) • Emotional states are intrinsically valenced, characterized by various negative or positive feelings	Channel functions • (*Discrete* information channels) • Cognitions are not valenced, characterized by information processing
Subconscious	Conscious
Non-computational consciousness • (Holistic feelings and action tendencies)	Computational consciousness • (Discreet information)
Intentions-in-action	Intentions-to-act
Action-to-perception	Perception-to-action
More emotionally deep and negativistic	More cognitively skilled and positivistic
Affects are more powerful and easier to induce in the young	Sophisticated cognitive activities prevail among adults
Based on Yogācāra School	
7th/emotional consciousness (*Manas*)	6th/cognitive consciousness
Capable of continuous distinction-making	Capable of distinction-making but is not continuous
Has 'defiling' effects on perception; generates fallacy (as a result of biases) because it is fallacy itself	Capable of veridical perception, inference and fallacy (not due to biases)
Self-consciousness	Is a recursive and reflexive processing mechanism
Learning to reduce fallacy with the help of cognitive consciousness	Fallacy due to processing bounded rationality can be reduced by using emotional consciousness as a numeraire

Note The word 'bounds' is a contronym and has two opposite senses in English: (a) a limit or boundary, and (b) something that restrains and confines. An increase in the first sense implies an reduction in the severity of the second sense. As a result, the term 'cognitive bounds' inherited such an ambiguity, and is used in both senses in this book. Fortunately, it causes negligible confusion, and its ambiguity can largely be overcome by context

Source (1) Author's own summary based on Panksepp (2003a, b, 2004), Xuanzang and Epstein (1986), and Harvey (2013), and other references mentioned in the previous sections. Terms in '[ ]' are explained Sect. 4.5

is discussed in Sect. 4.6. Along this line, bounded rationality should be referred to as *bounded rationalizing*, which is defined as the process of *manas* continuously rationalizing under cognitive bounds. In fact, even the word 'bounded' may be redundant since there is no need for 'rationalizing' if there are no bounds on cognition. Only through these moves can *manas* regain its status of being the 'master', and cognitive consciousness be relegated to its legitimate position as a 'servant'.

4.5 The Conceptual Separation of Cognitive Bounds from (Bounded) Rationalizing

4.5.1 *(Bounded) Rationality: Substantive Rationality vs Procedural Rationality*

While bounded rationality is a widely shared behavioral assumption across a wide spectrum of academic fields (Foss and Weber 2016b) and a key TCE assumption, it was treated as a black box in TCE since it was relegated to the background and was only *invoked*. Due to TCE's tacit positivist position and equilibrium analysis, it has largely been preoccupied with 'the extent to which appropriate courses of action are chosen', or 'substantive rationality', but not 'the effectiveness, in light of human cognitive powers and limitations, of the procedures used to choose actions', or 'procedural rationality' (Simon 1978: 9). Thus, TCE's version of bounded rationality is reduced to processing bounded rationality (cognitive bounds): were it not for cognitive bounds, the standard equilibrium model would hold and market contracting could continue (Slater and Spencer 2000; Williamson 1975: 22). Such models based on substantive rationality prevent TCE from being behavioral and can only provide poor guidance in managerial decision-making since they necessarily *abstract* from the real world (Simon 1996; cf. Subsect. 3.4.2).

In order to make decision models more practical, according to Mäki, Simon proposes that 'the neoclassical fully informed, maximizing firm should give way to the searching, information processing and satisficing firm. As to the notion of rationality in the study of decision-making, he advocates switching attention from what he calls perfect substantive rationality or results of choice to bounded procedural rationality or the process of choice' (Mäki 1989: 189; Simon 1976, 1978). Considering the close affinity between bounded rationality and procedural rationality (Simon 1976, 2001), a focus on procedural rationality not only accounts for bounded rationality but also bring procedural rationality within the compass of the rationalizing calculus (Simon 1978) since rationalizing is always procedural (Lindenberg 2001: 240). Some scholars point out that the term 'procedural rationality' better synthesizes Simon's view about rationality and that the term 'bounded rationality' serves mainly a critical and rhetorical function in relation to rationality in classical economics (Barros 2010). Thus, bounded rationality has lower degree of conceptual specificity and procedural rationality is believed to be of more importance in a behavioral theory.

Nevertheless, bounded rationality and procedural rationality can be viewed as the two faces of the same coin, and bounded rationality is a process (Simon 1976, 1978). Due to environmental complexity and cognitive limits, what is more important is the process of choice rather than the characteristics of choice. In fact, there is no such thing as 'rationality'. Instead of the attainment of the supposed 'rationality', it is the process moving toward the supposed rational direction that grasps the spirit of the concept of 'rationality': rationality is a process rather than an equilibrium state. Whether one can reach the final state of 'rationality' is not important so long as the process is rational because the 'rational' state is difficult even to define. As such, bounded rationality is a dynamic process through which economic agents approximate to 'rationality'.[9]

Such procedural rationality, though a step further in comparison with substantive rationality in TCE, is not genuinely conducive to a behavioral theory. There are two reasons. First, at the core of Simon's procedural rationality is the computational theory of the brain (Putnam 1963), in which the human brain is thought of as an information processing system, and thinking is synonymous with the activity of computing (Barros 2010; Levy and Hirschheim 2012), or in Simon's own words, 'a theory of rationality [is]...a theory of efficient computational procedures to find good solutions - a theory of procedural rationality' and 'the search for computational efficiency is a search for procedural rationality' (Simon 1976: 69 and 68). This is to say, Simon's bounded rationality considered largely only cognitive bounds (processing bounded rationality/the sixth consciousness) but did not specify the master of the 'bounded rationalizing process' (psychological bounded rationality/*manas* or the seventh consciousness). Since the sixth consciousness is the servant of the seventh consciousness, a focus on cognitive limits implies that Simon's bounded rationality is procedural but not behavioral in the sense of behavioral theories as described in Chapter 1 since it largely ignores emotion. Second,

Simon's bounded rationality is still a positivist form of bounded rationality. It meets all the criteria of positivism (Levy and Hirschheim 2012) as suggested by (Goles and Hirschheim 2000: 251–252). One of these criteria is that science and its process are value free,[10] which prevents the Simonian conception of bounded rationality from taking psychology into serious consideration. Even though Simon had anticipated increasing cross-pollination between management theories and psychology (Miller 2008), he personally did not do much in this direction.

However, we propose that the Simonian procedural rationality can be extended into a CR framework if (1) the value-free assumption, and thus the positivist straight jacket (Levy and Hirschheim 2012), is removed; and (2) the master of information computing and processing, i.e., the seventh consciousness or *manas*, is introduced. In so doing, the reconceptualized procedural rationality can be considered as reflecting ontological realism, fallibilist epistemology and judgmental rationality in CR (see Table 4.4).

Once procedural rationality is ontologically located and psychological biases are introduced to it, it in fact becomes an ecological rationality since 'ecological rationality locates that procedure in the world' (Wheeler 2018), or in the actual domain in the context of this book. Here, ecological rationality refers to adaptive behavior resulting from the fit between heuristics (the mind's mechanisms) and the structure of the information in the environment. According to ecological rationality, a heuristic is ecologically rational to the degree that it matches the structure of an environment (Gigerenzer and Gaissmaier 2015; Todd and Gigerenzer 2000). This is to say, decision procedures are not irrational or rational per se, rather, procedural rationality is relative to the environment. As such, contextualizing procedural rationality in a CR ontology brings environmental structure back in the original notion of bounded rationality (Todd and Gigerenzer 2000) as conceptualized by Simon (1990), who describe it a scissors whose two blades are cognitive limitation of an economic agent and the structure of task environments (Simon 1990: 7). Treating CR-informed procedural rationality as an ecological rationality has several advantages. First, it is in the actually domain of CR that Simon's procedural rationality becomes genuinely engaged with fallibilist epistemology, which is conducive to a behavioral approach to the study of organizations. Second, ecological rationality underscores the primacy of judgmental rationality. This is because a judgment has to be made whether the mind's heuristics match environmental structure and judgmental heuristics reflect judgmental rationality in the actual domain. The linking of judgmental rationality and ecological rationality thus implies an upside of bounded rationality. This point has been suggested by some

Table 4.4 The stratified ontology of rationality based on critical realism[1]

Domain	*Real*	*Actual*	*Empirical*
Meta-rationality (Generative mechanisms/tendencies) • Meta-rationality (Jungermann 1983; Singer 1991; Stanovich 2015) • Multiple mechanisms of rationality (Singer 1991) • Various interrelationships between the multiple mechanisms of rationality (Singer 1991) • Meta-rationality is a broader concept than procedural and substantive rationality ['Meta-rationality demands a broad view of life, a concern for task construal and the role of emotions in decision, as well as a concern for the expected utility of the outcome' (Stanovic 2015: 154) • 'Preferences about...preferences'; 'meta-rationality is rationality itself' (Schwartz 2015) • Intransitive <u>judgmental rationality</u> of domain of real (Platenkamp and Botterill 2013; Bhaskar 2008)	✓		
Procedural[2] rationality/Ecological rationality (Events) • 'The effectiveness...of the procedures used to choose actions' (Simon 1978: 9) • Concerns 'how to decide' (Simon 1979: 498)/'process of choice' & 'dynamics of rationality' (Simon 1978: 2&3) • Satisficing (to find 'good enough' solutions) (Simon 1976; 2001) • 'Social man'/'social rationality' (Lindenberg 2001: 241) • Institutional structure influences choice (Simon 1978:3) • Imperfect information • Bounded/subjective rationality (Zafirovski 1999) • 'The rationality and irrationality of persons' (Schwartz 2015) • Transitive and knowledge dependent (Levy and Hirschheim 2012) • Consider psychological bounded rationality • <u>Ecological rationality</u> of <u>judgmental heuristics</u>: 'ecological rationality locates that procedure in the world' (Wheeler 2018). Judgmental heuristics reflects judgmental rationality in the actual domain. • <u>Fallibilist epistemology</u>	✓	✓	

(continued)

scholars (e.g., Schmidt 2015), even though they paid no attention to ontological depths of various types of rationality. Third, ecological rationality redresses the tendency to focus on the cognitive side in theories of human inference, which equates the notion of bounded rationality

Table 4.4 (continued)

Domain	*Real*	*Actual*	*Empirical*
Substantive rationality (Experiences) • 'The extent to which appropriate courses of action are chosen' (Simon 1978: 9) • Concerns 'what to decide' (Simon 1979: 498)/'results of rational choice' (Simon 1978: 2) • Optimization (to find 'best' solutions) (Savage 1954; Simon 2001) • 'Rational man'/(Lindenberg 2001: 241) • Perfect information (Sargent 1993) • 'The rationality and irrationality of decisions' (Schwartz 2015) • Unbounded/objective rationality (Zafirovski 1999) • Rationality (which is based on social values) is reduced to positivist formal rationality[3] of reductivist reasoning (Zafirovski 1999) • Methodological individualism: 'individuals are preconstituted by an inherent instrumental rationality and that it is this rationality which is responsible for all social and cultural phenomena'(Fast 2012: 16) • 'Bounded rationality' is reduced to processing bounded rationality • Fallible ontology	✓	✓	✓

Source [1] Author's creation, summary and extension based on Bhaskar (2008: 2). [2] Not in Simon's (1976) sense. See Endnote 17 in Chapter 1. [3] 'Formal rationality' means that people's choices can be represented by a utility function, and substantive rationality requires that choices are optimal' (Frank 2002: 97)

with human cognitive limitation and thus, paradoxically, reassures classical rationality as the normative standard for bounded rationality (Gigerenzer and Goldstein 1996). Fourth, ecological rationality highlights the adaptive aspect of bounded rationality and enables our discussion of the implications of this book in terms of the evolutionary theory of the firm (Nelson and Winter 1982). We return to this point in Chapter 7.

4.5.2 The Need for More Precise Terms: Cognitive Bounds and Rationalizing

In the previous sections, we used terms like processing bounded rationality, substantive rationality, and cognitive consciousness interchangeably for convenience. Similarly, we also did not distinguish between terms like psychological bounded rationality, emotional consciousness, procedural rationality, and bounded rationality. However, in order to be more consistent with CR and to avoid confusion, more accurate terms are needed. We propose the use of 'cognitive bounds' and rationalizing' instead.

Since the term 'bounded rationality' serves mainly a rhetorical function in critique of rationality in classical economics and 'procedural rationality' is the one that better synthesizes Simon's view about rationality (Barros 2010), we propose that bounded rationality be reserved for rhetorical use when challenging the rationality assumption in classical economics. In the context of modeling bounded rationality, 'procedural rationality' rather than 'bounded rationality' should be used for its conceptual specificity and relevance to a behavioral theory. Furthermore, considering that (1) 'procedural' can mean 'administrative' (Augier and Sarasvathy 2004; Dew et al. 2008) and does not necessarily mean 'behavioral' in the sense of behavioral theories which focus on psychological biases (see Chapter 1), and (2) nouns denote states or qualities (and suggest of being 'material' [Habermas 1992]) and gerunds processes, we propose that the term 'rationalizing' be used instead of 'procedural rationality' since 'rationalizing' implies the existence of cognitive bounds[11] and a process towards 'rationality'. Since Simon's bounded rationality assumes that human brain can be thought of as an information processing system, and cognition is synonymous with the activity of computing (Levy and Hirschheim 2012; Putnam 1963), we propose that processing bounded rationality be referred to as 'cognitive bounds' instead. Information processing capacity is equal to cognitive bounds. As an extension of the use of the terms 'cognitive bounds' and 'rationalizing', we also suggest that 'bounded rationalizing' is apparently a better term in comparison with 'bounded rationality', since the former conveys a dynamic behavioral sense.

The use of 'cognitive bounds' and 'rationalizing' is largely consistent with recent development in understanding bounded rationality, according to which bounded rationality is consisted of three components (e.g., Foss and Weber 2016b): (1) processing capacity (e.g., Simon 1961), (2) cognitive economizing (e.g., Simon 1990), and (3) cognitive biases (e.g., Tversky and Kahneman 1974). These three components actually reflect the evolution[12] in bounded rationality research, which evolved from the introduction of satisficing, to the investigation of heuristics, and finally to the examination of biases arising from cognitive shortcuts (Foss and Weber 2016b). Nevertheless, the existing TCE research only incorporated processing capacity, the most basic component (Foss and Weber

2016b). Even though the new advances in bounded rationality research started to consider the other two components, a clear philosophical position is lacking, thus failing to free bounded rationality from the traps of substantive rationality and a cognition-centric approach. This is because that cognitive economizing tacitly assumes substantive rationality. The consideration of psychological biases, approached from the direction of 'expanding' processing bounded rationality (e.g., Foss and Weber 2016a; Weber and Mayer 2010) is less likely to make bounded rationality procedural (or more accurately, behavioral) due to the approach's untenable foundation on cognitive economizing and substantive rationality. In order to make bounded rationality behavioral, it has to be approached from the 'rationalizing' side by assuming a fallibilist ontology and epistemology and judgmental rationality in CR (see Table 4.4). This is to say, 'rationalizing' *manas* (psychological bounded rationality), the 'master', has to be moved to the front seat while cognitive bounds and its collateral cognitive economizing have to be relegated to the back seat reserved for the 'servant'. We discuss this point further below.

4.5.3 Moving 'Rationalizing' to the Front Seat

Seeing the limitations that processing bounded rationality places on TCE, scholars have been proposing to expand bounded rationality to include psychological bounded rationality (e.g., Foss and Weber 2016a; Weber and Mayer 2010). However, such efforts are not built on solid philosophical foundations and still center on cognitive bounds in a 'master'-absent manner which is not in line with the behavioral approach. Consequently, bounded rationality after incorporating its psychological portion is still a black box and can serve only a rhetorical role in theoretical arguments but not in empirical modeling. After the conceptual separation of cognitive bounds' and 'rationalizing', we propose that 'rationalizing' be moved to the front seat in order to facilitate the building of a behavioral TCE and the modeling of bounded rationality.

The prioritizing of 'rationalizing' (psychological bounded rationality) has several advantages. First, it is conceptually more convincing. Processing bounded rationality, or correctly speaking 'cognitive bounds', cannot be extended to include psychological bounded rationality or rationalizing since they are two different and distinct concepts. The servant who is used by the master cannot be 'expanded' to include the master. Second, Simon's own research was based on an analogy between the computer and the human brain (Barros 2010). Nevertheless, he was not specific who was the user of the 'computer' and thus cannot consider psychology in a serious manner. The use of 'cognitive bounds' and 'rationalizing' solved this problem of master-less rationalizing. Third, it opens up possibilities for *manas*, the continuously rationalizing (distinction-making) master, to expand 'cognitive bounds' socially and we discuss this point in Sect. 4.6. While cognitive bounds in the sense of the six consciousnesses do exist, we have no way of knowing it even at today's level of scientific development. But this does not prevent us from modeling our bounds if we can get access to some measures of the changes in mental bounds or factors which affect our mental bounds. Based on literature on socially extended mind, we propose that CD fits the bill for such a measure, as we discuss shortly. Only by putting the 'rationalizing' horse before the cart of 'cognitive bounds' can TCE be genuinely transformed into a behavioral theory which treats organization as an 'instrument for utilizing varying cognitive and behavioral propensities to best advantage' (Williamson 1998: 12).

4.6 The Social Extensibility of Cognitive Bounds

Previously, we treated the capacity of the cortex as a cognitive bounds of rationality. However, cognitive processes are not brain-bound, and such bounds can be extended, both instrumentally with tools (Clark and Chalmers 1998) and socially with rules and institutions (Gallagher 2013; Gallagher and Crisafi 2009; Hegel 1949).[13] In the former case, mental bounds are extended through such inventions as writing, printing, electronic communications and artificial intelligence (e.g., Simon 1978): thinking 'is not an event going on exclusively within the cortex.... Hands and feet, apparatus and appliances of all kinds are as much a part of it as changes within the brain' (Dewey 1916: 13–14). In the latter case, social institutions and cultural practices, which are constituted with cognition in mind through shared mental processes, are used instrumentally to extend our cognitive capacity (Gallagher 2013; Gallagher and Crisafi 2009).[14] As such, cultures and institutions are 'cognitive institutions', which serve as sources of low-cost heuristics that economizing on human cognitive bounds (Hayakawa 2000). The extended cognition is 'a set of processes that loop in and out of brains and social institutions' (Gallagher and Crisafi 2009: 49). Such social extension of human cognition is so important to us that institutions can 'take on a life of their own and allow us to engage in activities (often cognitive activities) that we are unable to do purely in the head, or even in many heads' (Gallagher and Crisafi 2009: 49–50). We run our cognitive processes on our externalized cognitive apparatus to facilitate and enhance our cognitive production. As a result, our cognitive bounds are greatly increased through institutions and cultural practices. The behavioral approach acknowledges that human decision-making is bounded not only by human but also by institutional limitations (Augier and March 2008). This may be one of the deeper mechanisms explaining why institutions can affect transaction costs by acting as 'shift parameters' (Williamson 2000).

The social extensibility of cognitive bounds in terms of institutions also suggests a reconceptualization of the relationship between institutional theory and TCE. While it is common to integrate these two theories in international business literature, the usual way is to treat them as vaguely defined 'complements' in an ontology which is collapsed into the empirical domain. Such an approach is positivist and cannot account for biases arising from cultural and institutional distances (see the following sections) and emic-etic interactions (see Sect. 3.3). This book suggests that subsuming institutional theory under the cognitive bounds in part of the bounded rationalizing process and treating institutions as affecting cognitive bounds in a CR framework may prove another way of productive integration of the two theories.

4.7 Cultural Distance Is Central to Transaction Cost Economics by Affecting Mental Bounds

The social extensibility argument has significant implications with regard to CD's role in TCE and international business research. While CD is an important variable in international business research based on TCE, its effects on governance structures have been consistently inconsistent (see Sect. 7.7.2). While various reasons have been suggested, one is particularly worth noting: 'cultural distance is not central to transaction cost economics' (Dikova and Brouthers 2009: 232; Gatignon and Anderson 1988: 311; Madhok 1997). Considering TCE's emphasis on the significant impacts of informal institutions (such as cultures, norms, values, etc.) on transaction costs and thus on decision-making (Hosseini 2015) and the importance of the construct of CD in international business, we think the claim that 'cultural distance is not central to transaction cost economics' is particularly misplaced. Our opinion is further buttressed by the fact that CD reflects cognitive bounds and thereby bounded rationality, as we discuss below. How can a concept at the foundation of TCE be not central to it?

Culture is generally understood as collectively shared structure of social cognition (Beckmann et al. 1997) and 'collective programming of the human mind' (Hofstede et al. 2010: 6). Different cultures can be regarded as different social minds. Institutional theory also suggests that the third pillar of institutions is the cultural-cognitive pillar, which refers to the established cognitive structures that are taken for granted and shared by the people in a culture (Scott 1995). Such cognitive structures facilitate 'cultural cognition' (Sunstein 2006) since they affect our range of possible choices of thought (Lopez and Potter 2001).

Since cultures and institutions constitute 'social cognition' (Lyre 2018), they extend human cognitive bounds by increasing the upper bounds of human information processing capacity. As such, people which share social norms and values in the same culture have each individually extended their minds. When MNCs internationalize, they have to leave their cultures and enter different cultures which have different cultural distances. If CD is low, their mental bounds may not be affected much. However if CD is high, their mental bounds would be significantly reduced, and cognitive loads be significantly increased.

As such, CD reflects change in cognitive bounds. While cognitive bounds in the sense of processing capability of cortex (i.e., the sixth consciousness) do exist, we have no way of knowing it even at today's level of scientific development. But this does not prevent us from modeling cognitive bounds if we can get access to some measures of the changes in mental bounds or factors which affect our mental bounds. Based on literature on socially extended mind, we propose that CD fits the bill for such a measure. This is an extremely important insight this study can provide. While CD has been widely used in international business literature, it is seldom *explicitly* viewed as a measure of cognitive bounds. This has significantly limited theoretical development and empirical testing along the line of bounded rationality, resulting in non-behavioral theories of the firm. In the empirical literature, CD is often inaccurately treated as a source of internal uncertainty (opportunism) and complexity (Beugelsdijk et al. 2018: 97), and its direct effect on governance structures was often the main concern. This practice ignored the more interesting diminishing interaction effects of CD vis-à-vis various uncertainties (controllable ones vs uncontrollable ones), which reflect the diminishing effects of cognitive bounds on governance structures with learning.

Because CD reflects cognitive bounds which in turn affect bounded rationality, and because of bounded rationality's fundamental position in TCE, CD should be considered central to TCE. While TCE has been extensively used in international business, and CD is an important variable in TCE-based international business research, the link between CD and TCE has not been studied in an ontologically deep manner. Some scholar pointed out that CD is only awkwardly incorporated TCE (e.g., Madhok 1997), and that a full incorporation will result in the possibility of opposing predictions between CD and governance structures (Dikova and Brouthers 2009: 232). We agree with these comments, but are quick to add that CD can in fact provide a tremendous opportunity to advance TCE in a CR framework, and that international business can become an even more fertile ground for TCE research, exactly for CD's centrality to TCE. The current confusions about CD and the inconclusiveness of the effects of CD arise from the positivist deductive approach adopted in the traditional TCE which does not have an ontological depth to accommodate various (potentially opposing) generative mechanisms in the real domain of CR. The positivist focus on event regularities rather than mechanisms shifted scholarly attention to CD itself rather than CD as a cognitive device vis-à-vis various uncertainties of varying levels of controllability.

It is worth noting here that 'central' does not mean 'centric'. We used the expression 'CD is central to TCE' to be consistent with the expression used in the literature (e.g., Dikova and Brouthers 2009: 232; Gatignon and Anderson 1988: 311; Madhok 1997). What it means is that 'CD is fundamental to TCE'. Nevertheless, as discussed in the previous sections and Endnote 5, we are against a CD-centric approach in the TCE-based international business literature. CD affects cognitive bounds, so it is a variable related to cognition. A behavioral theory should not be cognition-centric but emotion-centric or psychology-centric. After all, cognition is used by *manas* in human experiences.

Recent research supports our view in the above paragraph. Azar and Drogendijk (2019) suggest that the CD measure commonly used in international business is a measure of *objective* CD, which is different from *perceived* CD. As they empirically demonstrated, what is more important for MNC performance is the 'distance divergence' between objective CD and perceived CD. To re-phrase their view in terms our behavioral approach, the CD measure commonly used in international business research is cognition-centric since it is objective, and research attention should be focused on perceived CD, which is psychology-centric.

To conclude this section, we would like to point out that CD is not the only factor which affects cognitive bounds. We use treat cultural distance as central to TCE because CD maybe the most widely used construct in international business. As we discuss in Subsect. 7.7.4, there are a variety of other distance measures. Since these measures are highly correlated with CD, and the arguments supporting the relationships between CD and some common outcome variables can often be extended to these measures, some of them may similarly be regarded as reflecting cognitive bounds, such as institutional distance (cf. Sect. 4.6). In addition, a distance measure which reflects cognitive bounds does not need to be related to space in a geographic sense. What matters is whether it affects cognition. One of such distance which comes to our mind, for example, is technological distance in the technology space. For TCE to become behavioral, it is essential to subject it to various spatial dimensions which present challenges to cognition since humans act, or 'behave', in different spaces. We return to this point in Chapter 7.

4.8 Cultural Distance Contextualizes Effectuation

Since CD affects cognitive bounds, it will also lead to and affect effectuation since effectuation theory is based on the assumption of cognitive bounds and Herbert Simon's work on bounded rationality (Read and Sarasvathy 2005). In fact, effectuation theory was developed in close collaboration with Simon (Sarasvathy and Simon 2000). As mentioned in Sect. 2.8, effectuation theory was claimed to be the straight inversion of the traditional rational choice theory (or predictive or causal rationality) (Read and Sarasvathy 2005). In Sect. 2.9, we instead suggested that the relationship between prediction and effectuation should not be considered as an either-or choice. They should be considered as responses to different circumstances at different stages of firm development, and causal reasoning can be subsumed under the effectual process from a CR perspective, as a top-down reasoning logic (see Subsect. 2.9.1). Experienced firms are capable of using both modes well by interweaving causation and effectuation (Chetty et al. 2015). Bottom-up effectual action is preferred to causal reasoning in the early stages of a new investment and/or in new markets, while top-down causal reasoning becomes more relevant at latter stages and/or in mature markets (Sarasvathy

2008). In other words, whether firms are able to predict will determine the tendency of firms effectuating. Since CD reflects cognitive bounds and negatively affects firms' ability to predict, effectuation will be positively related to CD.

Treating CD as a measure of cognitive bounds serves to contextualize effectuation theory, which has been criticized for paying insufficient attention to social and cultural contexts and social structure/agency interaction that may significantly affect the effectuation process (Kitching and Rouse 2020). While CD is a widely used measure in international business research, its effects on effectuation have seldom been considered, resulting in a conspicuous gap and constituting a research direction of great potential.

Furthermore, considering CD in effectuation also brings attention to the potential biases in effectuation process, considering various biases arising from CD, as will be discussed in Sect. 4.11. While effectuation is a heuristic, and effectuation theory can be traced back to Simon's bounded rationality which originates from psychology research on heuristics and biases (Sarasvathy 2001), research on effectuation and psychological biases has ironically developed into separate streams of research over time (Zhang et al. 2018). This hinders understanding of how psychology biases effectuation decision-making process. CD serves to bring the consideration of biases back to effectuation. We will discuss this point further in Chapters 5 and 6.

4.9 Modeling Bounded Rationality: The Increasingly More Efficient Use of Cognitive Bounds

Because traditional TCE uses the concept of bounded rationality only rhetorically with no intention to operationalize and model it (Foss 2003a; Pessali 2006), the existing literature is not clear about how to model bounded rationality. While scholars have been advocating the reduction of bounded rationality as the key governance challenge (Foss and Weber 2016b; Verbeke 2003; Verbeke and Greidanus 2009), they unintentionally showed their understanding of bounded rationality as being substantive rather than behavioral. Even if some scholars suggested how to model bounded rationality, they treated bounded rationality as a standalone black box rather than as a behavioral process. For example, Verbeke et al. (2017: 41) suggest that 'bounded rationality...are likely functioning as mediators (and in some cases as moderators) with respect to the link between perceptions of distance and preferences for a particular alternative or course of action'. Insisting on modeling bounded rationality through its mediation or moderation effects in fact reflects the tacit positivism assumed by TCE scholars, which is unconscious of the self and thus cognition-centric and susceptible to 'the epistemic fallacy' (Bhaskar 1998: 27).

We suggest that bounded rationality cannot be modeled using either mediation or moderation because it is a process rather than a variable and because cognitive bounds (i.e., processing bounded rationality) do not change over time. As presented in previous sections, in order for TCE to become a behavioral theory, bounded rationality has to be modeled as the rationalizing process of *manas* using the recursive and reflexive cognitive capability of the cognitive consciousness (as reflected by 'cognitive bounds') vis-à-vis a decision context. Rationalizing is a behavioral process through which *manas* applies and economizes on the bounded cognitive capacity in sense-making. In the eight-consciousness model of mind, learning is a natural part of rationalizing due to cognitive recursivity and reflexivity of the cognitive consciousness. The cognitive bounds or information processing capacity is fixed so cannot be changed (but can be economized),[15] but the cognitive errors due to information processing limits and psychologic biases arising from *manas* can be reduced by learning as firms continually update 'what needs to be done' as an evolving response to uncertainty in a CR framework (Buckley 2018; Spender 1989). Such rationalizing process can be modeled by the increasingly more efficient, or more 'rational', use of cognitive bounds through the three-way interaction effect between cognitive bounds, organizational learning (e.g., experience over time) and any independent variable on a firm behavior of interest. Bounded rationality has to be disaggregated into cognitive bounds and psychological rationalizing for this purpose.

Rationalizing starts with effectuation in the form of an initial prereflective aspiration level, which is a subjective value judgment, based on the principle of satisficing. Satisficing plays a vital role in rendering TCE behavioral because it uses an effectuation reasoning[16] (Chandra 2007; Sarasvathy 2001; Simon 1957), and the process of rationalizing is a process of satisficing decision-making in an iterative manner (Joas and Beckert 2001). As suggested by the eight-consciousness model, *manas*, or the fallacy itself, is the master of the rationalizing process and it uses cognitive consciousness on an on-and-off basis. As such, thinking is first of all feeling, and rationality is first of all emotions (James 1977). Consequentially, decision-making starts from effectuation through satisficing.[17]

The initial governance structure based on TCE is not mission accomplished since it is derived based on bias-prone emotions. In addition, the very idea of 'cognitive bounds' implies that economic agents cannot achieve *real* rationality given complexity and/or time constraints which characterize most task environment (Dosi et al. 2005).[18] Hence, the pursuit of rationality cannot be divorced from value judgments which are emotions (Damasio 1994; Lo 2005; Solomon 1993). Satisficing, the common mechanism in bounded rationality, is emotional in nature. Without emotions, the neocortex will not know when to stop if information processing takes too long due to its processing bounds. As such, emotions are not irrationality or nonrationality, but they are central to rationality (Damasio 1994; de Sousa 1990). This is because 'human behavior is intendedly rational' (Simon 1961: 24) and 'intentions are the emotional thrust of goal pursuit' (Lewis and Todd 2005: 218). Emotions provide a kind of mental yardstick for economic actors to engage in a cost-benefit analysis of the various options open to them and thus facilitate the selection of advantageous behavior (Lo 2005; Rolls 1999). Turner (2007) suggests that emotions have their legitimate place in human decision-making process since 'it is the interaction between cognitive and emotional capacities that makes rationality and memory possible on a human scale' (p. 37) and that 'thought involves a constant tagging of images with emotional valences' (p. 59). This is in fact consistent with the eight-consciousness model and the CR theme of this chapter. In terms of bounded rationality, agents are *intendedly* rational, or they *value* rationality as a criterion of choice in the process of rationalizing (Barros 2010). This is judgmental rationality in CR.

Since it is the interaction between cognitive and emotional capacities that makes 'rationality' possible, the magnitude of emotional capabilities matters. An animal whose emotional range had not increased would not be more intelligent even though its neocortex grew in size (Turner 2007: 37). The extant research suggests that millions of years of evolution have expanded the emotional bounds of hominids together with the increase in their cognitive capacities (Turner 2007), and a mutually inseparable relationship emerges: emotions drive cognition, cognition feeds to emotions; cognition provides understanding of the world, emotions provide value judgment (Norman 2013). Hence, cognitive bounds (processing bounded rationality) and rationalizing (psychological bounded rationality) cannot exist without the presence of each other (Borsboom et al. 2011; Jones 1999). They can be considered as proportional to each other as an outcome of evolution.

While rationalizing is moved to the front seat and cognition to the back seat, both of them can only be inferred from observed choice behavior[19] (e.g., governance structures) (Kahneman 1994). Even though 'rationalizing' may imply that the initial governance structure may be misspecified because economic agents have to satisfice rather than optimize and satisficing is prone to biases, boundedly rational decision-makers are goal-driven and adaptive (Au and Kauffman 2003; Jones 1999), and will update their satisficing levels based on learning with the involvement of cognition (Jones 1999; Simon 1957). Due to judgmental rationality, such learning will drive choices toward more rational directions in the rationalizing process, and the changes in governance structure will reflect the reduction of psychological biases and cognitive inefficiencies and errors over time.

However, the relative proportion of the reduction of psychological biases vs. cognitive inefficiencies and errors is an empirical issue (cf. Jones 1999). Due to emotional biases, there often is a gap between the choice of the decision-maker and the 'rational' choice dictated by the task environment based on 'full' rationality (Jones 1999). This gap can be considered as psychological 'bounded rationality showing through' (Jones 1999; Newell and Simon 1972; Simon 1996). Because decision-makers are adaptive learners (e.g., Au and Kauffman 2003; Gigerenzer and Selten 2001), this gap will diminish with learning and the successively updated choice will converge on that 'rationally' required by the task environment.[20] As such, the diminishing gap reflects the process of 'rationalizing'.

Since emotional capacities are proportional to cognitive capacities (Turner 2007), the modeling of boundedly rational behavior necessitates measures which are related to cognitive bounds. As we discussed in Sects. 4.6 and 4.7, CD reflects change in cognitive bounds. The higher the levels of CD are, the narrower the cognitive bounds are, and the more serious the consequent emotional biases are. Thus, in the context of this book, boundedly rational behavior can be modeled by the increasingly more efficient, or more 'rational', use of cognitive bounds (or more accurately, bounded cognitive capacity). Methodologically speaking, such rationalizing process can be detected using the three-way interaction effect between CD (cognitive bounds), organizational learning (e.g., experience over time) and any independent variable of interest on governance structure (firm behavior) based on longitudinal data. We demonstrate this in Chapter 6.

4.10 The *Manas*-Centric, CR-Informed Approach Informs Penrose (1959)

In the previous sections, we identified the link between CR and the theory of the mind; and after the ontologization of the self in CR, we suggested a novel modeling strategy of bounded rationality. Considering that some scholars have tried to link CR to Penrose (1959) (e.g., Clark and Blundel 2007) and that Penrosean learning is fundamental to behavioral theories (see Chapter 1) such as our behavioral TCE in Chapter 5 and the proposed behavioral OLI paradigm in Chapter 7, we suggest that the *manas*-centric modeling strategy discussed in Sect. 4.9 has potential to inform Penrosean learning. We also suggest that CD can contextualize Penrose learning, similar to our argument that CD contextualizes effectuation theory, as discussed in Sect. 4.8.

The central insight offered in Penrose (1959) is that the rate of firm growth is constrained by the availability of managerial productive services—the so-called Penrose effect. Peng and Beamish (2016) demonstrated this effect vividly in an MNC sequential expansion study. Penrose distinguished between resources and services: the former can be defined independently of their use, while the latter are heterogeneous capabilities unique to each individual firm. Penrose argues that, '[s]trictly speaking, it is never resources themselves that are the 'inputs' in the production process, but only the services that the resources can render' and 'the very word 'service' implying a function, an activity' (Penrose 2009: 22). The availability of managerial services is affected by an endogenous intra-firm learning process which generates excess managerial capacity of productive services available for further strategic actions geared toward firm growth. We suggest that the Penrose effect is, in essence, a manifestation of *manas* itself. Please note here that, by saying 'the services that the resources can render', Penrose may have unintentionally conflated excess resources with available managerial services, to the contrary of what she intended (see Point 5 below).

Like *A Behavioral Theory of the Firm* (Cyert and March 1963), Penrose (1959) is believed to have opened up or entered the black box of the firm (Clark and Blundel 2007; Pitelis 2007). However, Penrose (1959) did not take the 'entering' to its end by entering the mind of the managers, and, as a result, there are some fundamental issues which remain to be addressed. These include:

1. While her 'method-epistemology involved a dynamic interplay between induction and deduction, structure and agency, in the context of a history-informed path-dependent evolutionary dynamic, shaped by actors' ***conscious***, yet path-dependent and structure-moulded actions, in the context of a purposive organization, the firm, operating under conditions of uncertainty' (Pitelis 2009: xxxiii. Italic added), the recognition of social structure and institutional contexts has not led to clear articulation thereof (Thompson and Valentinov 2017). Instead, it has largely transitioned from being a process theory concerned with how firms grow to being a variance theory (in the form of resource-based view) concerned with why firms grow (McKelvie et al. 2020: 709) and has tended to fixate on the issues of what activities are best suited to the firm's capability set (Thompson and Valentinov 2017). Pitelis (2009: xxxiii) pointed out that 'at least a variant of modern resource-based theory is about rents in equilibrium, which is far from Penrose's main theme'. It is of interest to know what caused this phenomenon.
2. Although Penrose did not use the term 'bounded rationality', the idea is believed to be there (Barca 2003). It is believed that, in contrast to the neoclassical theory, 'Penrose does not have conventional, rational optimizing agents, does not focus on efficient allocation of scarce resources alone, does not look for an equilibrium' (Pitelis 2009: xxx). Nevertheless, the literature is not clear about the nature of such bounded rationality, i.e., whether it is processing or psychological. A careful reading seems to suggest that the Penrose effect is cognition-centric and based on processing bounded rationality since psychological biases had not registered on its radar. If so, its potential with regard to organizational learning has not been fully developed and tapped.
3. Related to Point 2 above, while Penrose effect is believed to have taken into consideration a cognitive dimension (Pitelis 2011), it is not behavioral (Joseph and Wilson 2018; Pitelis 2007, 2009). It is

a perspective that implicitly assumes that managers qua managers can apply excess resources to a give set opportunities, in contrast to behavioral theories which focuses on the *allocation of attention* to various opportunities due to cognitive limits placed on managers (Cyert and March 1963; Joseph and Wilson 2018)[21] and potential conflicts in the allocation process (cf. Pitelis 2009). Furthermore, the psychological biases arising from cognitive bounds have not been serious taken into account in Penrose (1959).

4. While she suggested that the rate of firm growth is constrained by the availability of managerial productive services, what constrains the latter was not well articulated (Penrose 2009: 3–4). In a sense, the black box of the development of managerial services has not been opened up. The core of Penrose's theory is that, while the production of these services requires time thus constrains firm growth at a given time, it permits continuous and infinite extension of managerial knowledge and thus a firm's expansion plan (Pitelis 2009; Spender 1996). In other words, 'there is no limit to the size of the firm, but only to its rate of growth' (Pitelis 2009: xix; Penrose 2009). This is due to the fact that, while being firm-specific, managerial knowledge is a public good within the bounds of the firm, meaning that it is infinitely extensible and its use by one person does not deprive others of its use (Spender 1996). As such, Penrose's argument is not simply about the growth of the firm, rather it is an argument about the theory of the growth rate of managerial knowledge and thus service potentials.

   However, while acknowledging the limits to the growth rate of managerial services, Penrose failed to open up the black box of managerial services. She suggested that at present 'the validity of the theory of the limits to the rate of growth of firms lies entirely in the extent to which it is consistent with the theory of the process of growth, in its logic, and in its intuitive acceptability' (Penrose 2009: 4). This is because '[t]he analysis of the limits to growth—the factors determining the maximum rate of growth of firms—on the other hand, cannot, in its present formulation at any rate, be tested against the facts of the external world, partly because of the difficulties in expressing some of the concepts in quantitative terms and partly because of the impossibility of ever knowing for any given firm what is, or would have been, its maximum rate of growth' (Penrose 2009: 3). She only hoped that '[p]erhaps some of these difficulties will be overcome in different formulations constructed by others' (Penrose 2009: 3–4).

The difficulties that Penrose mentioned about the impossibility of ever knowing the maximum rate of growth apparently parallel the difficulties that we discussed about knowing the bounds of the sixth consciousness in previous sections. As we suggested in Sects. 4.6 and 4.7, while we have no way of knowing the bounds itself, we do know that various types of distance affect cognitive bounds and can thus be used as a measure for cognitive bounds. Similarly, while it will be impossible to ever know for certain the maximum rate of growth, we can still model the Penrose effect if we can find some measures which reflect the variation in the rate of growth. For this purpose, we suggest that CD, again, fits the bill for such a measure. An apparent shortcoming of Penrose (1959) is that it did not deal with locations and thus distances (Pitelis 2011). While some scholars have suggested to link distance to Penrose effect (e.g., Kay 2005), the suggestion was based on an etic understanding, which paid insufficient attention to the fundamental role of emic-etic interaction and psychological biases arising from distances. See next point.

5. In addition, available managerial services are often conflated with excess resources, sometimes even by Penrose (e.g., Penrose 2009: 22). While both are necessary for firm growth (Pitelis and Verbeke 2007: 143), what matter in Penrose effect is the former rather than the latter, and the two should not be conflated (Penrose 1959; Mahoney 2004). As we discussed in Chapter 3 and will discuss passim in the book, this conflation is a symptom of another emic-etic conflation. While Penrose did not use the words 'emic' and 'etic', her 'concept of the firm was more or less coterminous with the management team's emic knowledge - though she is widely cited today, incorrectly, as describing the firm as a bundle of etic resources' (Spender 2015: 65). In other words, her theory of the growth of the firm is more of an emic knowledge-based theory of the firm rather than an etic resource-based view. A question could be raised as to what causes these confusions.

We suggest that the above issues occur because that the black box of the mind and thus that of managerial services has not been opened, and that cognition is conflated with *manas*. This is largely due to the insufficient attention to ontological depth in Penrose (1959). While we do not repeat here, what we discussed in Sect. 2.8 can be readily extended to the case of Penrose effect (see Table 4.5), considering that effectuation theory hinges on Penrosean resources and parallels and extends Penrose (Chiles et al. 2008; Sarasvathy and Dew 2008), and that Penrosian process is consistent with the decision-making logic of 'resources in search of uses' of effectuation theory (Foss and Grandori 2020). While Penrose (1959) rightly suggested that the focus should be on how people use resources rather than on what counts as resources and recognized the importance of social structure and institutional contexts, its shallow ontology prevented it from achieving more fruitful advances.

According to Table 4.5, it is the insufficient attention to a CR-based ontology that has led scholars to adopt a positivist approach, to focus on processing bounded rationality, and to change the Penrosean focus on emic process to a focus on variance in etic resources, which, ironically, is contrary to what Penrose sought (Spender 1996). It is also for the same reason that managerial services and excess resources tend to be conflated since *manas* is conflated with cognition in a collapsed ontology. In other words, the Penrose effect had been understood in a cognition-centric manner. In fact, even recent efforts to integrate Penrose's (1959) theory of the growth of the firm and Cyert and March's (1963) behavioral theory of the firm in developing a behavioral theory of firm growth (e.g., Joseph and Wilson 2018) can at best be regarded as being cognition-centric and 'administrative' rather than *manas*-centric and 'behavioral'. This is because such efforts did not disaggregate cognition from *manas* and thus failed to consider psychological biases. Similarly, efforts in bridging Penrose with MNC theories based on distances (e.g., Kay 2005) were also carried out in a cognition-centric way, failing to consider emic-etic interaction which can only be considered after the theoretical separation of emic and etic perspectives.

After ontologizing the Penrose effect in CR and separating *manas* from cognition (cognitive bounds), we propose the adoption of a *manas*-centric approach to Penrosean learning, as shown in Table 4.5. In such an approach, the focus will be on the need for allocation of managerial attention due to bounded rationality (i.e., cognitive constraints) (Sherman et al. 2000), which give rise to psychological biases. Because cognition is separated from *manas*, and because *manas* is foregrounded, the psychological biases arising from cognitive constraints can be considered, and excess resources are differentiated from managerial services since the former is used by the latter and strictly speaking not central to Penrosean learning (Penrose 1995: 22; Mahoney 2004; Sarasvathy and Dew 2008).

Table 4.5 Ontologizing the Penrose effect based on critical realism

Domain	*Real*	*Actual*	*Empirical*
Generative mechanisms/tendencies *Alaya*/Volition '[T]emperamental' aspects of the quality of entrepreneurial services which are not amenable to economic analysis (Penrose 2009: 32; original emphasis): • Entrepreneurial versatility • Entrepreneurial ingenuity • Entrepreneurial ***ambition*** (emphasis added) • Entrepreneurial ***judgment*** (emphasis added) • Etic	✓		
Events *Manas*/Emotion • Managerial services: 'the services that the resources can render'; 'resources consist of a bundle of ***potential*** services' (Penrose 2009: 22; emphasis added) • '[D]ynamic interplay between induction and deduction, structure and agency, in the context of a history-informed path-dependent evolutionary dynamic, shaped by actors' conscious, yet path-dependent and structure-moulded actions, in the context of a purposive organization, the firm, operating under conditions of uncertainty' (Pitelis 2009: xxxiii) • 'Resources render (multiple) services. The heterogeneity of services from resources gives each firm its unique character' (Pitelis 2009: xx) • Knowledge as a process (Spender 1996) • Knowledge-based theory of the firm (Spender 2015) • Focus on 'knowledge speed'/the growth rate of managerial knowledge • The black box of the firm opened, but managerial services remain a black box • The black box of managerial services fully opened by foregrounding *manas* and considering various types of distance as reflecting cognitive bounds (this study) • Contextualized in cultural distance (this study) • Various types of distances are fundamental constraints to the development of managerial services (this study) • *Manas* applies resources in a way susceptible to biases resulting from cultural distance and other types of distance (this study) • The Penrose effect is fundamentally related to the reduction of psychological biases arising from distances (this study) • *Manas*-centric (this study) • Psychological bounded rationality (this study) • Emic x Etic: "[Penrose's] move opened up space for the constructive or emic agency of the 'management team'" (Spender 2015: 65); link to cultural distance-profile interaction (see Chapter 7)	✓	✓	

(continued)

Table 4.5 (continued)

Domain	*Real*	*Actual*	*Empirical*
Experiences Cognitive consciousness/Cognition • Resources • Resources can be defined 'independently of their use' (Penrose 2009: 22) • Knowledge as a resource (Spender 1996) • Resource-based view • Focus on 'resource scarcity' • Various types of distances not considered • Cognition-centric • Processing bounded rationality • Emic (imposed etic/pseudo-etic when applied in international settings)	✓	✓	✓

Source Author's creation based on Bhaskar (2008: 2)

More importantly, the *manas*-centric approach answers the question of what constrains the availability of managerial services in the first place. As we have discussed in Sect. 4.7, there are numerous types of distance which affect cognitive bounds. We suggest that it is distances that constrain the availability of managerial services since they pose challenge to managerial cognitive capacity, give rise to psychological biases, and necessitate the need for attention allocation until tasks are routinized with learning. This is a significant insight, especially in international settings, as we discuss in Chapter 7. In intra-country settings, firm growth can be viewed as '*added distance*' (cf. Hutzschenreuter et al. 2011) in some 'spatial' dimensions other than in a geographic sense, such as technological space, customer space, among others. While Penrose (1959) did not deal with locations and thus distances (Pitelis 2011), she did slightly hinted at the relevance of international context in the third edition of her 1959 book (Penrose 1995) by claiming that all theories of the MNC need to suitably adapt her ideas and account for the existence of national differences (Pitelis 2011). Nevertheless, she did not spell out the fundamental role of various types of distance in her theory and did not consider the psychological biases which arise from distances. She also did not disaggregate *manas* from cognition, and as a result, her theory did not achieve much along the behavioral line, as suggested by some scholars who called for the integration of her theory with that of Cyert and March (1963) in order to make the Penrosean learning behavioral (Joseph and Wilson 2018; Pitelis 2007). Our proposed *manas*-centric approach has potential to contribute to this stream of research.

The *manas*-centric approach foregrounds the emic perspective and thus places managerial agency at the center of analysis (Spender 2015). Due to the fact that *manas* applies cognition in a fallible manner, our *manas*-centric approach is naturally conducive to considering emic-etic interaction, and thus opens up the possibility of an coherent behavioral theory. In addition, the pivotal role of distances enables us to overcome the downside of such a theory, i.e., the inability to characterize, measure and evaluate the managerial team knowledge that is central to Penrose analysis (Spender 2015). As pointed out in Point 4 above, while Penrose (1959) opened up the black box of the firm and the possibility of an emic theory of firm growth, she did not pursue the opening up to the core to open up the mind of managers, or managerial teams, due to the impossibility of ever knowing the firm's maximum rate of growth (Penrose 2009: 3). Such impossibility results from the unknowability of the physiological cognitive bounds. By conceptualizing various types of distance as reflecting cognitive bounds, this study suggests that such impossibility can be circumvented. Since it was the difficulty in characterizing and measuring managerial knowledge that has caused scholars to overlook the time-dependency and periodicity of Penrosean analysis (Spender 2015) and thus to change the Penrosean focus on emic process to a focus on variance in etic resources (Spender 1996), casting distances in a new light as suggested by this book will enable a refocus on the time-dependency or periodicity of Penrosean analysis.

4.11 Boundedly Rational Behavior Arising from CD: Assimilation Bias and Contrast Bias

To prepare for the next two chapters, we discuss some fundamental biases arising from biased perception of CD due to bounded rationality. Existing literature suggest that significant boundedly rational human behavior can arise from biased perception of CD (e.g., Morris and Gelfand 2004). We focus on the link between CD and assimilation/contrast biases vis-à-vis controllable uncertainties and the similar link between CD and cultural overconfidence/discounting biases vis-à-vis uncontrollable uncertainties.

4.11.1 Assimilation Bias and Contrast Bias

Assimilation bias is defined as 'the perception of one's view being closer to another's view than they actually are'; contrast bias refers to the situation 'when a person holds a view relatively distant from another's, that person will likely perceive the opposing view as even more distant than it is in actuality' (Hart and Diehl 1994: 71; Secord and Backman 1964). The definitions of these two biases are closely linked to familiarity and thus CD (Hart and Diehl 1994; Parente et al. 2008). Extant research suggests that lower (higher) levels of CD lead to assimilation (contrast) biases, resulting in an overly optimistic (pessimistic) perception of risks, which affect managerial behavior accordingly (Fuchs and Gehring 2017; Huberman 2001; Guiso et al. 2009; Parente et al. 2008). Perceived 'familiarity' also intersects with risk/uncertainty controllability to define the space of risks (Johnson and Tversky 1984; Slovic 1987; Slovic et al. 1982; Vlek and Stallen 1981). As we explained in Chapter 2, risk familiarity refers to the epistemological side of risks and reflects bounded rationality, the modeling of which centers on CD.

Researchers have also suggested that trust/source creditability is the mechanism behind the link between CD and assimilation/contrast biases (Tormala and Clarkson 2007). Because low CD implies familiarity with the host country culture, MNC managers will perceive and attribute more trustworthiness to their host country partners than they actually are, resulting in assimilation biases (Hart and Diehl 1994). Conversely, high CD implies that there is little common ground between host and home managers. This will result in an inclination for exaggeration of partner discrepancies, which leads to contrast biases (Parente et al. 2008). Similarly, trust is also behind the relationship between CD and biased risk perception, and higher trust levels are believed to be more conducive to a more optimistic risk perception (Guiso et al. 2009). This is because trust can substitute for knowledge (Siegrist 2000). More recent risk perception literature suggests that trust should enter the equation, in addition to the well-known factors of risk familiarity and controllability (Sjöberg 2002; Slovic et al. 1991).

It is interesting to note that, in the above discussion about assimilation and contrast biases, CD is still treated as cognitive bounds. These biases arise from the perception of this cognitive bounds according to its different levels, or there is a 'separation' between the perceived CD and the actual CD (Azar and Drogendijk 2019; Parente et al. 2008: 320).

As such, these biases can be considered as biases produced by *manas* consciousness while it is applying its social cognition, the capacity of which is affected by CD. In addition, these two types of biases should not be treated as being separate from each other. Instead, organizations are deemed to be simultaneously subject to these competing biases along the gamut of CD where assimilation biases dominate when CD is low and contrast biases prevail when CD is high.

4.11.2 'Cultural Overconfidence Bias' (Over-Optimism) and 'Cultural Discounting Bias' (Over-Pessimism)

Another pair of biases are 'cultural overconfidence bias' and 'cultural discounting bias', which are based on perceived similarity between cultures and the consequential overly optimistic (pessimistic) perception of risks due to low (high) CD. These biases are very similar to the above-mentioned assimilation/contrast biases, but may be more customarily consistent with uncontrollable uncertainties according to ROT. While the potentially powerful influence of cultural values and norms on cognition and thus tendencies of managers to recognize, create and execute real options has been suggested (Chi et al. 2019), the potential biases arising from CD on ROT need to be more systematically integrated into ROT in a behavioral sense.

A widely known cognitive bias in the ROT literature is the time discounting bias, which suggests that individuals place a higher value on proximate events than more remote future events (Frederick et al. 2002). It is a temporal bias because 'people are apparently unable to produce an accurate and unbiased evaluation of experiences that extend over time' (Kahneman et al. 2004: 430). However, temporal remoteness is just one reason that makes evaluations difficult to make, and other factors that can generate 'psychological remoteness' will cause similar discounting bias (Trout 2007: 210). Considering the wide use of CD, a bias, which can be termed as 'cultural discounting bias', comes to our mind. We believe that this bias will be of particular relevance in the context of a behavioral ROT (see Chapter 5). For example, Miller and Shapira (2004) found that managers display a natural tendency to discount the values of their options relative to their expected pay-offs due to temporal remoteness. This tendency can naturally be extended the cultural dimension (Trout 2007: 210), and managers will display a tendency to discount their expected pay-offs in culturally remote locations.

When CD is low, however, 'cultural discounting bias' gradually lose its potency and 'cultural overconfidence bias' takes over. Existing literature suggest that, as a consequence of perceived cultural similarity, managers tend to expect that what works at home culture would also work in host counties, and as a result, cultural overconfidence may develop (Fenwick et al. 2003; O'Grady and Lane 1996). Cultural similarity can mask small, but important, differences (Zaheer et al. 2012), leading to biases. We leave further discussion on this topic to Chapter 5. Here, again, it should be noted that firms are subject to these two types of bias simultaneously along the gamut of CD, where cultural overconfidence bias dominates when CD is low and cultural discounting bias prevails when CD is high. The implications of this will be discussed in Chapter 7.

4.12 A Behavioral Theory Should Be a Self-Conscious Theory

To conclude this chapter, we would like to come back to Williamson's (1985: 387) comment about TCE that it is 'more self-conscious about its behavioral assumptions'. While he hit on an important insight into the key to a behavioral theory, he failed to pursue this insight further by disaggregating the brain, the mind and the self. Since the black box of 'self' is not opened up in TCE, bounded rationality in TCE can only be treated as a black box as well. As something standing alone, bounded rationality in TCE is not considered as an integral part of firm behavior, and as a result, TCE fell short of being a behavioral theory.

Adopting a CR stance, this study opens up the black box of the self and bounded rationality, thus providing ontological depth necessary for a behavioral theory to operate. It is in the actual domain of CR that TCE and effectuation theory can be contextualized and integrated, and psychological biases be genuinely considered. It is after its conceptual separation of cognitive bounds from bounded 'rationalizing' that the importance of CD can be genuinely appreciated in a manas-centic, ontologically deep behavioral TCE. This chapter suggests that we must seek to discover what went on in the black box of the 'self' by distinguishing between the self, the mind and the brain in order to develop empirically sound theories and to have an accurate understanding of economic processes. A behavioral theory of the firm should be a self-conscious theory, and the application of such a theory necessitates an ontologically deep psychoanalytic understanding of the self.

Notes

1. Maharshi (1985: 129) teaches: 'where is the brain? It is in the body. I say that the body itself is a projection of the mind. You speak of the brain when you think of the body. It is the mind which creates the body, the brain in it and also ascertains that the brain is its seat'.
2. We refrain from providing detailed explanation for space limitations. Interested readers can refer to books about CR and the Yogācāra School of Mahayana Buddhism.
3. A concise explanation can be found in Goleman (1996: 19).
4. There exists a debate about the locus of memory and thus how we learn (Langille and Brown 2018; Trettenbrein 2016). Some suggest that memory and learning arises from intracellular (intrinsic) plasticity rather than synaptic plasticity (e.g. Trettenbrein 2016). Langille and Brown (2018) does not see a contradiction in Hebb's theory because Hebb (1949) also mentioned 'some growth process or metabolic change' in the neuron which accompanies synaptic plasticity. Such growth process or metabolic change is 'intrinsic plasticity' (Sehgal et al. 2013). Without going into great detail, it is fair to say that the synapse plays an important role in memory and learning. Memory formation and learning can be a result of both synaptic plasticity and intracellular plasticity (Langille and Brown 2018).
5. While 'we still live in a cognition-centric era in the mind sciences', more and more recent research suggests an emotion-centric turn (Panksepp 2004, 2003a: 51). After all, if cognition is a new development in human evolution, it cannot be 'centric'. Panksepp (2003b: 9) notes that 'emotional responses, and apparently many basic affective tendencies, survive many forms of brain damage that severely impair cognitions'.
6. Panksepp (2003a: 54) notes that 'only with the emergence of cognitive neural mechanisms capable of resolving highly detailed perceptual fields in reiterative ways, did the possibility emerge of internally buffering decision making by higher executive processes (i.e. free will?)'.
7. Probably, the modern neuroscience just corroborated the ideas which were handed down from antiquity in various religions, and Buddhism in particular.
8. Wilson (2002: 24) observes that 'at any given moment [i.e., each second], our five senses are taking in more than 11,000,000 pieces of information...The most liberal estimate is that people can process consciously about 40 pieces of information per second'. This suggests that our subconsciousness (i.e., psychological 'machinery') manages six orders of magnitude more information than our cognitive consciousness can manage (Campbell 2011).

9. Boland (1998: 604) suggests that 'it is the process of moving toward an equilibrium rather than the attainment of the state of equilibrium that constitutes the only possible useful information one can obtain from a market'. Hayek (1945) shares a similar view.
10. Nevertheless, Barros (2010: 457) suggests that Simon defines rationality as 'a relation of conformance (efficacy) between preestablished ends and the means to reach them. To him, the specification of these ends is a question of value and, hence, is beyond the scope of science'.
11. Absent cognitive bounds, there will be no need for rationality or rationalizing (cf. Sect. 4.4).
12. This evolution was driven by developments in neuropsychology, social psychology, evolutionary psychology and behavioral economics (Foss and Weber 2016b).
13. The Yogācāra thought has particular affinity with this idea, considering that it considers the external world as the perceived part of the same consciousness.
14. Evolutionary psychology and sociology see both social institutions and brains as having been shaped by evolution (e.g., Wilson 1998).
15. No matter how hard one studies and learns, the bounds are not reduced since the brain, as an apparatus, is still an apparatus. Otherwise, all human beings have the potential of becoming super beings with unlimited rationality during their lifetime. We do not deny the possibility that cognitive capacity can be increased on an evolutionary time scale.
16. The theory of effectuation is related to and extends the work of Herbert Simon on the satisficing principle (Chandra 2007: 64). In fact, effectuation theory was developed in close collaboration with Simon (Sarasvathy and Simon 2000; Sarasvathy 2003).
17. Sarasvathy and Simon (2000) suggest that effectuation answers the question: 'Where do we find rationality when the environment does not independently influence outcomes or even rules of the game…the future is truly unpredictable…and the decision maker is unsure of his/her own preferences?'.
18. Experimental economists have found that choices are often affected by considerable emotional biases, even in quite simple settings (Kahneman and Tversky 1979).
19. This is consistent with the vast literature in economics based on the 'revealed preference' principle (Samuelson 1938).
20. Such choice 'rationally' required by the task environment is a tentative moving target rather than something fixed from the beginning. It is also a relative term since economic agents cannot achieve real rationality given cognitive bounds, task complexity and time constraints (Dosi et al. 2005) (cf. Sect. 4.5.1 for ecological rationality). As such, psychological biases are always in the front seat.

21. Even though Joseph and Wilson (2018) aim to integrate the views of Penrose and Cyert and March (1963) in developing a behavioral theory of firm growth, their approach can at best be regarded as being cognition-centric and administrative rather than *manas*-centric and 'behavioral', by which we mean behavior affected by human psychology. They did not consider psychological biases. We prefer to extend the concept of attention into a behavioral sense consistent with the theme of this book. See also Point 3 in Sect. 1.3.

References

Au, Y. A., & Kauffman, R. J. (2003). What do you know? Rational expectations in information technology adoption and investment. *Journal of Management Information Systems, 20*(2), 49–76.

Augier, M., & March, J. G. (2008). A retrospective look at a behavioral theory of the firm. *Journal of Economic Behavior & Organization, 66*(1), 1–6.

Augier, M., & Sarasvathy, S. D. (2004). Integrating evolution, cognition and design. *Strategic Organization, 2*(2), 169–204.

Azar, G., & Drogendijk, R. (2019). Ex-post performance implications of divergence of managers' perceptions of 'distance' from 'reality' in international business. *Management International Review, 59*(1), 67–92.

Barca, M. (2003). *Economic foundations of strategic management*. Aldershot: Ashgate.

Barros, G. (2010). Herbert A. Simon and the concept of rationality. *Brazilian Journal of Political Economy, 30*(3), 455–472.

Beckmann, S. C., Kilbourne, W. E., van Dam, Y., & Pardo, M. (1997. Anthropocentrism, value systems, and environmental attitudes. In P. Andersson (Ed.), *Proceedings of the 27th Annual European Marketing Academy Conference.*

Bell, D. E., Raiffa, H., & Tversky, A. (1988). *Decision making*. Cambridge: Cambridge University Press.

Beugelsdijk, S., Kostova, T., Kunst, V. E., Spadafora, E., & van Essen, M. (2018). Cultural distance and firm internationalization. *Journal of Management, 44*(1), 89–130.

Bhaskar, R. (1998). Philosophy and scientific realism. In M. Archer, R. Bhaskar, A. Collier, T. Lawson, & A. Norrie (Eds.), *Critical realism: Essential readings* (pp. 16–47). London: Routledge.

Bhaskar, R. (2008). *A realist theory of science*. London: Routledge.

Blanco, I. M. (2018). *The unconscious as infinite sets*. New York: Routledge.

Boland, L. A. (1998). Knowledge in economics. *Scottish Journal of Political Economy, 45*(5), 604–613.

Borsboom, D., Wagenmakers, E. J., & Romeijn, J. W. (2011). Mechanistic curiosity will not kill the Bayesian cat. *Behavioral and Brain Sciences, 34*(4), 192–193.

Buckley, P. J. (2018). How theory can inform strategic management education and learning. *Academy of Management Learning & Education, 17*(3), 339–358.

Camerer, C. F., Loewenstein, G., & Prelec, D. (2004). Neuroeconomics. *Scandinavian Journal of Economics, 106*(3), 555–579.

Campbell, P. L. (2011). *Peirce, pragmatism, and the right way of thinking*. Albuquerque: Sandia National Laboratories.

Chandra, Y. (2007). *Internationalization as an entrepreneurial process* (Doctoral dissertation). Australia: University of New South Wales.

Chetty, S., Ojala, A., & Leppaaho, T. (2015). Effectuation and foreign market entry of entrepreneurial firms. *European Journal of Marketing, 49*(9), 1436–1459.

Chi, T., Li, J., Trigeorgis, L. G., & Tsekrekos, A. E. (2019). Real options theory in international business. *Journal of International Business Studies, 50*(4), 525–553.

Chiles, T. H., Gupta, V. K., & Bluedorn, A. C. (2008). On Lachmannian and effectual entrepreneurship: A rejoinder to Sarasvathy and Dew (2008). *Organization Studies, 29*(2), 247–253.

Churchland, P. S., & Sejnowski, T. (1992). *The computational brain*. Cambridge: MIT Press.

Clark, A., & Chalmers, D. J. (1998). The extended mind. *Analysis, 58*(1), 7–19.

Clark, P., & Blundel, R. (2007). Penrose, critical realism and the evolution of business knowledge. *Management & Organizational History, 2*(1), 45–62.

Cook, F. H. (1999). *Three texts on consciousness only*. Berkeley, CA: Bukkyō Dendō Kyōkai and Numata Center for Translation and Research.

Coseru, C. (2017). Mind in Indian Buddhist philosophy. In E. N. Zalta (Ed.), *The Stanford encyclopedia of philosophy*. https://plato.stanford.edu/archives/spr2017/entries/mind-indian-buddhism/.

Cyert, R. M., & March, J. G. (1963). *A behavioral theory of the firm*. Oxford: Blackwell.

Damasio, A. R. (1994). *Descartes' error*. New York: G. P. Putnam.

de Sousa, R. (1990). *The rationality of emotion*. Cambridge: MIT Press.

Dean, J. W., & Sharfman, M. P. (1993). The relationship between procedural rationality and political behavior in strategic decision making. *Decision Sciences, 24*(6), 1069–1083.

Deigh, J. (1994). Cognitivism in the theory of emotions. *Ethics, 104*(4), 824–854.

Dew, N., Read, S., Sarasvathy, S. D., & Wiltbank, R. (2008). Outlines of a behavioral theory of the entrepreneurial firm. *Journal of Economic Behavior & Organization, 66*(1), 37–59.
Dewey, J. (1916). *Essays in experimental logic*. Chicago: University of Chicago Press.
Dikova, D., & Brouthers, K. D. (2009). Establishment mode choice. In M. Kotabe & K. Helsen (Eds.), *SAGE Handbook of International Marketing* (pp. 218–237). London: Sage.
Dosi, G., Marengo, L., & Fagiolo, G. (2005). Learning in evolutionary environments. In K. Dopfer (Ed.), *The evolutionary foundations of economics* (pp. 255–338). Cambridge: Cambridge University Press.
Fast, T. W. (2012). *The profound hegemony of neoliberalism* (Unpublished Doctoral Dissertation). Toronto: York University.
Fenwick, M., Edwards, R., & Buckley, P. J. (2003). Is cultural similarity misleading? *International Business Review, 12*(3), 297–309.
Foss, N. J. (2003). The rhetorical dimensions of bounded rationality. In S. Rizzello (Ed.), *Cognitive developments in economics* (pp. 158–176). London: Routledge.
Foss, N. J., & Grandori, A. (2020). Entrepreneurship and the firm. *Industrial and Corporate Change, 29*(3), 581–598.
Foss, N. J., & Weber, L. (2016a). Expand bounded rationality. *Academy of Management Review, 41*(4), 741–744.
Foss, N. J., & Weber, L. (2016b). Moving opportunism to the back seat. *Academy of Management Review, 41*(1), 61–79.
Frank, B. (2002). The unimportance of the choice-value thesis in economics. *International Advances in Economic Research, 8*(2), 97–106.
Frederick, S., Loewenstein, G., & O'Donoghue, T. (2002). Time discounting and time preference. *Journal of Economic Literature, 40*(2), 351–401.
Fuchs, A., & Gehring, K. (2017). The home bias in sovereign ratings. *Journal of the European Economic Association, 15*(6), 1386–1423.
Gallagher, S. (2013). The socially extended mind. *Cognitive Systems Research, 25*(26), 4–12.
Gallagher, S., & Crisafi, A. (2009). Mental institutions. *Topoi, 28*(1), 45–51.
Gatignon, H., & Anderson, E. (1988). The multinational corporation's degree of control over foreign subsidiaries. *Journal of Law Economics and Organization, 4*(2), 305–336.
Gigerenzer, G., & Gaissmaier, W. (2015). Decision making: Nonrational theories. In J. D. Wright (Ed.), *International encyclopedia of the social and behavioral sciences* (pp. 911–916). Amsterdam: Elsevier.
Gigerenzer, G., & Goldstein, D. G. (1996). Reasoning the fast and frugal way. *Psychological Review, 103*(4), 650–669.

Gigerenzer, G., & Selten, R. (2001). *Bounded rationality*. Cambridge: MIT Press.

Goldberg, A. (2015). *The brain, the mind and the self*. New York: Routledge.

Goleman, D. (1996). *Emotional intelligence*. New York: Bantam Books.

Goles, T., & Hirschheim, R. (2000). The paradigm is dead. *Omega, 28*(3), 249–268.

Guiso, L., Sapienza, P., & Zingales, L. (2009). Cultural biases in economic exchange? *Quarterly Journal of Economics, 124*(3), 1095–1131.

Habermas, J. (1992). *Postmetaphysical thinking*. Cambridge: MIT Press.

Hart, B., & Diehl, V. (1994). Position reversal. *Journal of Psychology, 128*(1), 71–87.

Harvey, P. (2013). *An introduction to Buddhism*. Cambridge: Cambridge University Press.

Hayakawa, H. (2000). Bounded rationality, social and cultural norms, and interdependence via reference groups. *Journal of Economic Behavior & Organization, 43*(1), 1–34.

Hayek, F. A. (1945). The use of knowledge in society. *American Economic Review, 35*(4), 519–530.

Healey, M. P., & Hodgkinson, G. P. (2014). Rethinking the philosophical and theoretical foundations of organizational neuroscience. *Human Relations, 67*(7), 765–792.

Hebb, D. O. (1949). *The organization of behavior*. New York: Wiley.

Hegel, G. W. F. (1949). *Philosophy of right*. Oxford: Clarendon.

Herrmann, N. (1996). *The whole brain business book*. New York: McGraw-Hill.

Hofstede, G., Hofstede, G. J., & Minkov, M. (2010). *Cultures and organizations*. London: McGraw-Hill.

Hosseini, H. (2015). Williamson, Oliver (-1932). In M. Altman (Ed.), *Real-world decision making: An encyclopedia of behavioral economics*. ABC-CLIO: Denver, CO.

Huberman, G. (2001). Familiarity breeds investment. *Review of Financial Studies, 14*(3), 659–680.

Hutzschenreuter, T., Voll, J. C., & Verbeke, A. (2011). The impact of added cultural distance and cultural diversity on international expansion patterns: A Penrosean perspective. *Journal of Management Studies, 48*(2), 305–329.

James, W. (1977). *The writings of William James*. Chicago: The University of Chicago Press.

Johnson, E. J., & Tversky, A. (1984). Representations of perceptions of risks. *Journal of Experimental Psychology: General, 113*(1), 55–70.

Jones, B. D. (1999). Bounded rationality. *Annual Review of Political Science, 2*(1), 297–321.

Joseph, J., & Wilson, A. J. (2018). The growth of the firm: An attention-based view. *Strategic Management Journal, 39*(6), 1779–1800.

Jungermann, H. (1983). The two camps on rationality. In R. W. Scholz (Ed.), *Decision making under uncertainty* (pp. 63–86). New York: North Holland.

Kahneman, D. (1994). New challenges to the rationality assumption. *Journal of Institutional and Theoretical Economics, 150*(1), 18–36.

Kahneman, D. (2011). *Thinking fast and slow*. New York: Farrar, Straus and Giroux.

Kahneman, D., Krueger, A. B., Schkade, D., Schwarz, N., & Stone, A. (2004). Toward national well-being accounts. *American Economic Review, 94*(2), 429–434.

Kahneman, D., & Tversky, A. (1979). Prospect theory. *Econometrica, 47*(2), 263–291.

Kay, N. M. (2005). Penrose and the growth of multinational firms. *Managerial and Decision Economics, 26*(2), 99–112.

Kern, I. (1988). The structure of consciousness according to Xuanzang. *Journal of the British Society for Phenomenology, 19*(3), 282–295.

Kitching, J., & Rouse, J. (2020). Contesting effectuation theory. *International Small Business Journal, 38*(6), 515–535.

Kochumuttom, T. A. (1982). *A Buddhist doctrine of experience*. Delhi: Motilal Banarsidass.

Langille, J. J., & Brown, R. E. (2018). The synaptic theory of memory. *Frontiers in Systems Neuroscience, 12*, Article 52.

LeDoux, J. E., & Brown, R. (2017). A higher-order theory of emotional consciousness. *Proceedings of the National Academy of Sciences, 114*(10), E2016–E2025.

Levy, M., & Hirschheim, R. (2012). Removing the positivist straight jacket from information systems design science research. *ECIS 2012 Proceedings*, Article 9.

Lewis, M. D., & Todd, R. M. (2005). Getting emotional. *Journal of Consciousness Studies, 12*(8/9), 213–238.

Liao, J. S., & Chien, C. S. (2017). The eight-consciousness model of ethical decision making. *Review of Social Sciences, 2*(9), 1–10.

Lindenberg, S. (2001). Social rationality as a unified model of man (including bounded rationality). *Journal of Management and Governance, 5*(3/4), 239–251.

Lo, A. W. (2005). Reconciling efficient markets with behavioral finance. *Journal of Investment Consulting, 7*(2), 21–44.

Lopez, J., & Potter, G. (2001). *After Postmodernism*. London: Athlone Press.

Lyre, H. (2018). Socially extended cognition and shared intentionality. *Frontiers in Psychology, 9*, Article 831.

MacLean, P. D. (1990). *The triune brain in evolution*. New York: Plenum.

Madhok, A. (1997). Cost, value and foreign market entry mode. *Strategic Management Journal, 18*(1), 39–61.

Maharshi, S. R. (1985). *Be as you are*. London: Arkana.
Mahoney, J. T. (2004). *Economic foundations of strategy*. London: Sage.
Mäki, U. (1989). On the problem of realism in economics. *Richerche Economiche, 43*(1–2), 176–198.
Mascolo, M. F., Fischer, K. W. (2010). The dynamic development of thinking, feeling, and acting over the life span. In W. F. Overton & R. M. Lerner (Eds.), *Handbook of life-span development* (Vol. 1, pp. 149–194). Hoboken, NJ: Wiley.
McKelvie, A., Chandler, G. N., DeTienne, D. R., & Johansson, A. (2020). The measurement of effectuation: highlighting research tensions and opportunities for the future. *Small Business Economics, 54*(3), 689–720.
McKinney, M. L. (1998). Cognitive evolution by extended brain development. In J. Langer & M. Killen (Eds.), *Piaget, evolution, and development* (pp. 9–32). Mahwah, NJ: Lawrence Erlbaum.
Miller, K. D. (2008). Simon and Polanyi on rationality and knowledge. *Organization Studies, 29*(7), 933–955.
Miller, K. D., & Shapira, Z. (2004). An empirical test of heuristics and biases affecting real option valuation. *Strategic Management Journal, 25*(3), 269–284.
Morris, M. W., & Gelfand, M. J. (2004). Cultural differences and cognitive dynamics. In M. J. Gelfand & J. M. Brett (Eds.), *Handbook of negotiation and culture* (pp. 45–70). Stanford, CA: Stanford University Press.
Nelson, R. R., & Winter, S. G. (1982). *An evolutionary theory of economic change*. Cambridge, MA: Belknap Press of Harvard University Press.
Newell, A., & Simon, H. A. (1972). *Human problem solving*. Englewood Cliffs, NJ: Prentice Hall.
Ni, L. (2004). Self-consciousness (svasamvittibhaga) and ego-consciousness (*manas*) in Yogācāra Buddhism and in Husserl's phenomenology. In D. Carr & C. F. Cheung (Eds.), *Space, time, and culture* (pp. 219–233). Dordrecht: Springer.
Norman, D. (2013). *The design of everyday things*. New York: Basic Books.
O'Grady, S., & Lane, H. W. (1996). The psychic distance paradox. *Journal of International Business Studies, 27*(2), 309–333.
Panksepp, J. (2003a). An archaeology of mind. *Soundings: An Interdisciplinary Journal, 86*(1/2), 41–69.
Panksepp, J. (2003b). At the interface of the affective, behavioral, and cognitive neurosciences. *Brain and Cognition, 52*(1), 4–14.
Panksepp, J. (2004). *Affective neuroscience*. Oxford: Oxford University Press.
Parente, R., Baack, D. W., & Almeida, V. (2008). Psychic distance and directional equivalence. In S. Tallman (Ed.), *A new generation in international strategic management* (pp. 308–325). Cheltenham: Edward Elgar.

Peng, G. Z., & Beamish, P. W. (2016). Sequential entry timing and the survival of MNC subsidiaries. *Academy of Management Proceedings, 2016*(1), Article 15064.

Penrose, E. T. (1959). *The theory of the growth of the firm*. Oxford: Oxford University Press.

Penrose, E. T. (1995). *The theory of the growth of the firm* (3rd ed.). Oxford: Oxford University Press.

Penrose, E. T. (2009). *The theory of the growth of the firm* (4th ed.). Oxford: Oxford University Press.

Pessali, H. F. (2006). The rhetoric of Oliver Williamson's transaction cost economics. *Journal of Institutional Economics, 2*(1), 45–65.

Peters, F. (2014). Consciousness should not be confused with qualia. *Logos & Episteme, 5*(1), 63–91.

Pinker, S. (2009). *How the mind works*. New York: Norton.

Pitelis, C. N. (2007). A behavioral resource-based view of the firm: The synergy of Cyert and March (1963) and Penrose (1959). *Organization Science, 18*(3), 478–490.

Pitelis, C. N. (2009). Introduction: 'Edith Penrose's 'the theory of the growth of the firm' fifty years later. In E. Penrose (Ed.), *The theory of the growth of the firm* (4th ed., pp. ix–xlvii). Oxford: Oxford University Press.

Pitelis, C. N. (2011). A knowledge: Learning-based perspective on foreign direct investment and the multinational enterprise. In P. Nijkamp & I. Siedschlag (Eds.), *Innovation, growth and competitiveness* (pp. 221–234). Berlin: Springer.

Pitelis, C. N., & Verbeke, A. (2007). Edith Penrose and the future of the multinational enterprise. *Management International Review, 47*(2), 139–149.

Platenkamp, V., & Botterill, D. (2013). Critical realism, rationality and tourism knowledge. *Annals of Tourism Research, 41*, 110–129.

Pogliano, C. (2017). Lucky triune brain. *Nuncius, 32*(2), 330–375.

Putnam, H. (1963). Brains and behavior. In R. J. Butler (Ed.), *Analytical philosophy* (pp. 211–235). Oxford: Basis Blackwell.

Rao, K. R., & Paranjpe, A. C. (2016). *Psychology in the Indian tradition*. New York: Springer.

Read, S., & Sarasvathy, S. D. (2005). Knowing what to do and doing what you know. *Journal of Private Equity, 9*(1), 45–62.

Rolls, E. T. (1999). *The brain and emotion*. Oxford: Oxford University Press.

Samuelson, P. A. (1938). A note on the pure theory of consumer's behavior. *Economica, 5*(1), 61–71.

Sarasvathy, S. D. (2001). Causation and effectuation. *Academy of Management Review, 26*(2), 243–263.

Sarasvathy, S. D. (2003). Entrepreneurship as a science of the artificial. *Journal of Economic Psychology, 24*(2), 203–220.

Sarasvathy, S. D. (2008). *Effectuation: Elements of entrepreneurial expertise*. Cheltenham: Edward Elgar.
Sarasvathy, S. D., & Dew, N. (2008). Is effectuation Lachmannian? A response to chiles, Bluedorn, and Gupta (2007). *Organization Studies, 29*(2), 239–245.
Sarasvathy, S. D., & Simon, H. A. (2000). *Effectuation, near-decomposability, and the creation and growth of entrepreneurial firms*. University of Maryland: The first annual research policy technology entrepreneurship conference.
Sargent, T. J. (1993). *Bounded rationality in macroeconomics*. Oxford: Oxford University Press.
Savage, L. J. (1954). *The foundations of statistics*. New York: Wiley.
Schmidt, J. (2015). Cognition, resources, and opportunities. In G. Gavetti & W. Ocasio (Eds.), *Advances in strategic management* (Vol. 32, pp. 549–575). Bingley: Emerald.
Schwartz, B. (2015). What is rationality? *Journal of Marketing Behavior, 1*(2), 175–183.
Scott, W. R. (1995). *Institutions and organizations*. Thousand Oaks, CA: Sage.
Secord, P. F., & Backman, C. W. (1964). *Social psychology*. New York: McGraw-Hill.
Sehgal, M., Song, C., Ehlers, V. L., & Moyer, J. R. (2013). Learning to learn-intrinsic plasticity as a metaplasticity mechanism for memory formation. *Neurobiology of Learning and Memory, 105*, 186–199.
Sejnowski, T. J. (1999). The book of Hebb. *Neuron, 24*(4), 773–776.
Sharp, P. E. (2011). Buddhist enlightenment and the destruction of attractor networks. *Journal of Consciousness Studies, 18*(3/4), 137–169.
Shatz, C. J. (1992). The developing brain. *Scientific American, 267*(3), 60–67.
Sheldrake, R. (2012). *Science set free*. New York: Deepak Chopra.
Sherman, J. W., Macrae, C. N., & Bodenhausen, G. V. (2000). Attention and stereotyping: Cognitive constraints on the construction of meaningful social impressions. *European Review of Social Psychology, 11*(1), 145–175.
Siegrist, M. (2000). The influence of trust and perceptions of risks and benefits on the acceptance of gene technology. *Risk Analysis, 20*(2), 195–203.
Simon, H. A. (1957). *Models of man*. New York: Wiley.
Simon, H. A. (1961). *Administrative behavior*. New York: Macmillan.
Simon, H. A. (1976). From substantive to procedural rationality. In T. J. Kastelein, S. K. Kuipers, W. A. Nijenhuis, & G. R. Wagenaar (Eds.), *25 Years of economic theory* (pp. 65–86). Boston, MA: Springer.
Simon, H. A. (1978). Rationality as process and as product of thought. *American Economic Review, 68*(2), 1–16.
Simon, H. A. (1979). Rational decision making in business organizations. *American Economic Review, 69*(4), 493–513.
Simon, H. A. (1990). Invariants of human behavior. *Annual Review of Psychology, 41*(1), 1–19.

Simon, H. A. (1996). *The sciences of the artificial*. Cambridge: MIT Press.
Simon, H. A. (1997a). *An empirically based microeconomics*. Cambridge: Cambridge University Press.
Simon, H. A. (1997b). *Models of bounded rationality* (Vol. 3). Cambridge: MIT Press.
Simon, H. A. (2000). Bounded rationality in social science. *Mind & Society, 1*(1), 25–39.
Simon, H. A. (2001). Rationality in Society. In N. Smelser & P. Baltes (Eds.), *International encyclopedia of the social & behavioral sciences* (pp. 782–786). Oxford: Elsevier Science.
Singer, A. E. (1991). Meta-rationality and strategy. *Omega, 19*(2–3), 101–112.
Sjöberg, L. (2002). Attitudes toward technology and risk. *Policy Sciences, 35*(4), 379–400.
Slater, G., & Spencer, D. A. (2000). The uncertain foundations of transaction costs economics. *Journal of Economic Issues, 34*(1), 61–87.
Slovic, P. (1987). Perception of risk. *Science, 236*(4799), 280–285.
Slovic, P., Fischhoff, B., & Lichtenstein, S. (1982). Why study risk perceptions? *Risk Analysis, 2*(2), 83–93.
Slovic, P., Flynn, J. H., & Layman, M. (1991). Perceived risk, trust, and the politics of nuclear waste. *Science, 254*(5038), 1603–1607.
Solomon, R. (1993). *The passions*. Indianapolis, IN: Hackett.
Spender, J. C. (1989). *Industry recipes*. Oxford, UK: Basil Blackwell.
Spender, J. C. (1996). Making knowledge the basis of a dynamic theory of the firm. *Strategic Management Journal, 17*(S2), 45–62.
Spender, J. C. (2015). The theory of the managed firm (TMF). *Human Systems Management, 34*(1), 57–80.
Sperry, R. W. (1975). Left-brain, right-brain. *Saturday Review, 2*(23), 30–32.
Stanovich, K. E. (2015). Meta-rationality in cognitive science. *Journal of Marketing Behavior, 1*(2), 147–156.
Sunstein, C. R. (2006). Misfearing. *Harvard Law Review, 119*(4), 1110–1125.
Suzuki, D. T. (1978). *The Lankavatara Sutra*. Boulder, CO: Prajna Press.
Thompson, S., & Valentinov, V. (2017). The neglect of society in the theory of the firm: A systems-theory perspective. *Cambridge Journal of Economics, 41*(4), 1061–1085.
Todd, P. M., & Gigerenzer, G. (2000). Précis of simple heuristics that make us smart. *Behavioral and Brain Sciences, 23*(5), 727–741.
Tola, F., & Dragonetti, C. (2005). Philosophy of mind in the Yogācāra Buddhist idealistic school. *History of Psychiatry, 16*(4), 453–465.
Toomela, A. (2008). Variables in psychology. *Integrative Psychological and Behavioral Science, 42*(3), 245–265.
Tormala, Z. L., & Clarkson, J. J. (2007). Assimilation and contrast in persuasion. *Personality and Social Psychology Bulletin, 33*(4), 559–571.

Trettenbrein, P. C. (2016). The demise of the synapse as the locus of memory. *Frontiers in Systems Neuroscience, 10*, Article 88.
Trout, J. D. (2007). The psychology of discounting. *Public Affairs Quarterly, 21*(2), 201–220.
Turner, J. H. (2007). *Human emotions*. New York: Routledge.
Tversky, A., & Kahneman, D. (1974). Judgment under uncertainty. *Science, 185*(4157), 1124–1131.
Verbeke, A. (2003). The evolutionary view of the MNE and the future of internalization theory. *Journal of International Business Studies, 34*(6), 498–504.
Verbeke, A., Greidanus, N. S. (2009). The end of the opportunism vs. trust debate. *Journal of International Business Studies, 40*(9), 1471–1495.
Verbeke, A., van Tulder, R., & Puck, J. (2017). Distance in international business studies. In A. Verbeke, J. Puck, & R. Tulder (Eds.) *Progress in international business research* (Vol. 12, pp. 17–43). London: Emerald.
Vlek, C., & Stallen, P. J. (1981). Judging risks and benefits in the small and in the large. *Organizational Behavior and Human Performance, 28*(2), 235–271.
Weber, L., & Mayer, K. (2010). *Expanding the concept of bounded rationality in TCE*. cor.web.uci.edu/files/2013/02/Weber-Mayer-2010_BR.docx. Accessed 25 December 2015.
Wheeler, G. (2018). Bounded rationality. In E. N. Zalta (Ed.), *Stanford encyclopedia of philosophy*. Stanford, CA: Metaphysics Research Lab, Stanford University.
Williamson, O. E. (1975). *Markets and hierarchies*. New York: Free Press.
Williamson, O. E. (1985). *The economic institutions of capitalism*. New York: Free Press.
Williamson, O. E. (1998). *Human actors and economic organization*. Paris: ISNIE conference.
Williamson, O. E. (2000). The new institutional economics. *Journal of Economic Literature, 38*(3), 595–613.
Wilson, E. O. (1998). *Consilience*. New York: Knopf.
Wilson, T. D. (2002). *Strangers to ourselves*. Cambridge, MA: Belknap Press of Harvard University Press.
Xuanzang, T. M., & Epstein, R. (1986). Verses delineating the eight consciousnesses. *Vajra Bodhi Sea: A Monthly Journal of Orthodox Buddhism*, on various issues in 1997 and 1998.
Xuanzang, T. M., & Wei, T. (1973). *Ch'eng wei shih lun*. Hong Kong: The Ch'eng Wei Shih Lun Publication Committee.
Yuste, R. (2015). From the neuron doctrine to neural networks. *Nature Reviews Neuroscience, 16*(8), 487–497.
Zafirovski, M. (1999). What is really rational choice? *Current Sociology, 47*(1), 47–113.

Zaheer, S., Schomaker, M. S., & Nachum, L. (2012). Distance without direction: Restoring credibility to a much-loved construct. *Journal of International Business Studies, 43*(1), 18–27.

Zhang, S. X., Foo, M. D., & Vassolo, R. (2018). *Effectuation is a heuristic, then how about its biases?* https://ssrn.com/abstract=3271633 or http://dx.doi.org/10.2139/ssrn.3271633.

CHAPTER 5

Toward Behavioral Transaction Cost Economics and Beyond

5.1 A Recap of Proposals Developed in Previous Chapters to Render TCE Behavioral

In the previous three chapters, we made multiple proposals to lay the foundation for a behavioral TCE. In Chapter 2, we clarified some key TCE terms and proposed a way to get rid of the serious conflations among them. We attributed the cause of such conflations to TCE's unclear philosophical foundations and called for critical realism for its conduciveness to behavioral considerations. In Chapter 3, we proposed that the TCE assumptions of opportunism and bounded rationality be tackled at an attitude level so that they become amenable to institutional contextualization and thus measurement. We recommended that national ethical attitude (NEE) and cultural distance (CD) be used as the respective measures for opportunism and cognitive bounds. In Chapter 4, we discussed how to model bounded rationality in a self-conscious manner consistent with a behavioral theory approach. We pointed out that bounded rationality cannot be modeled either as a mediator or moderator since bounded rationality is a process rather than a variable. Instead, we highlighted the needs to use more accurate terms and to conceptually separate cognitive bounds from 'rationalizing', which are often hooped together in the widely used term of bounded rationality. Only after doing so can bounded rationality be modeled as a 'rationalizing' process wherein organizations economize on cognitive bounds and reduce cognitive biases through

G. Z. Peng, *Toward Behavioral Transaction Cost Economics*,
International Marketing and Management Research,
https://doi.org/10.1007/978-3-030-46878-1_5

learning. At the end of Chapter 4, we also presented some common cognitive biases arising from CD.

5.2 Prospect Theory Provides the Overarching Generative Mechanisms in Decision-Making

As we discussed in previous chapters, we propose that bounded rationalizing should take the center stage in a behavioral theory of the firm and various cognitive biases should be considered. However, there is a wide array of cognitive biases, which are often contradictory to each other (see Blumenthal-Barby and Krieger 2015; Caputo 2013; and Pohl 2017 for reviews). For example, the same investor may sometimes avoid risks (risk aversion) while at other times embraces them (risk seeking/risk tolerance). In the context of MNC ownership research, as we explained previously, two types of uncertainty, controllable uncertainty and uncontrollable uncertainty, have opposite effects on subsidiary ownership levels. As we explain shortly, this is due to competing problem frames resulting from varying degrees of uncertainty controllability.

Considering that traditional TCE is incapable of simultaneously accounting for both types of uncertainties due to its shallow ontology and assumptional asymmetry, merely putting bounded rationality at the center of theorizing, even after moving psychological processes to the front seat, will not automatically make TCE behavioral since 'rationalizing' needs to be contextualized. An overarching theory which can integrate various contradictory firm behaviors and consider symmetrical assumptions should first be applied before bounded rationalizing can take place. We propose that the framing effects in prospect theory fit the bill since prospect theory can accommodate different risk behaviors under different problem frames according to how investors perceive risks differently. Without cross-fertilization with prospect theory, a behavioral TCE risks being ad hoc even if it centers on bounded rationality because it cannot seriously accommodate competing risk mechanisms as a result of its assumption-omitted theorization and empirical testing (e.g., Tsang 2006).

Nevertheless, as we discuss in Subsect. 5.2.2, prospect theory has collapsed the real and the actual domains into the empirical domain of CR. It thus needs to be contextualized (Bruch and Feinberg 2017) and properly ontologized. Despite this, we argue that prospect theory, once properly ontologized, can provide valuable insights into competing generative mechanisms of organizational decision-making in the real domain. These generative mechanisms include risk aversion and risk tolerance (or risk seeking), as opposed to expected utility under the assumption of risk neutrality which deprived traditional TCE of a focus on and a clear understanding of its generative mechanisms (cf. Sect. 2.7). It is also worth noting that, while prospect theory is a formal model of individual decision-making under uncertainty (Kahneman and Tversky 1979), it accurately describes the behavior of organizations as well (see Fiegenbaum and Thomas 1988, for a review; Whyte 1993). There has been a steady trend of applying prospect theory at various levels of analysis.

Prospect theory can be regarded as an overarching grand theory because it can be linked to judgmental rationality of CR which is located in the real domain (see Table 4.4). Judgmental rationality suggests that 'there are some theoretical and methodological tools we can use in order to discriminate among theories regarding their ability to inform us about external reality' (Danermark et al. 2019: 10; Hu 2018). Prospect theory can be regarded as a tool which helps us to discriminate among theories which can account for competing risk logics vis-à-vis uncertainties of varying levels of controllability (this chapter passim). While the potential of prospect as an overarching grand theory has been suggested (e.g., Miller and Bamberger 2016), the reasons were not well articulated. We map the various theories used in this book in Table 5.1.

Table 5.1 Mapping various theories into critical realism domains

Domain	*Real*	*Actual*	*Empirical*
Judgmental rationality	✓		
Prospect theory			
Epistemological relativism (fallibilist epistemology)	✓	✓	
Effectuation/behavioral TCE/behavioral ROT			
Behavioral OLI$^{(1)}$			
Ontological realism (fallibilist ontology)	✓	✓	✓
Transaction cost economics (TCE)			
Real options theory (ROT)			

Note (1) See Sect. 7.3
Source Author's creation based on Bhaskar (2008: 2). See this chapter passim

5.2.1 *Prospect Theory in a Nutshell*

As a behavioral theory of decision-making under uncertainty, prospect theory makes two related statements about how decision-makers make decisions in a way which departs from rationality of traditional economics. First, decision-makers make decisions based on whether a given course of action will yield a loss or a gain relative to their specific situation (the reference point) rather than based on the total expected utility thereof in absolute terms. Second, it contends that how a situation is framed will affect decision-makers' risk preferences since they value losses and gains differently (Kahneman and Tversky 1979; Wakker 2010). They tend to be risk seeking in a loss frame and risk-averse in a gain frame. This idea is vividly expressed in the dictum that 'losses loom larger than gains' (Kahneman and Tversky 1979: 279) and in Jimmy Conners' quote that 'I hate to lose more than I like to win'. On the one hand, decision-makers show risk aversion when decision outcomes are framed in the positive for example, as a choice between a sure gain and a larger gain which is less certain. On the other hand, decision-makers display risk seeking tendency when decision outcomes are framed in the negative. When faced with a decision between a sure loss and a gamble which could decrease or increase the sure loss, decision-makers prefer the gamble even when its expected value is less than the sure loss. As such, decision-makers exhibit preference reversal under different problem frames (Tversky and Kahneman 1981).

Prospect theory assumes that gains and losses are defined 'relative to some neutral reference point' (Kahneman and Tversky 1979: 274) and 'perception is reference dependent' (Kahneman 2003: 703). Outcomes perceived to be above the reference point are viewed as gains, and outcomes perceived to be below it are viewed as losses (Tversky and Kahneman 1981). Generally, prospect theory assumes the status quo as the reference point (Bendor et al. 2011), but factors like expectations and aspirations can shape the reference point (Holmes et al. 2011). Increases in aspirations will be associated with increases in risk taking, and increases in expectations (anticipated returns) will be associated with decreases in risk taking (Bromiley 1991).

While prospect theory is often considered as a behavioral theory of decision-making under uncertainty (see Chapter 1) and discussed as an alternative to classical rational choice modeling, it is worthwhile noting that prospect theory overlaps with rational choice theory in considerable ways (Berg and Gigerenzer 2010; Bendor et al. 2011). First, prospect theory is forward-looking, even though it compares expected payoffs with a reference point. Second, once a reference point is set, choice is made based on utility maximization in the context of a frame or representation, even though different frames imply different utility functions. Third, prospect theory assumes that the economic agent follows an algorithm that completely specifies her or his behavior for the choice problem of concern. As such, prospect theory is only limitedly 'behavioral' in terms of its problem frames which depart from the risk neutrality assumption of classical economics. In order for it to become truly behavioral, further psychosocial biases in the form of heuristics and satisficing have to be brought in whichever frame wherein the choice decision process takes place (Bendor et al. 2011). This requires ontological deepening and contextualization, as we discuss in Subsects. 5.2.2–5.2.4. Otherwise, the utility of prospect theory in our behavioral endeavor is limited as an 'actualizing' principle which determines the relevant problem frame (loss or gain) and risk preference.

5.2.2 *Prospect Theory Needs to Be Contextualized in Critical Realism*

While prospect theory can be regarded as an overarching grand theory (Miller and Bamberger 2016) which accounts for competing risk logics, it lacks a clear ontological understanding and tends to focus on individual decision-making within a given context and pay insufficient attention to variation in social contexts (Boettcher 1995). Such a lack contributes to its considerable overlap with the neoclassical approach of expected utility and rational choice which is deductive and based on an explicit set of axioms (Berg and Gigerenzer 2010; Newman 1980), even though the former has been developed in challenge to the latter (Bendor et al. 2011). Thus, prospect theory poorly informed by CR tends to collapse the real and the actual domain into the empirical domain of CR and thus to be used in a deductive way (Berejikian 2002; Miller and Bamberger 2016). As a result, prospect theory literature often tacitly assumes that problem frames are given (Bruch and Feinberg 2017) and ignores the role of environment and social contexts in the actual domain as explanatory variables which determine problem frames (Berg and Gigerenzer 2010).

We suggest that CR can inform prospect theory with a deep ontology, as shown in Table 5.2. In the following subsections, we provide more

Table 5.2 Critical realism informs prospect theory with a deep ontology

Domain	*Real*	*Actual*	*Empirical*
Mechanisms Risk aversion/risk tolerance [Mechanisms that may enhance or counteract each other]	✓		
Events Contingent social conditions [Uncertainty controllability and cultural distance]	✓	✓	
Experiences Experienced behavior in one context	✓	✓	✓

Note Uncertainties are social contexts (Horst and Grabska 2015; Kitching and Rouse 2020)
Source Author's creation based on Bhaskar (2008: 2)

explanations on this. We suggest that uncertainty controllability and CD can be used to contextualize and deepen the ontology of prospect theory. Only through a more committed engagement with the actual domain of various social contexts and structures can prospect theory regain its original abductive momentum (Levy 2000; Newman 1980) toward a descriptive theory which accounts for what people actually do, i.e., a behavioral theory of decision-making under uncertainty. While recent literature has started to pay attention to social and cultural contexts (Bruch and Feinberg 2017; Müller and Rau 2019; Rieger et al. 2015) which affect individual and organizational risk behaviors, the central role of CD has been neglected.

5.2.3 Uncertainty Controllability and the Framing Effect

Prospect theory is a theory about how varied problem frames affect individual behavior under uncertainty (Kahneman and Tversky 1979; Wakker 2010). It tends to assume that the problem frames are given. However, for individuals and organizations to respond to risks and uncertainties, they need first to interpret the environment and frame the problem. As such, it is important to understand the determinants of risk perceptions and the formation of frames (Bazerman 1984).

In Chapter 2, we distinguished between 'controllable uncertainty' and 'uncontrollable uncertainty'. The risk perception literature suggests that the controllability of risk and uncertainty is one of the most important determinants of frame formation (Hendrickx and Vlek 1991; Johnson and

Tversky 1984). Risk perception and framing is a subjective concept about its controllability (Sitkin and Pablo 1992). The perceived controllability determines whether decision-makers are under optimistic or pessimistic biases (Harris 1996) and thus frame formation (Nabi et al. 2019; Yacoub 2012). Controllability and uncontrollability are, respectively, related to 'gain framing' and 'loss framing', because risk is perceived to be lower and more acceptable in situations where decision-makers can influence outcomes than in situations where outcomes occur purely by chance (Ali et al. 2018; Alpers 2019; Anderson 1985; Shen et al. 2017; Sitkin and Pablo 1992; Vertzberger 1995). In Sect. 5.3, we use these different frames to facilitate the construction of a behavioral framework which includes behavioral TCE as one side of a bigger picture.

5.2.4 *Coping with Uncertainties: The Impacts of Optimism/Pessimism Arising from CD*

Given the distinction between controllable uncertainties (e.g., partner opportunism) and uncontrollable uncertainties (e.g., environmental uncertainties), how firms cope with different uncertainties will impact their governance structures. Existing studies in psychology suggest that coping strategies are significantly affected by whether economic actors have an optimistic or pessimistic perception about uncertainties. It is generally accepted that optimism is positively related to 'approach' or engagement coping strategies, which seek to reduce, manage, or eliminate uncertainties; and negatively related to 'avoidance' or disengagement coping strategies, which aim to avoid, ignore, or withdraw from uncertainties (Carver et al. 2010; Nes and Segerstrom 2006).

As we discussed in Sect. 4.11, higher (lower) levels of CD will lead to contrast (assimilation) biases or cultural discounting (overconfidence) biases, and consequently result in over-pessimism (optimism). As such, CD may interact with uncertainty controllability. In the case of high CD, firms will be affected by over-pessimism. They will tend to adopt disengagement strategy in order to avoid uncertainties. When uncertainties are perceived to be uncontrollable, firms will likely use low control governance structures in order to withdraw from uncertainties and adopt a wait-and-see strategy (cf. Miller 1992), consistent with real options theory (ROT). When the uncertainties are controllable types, firms will likely adopt high control mode of governance and increase ownership levels in order to disengage from local partners.

Table 5.3 The interaction between uncertainty controllability and cultural distance on tendency for high/low control governance structure

Controllable uncertainties	↓	↑
Uncontrollable uncertainties	↑	↓
Coping strategy	'Approach' (engagement)	'Avoidance' (disengagement)
Bias type	'Assimilation' (over-optimism)	'Contrast' (over-pessimism)
Cultural distance	Low	High

Source Author's own creation

In the case of low CD, firms will be affected by over-optimism. They will likely adopt engagement strategy in order to reduce uncertainties. When uncertainties are perceived to be controllable, they will likely use low control governance structures in order to engage local partners and reduce partner uncertainty by 'doing'. When the uncertainties are uncontrollable types, firms will likely adopt high control mode of governance and increase ownership levels in order to more effectively engage with the external environment (cf. Miller 1992). The preceding arguments can be summarized in Table 5.3. The most important thing to note is that optimism/pessimism will affect firm behavior differently according to perceived uncertainty controllability.

5.3 A Broader Behavioral Framework: Behavioral TCE and Behavioral ROT as Two Sides of the Same Coin

Based on all the contents that we have discussed up to this point, a behavioral TCE framework comes into view which is grounded in CR. This framework has two sides and would not be complete if we ignore the side other than the behavioral TCE side. As we suggested in Sect. 2.5, TCE is not well suited to the study of uncontrollable uncertainties, and ROT has to be introduced in order for us to understand the fuller decision-making process in determining governance structures. While the integration of TCE and ROT considerations is not novel (Barney and Lee 2000; Chi and McGuire 1996; Folta 1998; Leiblein 2003; Sanchez 2003), our framework goes a significant step further: It uses prospect theory to consider generative mechanisms in the real domain and to integrate *behavioral* TCE and *behavioral* ROT in the actual domain by accounting for psychological biases arising from cultural distance vis-à-vis perceived uncertainty controllability. As such, our integration is ontologically deeper and behavioral theory-friendly. This framework is shown in Fig. 5.1. We also present the comparison of (behavioral) TCE and (behavioral) ROT in Table 5.4.

It should be noted that, while we have not focused on the need for a behavioral ROT, what we discussed in support of a behavior TCE can be applied analogously, but in opposite direction, to the case of a behavioral ROT. For example, Miller and Shapira (2004) and Howell and Jägle (1997) highlight the impact of biased risk perceptions on managerial real options valuation. This stream of literature suggests that real option valuation is also affected by heuristics and biases. More recent studies have called for the continued consideration of biased in real options (e.g., Chi et al. 2019; Leiblein et al. 2017; Posen et al. 2018; Trigeorgis 2014).

Based on Fig. 5.1 and Table 5.4, we can say that behavioral TCE and behavioral ROT are mirror images of each other. They showed identical patterns, except that the relationships are reversed according to uncertainty controllability. Below, we explain the behavioral TCE side of our framework for controllable uncertainty based on Fig. 5.1, and interested readers can easily do the same for the behavioral ROT side on their own.

When faced with uncertainties, *manas* of economic agents will make the distinction whether the uncertainties of concern are perceived to be controllable or not. If the uncertainties are perceived to be controllable, then a gain frame is formed and behavioral TCE should be applied. Next, *manas* will apply its cognitive capabilities based on its cognitive bounds. Due to the bounds of its cognition, *manas* will be biased according to the varying degrees of boundedness, and either contrast or assimilation bias will take effect depending on the varying levels of CD (see Sect. 4.11).

As suggested by effectuation theory, at the beginning of an investment and/or in a new international market, firms simply cannot predict and have to effectuate[1] (Sarasvathy 2008; Sarasvathy and Simon 2000). This is to say, transaction costs are indeterminate in a traditional TCE way. Some scholars suggest that firms will effectuate by making precommitments, that is, ex ante high commitments to deter ex post opportunism (Read and Sarasvathy 2005; Sarasvathy 2008).[2] However, effectuation theory suffers from several shortcomings. First, it does not distinguish between different types of uncertainties and has not clearly specified what kind of uncertainties it is concerned with. Based on a

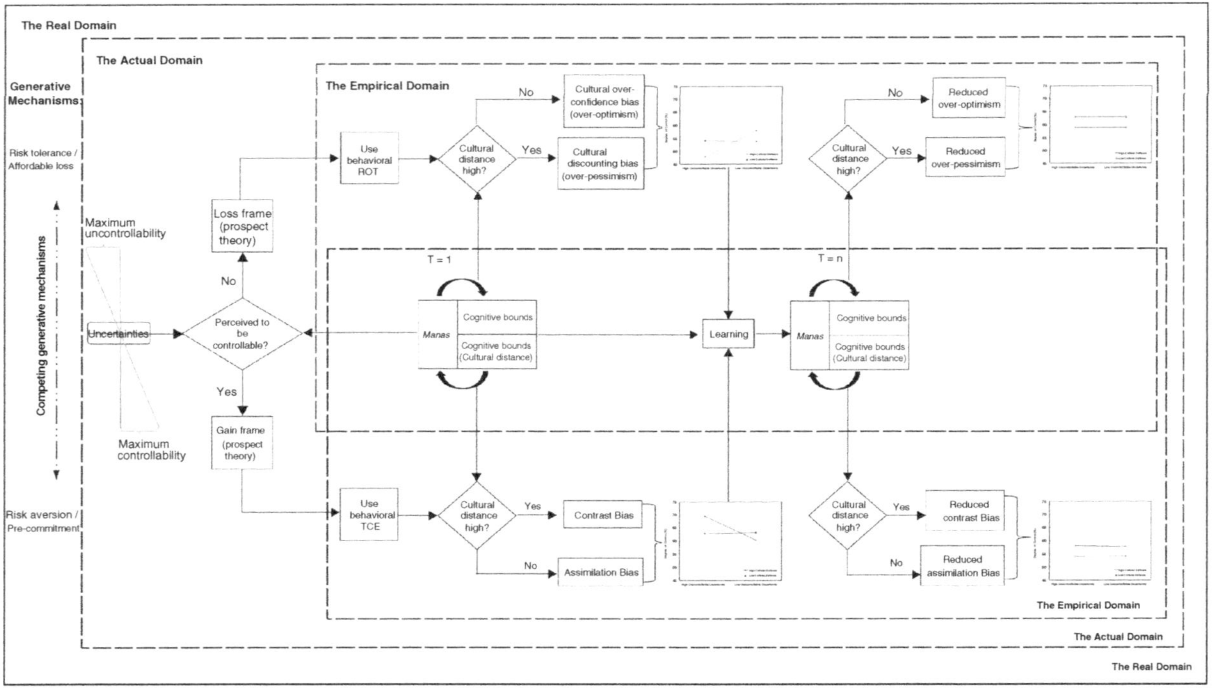

Fig. 5.1 An assumption-symmetrical behavioral framework of organizational decision-making (*Notes* [1] As mentioned in Chapters 1 and 2, TCE assumes controllable uncertainty. Nevertheless, as discussed in Subsects. 2.3.2 and 7.7.6 uncertainty controllability should be treated as a continuous variable. The colored lines in this figure reflect this point. [2] While cultural distance is the most studied type of distance, there are many other distance measures, such as geographic, institutional and psychic distances, among others. Cultural distance in this figure can be extended to other types of distances. See Subsects. 4.7, 4.10, 7.7.3 and 7.7.4. [3] The behavioral TCE part of the figure is broader in scope than the behavioral OLI paradigm [see Subsect. 7.3.2] in that the former can consider distances such as 'technological proximity' or 'distance in technology space', which may not necessarily be related to locations in a geographic sense. *Source* Author's creation)

Table 5.4 A comparison of (behavioral) transaction cost economics and (behavioral) real options theory[1]

Theory	*Transaction cost economics (TCE)*	*Behavioral TCE*	*Behavioral ROT*[2]	*Real options theory (ROT)*
Philosophical position	• Positivism	• Critical realism (cf. Pratten 1997)	• Critical realism (cf. Buckley 1998; Kitching and Rouse 2020)	• Positivism
Human assumption	• *Homo Economicus*	• *Homo sapiens*	• *Homo sapiens*	• *Homo Economicus*
Focus on nature or human action?	• Nature (Sarasvathy 2001)	• Human action (Sarasvathy 2001)	• Human action (Sarasvathy 2001)	• Nature (Sarasvathy 2001)
General application	• Decision-making under uncertainty (Williamson 1985)	• Sequential decision-making process under uncertainty	• Sequential decision-making process under uncertainty (Trigeorgis and Mason 1987)	• Decision-making under uncertainty (Driouchi and Bennett 2011)
Unit of analysis	• Transaction	• Transaction relations (Nooteboom 1992)	• Sequential real options in the form of investment sequence [In a critical realist sense]	• Real options in the form of investment sequence (Cuypers and Martin 2007; Folta 1998; Kogut 1991) [In a positivist sense]
Approach to decision-making	• Causation based on the logic of prediction (Sarasvathy 2001; Wiltbank et al. 2006) • Goal-driven: 'Causation processes take a particular effect as given and focus on selecting between means to create that effect'(Sarasvathy 2001)	• Effectual decision-making • Means-driven: 'Effectuation processes take a set of means as given and focus on selecting between possible effects that can be created with that set of means' (Sarasvathy 2001) • Acceptable decision-making (Larimo 1995)	• Effectual decision-making • Means-driven: 'Effectuation processes take a set of means as given and focus on selecting between possible effects that can be created with that set of means' (Sarasvathy 2001) • Acceptable decision-making	• Causation based on the logic of prediction (Sarasvathy 2001; Wiltbank et al. 2006) • Goal-driven: 'Causation processes take a particular effect as given and focus on selecting between means to create that effect'(Sarasvathy 2001)

(continued)

Table 5.4 (continued)

Theory	*Transaction cost economics (TCE)*	*Behavioral TCE*	*Behavioral ROT*[(2)]	*Real options theory (ROT)*
	• Causation has connotations of ex ante rational planning (Harms and Schiele 2012) • Prediction based on a priori probability distribution (Dew et al. 2009; Wiltbank et al. 2009) • Transactions come first (Cohendet and Llerena 2005)	• Effectuation based on the logic of control (Sarasvathy 2001; Wiltbank et al. 2006) • Effectuation is associated with ex post emergent or non-predictive processes (Harms and Schiele 2012) • Control based on probability alterability (Dew et al. 2009; Wiltbank et al. 2009) • Psychological processes come first (Cohendet and Llerena 2005)	• Effectuation based on the logic of control[(3)] (Sarasvathy 2001; Wiltbank et al. 2006) • Effectuation is associated with ex post emergent or non-predictive processes (Harms and Schiele 2012) • Control based on probability alterability (Dew et al. 2009; Wiltbank et al. 2009) • Psychological processes come first (Dew et al. 2009; Martina 2020)	• Causation has connotations of ex ante rational planning (Harms and Schiele 2012) • Prediction based on a priori probability distribution (Dew et al. 2009; Wiltbank et al. 2009) • Options come first
Behavioral approach?	• Not behavioral • Geared toward analysis	• Behavioral • Geared toward action	• Behavioral (Dew et al 2009) • Geared toward action	• Not behavioral (Dew et al 2009) • Geared toward analysis
Process view?	• Structure of inter-organizational exchange relationships (Zajac and Olsen 1993)	• Process of inter-organizational exchange relationships (Zajac and Olsen 1993)	• Process of structuring options and portfolios of options	• Structure of investments and investment portfolios (Reuer and Tong 2007)
Equilibrium analysis?	• Equilibrium (Slater and Spencer 2000)	• Disequilibrium (Chiles et al. 2008)	• Disequilibrium (Chiles et al. 2008)	• Equilibrium (Tourinho 2013)
Concerned with…	• What to decide and why	• How to decide	• How to decide (Hunt and Song 2015)	• What to decide and why (McGrath 1999)
Time preference	• Timeless (Slater and Spencer 2000) or time-consistent	• Time-inconsistent (cf. Verbeke and Greidanus 2009)	• Time-inconsistent (Grenadier and Wang 2007)	• Time-consistent (Grenadier and Wang 2007)

Theory	*Transaction cost economics (TCE)*	*Behavioral TCE*	*Behavioral ROT*(2)	*Real options theory (ROT)*
Predisposition toward risk/return	• Transaction cost (Williamson 1985)	• Transaction value	• Affordable loss or acceptable risk (Dew et al 2009; Sarasvathy 2001)	• Expected return (Dew et al 2009), downside risk is not the focus (Read and Sarasvathy 2005)
Core applications (in general)	• Mainly concerned with firm boundaries (Williamson 1975) and the governance of contractual relations (Williamson 1993) • Comparison of discrete institutional alternatives/governance structures (Williamson 1985; Pratten 1997) • Performance implications of investment mode decisions (Leiblein 2003)	• Same as in the left column	• Same as in the right column	• Investment and divestment decisions (Li et al. 2007) • Investment mode decisions (Li et al. 2007) • Performance implications of investment/divestment and investment mode decisions (Li et al. 2007)
Core applications (international business)	• Entry mode/ownership decisions (Zhao et al. 2004) • Performance implications of entry mode (Brouthers et al. 2003)	• Same as in the left column	• Same as in the right column	• Timing and scale of market entry/exit (Chi et al. 2019) • Governance structure (e.g. entry mode) (Chi et al. 2019) • MNC network configuration and subsidiary portfolio (Chi et al. 2019) • Performance implications (Chi et al. 2019)

(continued)

Table 5.4 (continued)

Theory	*Transaction cost economics (TCE)*	*Behavioral TCE*	*Behavioral ROT*(2)	*Real options theory (ROT)*
'Goal'	• Minimization of transaction cost: A cost focus (Williamson 1985)	• Satisficing (cf. Chandra 2007) • 'Rationalizing' the process of achieving transaction value	• Satisficing • 'Rationalizing' the process of managing downside risk	• Maximization of (risk adjusted) expected value: A value focus (Read and Sarasvathy 2005)
Assumptions (Core)	• Bounded Rationality (treated in a positivist rational way) • Opportunism • Risk Neutrality	• Bounded rationality • Uncertainty • Intelligent altruism (Sarasvathy 2004; Simon 1993)	• Bounded rationality (Tiwana et al. 2007; Trigeorgis 2014) • Uncertainty • Intelligent altruism (Sarasvathy 2004; Simon 1993)	• Uncertainty (Kogut and Kulatilaka 2001) • Managerial flexibility or discretion (Chi et al. 2019; Kogut and Kulatilaka 2001) • Irreversibility (Dixit and Pindyck 1994)
Assumptions about market	• Known market (Karami 2020) • Stable market (Rese and Roemer 2004) • Competitive market (Dow 1987; Langlois 1984)	• Unknown market (Kalinic et al. 2014; Karami 2020) • New or newly created market/international market (Kalinic et al. 2014)	• Unknown market (Kalinic et al. 2014; Karami 2020) • New or newly created market/international market (Kalinic et al. 2014)	• Perfect and complete markets (Rese and Roemer 2004)
Assumptions about system	• Closed system (Pratten 1997; Slater and Spencer 2000) • Exogenous environment	• Open system (Pratten 1997; Slater and Spencer 2000) • Endogenous environment	• Open system (Kitching and Rouse 2020) • Endogenous environment	• Closed system (Loasby 2002) • Exogenous environment
Adaptability	• External focus (White 2000) • Reactive • Adaptive	• Internal focus • Enactive • Exaptive	• External focus (Boyd and Brown 2012) • Enactive • Exaptive	• Internal focus (Boyd and Brown 2012) • Reactive • Adaptive

Theory	*Transaction cost economics (TCE)*	*Behavioral TCE*	*Behavioral ROT*[(2)]	*Real options theory (ROT)*
Form of rationality	• Rationality [semi-strong form, or bounded rationality treated in a positivist rational way] (Rese and Roemer 2004) • Managerial foresight (Williamson 1985)	• Bounded rationality • Effectuation is rooted in bounded rationality (Kalinic et al. 2014)	• Bounded rationality (Galkina and Lundgren-Henriksson 2017; Tiwana et al. 2007; Trigeorgis 2014); effectuation is rooted in bounded rationality (Kalinic et al. 2014) • Procedural rather than substantive rationality (Dew et al. 2009)	• Rationality (strong form) (Rese and Roemer 2004) • Managerial foresight (Chi and McGuire 1996) • Ability to specify an a priori probability distribution of expected returns (Leiblein 2003)
Type of uncertainty considered	• Controllable uncertainty • Fails to sufficiently consider environmental uncertainty [applicable only if environmental uncertainty is low] (Rese and Roemer 2004) • The higher the controllable uncertainty is, the more efficient the internal organization of transactions is	• Controllable uncertainty	• Uncontrollable uncertainty • Risk is a product of uncontrollability (Dew et al. 2009)	• Uncontrollable uncertainty • Omits behavioral uncertainty arising from human interactions (Rese and Roemer 2004) • Environmental uncertainty, under which larger flexibility is favored (Rese and Roemer 2004). The higher the uncontrollable uncertainty is, the more valuable an option becomes

(continued)

Table 5.4 (continued)

Theory	*Transaction cost economics (TCE)*	*Behavioral TCE*	*Behavioral ROT*(2)	*Real options theory (ROT)*
Emphasized side of uncertainty	• Uncertainty as cost • The downside cost associated with uncertainty (Leiblein 2003; Williamson 1985) • TCE seeks effective governance structure which minimizes transaction cost while maintaining transaction value	• Ex ante commitment (pre-commitment) (Sarasvathy 2008) shifts attention away from concerns about transaction cost to the process of actively enhancing ex post transaction value • After making the large initial commitment, the firm can iteratively reduce ownership level for ex post cooperative gains. In so doing, the firm can increase transaction value while limiting transaction cost	• 'Affordable loss' shifts attention away from profit expectations to the process of actively managing the downside risk (Freiling 2019; Read and Sarasvathy 2005) • To reduce downside risk while maintaining upside potential (Miller and Reuer 1996). Firms adopting the affordable loss approach experience a significantly lower number of investment failures without a reduction in the number of overall successes (Dew et al. 2009; Wiltbank et al. 2009) • By investing only what it can afford to lose, the firm can iteratively push to expand the upside potential of what has just been made possible (Sarasvathy 2013)	• Uncertainty as value/opportunity • The upside profit creating opportunities associated with uncertainty (Leiblein 2003) • ROT aims for structuring a sequence of investments in order to exploit the upside potential while limiting the downside risk (Dixit and Pindyck 1994)

Theory	*Transaction cost economics (TCE)*	*Behavioral TCE*	*Behavioral ROT*[(2)]	*Real options theory (ROT)*
Way to reduce bounded rationality (Type of learning)	• Act and see (passive and deterministic action) • Learning by doing (Cohendet and Llerena 2005) • Passive learning (Cohendet and Llerena 2005) or no learning (Slater and Spencer 2000) • Controllable uncertainty is reduced by actions of the firm since 'doing' reveals additional information with time passing (Folta 1998)	• Effectuate and see • Active learning (Zajac and Olsen 1993) • Internal locus of control leads to active learning • Satisficing facilitates momentum toward	• Effectuate and see • Active learning • Exploratory learning (Cai et al. 2017) • Affordable loss facilitates exploratory learning (Cai et al. 2017)	• Wait and see (Adner and Levinthal 2004) • Learning by waiting (Mun 2002) • Passive learning (Chi et al. 2019) • Uncontrollable uncertainty can only be resolved with the passage of time, thus making market more attractive since 'waiting' provides the firm with the new information (Folta 1998)
Exploration or exploitation mindset?	• Exploitation (Zajac and Olsen 1993) • 'Going by the book': Causal exploitation of pre-existing knowledge (Galkina and Lundgren-Henriksson 2017) • Exploiting current resources and capabilities (Harms and Schiele 2012; Sarasvathy 2001)	• Exploration • Exploring contingencies in order to control the emerging situation (Galkina and Lundgren-Henriksson 2017)	• Exploration: The effectuation mindset leads to more explorative activities in search of options that can create more options for the future rather than maximizing present returns (Dew et al. 2009; Hunt and Song 2015; Yang et al. 2019) • Exploring emergent contingencies (Harms and Schiele 2012; Sarasvathy 2001)	• Exploitation (Adner and Levinthal 2001) • Exploiting current resources and capabilities (Harms and Schiele 2012; Sarasvathy 2001)

(continued)

Table 5.4 (continued)

Theory	*Transaction cost economics (TCE)*	*Behavioral TCE*	*Behavioral ROT*[(2)]	*Real options theory (ROT)*
Nature of assets[(4)]	• Specific (Williamson 1985)	• Specific	• Irreversible	• Irreversible (Chi et al. 2019)
Focus on what aspect of assets[(5)]	• Asset specificity (Rese and Roemer 2004; Sanchez 2003)	• Asset specificity (Rese and Roemer 2004; Sanchez 2003)	• Asset flexibility (Rese and Roemer 2004; Sanchez 2003)	• Asset flexibility (Rese and Roemer 2004; Sanchez 2003)
Problem frame	• n.a.	• Gain framing • TCE assumes adaptive gains from hierarchy (Henisz and Williamson 1999; Williamson 1985)	• Loss framing (Boyd and Brown 2012; Sarasvathy et al. 2020)	• n.a.
Reference point[(6)]	• n.a.	• Status quo[(7)] (Ambos et al. 2020; Sarasvathy et al. 2020)	• Affordable loss (Sarasvathy et al. 2020)	• n.a.
Risk attitude	• Risk neutral (Allen and Lueck 1995; Chiles and McMackin 1996; Rindfleisch and Heide 1997; Williamson 1985)	• Risk averse (Martynov and Schepker 2017; Stoiko et al. 2019) • Adaptive gain assumed in TCE can be regarded as an ex ante sure gain, and potential larger gain arising from ex post cooperation are regarded as less certain. Consequently, firms will be risk averse as a result of gain framing	• Risk seeking (Babenko and Tserlukevich 2019; Brady 2015; Miller and Shapira 2004) or risk tolerant (Read et al. 2015) • The affordable loss principle takes risk and failure for granted (Yang et al. 2019) • Affordable loss incorporates the notion of reference levels, which determines risk preference (Dew et al. 2009; Miller and Reuer 1996; Reuer and Leiblein 2000)	• Risk neutral (Garvin and Ford 2012)

Theory	*Transaction cost economics (TCE)*	*Behavioral TCE*	*Behavioral ROT*[(2)]	*Real options theory (ROT)*
			• Firms would start with an affordable loss and then take risk within such range (Sarasvathy 2003) • High flexibility under affordable loss means entrepreneurs can tolerate more risk (rather than taking more risk) (Read et al. 2015)	
Behavior measuring risk attitude	• n.a.	• Higher ownership levels reflect risk aversion • At the beginning of a transaction firms simply cannot predict motives of partners or even their own. As such, they will make ex ante high commitments in the form of high ownership levels to deter ex post opportunism (Sarasvathy 2008; Sarsvathy and Simon 2000) • Effectual logic allows firms to rapidly increase the level of commitment in the foreign market and may assist in overcoming liabilities of foreignness (Kalinic et al. 2014)	• Lower ownership levels reflect risk seeking • Affordable loss leads to significantly smaller investments than predictions based on traditional ROT (Dew et al. 2009) • Under the affordable loss principle, firms make small bets to ensure that their failure is not catastrophic (Yang et al. 2019) • Investment may increase over time, but the overall size of investment will likely be lower than predictions based on traditional ROT (Wiltbank et al. 2009)	• n.a.

(continued)

Table 5.4 (continued)

Theory	*Transaction cost economics (TCE)*	*Behavioral TCE*	*Behavioral ROT*[2]	*Real options theory (ROT)*
Focus on competition or cooperation?	• Pie division (Peng and Beamish 2014) • Competition (Read and Sarasvathy 2005)	• Pie expansion (Peng and Beamish 2014); Intelligent altruism leads to the co-creation of the pie, which allows for more flexible and innovative outcomes (Galkina and Lundgren-Henriksson 2017) • Cooperation (Read and Sarasvathy 2005)	• Pie expansion (Galkina and Lundgren-Henriksson 2017) • 'New markets created through alliances and other cooperative strategies' (Sarasvathy 2001)	• Pie division • 'Market share in existent markets through competitive strategies' (Sarasvathy 2001)
Focus on information processing or knowledge creation?	• Firm as passive processor of information[8] (Cohendet and Llerena 2005)	• Firm as active producer of knowledge (Cohendet and Llerena 2005)	• Firm as active producer of knowledge (Cohendet and Llerena 2005)	• Firm as passive processor of information (Cohendet and Llerena 2005)
Link with prospect theory?	• No	• Yes	• Yes	• No

Notes

1. TCE (ROT) and behavioral TCE (behavioral ROT), respectively reflecting causal and effectual reasoning, are not an either-or choice. They should be considered as responses to different circumstances at different stages of firm development, and causal reasoning can be subsumed under the effectual process from a critical realist perspective, as discussed in previous chapters. Experienced firms are capable of using both modes well. Effectual action is preferred to causal reasoning in the early stages of a new investment, while causal reasoning becomes more relevant at latter stages (Sarasvathy 2008)

2. While behavioral ROT is not the focus of the current book, we include ROT and behavioral ROT in this table to complete the full picture of the integrative framework. The behavioral ROT that we propose makes the shift from the traditional ROT toward the affordable loss principle which is firmly grounded in behavioral theory (Dew et al. 2009). In addition, as suggested by Kitching and Rouse (2020), the affordable loss principle needs to be informed by critical realism in order for it to be able to account for cultural and social structures, and the intrinsically dynamic social processes between structure and agency (cf. Pratten 1997)

3. Here, 'the logic of control' does not conflict with the assumption of uncontrollable uncertainty of (behavioral) ROT. The principle of affordable loss suggests that firms can control their exposure to uncontrollable uncertainties. Moreover, Goodie(2003) defined control as characterized by 'probability alterability', which involved 'seeking favorable outcomes by altering probabilities in event spaces and by actions that construct entirely new event spaces' (Wiltbank et al. 2009)

4. Irreversibility and specificity of investments are largely synonymous in the two theories (Rese and Roemer 2004). Both are strongly related to the notion of sunk costs (Dixit and Pindyck 1994; Williamson 1996)
5. Asset specificity and asset flexibility are the two faces of the same coin (Rese and Roemer 2004). The two theories have different focuses due to their focuses on different uncertainties
6. Firms may take several risks simultaneously and accordingly have multiple reference points (Holmes et al. 2011)
7. Prospect theory generally assumes the status quo as the reference point. Factors like social comparison, norms, expectations and aspirations can shape the reference point (Holmes et al. 2011)
8. As Dahlman (1979) and Langlois (1992) suggest, all transaction costs are basically information costs

Source Author's own creation

CR-informed understanding of the effectuation literature, we propose that effectuation theory can be made more coherent based on uncertainty controllability (cf. Sect. 2.10). As can be seen from Fig. 5.1 and Table 2.5, different generative mechanisms (experiment logics) are activated according to uncertainty controllability. It is only in the case of controllable uncertainties such as partner opportunism that effectuation starts with high commitments according to the logic of pre-commitment. Second, effectuation theory pays insufficient attention to cultural contexts and social structures which contextualize the effectuation process (Kitching and Rouse 2020), despite its affinity to CR (Kitching and Rouse 2020) and sociological approaches (Sarasvathy et al. 2020). As a result, how firms effectuate differently according to their socio-cultural contexts has been given short shrift. Third, CD, as an important factor which contextualizes effectuation [see Sect. 4.8], has seldom been considered. Since CD gives rise systematic biases as discusses in previous sections and in Sect. 4.11, lack of attention to CD may have contributed to inadequate attention to biases in effectuation, which has constituted a significant research gap (Zhang et al. 2018).

As such, effectuation should be contextualized in CD. For uncertainties which are perceived to be controllable, such as partner opportunism, the effectuation process of MNC subsidiary entry will start with a tendency for high ownership levels as ex ante pre-commitments (Read and Sarasvathy 2005; Sarasvathy 2008), even though such commitments may be means-constrained. Furthermore, such a tendency will be affected by CD and the assimilation/contrast biases which arise from CD. When CD is high, firms will suffer from contrast bias, which will lead to even higher pre-commitment levels. In comparison, firms will assume lower pre-commitment levels in locales with lower CD as a result of assimilation bias. This will result in the effectuated patterns of governance structure for the initial time period ($T = 1$), as shown in Fig. 5.1. Once the governance structure for $T = 1$ is assumed, economic agents will learn with this structure (or use it as an explanans or instrument for adaptation) and gradually reduce biases over time in a recursive and reflexive process, thus bringing governance structure toward the more rational direction.

Please note that the adjustment of governance structure toward the more rational direction is based on transaction value and ecological rationality rather than the vague conceptualization of bounded rationality in traditional TCE. As mentioned in Chapters 1 and 4, Williamson's TCE suffers from a contradiction in which transaction cost determines firm behavior, and such a view is untenable and unrealistic since firms can only 'behave' vis-à-vis an external environment and their behavior can only be justified based on ecological rationality according to transaction value rather than transaction cost alone. Because the overall tendency of firms making biased higher than necessary pre-commitments, the overall rational behavior is for them to reduce their commitment and control levels with learning to optimize their value creation potential over time, until the governance structure converges on what is dictated by ecological rationality at a certain time period (T = *n*). The behavioral framework shown in Fig. 5.1 should be considered together with Table 5.3 and be understood based on ecological rationality in a transaction value perspective. The transaction value-consistent firm behavior is also consistent with the idea of behavioral Penrosean learning discussed in Sect. 4.10. Considering that Fig. 5.1 involves several types of biases and the resulting patterns of firm behavior are somewhat too complicated to explain without an example, we leave more detailed explanation to Chapters 6 and 7. In particular, Figs. 6.1—6.3 are especially important in helping us to explain the ideas in this book.

5.4 Advantages of the Behavioral TCE Framework

We conclude this chapter by pointing out some advantages of our behavioral framework, particularly the TCE side. First, as suggested by Noorderhaven (1996: 925), 'a behavioral theory of transaction governance...should address the consequences of bounded rationality more radically than is customary in TCE'. Our framework is radically different from the traditional TCE. It starts from the psychology of human choice and effectuation. Instead of expanding the 'rational' processing bounded rationality to include psychological bounded rationality (Foss and Weber 2016; Weber and Mayer 2010), we propose a radical revision and overhaul of TCE from its philosophical foundation, and approach bounded rationality by taking a *manas*-centered approach based on CR. Such an approach moves psychological bounded rationality to the center stage and relegates processing bounded rationality to the status of a cognitive tool used by *manas*. It is also a process-based psychological approach which can incorporate framing effects and organizational learning in a seamless realistic way. According to Chapter 1, our approach is genuinely behavioral.

Second, our behavioral framework emphasizes the importance of perception for a behavioral TCE. It starts out by distinguishing between controllable and uncontrollable uncertainties, which are respectively related to 'gain framing' and 'loss framing'. As a result, prospect theory is introduced as the backbone of the comprehensive framework. According to Chapter 1, this further contributes to render TCE behavioral. In so doing, the behavioral TCE approach can redress the traditional TCE assumption of risk neutrality, which is not only unrealistic but also prevents TCE from being a behavioral theory.

Third, our behavioral framework is centered on uncertainty as it starts from *manas*' perception of whether the uncertainty of concern is controllable or not. As is well-known, uncertainty should be central to TCE because, without uncertainty, the firm and many potential issues in comparative institutional assessments will not arise (Coase 1937; Hayek 1945; Williamson 1985). Nevertheless, it has been suggested that Williamson's (1975, 1985) version of TCE actually focused on information processing and complexity instead of uncertainty as suggested in Coase's 1937 piece (Alvarez et al. 2018; Slater and Spencer 2000; Spender 2018). Due to such a focus, traditional TCE has not departed much from the neoclassical paradigm since bounded rationality in traditional TCE can be reduced to neoclassical optimization (Langlois 1984). Our behavioral approach brings the focus back on uncertainty. In additions, uncertainties in our framework are conceptually broader than TCE's partner opportunism, which is only one type of a broad spectrum of uncertainties. A behavioral theory of the firm should focus on how firms deal with uncertainties in a broader sense according to uncertainty controllability because uncertainty management is the essence of organizational processes (Thompson 1967: 159). A theory that fails to incorporate uncertainty would never be helpful in understanding how firms actually make decisions in real world and, thus, uncertainty should be a core concept in the study of organizations (Alvarez et al. 2018). Our behavioral framework can be considered as a comprehensive integrated uncertainty management tool since it is able to consider various types of uncertainties.

Fourth, as suggested in Sect. 2.5, TCE is not well suited to the study of uncontrollable uncertainties. Our framework suggests that behavioral TCE constitutes only one side of a full two-sided, assumption-symmetrical behavioral framework of organizational decision-making, and a behavioral ROT side needs to be introduced to complement behavioral TCE and to complete the full picture of organizational uncertainty management. At the core of this integration is *manas*, which 'applies' prospect theory and determines the applicability of either behavioral TCE or behavioral ROT according to perceived risk controllability. Because *manas* (psychological bounded rationality) uses cognitive bounds (processing bounded rationality) in a recursive and reflexive manner, the framework is further linked to organizational learning. Thus, based on prospect theory, *manas* (psychological bounded rationality) serves to integrate behavioral TCE, behavioral ROT, and organizational learning into a behavioral framework of organizational adaptation. This is consistent with Simon's (1957) idea that behavioral decision theory should center on bounded rationality, which is even considered synonymous with behavioral decision theory (Jankowski 2018).

Fifth, our framework is consistent with the critical realist position that we adopt. It moves psychological bounded rationality to the center stage and relegates processing bounded rationality to the status of a cognitive tool used by *manas*. The biases of *manas* are consistent with a fallibilist epistemology. Due to decision-making biases arising from *manas*, there often is a mismatch between the choices of the decision-makers and those dictated by the task environment (Jones 1999). However, due to decision-makers' adaptive leaning capability (Au and Kauffman 2003; Gigerenzer and Selten 2001), this mismatch will diminish with learning and the chosen choices will converge on those required by the task environment as a result of a realist ontology and decision-makers' judgmental rationality. We have explained this in Chapter 4 and will apply this idea in an empirical demonstration in the next chapter.

Sixth, the theoretical exercise in a CR framework showed that theoretical progress can come about as a result of a more ontologically grounded examination of assumptions by considering factors like contrastive explanation (Tsang and Ellsaesser 2011), assumptional symmetry, and ontological unification (Foss and Hallberg 2014; see next section), even in the absence of falsifying or corroborating empirical evidence (Foss and Hallberg 2017). What's more, we contend, a thorough examination of assumptional symmetry is even more important in the presence of a glut of empirical 'findings' derived from mechanisms-absent and assumption-omitted testing. Such findings tend to mislead research to the direction of focusing on one-sided empirical regularities instead of 'mechanismic explanations' (Bunge 1997; Tsang 2006). But without a clear awareness of various generative mechanisms, replication and accumulation of findings bases on positivist reduced models only tend to entrench an undesirable partial understanding of real management phenomena and to inflate false confidence in the 'evidence' derived based on partial assumptions (Miller and Tsang 2011). The mechanism-unaware normative application of such findings would have detrimental effects on management: 'A faulty explanation would be likely to lead to faults in corporate strategy and in the design of governance structures' (Hodgson 2004: 404). In the following section, we discuss further the theoretical and empirical implications of assumptional symmetry considering its significance for theoretical advancement and empirical modeling.

5.5 Implications of Assumptional Symmetry: Structural Model Vs. Reduced Model

As shown in Fig. 5.1, our framework is aesthetically symmetrical (Foss and Hallberg 2014) based on uncertainty controllability which contingently activates different generative mechanisms in the real domain of CR. An advantage of such a framework based on CR is its deep ontology and attention to competing generative mechanisms, and as a result, it provides ontological depth for (a) the theoretical consideration of symmetrical assumptions, which facilitates better causal articulation and thus advances theory (Foss and Hallberg 2014, 2017), and (b) the adoption of structural model instead of reduced model in empirical testing (Tsang 2006). We discuss them separately.

5.5.1 Assumptional Symmetry and Theoretical Advancement

In the study of management phenomena, management theories tend to focus on specific economic actors and their interaction with certain social domains (Foss and Hallberg 2014). Traditional TCE is such an example. It highlights opportunism (or more accurately, a type of controllable uncertainty) as its domain of concern and studies the choice of different governance structures based on some transaction characteristics. Nevertheless, it treats uncontrollable uncertainty (a different domain) and the interaction between transaction characteristics and uncontrollable uncertainty as indeterminate or peripheral to the explanation of governance structures. Such treatment of assumptions is asymmetrical and literally forces scholars to rely on opportunism for explanations of governance structures in isolation from other uncontrollable uncertainties which may matter significantly to governance decisions, as evidenced by the 'uncertainty paradox', which is to be discussed in Sect. 7.7.1. Assumptional symmetry obtains when assumptions made about certain economic actors and their interactions in one of the application domains of the theory are also made about the same economic actors and their interactions in other application domains of the theory (Foss and Hallberg 2014).

As mentioned in Sect. 5.4, the framework in Fig. 5.1 suggests that greater importance should be attached to assumptional symmetry since making assumptions symmetrical is typically associated with theoretical advancement in the sense of yielding new insights into the management phenomena of concern (Foss and Hallberg 2014, 2017). There can be several arguments for this. First, theoretical progress can result purely from an examination of assumptional symmetry, without reference to the corroborating or falsifying evidence (Foss and Hallberg 2014, 2017). This is what we have done in this chapter. Second, a re-examination of assumptional symmetry is even more important after considerable effort in theory falsification and accumulation of empirical evidence. Questions should be asked about whether assumptional symmetry has been considered and whether the potential empirical inconclusiveness in the accumulated literature may have resulted from asymmetrical assumptions. If the answers are believed to be respectively no and yes, then there is potential for achieving theoretical advancement in obtaining assumptional symmetry. In the context of this book, we can suggest two related examples of empirical inconclusiveness which may have arisen from assumptional asymmetry: One is the inconclusive relationship between uncertainty and governance structure, which we label as 'uncertainty paradox'; and the other is the 'cultural distance paradox'. We discuss them in Sect. 7.7. Third, there is a mutually enhancing relationship between theory falsification through empirical testing and the examination of assumptional symmetry. While we agree with Foss and Hallberg (2014, 2017) on the importance of assumptional symmetry, we do not deny that empirical testing is also important. On the one hand, we believe that the former can improve the 'sense' and effectiveness of empirical falsification. It does not make much sense to 'falsify' a partial theory by keeping replicating empirical findings based on partial assumptions since no amount of replication can solve the problem associated with reduced models. Repetitive assumption-unaware testing can lead to the entrenchment of undesirable partial understanding of real management phenomena based on event regularities and give rise to faulty organizational strategy (Hodgson 2004). On the other hand, theorizing cannot happen in a vacuum, and no amount of rigorous theorization can replace the importance of empirical testing (Tsang 2006). A valid scientific social science should be based on periodical examination of both empirical findings and theory assumptions. Unfortunately, traditional TCE seems to have focused on replicating empirical findings through 'falsification' based on asymmetrical assumptions, and such a practice is a flawed enterprise.

In order to obtain assumptional symmetry and increase causal articulation about generative mechanisms, deeper ontology is a must. There are two reasons. First, the consideration of assumptional symmetry is something like ***assumptions about assumptions***, which is reflexive and cannot be done in the empirical domain since empirical tests in it are by definition positivist and deductive, based on a set of given assumptions. The inclusion of symmetrical assumptions requires the application of a theory of concern in different yet unexperienced contexts, which can only be found in the actual domain of CR. Second, in the empirical domain, scholars tend to focus on 'rigorizing' empirical tests and falsifying hypotheses about event regularities in a positivist way based on a fixed set of assumptions which are often omitted in testing (Tsang 2006). But as previously mentioned, hypotheses based on asymmetrical assumptions are relationships about event regularities as a result of inattention to causal mechanisms. Falsification of empirical regularities is *false* falsification since empirical regularities are not 'mechanismic explanations' (Bunge 1997; Tsang 2006). One cannot falsify something which is itself false due to its partial assumptional basis.

Figure 5.1 suggests that CR can greatly contribute to obtaining assumptional symmetry and increasing causal articulation for its deep ontology, which can easily account for competing generative mechanism and new assumptions, and provide contexts for different assumptions to apply.

5.5.2 *Assumptional Symmetry and Structure Model vs Reduced Model*

Assumptional symmetry has direct bearing on empirical modeling with regard to the distinction between structural model and reduced model (e.g., Chow 1983). The former refers to the relationship between a dependent variable to its independent variables at various levels, expressed through a set of hierarchical equations, while the latter refers to the ultimate relationship between the dependent variable and the lowest-level independent variables after subsequently substituting lower level equations into the higher level formula (Tsang 2006). The structural form takes the following shape (Tsang 2006):

$$z = f(x, y) \tag{1a}$$

where

$$x = g(u), \text{ and } y = h(v) \tag{1b}$$

Substituting Eq. 1b into Eq. 1a yields the corresponding reduced model:

$$z = \varphi(u, v) \tag{2}$$

These two types of models differ in two crucial ways (Bunge 1997; Tsang 2006). First, the reduced model can be derived from the structural model but not vice versa because the attempt to work out the structural model from the reduced model will yield indefinite number of solutions. Second, Eq. 1b 'explain' the intermediary variables *x* and *y*, which are not even contained in Eq. 2. Thus, the reduced model is shallower and simpler than the structural model for skipping the intermediary variables, which explain the mechanism through which *u* and *v* affect the dependent variable. Tsang (2006) illustrated using examples that behavioral assumptions are often eliminated in the process of converting a structural model into its reduced form, which is often much less informative with regard to causal mechanisms than the structural model. Based on some comprehensive literature reviews (e.g., Macher and Richman 2008; David and Han 2004), he also concludes that the empirical TCE literature has been dominated by assumption-omitted testing based on reduced models. He consequently cast doubt over Williamson's (1999: 1092) claim that TCE 'is an empirical success story': How can a theory that has been based predominantly on testing using reduced models be an empirical success story if there are indefinite number of alternative explanations when attributing empirical findings based on reduced models to the structural model level (Bunge 1997)? For example, management scholars often find that firm boundary decisions are driven more by 'competences', 'capabilities', and 'dynamic capabilities' of firms than by transaction cost considerations (e.g., Augier and Teece 2008). Due to the absence of mechanism explanation, confirmatory findings based on reduced models may not offer any significant empirical support for the structural model entailed by the theory other than a confirmation of empirical regularity which is devoid of any insights into decision-making mechanism (Tsang 2006).

As previously discussed passim, the reduced model-based testing and hypothesis development in the TCE literature can be attributed to its positivist deductive stance as a result of its shallow ontology. In the empirical domain and from a positivist perspective, it is inconvenient to consider competing generative assumptions and to pay attention to the effect of assumptional symmetry and ontological unification (Foss and Hallberg 2014). As a result, there has been little theoretical and methodological progress, despite a continuously growing body of empirical studies. Figure 5.1 suggests that CR can not only facilitate assumptional symmetry by considering both controllable and uncontrollable uncertainty, it is also conducive to structural model-based empirical testing by providing ontological depth and width wherein the mechanisms which cause the use of certain governance structure can be explored without being forced to drop out. Consequently, structural models can be used and more sensible and effective falsification can be expected. We demonstrate this point in part in an empirical application in Chapter 6, which tests directly the effects of the opportunism and bounded rationality assumptions of TCE.

Notes

1. Effectuation is fundamentally different from TCE' remediability or remediableness criterion, which argues that all feasible governance structures are flawed and there is no optimal governance structure, thus bounding 'optimal' efficiency tentatively to the governance structure with net gains but no superior alternative. More information on this point can be found in Endnote 12 of Chapter 1.
2. Pre-commitment is usually through specific assets. It is particularly effective in new or international markets which can be considered more nonergodic environments. Davidson and Davidson (1984) suggest that '[a]sset specificity can ...play a useful role in creating an environment for contractual agreements in a nonergodic world' (cited in Dunn 2002: 80).

References

Adner, R., & Levinthal, D. A. (2004). What is not a real option. *Academy of Management Review, 29*(1), 74–85.

Ali, Z., Zhu, F., & Hussain, S. (2018). Risk assessment of ex-post transaction cost in construction projects using structural equation modeling. *Sustainability, 10*(11), Article 4017.

Allen, D. W., & Lueck, D. (1995). Risk preferences and the economics of contracts. *American Economic Review, 85*(2), 447–451.

Alpers, I. (2019). *Managing the 'unknowns'* (Doctoral dissertation). University of St. Gallen.

Alvarez, S. A., Afuah, A., & Gibson, C. (2018). Should management theories take uncertainty seriously? *Academy of Management Review, 43*(2), 69–72.

Ambos, T. C., Cesinger, B., Eggers, F., & Kraus, S. (2020). How does de-globalization affect location decisions? *Global Strategy Journal, 10*(1), 210–236.

Anderson, E. (1985). The salesperson as outside agent or employee. *Marketing Science, 4*(3), 234–254.

Au, Y. A., & Kauffman, R. J. (2003). What do you know? Rational expectations in information technology adoption and investment. *Journal of Management Information Systems, 20*(2), 49–76.

Augier, M., & Teece, D. J. (2008). Strategy as evolution with design. *Organization Studies, 29*(8/9), 1187–1208.

Babenko, I., & Tserlukevich, Y. 2019. *Embracing risk: Hedging policy for firms with real options*. Available at SSRN: https://ssrn.com/abstract=1785334 or http://dx.doi.org/10.2139/ssrn.1785334.

Barney, J. B., & Lee, W. (2000). Multiple considerations in making governance choices. In N. J. Foss & V. Mahnke (Eds.), *Competence, governance, and entrepreneurship* (pp. 304–317). Oxford: Oxford University Press.

Bazerman, M. H. (1984). The relevance of Kahneman and Tversky's concept of framing to organizational behavior. *Journal of Management, 10*(3), 333–343.

Bendor, J., Diermeier, D., Siegel, D. A., & Ting, M. M. (2011). *A behavioral theory of elections*. Princeton, NJ: Princeton University Press.

Berejikian, J. D. (2002). Model building with prospect theory. *Political Psychology, 23*(4), 759–786.

Berg, N., & Gigerenzer, G. (2010). As-if behavioral economics: neoclassical economics in disguise? *History of Economic Ideas, 18*(1), 133–165.

Blumenthal-Barby, J. S., & Krieger, H. (2015). Cognitive biases and heuristics in medical decision making. *Medical Decision Making, 35*(4), 539–557.

Boettcher, W. A. (1995). Context, methods, numbers, and words. *Journal of Conflict Resolution, 39*(3), 561–583.

Boyd, D. E., & Brown, B. P. (2012). Marketing control rights and their distribution within technology licensing agreements. *Journal of the Academy of Marketing Science, 40*(5), 659–672.

Brady, N. D. (2015). *An analysis of the effects of risk biases on real options pricing* (Doctoral dissertation). University of Newcastle, Australia.

Bromiley, P. (1991). Testing a causal model of corporate risk taking and performance. *Academy of Management Journal, 34*(1), 37–59.

Brouthers, K. D., Brouthers, L. E., & Werner, S. (2003). Transaction cost-enhanced entry mode choices and firm performance. *Strategic Management Journal, 24*(12), 1239–1248.

Bruch, E., & Feinberg, F. (2017). Decision-making processes in social contexts. *Annual Review of Sociology, 43*, 207–227.

Buckley, A. (1998). *International investment*. Copenhagen: Handelshøjskolens Forlag/Copenhagen Business School Press.

Bunge, M. (1997). Mechanism and explanation. *Philosophy of the Social Sciences, 27*(4), 410–465.

Cai, L., Guo, R., Fei, Y., & Liu, Z. (2017). Effectuation, exploratory learning and new venture performance. *Journal of Small Business Management, 55*(3), 388–403.

Caputo, A. (2013). A literature review of cognitive biases in negotiation processes. *International Journal of Conflict Management, 24*(4), 374–398.

Carver, C. S., Scheier, M. F., & Segerstrom, S. C. (2010). Optimism. *Clinical Psychology Review, 30*(7), 879–889.

Chandra, Y. (2007). *Internationalization as an entrepreneurial process* (Doctoral dissertation). University of New South Wales, Australia.

Chi, T., Li, J., Trigeorgis, L. G., & Tsekrekos, A. E. (2019). Real options theory in international business. *Journal of International Business Studies, 50*(4), 525–553.

Chi, T., & McGuire, D. J. (1996). Collaborative ventures and value of learning. *Journal of International Business Studies, 27*(2), 285–307.

Chiles, T. H., Gupta, V. K., & Bluedorn, A. C. (2008). On Lachmannian and effectual entrepreneurship. *Organization Studies, 29*(2), 247–253.

Chiles, T. H., & McMackin, J. F. (1996). Integrating variable risk preferences, trust, and transaction cost economics. *Academy of Management Review, 21*(1), 73–99.

Chow, G. C. (1983). *Econometrics*. Singapore: McGraw-Hill.

Coase, R. H. (1937). The nature of the firm. *Economica, 4*(16), 386–405.

Cohendet, P., & Llerena, P. (2005). A dual theory of the firm between transactions and competences. *Revue D'Économie Industrielle, 110*(1), 175–198.

Cuypers, I. R. P., & Martin, X. (2007). Joint ventures and real options. In J. J. Reuer & T. W. Tong (Eds.), *Advances in strategic management* (Vol. 24, pp. 107–148). Amsterdam: Elsevier.

Dahlman, C. J. (1979). The problem of externality. *Journal of Law and Economics, 22*(1), 141–162.

Danermark, B., Ekström, M., & Karlsson, J. C. (2019). *Explaining society: Critical realism in the social sciences*. London: Routledge.

David, R. J., & Han, S. (2004). A systematic assessment of the empirical support for transaction cost economics. *Strategic Management Journal, 25*(1), 39–58.

Davidson, P., & Davidson, G. S. (1984). Financial markets and Williamson's theory of governance. *Quarterly Review of Economics and Business, 24*(4), 50–63.

Dew, N., Sarasathy, S., Read, S., & Wiltbank, R. (2009). Affordable loss. *Strategic Entrepreneurship Journal, 3*(2), 105–126.

Dixit, A. K., & Pindyck, R. S. (1994). *Investment under uncertainty*. Princeton, NJ: Princeton University Press.

Dow, G. K. (1987). The function of authority in transaction cost economics. *Journal of Economic Behavior & Organization, 8*(1), 13–38.

Driouchi, T., & Bennett, D. (2011). Real options in multinational decision-making. *Journal of World Business, 46*(2), 205–219.

Dunn, S. P. (2002). A post Keynesian approach to the theory of the firm. In S. C. Dow & J. Hillard (Eds.), *Post Keynesian econometrics, microeconomics and the theory of the firm* (pp. 60–80). Cheltenham, UK: Edward Elgar.

Fiegenbaum, A., & Thomas, H. (1988). Attitudes toward risk and the risk-return paradox. *Academy of Management Journal, 31*(1), 85–106.

Folta, T. B. (1998). Governance and uncertainty. *Strategic Management Journal, 19*(11), 1007–1028.

Foss, N. J., & Weber, L. (2016). Expand bounded rationality. *Academy of Management Review, 41*(4), 741–744.

Foss, N. J., & Hallberg, N. L. (2014). How symmetrical assumptions advance strategic management research. *Strategic Management Journal, 35*(6), 903–913.

Foss, N. J., & Hallberg, N. L. (2017). Changing assumptions and progressive change in theories of strategic organization. *Strategic Organization, 15*(3), 410–422.

Freiling, J. (2019). Leadership concepts for diaspora entrepreneurship. In M. Elo & I. Minto-Coy (Eds.), *Diaspora networks in international business* (pp. 323–336). Berlin: Springer.

Galkina, T., & Lundgren-Henriksson, E. L. (2017). Coopetition as an entrepreneurial process. *Industrial Marketing Management, 67,* 158–173.

Garvin, M. J., & Ford, D. N. (2012). Real options in infrastructure projects. *Engineering Project Organization Journal, 2*(1/2), 97–108.

Gigerenzer, G., & Selten, R. (2001). *Bounded rationality*. Cambridge, MA: MIT Press.

Goodie, A. S. (2003). The effects of control on betting. *Journal of Experimental Psychology, 29*(4), 598–610.
Grenadier, S. R., & Wang, N. (2007). Investment under uncertainty and time-inconsistent preferences. *Journal of Financial Economics, 84*(1), 2–39.
Harms, R., & Schiele, H. (2012). Antecedents and consequences of effectuation and causation in the international new venture creation process. *Journal of International Entrepreneurship, 10*(2), 95–116.
Harris, P. (1996). Sufficient grounds for optimism? *Journal of Social and Clinical Psychology, 15*(1), 9–52.
Hayek, F. A. (1945). The use of knowledge in society. *American Economic Review, 35*(4), 519–530.
Hendrickx, L., & Vlek, C. (1991). Perceived control, nature of risk information and risk taking. *Journal of Behavioral Decision Making, 4*(4), 235–247.
Henisz, W. J., & Williamson, O. E. (1999). Comparative economic organization. *Business and Politics, 1*(3), 261–277.
Hodgson, G. M. (2004). Opportunism is not the only reason why firms exist. *Industrial and Corporate Change, 13*(2), 401–418.
Holmes, R. M., Bromiley, P., Devers, C. E., Holcomb, T. R., & McGuire, J. B. (2011). Management theory applications of prospect theory. *Journal of Management, 37*(4), 1069–1107.
Horst, C., & Grabska, K. (2015). Flight and exile—Uncertainty in the context of conflict-induced displacement. *Social Analysis, 59*(1), 1–18.
Howell, S. D., & Jägle, A. J. (1997). Laboratory evidence on how managers intuitively value real growth options. *Journal of Business Finance & Accounting, 24*(7/8), 915–935.
Hu, X. (2018). Methodological implications of critical realism for entrepreneurship research. *Journal of Critical Realism, 17*(2), 118–139.
Hunt, R., & Song, Y. (2015). *Internationalizing entrepreneurs: Bridging real options reasoning and affordable loss logics*. Briarcliff Manor, NY: Academy of Management Conference.
Jankowski, P. (2018). Behavioral decision theory in spatial decision-making models. In D. R. Montello (Ed.), *Handbook of behavioral and cognitive geography* (pp. 41–55). Cheltenham, UK: Edward Elgar.
Joas, H., & Beckert, J. (2001). Action theory. In J. H. Turner (Ed.), *Handbook of sociological theory* (pp. 269–285). New York: Springer.
Johnson, E. J., & Tversky, A. (1984). Representations of perceptions of risks. *Journal of Experimental Psychology: General, 113*(1), 55–70.
Jones, B. D. (1999). Bounded rationality. *Annual Review of Political Science, 2*(1), 297–321.
Kahneman, D. (2003). A perspective on judgment and choice. *American Psychologist, 58*(9), 697–720.

Kahneman, D., & Tversky, A. (1979). Prospect theory. *Econometrica, 47*(2), 263–291.
Kalinic, I., Sarasvathy, S. D., & Forza, C. (2014). Expect the unexpected. *International Business Review, 23*(3), 635–647.
Karami, M. (2020). Effectual versus causal international opportunity discovery and creation. In V. Ratten (Ed.), *Entrepreneurship and the community* (pp. 29–48). Cham: Springer.
Kitching, J., & Rouse, J. (2020). Contesting effectuation theory. *International Small Business Journal, 38*(6), 515–535.
Kogut, B. (1991). Joint ventures and the option to expand and acquire. *Management Science, 37*(1), 19–33.
Kogut, B., & Kulatilaka, N. (2001). Capabilities as real options. *Organization Science, 12*(6), 744–758.
Langlois, R. N. (1984). Internal organization in a dynamic context. In M. Jussawalla & H. Ebenfield (Eds.), *Communication and information economics* (pp. 23–49). Amsterdam: North-Holland.
Langlois, R. N. (1992). Transaction cost economics in real time. *Industrial and Corporate Change, 1*(1), 99–127.
Larimo, J. (1995). The foreign direct investment decision process. *Journal of Business Research, 33*(1), 25–55.
Leiblein, M. J. (2003). The choice of organizational governance form and performance. *Journal of Management, 29*(6), 937–961.
Leiblein, M. J., Chen, J. S., & Posen, H. E. (2017). Resource allocation in strategic factor markets. *Journal of Management, 43*(8), 2588–2608.
Levy, J. S. (2000). Loss aversion, framing effects, and international conflict. In M. I. Midlarsky (Ed.), *Handbook of war studies II* (pp. 193–221). Ann Arbor: University of Michigan Press.
Li, Y., James, B. E., Madhavan, R., & Mahoney, J. T. (2007). Real options. In J. J. Reuer & T. W. Tong (Eds.), *Advances in strategic management* (Vol. 24, pp. 31–66). Amsterdam: Elsevier.
Loasby, B. J. (2002). *Options and evolution.* Helsingør, Denmark: DRUID Summer Conference.
Macher, J. T., & Richman, B. D. (2008). Transaction cost economics. *Business and Politics, 10*(1), Article 1.
Martina, R. A. (2020). Toward a theory of affordable loss. *Small Business Economics, 54*(3), 751–774.
Martynov, A., & Schepker, D. J. (2017). Risk preferences and asset ownership. *Managerial and Decision Economics, 38*(2), 125–143.
McGrath, R. G. (1999). Falling forward. *Academy of Management Review, 24*(1), 13–30.

Miller, C. C., & Bamberger, P. (2016). Exploring emergent and poorly understood phenomena in the strangest of places. *Academy of Management Discoveries, 2*(4), 313–319.

Miller, K. D. (1992). A framework for integrated risk management in international business. *Journal of International Business Studies, 23*(2), 311–331.

Miller, K. D., & Reuer, J. J. (1996). Measuring organizational downside risk. *Strategic Management Journal, 17*(9), 671–691.

Miller, K. D., & Shapira, Z. (2004). An empirical test of heuristics and biases affecting real option valuation. *Strategic Management Journal, 25*(3), 269–284.

Miller, K. D., & Tsang, E. W. (2011). Testing management theories. *Strategic Management Journal, 32*(2), 139–158.

Müller, S., & Rau, H. A. (2019). Decisions under uncertainty in social contexts. *Games and Economic Behavior, 116*, 73–95.

Mun, J. (2002). *Real options analysis*. New York: Wiley.

Nabi, R. L., Walter, N., Oshidary, N., Endacott, C. G., Love-Nichols, J., Lew, Z. J., Aune, A. (2019). Can emotions capture the elusive gain-loss framing effect? *Communication Research*. https://doi.org/10.1177/0093650219861256.

Newman, D. P. (1980). Prospect theory: Implications for information evaluation. *Accounting, Organizations and Society, 5*(2), 217–230.

Nes, L. S., & Segerstrom, S. C. (2006). Dispositional optimism and coping. *Personality and Social Psychology Review, 10*(3), 235–251.

Noorderhaven, N. G. (1996). How to make transaction cost economics more balanced and realistic. *Academy of Management Review, 21*(4), 924–925.

Nooteboom, B. (1992). Towards a dynamic theory of transactions. *Journal of Evolutionary Economics, 2*(4), 281–299.

Peng, G. Z., & Beamish, P. W. (2014). The effect of host country long term orientation on subsidiary ownership and survival. *Asia Pacific Journal of Management, 31*(2), 423–453.

Pohl, R. (2017). *Cognitive illusions*. London: Psychology Press.

Posen, H. E., Leiblein, M. J., & Chen, J. S. (2018). Toward a behavioral theory of real options. *Strategic Management Journal, 39*(4), 1112–1138.

Pratten, S. (1997). The nature of transaction cost economics. *Journal of Economic Issues, 31*(3), 781–803.

Read, S., & Sarasvathy, S. D. (2005). Knowing what to do and doing what you know. *Journal of Private Equity, 9*(1), 45–62.

Read, S., Sarasvathy, S. D., Dew, N., & Wiltbank, R. (2015). *Unreasonable assumptions in ASB*. www.effectuation.org.

Rese, M., & Roemer, E. (2004). Managing commitments and flexibility by real options. *Industrial Marketing Management, 33*(6), 501–512.

Reuer, J. J., & Leiblein, M. J. (2000). Downside risk implications of multinationality and international joint ventures. *Academy of Management Journal, 43*(2), 203–214.

Reuer, J. J., & Tong, T. W. (2007). How do real options matter? In J. J. Reuer & T. W. Tong (Eds.), *Advances in strategic management* (Vol. 24, pp. 145–173). Amsterdam: Elsevier.

Rieger, M. O., Wang, M., & Hens, T. (2015). Risk preferences around the world. *Management Science, 61*(3), 637–648.

Rindfleisch, A., & Heide, J. B. (1997). Transaction cost analysis. *Journal of Marketing, 61*(4), 30–54.

Sanchez, R. (2003). Integrating transaction costs theory and real options theory. *Managerial and Decision Economics, 24*(4), 267–282.

Sarasvathy, S. D. (2001). Causation and effectuation. *Academy of Management Review, 26*(2), 243–263.

Sarasvathy, S. D. (2003). Entrepreneurship as a science of the artificial. *Journal of Economic Psychology, 24*(2), 203–220.

Sarasvathy, S. D. (2004). Making it happen. *Entrepreneurship Theory and Practice, 28*(6), 519–531.

Sarasvathy, S. D. (2008). *Effectuation: Elements of entrepreneurial expertise*. Cheltenham, UK: Edward Elgar.

Sarasvathy, S. D. (2013). Entrepreneurial effectuation. In E. H. Kessler (Ed.), *Encyclopedia of management theory* (Vol. 1, pp. 239–240). Thousand Oaks: Sage.

Sarasvathy, S. D., Forster, W. R., & Ramesh, A. (2020). From Goldilocks to Gump. *Revista de Empreendedorismo e Gestão de Pequenas Empresas, 9*(1), 189–220.

Sarasvathy, S. D., & Simon, H. A. (2000). *Effectuation, near-decomposability, and the creation and growth of entrepreneurial firms*. University of Maryland: the first annual research policy technology entrepreneurship conference.

Shen, Z., Puig, F., & Paul, J. (2017). Foreign market entry mode research. *International Trade Journal, 31*(5), 429–456.

Simon, H. A. (1957). *Models of man*. New York: Wiley.

Simon, H. A. (1993). Altruism and economics. *American Economic Review, 83*(2), 156–161.

Sitkin, S. B., & Pablo, A. L. (1992). Reconceptualizing the determinants of risk behavior. *Academy of Management Review, 17*(1), 9–38.

Slater, G., & Spencer, D. A. (2000). The uncertain foundations of transaction costs economics. *Journal of Economic Issues, 34*(1), 61–87.

Spender, J. C. (2018). Managing—According to Williamson, or to Coase? *Kindai Management Review, 6*, 13–34.

Stoiko, M., Egan, T., & Duane, A. (2019). Entrepreneurial internationalization takes the effectuation turn. *SSRN* 3453813.

Thompson, J. D. (1967). *Organizations in action*. New York: McGraw-Hill.
Tihanyi, L., Griffith, D. A., & Russell, C. J. (2005). The effect of cultural distance on entry mode choice, international diversification, and MNE performance. *Journal of International Business Studies, 36*(3), 270–283.
Tiwana, A., Wang, J., Keil, M., & Ahluwalia, P. (2007). The bounded rationality bias in managerial valuation of real options. *Decision Sciences, 38*(1), 157–181.
Tourinho, O. A. F. (2013). Revisiting the Tourinho real options model. *European Journal of Finance, 19*(7–8), 591–603.
Trigeorgis, L. (2014). *Real options with bounded rationality* (Working Paper).
Trigeorgis, L., & Mason, S. P. (1987). Valuing managerial flexibility. *Midland Corporate Finance Journal, 5*(1), 14–21.
Tsang, E. W. K. (2006). Behavioral assumptions and theory development. *Strategic Management Journal, 27*(11), 999–1011.
Tsang, E. W. K., & Ellsaesser, F. (2011). How contrastive explanation facilitates theory building. *Academy of Management Review, 36*(2), 404–419.
Tversky, A., & Kahneman, D. (1981). The framing of decisions and the psychology of choice. *Science, 211*(4481), 453–458.
Verbeke A, Greidanus NS. 2009. The end of the opportunism vs. trust debate. *Journal of International Business Studies* **40**(9): 1471–1495.
Vertzberger, Y. Y. (1995). Rethinking and reconceptualizing risk in foreign policy decision-making. *Political Psychology, 16*(2), 347–380.
Wakker, P. P. (2010). *Prospect theory for risk and uncertainty*. Cambridge: Cambridge University Press.
Weber, L., & Mayer, K. (2010). *Expanding the concept of bounded rationality in TCE*. cor.web.uci.edu/files/2013/02/Weber-Mayer-2010_BR.docx. Accessed 25 December 2015.
White, S. (2000). Competition, capabilities, and the make, buy, or ally decisions of Chinese state-owned firms. *Academy of Management Journal, 43*(3), 324–341.
Whyte, G. (1993). Escalating commitment in individual and group decision making. *Organizational Behavior and Human Decision Processes, 54*(3), 430–455.
Williamson, O. E. (1975). *Markets and hierarchies*. New York: Free Press.
Williamson, O. E. (1985). *The economic institutions of capitalism*. New York: Free Press.
Williamson, O. E. (1993). Transaction cost economics and organization theory. *Industrial and Corporate Change, 2*(2), 107–156.
Williamson, O. E. (1996). *The mechanisms of governance*. Oxford: Oxford University Press.
Williamson, O. E. (1999). Strategy research: Governance and competence perspectives. *Strategic Management Journal, 20*(12), 1087–1108.

Wiltbank, R., Dew, N., Read, S., & Sarasvathy, S. D. (2006). What to do next? The case for non-predictive strategy. *Strategic Management Journal, 27*(10), 981–998.

Wiltbank, R., Read, S., Dew, N., & Sarasvathy, S. D. (2009). Prediction and control under uncertainty. *Journal of Business Venturing, 24*(2), 116–133.

Yacoub, M. (2012). *Emotional framing: How do emotions contribute to framing effects?* (Doctoral dissertation). University of North Carolina, Chapel Hill.

Yang, X., Sun, S. L., & Zhao, X. (2019). Search and execution: examining the entrepreneurial cognitions behind the lean startup model. *Small Business Economics, 52*(3), 667–679.

Zajac, E. J., & Olsen, C. P. (1993). From transaction cost to transactional value analysis. *Journal of Management Studies, 30*(1), 131–145.

Zhang, S. X., Foo, M. D., & Vassolo, R. (2018). *Effectuation is a heuristic, then how about its biases?* https://ssrn.com/abstract=3271633 or http://dx.doi.org/10.2139/ssrn.3271633.

Zhao, H., Luo, Y., & Suh, T. (2004). Transaction cost determinants and ownership-based entry mode choice. *Journal of International Business Studies, 35*(6), 524–544.

CHAPTER 6

An Empirical Application to MNC Subsidiary Ownership

In this chapter, we apply the behavioral TCE side of the framework shown in Fig. 5.1 to the empirical study of MNC subsidiary ownership decision-making process.[1] Considering the frequent *invocation* of opportunism in traditional TCE and the central role of bounded rationality in behavioral theories, and considering the surprising lack of testing of both (David and Han 2004; Tsang 2006; Verbeke and Greidanus 2009), we focus on their separate and joint effects on subsidiary ownership decisions. This focus was chosen also because there has been a long-standing debate about whether the control of opportunism or the reduction of bounded rationality should be the key governance challenge in TCE (Williamson 1985; Kogut and Zander 1993; Verbeke 2003). We aim to contribute to the resolution of this debate. As discussed in previous chapters, we use NEA and CD to proxy opportunism and cognitive bounds, respectively. As such the hypotheses will be on the separate and joint effects of NEA and CD on subsidiary ownership decisions.

6.1 Hypothesis Development

6.1.1 National Ethical Attitude and Subsidiary Ownership Level

TCE advocates that firms select governance structures (e.g., subsidiary ownership levels) that can minimize the transaction costs associated with partner opportunism (Williamson 1975). It is generally accepted that

G. Z. Peng, *Toward Behavioral Transaction Cost Economics*,
International Marketing and Management Research,
https://doi.org/10.1007/978-3-030-46878-1_6

when the risk of partner opportunism is high, MNCs should assume higher ownership levels in their subsidiaries. This relationship is considered to be fundamental to a broad range of TCE empirical studies which spans several decades (Dow et al. 2019). Nevertheless, this relationship is usually only rhetorically invoked (Foss 2003; Pessali 2006) and has seldom been empirically tested directly (David and Han 2004; Tsang 2006; Verbeke and Greidanus 2009).

As discussed in Chapter 3, the lack of empirical tests on the relationship between opportunism and governance structure arises largely from TCE's failure to differentiate between opportunism as a value, opportunism as an attitude, and opportunism as a behavior. We proposed there that opportunism in TCE should be considered as an attitude since treating opportunism as a behavior requires the paradoxical, ex ante observation of ex post opportunism, which is 'state unobservable' (Godfrey and Hill 1995). The dominant concern of TCE is to make provisions for and mitigate against potential ex post opportunistic behavior in the ex ante organizational design (David and Han 2004; Geyskens et al. 2006; Godfrey and Hill 1995; Richter 2005; Rindfleisch and Heide 1997; Williamson 1998). Thus, it is the perceived threat of opportunism that TCE considers in the calculation of ex post transaction cost (Godfrey and Hill 1995), and such perception is largely based on attitude. As such, opportunism should be treated as an attitude, or potential behavior, and governance structure may then be devised accordingly.

We also suggested in Chapter 3 that an institutional approach be taken in order to measure opportunism as an attitude. Economic agents' opportunistic behavior is conditioned by their institutional context (Lubatkin et al. 2007). Collective sanctions of members who violate institutional norms reduce transaction costs by increasing the costs of opportunistic behavior and decreasing the costs of monitoring. Because ethical institutions in a country serve to constrain economic agents' opportunistic behavior (Nooteboom 2004), NEA in host countries will thus reduce opportunistic behavior at the firm level. As such, the relationship between the propensity of opportunistic behavior and high ownership levels can be extended to the relationship between NEA and subsidiary ownership. We thus hypothesize a negative relationship between NEA and subsidiary ownership level.

It should be noted that this relation can stand independent of bounded rationality. Opportunism is a sufficient condition to explain the ownership of assets (Foss 1996a; Foss and Weber 2016a, b) regardless of bounded rationality. In determining ownership levels in the context of this hypothesis, the relevant question is whether opportunism alone can generate transaction costs, not whether bounded rationality is present or not. We developed this hypothesis exactly because traditional TCE seriously conflates bounded rationality and opportunism, and the separate and joint effects of bounded rationality and opportunism were only invoked with no intention to operationalize and model them (Foss 2003; Pessali 2006). In the case of full rationality or total absence of bounded rationality, opportunism as an attitude would be an objective type without being perceptually biased (Weaver and Dickson 1998). Opportunism is 'the rational pursuit by economic actors of their own advantage, with all means at their command, including guile and deceit' (Granovetter 1985: 494). When opportunism is contextualized using NEA, MNCs can objectively differentiate potential opportunists from potential non-opportunists ex ante without affecting their behavior, and assume appropriate ownership levels.[2] This will fully enable us to measure transaction cost *a priori* and generate falsifiable hypotheses (Dow 1987: 18),[3] thus making TCE more scientific and empirically relevant (Aldrich 2015; Popper 1959; Shelanski and Klein 1995).

Hypothesis 1 There will be a negative relationship between national ethical attitude and subsidiary ownership level.

6.1.2 *Cultural Distance and Subsidiary Ownership Level—A Reconceptualization*

While CD is one of the most widely used constructs in international business (Zaheer et al. 2012), and the subsidiary ownership literature in particular (Zhao et al. 2004), it is also one of the most confusing, both theoretically and empirically. Theoretically, due to the serious conflation of opportunism, bounded rationality, and uncertainty in TCE (see Chapter 2), CD has been incorrectly used as a proxy for opportunism and uncertainty (see Endnote 10 of Chapter 3). Empirically, in spite of an extensive literature about the relationship between CD and subsidiary ownership level/entry mode, multiple meta-review papers have consistently documented the inconclusiveness of this relationship (e.g., Beugelsdijk et al. 2018; Kirkman et al. 2006; Magnusson et al. 2008; Morschett et al. 2010; Tihanyi et al. 2005; Zhao et al. 2004), even though a positive relationship appears to be the empirical regularity.

While various reasons have been suggested, including that 'cultural distance is not central to transaction cost economics' (Dikova and Brouthers 2009), this book suggests, to the contrary, that CD is central to TCE. We argue that it is misguided to focus on the effect of CD on ownership since CD is only a measure of cognitive bounds, as discussed in Chapter 4. It is the positivist fixation on partial event regularities instead of mechanisms that shifted scholarly attention to CD itself rather than CD as a cognitive device vis-à-vis various uncertainties of varying levels of controllability. Cognitive bounds itself do not have a consistent relationship with ownership levels because it is used by *manas* vis-à-vis different contingencies which activate different generative mechanisms and consequently have competing effects on ownership levels, as discussed in Chapter 5. Hence, the inconclusiveness in the literature is not a surprise but a logical outcome which is consistent with CR. The failed struggle to find a consistent relationship between CD and ownership vividly demonstrates TCE's positivist limitations of focusing on partial event regularity in the empirical domain, through which it is unlikely to identify and explain the various (potentially opposing) generative mechanisms in the real domain of CR due to TCE's ontological shallowness (Downward et al. 2002).

While the purpose of science is to identify and explain the generative mechanisms in the real domain rather than to make empirical predictions about events regularities in the empirical domain (Downward et al. 2002: 495), it is still desirable to account for the event regularity which *prima facie* shows a positive relationship between CD and ownership level or high control mode, despite the inconclusiveness of this relationship. But a hypothesis about such empirical regularity should not be argued in a way similar to those adopted in the literature because they conflate CD with opportunism and uncertainty. In addition, most arguments used to argue for a certain relationship based on TCE can be readily used to argue for the opposite relationship based on ROT, as shown in the two-sided, assumption-symmetrical behavioral framework presented in Chapter 5. As such, we cannot develop a hypothesis using arguments in line with the existing literature. We can arrive at a pair of competing hypotheses, though.

Since the empirical regularity of the positive relationship between CD and ownership level is consistent with behavior in a gain frame and thus TCE, the relationship has to be justified by finding what causes MNCs to have a gain frame in most of cases, considering multiple factors which may determine frame formation. Further, we cannot use uncertainty controllability as the determinant of frame formation as discussed in Subsection 5.2.3, since the current hypothesis has to be independent of uncertainty (opportunism) to avoid conflating CD and uncertainty (opportunism). Instead, the determinant of the gain frame has to be found internally within the economic actor. We suggest that the overall gain frame in the partial empirical regularity found in the literature about the relationship between CD and governance structure is consistent with the fact that loss aversion and gain framing are the norm for most transactions (Hwang and Satchell 2010; Martynov and Schepker 2017), and in international business in particular (Stoiko et al. 2019). In the case of MNC subsidiaries, the decisions to invest in culturally distant countries reflect a gain framing; otherwise MNCs would not invest in culturally distant countries which are not considered attractive investment locales, ceteris paribus (Ambos et al. 2020). This is consistent with the widely accepted view in international business that most MNCs invest abroad to exploit their ownership advantages through dominant strategies rather than to gamble. For example, Dunning (1998) identified four types of foreign direct investment: resource-, market-, efficiency- and strategic asset-seeking. Neither of these types tolerates a gambling mentality. It is because of the ubiquitous loss aversion and gain framing in the business world that TCE gained its status as a dominant theory of the firm. TCE takes the adaptive gains from governance structures as given and regard governance structures as the means to allocate the gains from joint profit-maximizing transactions among transaction parties (Alchian and Woodward 1988; Henisz and Williamson 1999; Hill 1990; Williamson 1985). However, transaction parties are risk-averse under the gain framing because they face uncertainty about the allocation of such adaptive gains due to transaction partners' tendency to engage in self-interested bargaining in the allocation process (Williamson 1985; Riordan and Williamson 1985).

Once the empirically regular gain frame is justified, we can hypothesize a positive relationship between CD and ownership level. It should be emphasized here that the 'hypothesis' is about an 'event regularity', which reflects the overall effect of multiple generative mechanisms, even though TCE rationale may dominate. In essence, the positive relationship reflects the ratio of the number of serious loss-averse investors to that of gamblers; or in other word, it reflects the aggregated effect of two competing hypotheses. As discussed in Chapter 4, CD affects cognitive bounds. Because cultures are an extension of human cognition, they can be considered as information processing mechanisms. Since MNCs cannot readily apply their home country cultural heuristics in culturally distant locales, increasing CD will lead to reduced cognitive bounds or higher processing bounded rationality, thus resulting in increasing information processing costs (Morschett et al. 2010). Because ownership levels that 'make large demands on cognitive competence are relatively disfavored' (Williamson 1985: 46), TCE suggests that higher ownership levels would be more desirable with increasing CD (Erramilli and Rao 1993; Morschett et al. 2010). This is because lower ownership levels would strain MNCs' cognitive capabilities since they have to interact more with the local partner.

In addition to processing bounded rationality, CD also reflects psychological bounded rationality, which coexists with and is proportional to processing bounded rationality (Turner 2007). As is well-known, MNCs have to manage subjectively in culturally remote locales (Erramilli and Rao 1993). In the presence of information asymmetry, boundedly rational economic agents use heuristics instead of optimization rules to process information and make decisions (Kahneman and Tversky 1979; Kahneman et al. 1982; Weber and Mayer 2014). However, such heuristics can cause systematic decision biases, among which the framing bias has been identified as one of the most fundamental (Foss and Weber 2016b; Kahneman and Tversky 1979; Kahneman et al. 1982). According to prospect theory (Kahneman and Tversky 1979; Tversky and Kahneman 1981), how a situation is framed will affect decision-makers' risk behavior. On the one hand, decision-makers show risk aversion when decision outcomes are framed in the positive, for example as a choice between a sure gain and a larger gain which is less certain. On the other hand, decision-makers display risk seeking tendency when decision outcomes are framed in the negative. When faced with a decision between a sure loss and a gamble which could decrease or increase the sure loss, decision-makers prefer the gamble even when its expected value is less than the sure loss.

As mentioned previously, risk aversion and gain framing are the empirical regularity in the real world. Under such circumstances, prospect theory suggests that risk aversion propensity can significantly affect the preferred subsidiary governance structure (Buckley and Strange 2011;

Chiles and McMackin 1996). Specifically, the MNC subsidiary ownership decision can be viewed as a choice between a sure gain (in a competitive mentality) and an uncertain larger gain (in a cooperative mentality) which is less certain since it is dependent on mutual cooperation (Peng and Beamish 2014b). Although it is always in the mutual benefits of transaction parties to increase adaptive gains efficiently (Peng and Beamish 2014b), MNCs may forego some potentially beneficial adaptations (Riordan and Williamson 1985: 368) because they are more sensitive to loss of some initial entitlement in the form of control rights than to foregone gains of not obtaining the alternative entitlement of cooperative gains (Kahneman and Tversky 1984). As such, MNCs will tend to increase their subsidiary ownership levels with increasing psychological bounded rationality, which increases with CD.

It should be noted that the above arguments are strictly for the relationship between CD (and thus bounded rationality) and ownership levels, independent of opportunism. While early TCE literature suggests that bounded rationality would not be a serious problem if opportunism does not exist (Williamson 1979), more recent literature suggests that opportunism is a sufficient but not necessary condition to explain ownership of assets (Foss 1996a, b; Foss and Weber 2016a, b; Hodgson 2004; Love 1995, 2005; Madhok 1996; Martynov and Schepker 2017; Weber and Mayer 2014).[4] In Chapter 2, we also suggested that opportunism is only one out of many controllable uncertainties. As such, the right question to ask in the development of the current hypothesis is not about whether opportunism is present or not, but whether bounded rationality alone can generate transaction costs or not. According to this criterion, TCE should predict higher ownership levels based either on processing bounded rationality or psychological bounded rationality, independent of opportunism.[5] On the one hand, it has long been suggested that, in the absence of opportunism, processing bounded rationality determines the choice of governance mechanisms (Coase 1937; Scott and Davis 2016; Thompson 1967). With increasing CD, realistic risks can arise from misunderstanding and disagreement between honest and ethical partners, resulting in increased transaction costs and thus the need for integration (Alchian and Woodward 1988; Ketokivi and Mahoney 2016). Thus, processing bounded rationality alone can be used in generating falsifiable hypotheses,[6] thus making TCE more scientific and empirically relevant (Aldrich 2015; Popper 1959; Shelanski and Klein 1995).

As for psychological bounded rationality, it can generate considerable transaction cost according to prospect theory (Foss 2004; Foss and Weber 2016b). The perceived risk does not necessarily need to come from concerns for opportunism, since partner opportunism is only one out of many uncertainties which are perceived to be controllable, as we discussed in Chapter 2. The positive relationship between CD and ownership level can be readily explained by an effectuation logic, according to which psychological process comes first. When investing in a foreign location, MNCs simply cannot predict partner motives or even their own intentions and thus will not rely too much on prediction, which necessitates an understanding of uncertainties in the host environment. As such, they will effectuate by making ex ante high commitments within their means (Sarasvathy 2008; Sarasvathy and Simon 2000; see Tables 5.3 and 5.4), and this tendency to assume higher ownership levels will be positively related to CD since it affects the ability of MNCs' ability to predict. The lower the ability to predict, the more likely MNCs will have to effectuate (Sarasvathy 2001, 2008). CD will also determine whether assimilation or contrast bias impacts the effectuation process, as discussed in Sects. 4.11 and 5.3. When CD is high, firms will suffer from contrast bias, which leads to even higher pre-commitment levels. In comparison, firms will assume lower pre-commitment levels in locales with lower CD as a result of assimilation bias. Thus, we propose the following hypothesis.

Hypothesis 2 There will be a positive relationship between cultural distance and subsidiary ownership level [*This hypothesis is about empirical regularity*].

6.1.3 The Interaction Between National Ethical Attitude and Cultural Distance

While TCE *rhetorically* assumes that transaction costs arise from the joint effect of opportunism and bounded rationality (Williamson 1985), it makes no mention of their potential interaction effect (Foss 2004). This is not surprising considering that TCE conflates opportunism and bounded rationality. How can TCE study the joint effect of opportunism and bounded rationality if it is not even clear about how to study their individual effects? Consequently, this interaction effect has been sadly neglected in the empirical research (Dow et al. 2019). Even after the conceptual separation between them, traditional TCE still precludes the potential interaction effect, for two potential reasons. First, opportunism in TCE is ***invoked*** as a value and treated as a ***ceteris paribus*** fixed background condition. Second, bounded rationality in TCE refers only to processing bounded rationality, which implies a main effect only. Fundamentally, the inability for TCE to have a clear say about its own 'assumptions' can be attributed to its positivist entrapment in the empirical domain of CR and a collapsed ontology. The interaction effect can only be argued in the actual domain of CR where opportunism and bounded rationality can be contextualized and bounded rationality can be truly treated as a boundedly rationalizing process which involves satisficing and effectuation. Because this book uses NEA and CD to proxy opportunism and cognitive bounds, the interaction between opportunism and bounded rationality is going to be reflected in the interaction effect between NEA and CD in the actual domain which considers various biases arising from CD. This interaction effect can be argued in multiple ways below.

(1) It can be argued based on the 'framing effect' in prospect theory (Foss 2004) and using an effectuation logic (Sarasvathy 2008), after putting *manas* or psychological processes at the front seat, as we have discussed in Chapter 4. MNCs have to effectuate at the beginning of their investments and/or in a new market since they cannot predict the motives of their partners (Sarasvathy 2008; Sarasvathy and Simon 2000); and in the case of controllable uncertainties, they effectuate by making ex ante high commitments (pre-commitments) to deter ex post opportunism, and such effectuation will be biased by CD because CD affects the ability of MNCs making predictions (see Chapters 4 and 5).

In the presence of *manas*, opportunism can be broken into two portions, objective and perceived (Weaver and Dickson 1998). Given varying levels of bounded rationality due to CD, MNCs will effectuate their ownership decisions based on how they *perceive* the potential opportunism of local partners. Here, psychological bounded rationality takes effect. Because MNCs have a gain frame when investing in culturally distant locales (Ambos et al. 2020), and potential partner opportunism 'provokes the feeling of loss' (Chaserant 2003: 172), decision-makers will display 'opportunism aversion' and become over-protective if the perceived opportunism is high due to high psychological bounded rationality as a result of CD. With increasing bounded rationality, the inability to monitor economic agents becomes a more serious challenge, amplifying the perceptions of threat of opportunism and the psychological need for higher control (Dow et al. 2019). For example, Luo (2007) finds that firms attribute greater opportunism to partners that are culturally distant. Thus, MNCs will assume higher levels of ownership for the same levels of opportunism in host countries where the levels of CD are higher due to higher *perceived* opportunism with increasing bounded rationality. This is to say, CD 'magnifies' the threat of opportunism (Dow et al. 2019). Such a magnifying effect is an interaction.

(2) The aforementioned magnifying effect considered cognitive biases only in a coarse-grained manner. Chapters 4 and 5 have provided more developed and nuanced arguments for the interaction effect, both with regard to opportunism and bounded rationality. We first argue from the opportunism side. Decision-makers are known for biased information processing due to bounded rationality: They tend to underreact to many environmental stimuli until they have to overreact (Jones 2001). Transaction partner opportunistic behavior is one such stimulus (Arıkan 2020). Under the assumption of bounded rationality, economic agents make judgments about and react to potential opportunism not based on stimuli intensity but on how they perceive it (Arıkan 2020). When host country opportunism is perceived to be low, MNCs are likely to underreact to it and assume lower-than-rational ownership levels; however, once opportunism is perceived to be high, MNCs will assume higher-than-rational ownership levels. Such behavior will turn the relationship in Hypothesis 1 clockwise, and the steepness of the slope will increase with CD. Thus, there will be an interaction effect between opportunism and bounded rationality. Second, the interaction effect can also be corroborated by the observation that economic agents behave differently at different levels of bounded rationality. Bounded rationality can be broken down into two regions: a 'simple' region where information asymmetry is negligible and a 'complex' region where information asymmetry is rather significant (Yao and Li 2013). When CD is at low levels, economic agents behave with overconfidence (e.g., O'Grady and Lane 1996). This is because that they perceive that their expertise or experience about the home culture can be applied to culturally closer host countries with ease (Mahajan 1992; Peng 2009). Thus, the effect of opportunism on ownership levels will be dampened. However, as CD increases, information asymmetry becomes significant and risk aversion becomes the dominant concern, and the relationship between opportunism and ownership level will be amplified. As such, there will be an interaction effect between opportunism and

bounded rationality, and such interaction effect may be in the form of a disordinal interaction[7] (Aiken and West 1991: 22).

(3) The interaction effect can further be argued from bounded rationality as an attitude, which can bias information processing (Houston and Fazio 1989). Attitudes affect behavior in two ways: a spontaneous way and a deliberate way (Fazio 1990). When CD is low, MNCs are more likely to maintain and apply their home country habits in an involuntary way. In such a case, organizations tend to evaluate counter-habitual information negatively and are less likely to act on new information (Fazio 1990). As such, MNCs will under-respond to host country opportunism. However, when CD is high, MNCs have to switch to the deliberate mode because their home country-based habits become increasingly irrelevant. However, deliberative processing requires considerable cognitive work. Due to cognitive bounds, strained cognition will result in unproportional psychological bias, which will lead MNCs to over-respond to host country opportunism (Fazio 1990). Based on the multiple arguments above, we hypothesize:

Hypothesis 3 There will be a negative interaction between national ethical attitude and cultural distance on subsidiary ownership level such that the negative relationship between subsidiary ownership level and national ethical attitude will be more salient with increasing cultural distance.

6.1.4 *The Three-Way Interaction Between National Ethical Attitude, Cultural Distance, and Host Country Experience*

The focus of Hypothesis 3 was on how psychological biases distort effectuation in new markets where MNCs cannot predict and thus have to effectuate (Sarasvathy 2008; Sarasvathy and Simon 2000). Thus, the effect of organizational learning on the reduction of psychological biases and on effectuation was not considered. However, since effectuation is affected by both perceived uncertainty and by experience (Harms and Schiele 2012) and the ability of MNCs making predictions will improve with host country experience, how host country experience affects Hypothesis 3 is of interest.

A common critique against TCE is its static nature, which pays insufficient attention to the role of learning on the evolution of firm boundaries (Foss and Klein 2010; Hodgson 2010). Although processing bounded rationality is recognized as a *constraint* (Williamson 1985: 8), how managers may improve their cognitive efficiencies and reduce psychological biases is left unanswered. This shortcoming is not limited to TCE, since 'economics has largely been preoccupied with the results of [...] choice rather than the process of choice' (Simon 1978: 2). However, it is essential to treat 'rationality as process' (Simon 1978) in order to gain more behaviorally realistic understanding of organizational decision-making.

This gap can be filled by bringing in organizational learning. Bounded rationality represents a level of rationality at which firms can learn and *consciously* adapt to external environments (Nonaka et al. 2000). This is because human rationality is not only constrained by limited cognitive capabilities but also by limited decision time (Gigerenzer and Selten 2001; Simon 1956, 1991). Through learning over time, bounded rationality can be reduced. For MNCs, their host country experience is an important measure of learning with regard to their subsidiaries in the host country (Luo 1999; Peng 2009). Because CD and host country experience can be respectively viewed as measures of cognitive bounds and organizational learning, host country experience can reduce the effect of psychological biases arising from CD on subsidiary ownership levels.

The above arguments, however, have not differentiated between processing bounded rationality and psychological bounded rationality, and thus do not necessarily lead to a three-way interaction between NEA, CD, and host country experience if only processing bounded rationality is considered. The reduction in ownership levels due to reduced processing bounded rationality simply implies that the two-way interaction effect in Hypothesis 3 is shifted downward with no change in its pattern. This is because, as previous explained, processing bounded rationality in TCE refers to rationality commonly assumed in neoclassical economics theories, albeit with positive information costs.[8] Because bounded rationality in TCE implies only a main effect in Hypothesis 3, the reduction in processing bounded rationality implies only a main effect in the current hypothesis as well. The reduction of the processing portion of bounded rationality should apply over the whole range of NEA.

We contend that the reduction in psychological bounded rationality and its effect on subsidiary control would be necessary to justify a three-way interaction. As explained in detail in the development of Hypothesis 3, the two-way interaction effect was a result of psychological bounded rationality. Due to psychological bounded rationality as a result of CD,

MNCs have to effectuate by assuming higher ownership levels than necessary to exert control and thus deter ex post partner opportunism in culturally distant locations. In addition, effectuation will be differently biased vis-à-vis various levels of partner opportunism. As such, MNCs' ownership decision deviated from the levels dictated rationally by the external environment. However, such deviation from rationality can be reduced with learning, and the more the deviation is from rationality, the more reduction can be made because learning will drive goal-oriented and adaptive decision-makers to converge on rationality (Jones 1999; Simon 1957). At higher levels of organizational learning, MNCs' ability to making predictions will improve and the need for effectuation will decrease. As such, it is more likely to make ownership decisions based on rational economic considerations. As such, we hypothesize:

Hypothesis 4 There will be three-way interaction between national ethical attitude, cultural distance, and parent firm host country experience on subsidiary ownership level such that the negative interaction effect between national ethical attitude and cultural distance on subsidiary ownership level is more salient when parent firm host country experience is low.

6.2 Date and Measures

A longitudinal dataset was collected from multiple sources in order to conduct analysis of how MNCs adapt to host country environment by dynamically adjusting their subsidiary ownership levels (Shelanski and Klein 1995). Parent firm information was collected from the Nikkei NEEDS tapes. The sources of subsidiary level data are various editions of the Handbook of Japanese Overseas Investments published by Toyo Keizai. Other data sources will be described in the variables subsections. We use the data for the years 1996–2005 because the NEA measure used in this study was developed based on the 1999–2002 World Values Survey data. We chose the 1996–2005 data window because the World Values Surveys happened in the middle of the time period, thus minimizing concerns caused by data mismatch. The final dataset consists of 58,132 observations on 10,687 Japanese affiliates founded in 43 host countries.

6.2.1 *Dependent and Independent Variables*

The dependent variable is the percentage ownership of the Japanese parent in the subsidiary. The independent variables include a cross-national measure of NEA taken from Franke and Nadler (2008: 259) to proxy partner opportunism (Peng 2018; Peng and Beamish 2012), CD to proxy cognitive bounds, and parent firm host country for experience. The NEA measure and CD had been introduced in Sect. 3.5. CD was calculated according to Kogut and Singh (1988) based on data collected from Hofstede's website at http://www.geert-hofstede.com/. Parent firm host country experience was operationalized as the total number of subsidiary years of operation in the host country.

6.2.2 *Control Variables*

A series of control variables were included based on multiple review papers on previous studies (e.g., Canabal and White 2008; Morschett et al. 2010; Tihanyi et al. 2005; Zhao et al. 2004). Seven host country level controls were included. Host country GDP, GDP growth rate, trade ratio, and GDP per capita data were collected from the World Bank's World Development Indicators. Host country risk was measured with the yearly country credit ratings published in *Institutional Investor*. Host country economic freedom was measured using the Index of Economic Freedom published by the Heritage Foundation. FDI legitimacy was measured with the foreign ownership/investment restrictions sub-component of the Economic Freedom of the World Index by the Fraser Institute (Peng 2012).

Parent firm level controls include ROA, R&D intensity, marketing intensity, international experience, host country experience, and parent firm size. Subsidiary level controls include subsidiary size and age, and dummy variables for subsidiary industry. Dummy variables for year were also included. The parent firm's international experience was operationalized as the total number of subsidiary years of operation around the world. R&D and marketing intensity were operationalized as the ratio of R&D and advertising expenses to sales revenues, respectively. Parent firm and subsidiary size was operationalized using the number of parent firm and subsidiary employees, respectively.

The inclusion of the above-mentioned variables was based on various justifications. Host country GDP and GDP growth rate were included to proxy for market size and potential (Chen and Hu 2002; Peng and Beamish 2008). Host country risk (e.g., Hill et al. 1990), economic freedom (Meyer et al. 2009), trade ratio (Peng 2012), and FDI legitimacy (Gomes-Casseres 1989; Peng 2021; Peng and Beamish 2019) were included because they reflect different aspects of the host country institutional environment, which affect transaction costs. Because there are numerous institutional factors and we cannot include all of them in one study, we used GDP per capita as an additional control since it can proxy the overall levels of multifaceted institutional development in host countries (Nafziger 2006: 107). Parent firm size and ROA were included to proxy for its capabilities and profitability (Meyer 2001). Existing studies also routinely control for subsidiary size (Peng and Beamish 2014a) and age (Peng and Beamish 2017; Wilkinson et al. 2008), and we did so accordingly. All the other variables were included because they are frequently used TCE explanatory variables (Zhao et al. 2004). R&D intensity, country risk, international experience, and marketing intensity were used to control for asset specificity, external uncertainty, internal uncertainty, and free-riding potential, respectively (Zhao et al. 2004).

6.3 Method

The cross-sectional time-series dataset used in this study may suffer from within-subject correlation. There are two modeling approaches for addressing such correlated data: population-averaged and subject-specific models (Neuhaus et al. 1991). If interest lies in the average response over the population to changes in the covariates, population-averaged models are most appropriate to assess such between subject effects. In contrast, if interest lies in within-subject comparisons, then subject-specific approaches are most appropriate. We used Liang and Zeger's (1986) method of generalized estimating equation (GEE), which fits population-averaged models. GEE is deemed appropriate because we are interested in estimating the average effect of NEA and CD on subsidiary ownership levels across multiple host countries.

However, subject-specific models may also be used for Hypothesis 4 which involves parent firm host country experiences. It is of interest to study the time course of subsidiary ownership levels for each subsidiary with increasing host country experience, even though GEE results can provide indirect insights into such within-subject relationships. For this purpose, subject-specific models are needed because population-averaged models cannot provide estimates of changes within subjects over time (Neuhaus et al. 1991). While we have the choice of random effects (RE) and fixed effects (FE) subject-specific models, FE models do not allow for the estimation of variables that are constant within unit, such as NEA and CD. As such, we also used RE models in testing our hypotheses.

6.4 Results

Table 6.1 presents the descriptive statistics and correlation matrix of variables. The GEE and RE model results are presented in Table 6.2 and Table 6.3, respectively. Since GEE and RE results are consistent, we report hypothesis test results below based on GEE results.

Hypothesis 1 predicted that there will be a negative relationship between NEA and subsidiary ownership. Hypothesis 2 proposed that there will be a positive relationship between CD and subsidiary ownership. We test them using Model 1 and Model 2 in Table 6.2. Model 1 is the base model with all the control variables. In Model 2, NEA and CD were entered. As suggested by Aiken and West (1991), host country experience was also entered in this main effect model because it is involved in a higher-order three-way interaction effect hypothesized in Hypothesis 4.

The models fit well since the model χ^2 values were significant at the $p < 0.001$. The χ^2 change from Model 1 to Model 2 is significant at $p < 0.001$, indicating that the inclusion of the three terms significantly improved the model. In Model 2, NEA was significant at $p < 0.05$ with a negative sign, supporting Hypothesis 1. CD was significant at $p < 0.001$ with a positive sign, supporting Hypothesis 2.

Hypothesis 3 predicted that the negative relationship between subsidiary ownership level and NEA will be more salient with increasing CD. This hypothesis was tested by entering the interaction term between NEA and CD in Model 3. The interaction effect between CD and host country experience and that between NEA and host country experience was also included because they are involved in a higher-order three-way interaction effect in Hypothesis 4 (Aiken and West 1991).

The models fit well, as the model χ^2 values were significant at the $p < 0.001$. The inclusion of the interaction terms significantly improved the model as the χ^2 change from Model 2 to Model 3 was significant at $p < 0.001$. The interaction term between NEA and CD was significant at $p < 0.05$ with the expected negative sign, supporting Hypothesis 3. We illustrate the interaction effect in Fig. 6.1.

Hypothesis 4 predicted that the interaction effect between NEA and CD on subsidiary ownership is more salient when parent firm host

Table 6.1 Descriptive statistics and correlation matrix

Variable	*Mean*	*SD*	*1*	*2*	*3*	*4*	*5*	*6*	*7*	*8*	*9*	*10*	*11*	*12*	*13*	*14*	*15*	*16*	*17*
1. Ownership level	61.10	40.48																	
2. GDP per capita	17971	13565	.083																
3. Country GDP	12.11	0.69	−.016	.622															
4. GDP growth rate	4.20	3.22	−.059	−.487	−.010														
5. Host country risk	75.19	20.95	.086	.887	.598	−.349													
6. Trade ratio	67.39	77.78	.110	−.044	−.551	−.044	.041												
7. Economic freedom	2.52	0.76	−.120	−.907	−.361	.574	−.861	−.176											
8. FDI legitimacy	2.41	0.87	−.106	−.685	−.100	.631	−.624	−.308	.823										
9. Parent firm ROA	0.01	0.04	.012	.020	.020	−.020	.016	−.031	−.015	−.019									
10. R&D intensity	0.02	0.03	−.034	.050	.050	−.032	.066	−.002	−.039	−.033	.071								
11. Marketing intensity	0.01	0.02	.026	.000	.009	−.006	.017	−.021	.007	.010	.007	.125							
12. International experience	2.37	0.65	−.196	−.039	−.111	−.054	−.044	−.005	.002	−.014	−.081	−.018	−.064						
13. No. parent firm employees	3.53	0.58	−.157	−.023	−.068	−.048	−.026	−.052	.003	−.015	−.006	.132	.075	.600					

(continued)

Table 6.1 (continued)

Variable	*Mean*	*SD*	*1*	*2*	*3*	*4*	*5*	*6*	*7*	*8*	*9*	*10*	*11*	*12*	*13*	*14*	*15*	*16*	*17*
14. No. subsidiary employees	1.61	0.81	−.144	−.279	−.079	.172	−.286	−.060	.303	.255	.020	.079	.042	.103	.204				
15. Subsidiary age	12.16	9.47	.126	.246	.028	−.270	.162	.045	−.269	−.246	−.051	−.004	.016	.167	.059	.113			
16. CD	3.24	1.20	.075	−.007	−.310	.089	.027	.558	−.086	−.114	−.019	−.026	−.024	−.031	−.039	−.058	−.063		
17. Host country experience	1.43	0.51	−.163	.291	.306	−.070	.232	−.102	−.239	−.126	−.097	−.054	−.057	.660	.368	.060	.328	−.024	
18. NEA	0.13	0.50	−.074	−.422	−.015	.526	−.317	−.067	.500	.439	−.023	−.049	−.010	−.064	−.057	.203	−.248	.087	−.060

Notes (1) Two-tailed Pearson correlation coefficients are reported. (2) In case of missing values, cases are excluded list wise. (3) $n = 58{,}132$ list wise. (4) Correlations more than 0.008 or less than −0.008 are significant at 5% level or lower; other correlations are not significant. (5) Dummies are not included. (6) Country GDP, numbers of parent and subsidiary employees, and parent firm international experience and host country experience are in logarithm

Source Author's own creation

Table 6.2 Generalized estimating equation (GEE) regression results

Variable	*Model 1*		*Model 2*		*Model 3*		*Model 4*	
	Coefficient	*SE*	*Coefficient*	*SE*	*Coefficient*	*SE*	*Coefficient*	*SE*
GDP per capita	−0.000	0.000	0.000*	0.000	0.000†	0.000	0.000	0.000
Country GDP	−0.146**	0.944	3.697***	1.021	3.291**	1.025	2.937**	1.032
GDP growth rate	0.046	0.029	0.006	0.030	0.005	0.030	0.006	0.030
Host country risk	0.008	0.025	−0.003	0.025	−0.018	0.025	−0.012	0.026
Trade ratio	0.046***	0.006	0.046***	0.006	0.048***	0.007	0.045***	0.007
Economic freedom	−1.997**	0.646	−2.292***	0.650	−1.922**	0.656	−1.815**	0.657
FDI legitimacy	0.348	0.253	0.515*	0.254	0.466†	0.255	0.435†	0.256
ROA	−1.490	1.594	−1.620	1.594	−1.602	1.595	−1.581	1.595
R&D intensity	−42.838***	6.405	−44.283***	6.399	−44.358***	6.399	−44.389***	6.400
Marketing intensity	30.207**	10.753	30.192**	10.728	30.073**	10.726	29.901**	10.726
International experience	−9.411***	0.535	−5.456***	0.660	−5.569***	0.660	−5.534***	0.660
No. of parent firm employees	−2.553***	0.636	−2.624***	0.633	−2.657***	0.633	−2.655***	0.633

(continued)

Table 6.2 (continued)

Variable	*Model 1*		*Model 2*		*Model 3*		*Model 4*	
	Coefficient	*SE*	*Coefficient*	*SE*	*Coefficient*	*SE*	*Coefficient*	*SE*
No. of subsidiary employees	−1.849***	0.282	−1.722***	0.282	−1.713***	0.283	−1.724***	0.283
Subsidiary age	0.366***	0.035	0.471***	0.036	0.483***	0.036	0.477***	0.036
CD (B)			2.105***	0.464	1.256*	0.586	1.460*	0.590
Host country experience (C)			−3.876***	0.379	−3.902***	0.384	−3.917***	0.384
NEA (A)			−1.042*	0.439	−1.240**	0.450	−1.105*	0.452
A × B					−1.403*	0.558	−1.260*	0.559
A × C					0.895***	0.249	1.076***	0.256
B × C					−0.140	0.308	0.497	0.371
A × B × C							1.141**	0.371
Wald χ^2	1039.48***		1177.90***		1200.91***		1211.44***	
Change in Wald χ^2			138.42***		23.01***		10.53**	

Notes [a]Dummies for industry and year are included in all models but not presented in the table. [b]$N = 8916$ subsidiaries; 53,765 observations. [c]$^{\dagger}p < 0.1$; $^{*}p < 0.05$; $^{**}p < 0.01$; $^{***}p < 0.001$

Source Author's own creation

Table 6.3 Random effects (RE) regression results

Variable	*Model 1a*		*Model 2a*		*Model 3a*		*Model 4a*	
	Coefficient	*SE*	*Coefficient*	*SE*	*Coefficient*	*SE*	*Coefficient*	*SE*
GDP per capita	−0.000	0.000	−0.000†	0.000	0.000	0.000	−0.000	0.000
Country GDP	0.384	0.807	3.630***	0.892	2.846**	0.911	2.613**	0.913
GDP growth rate	0.075*	0.036	0.056	0.036	0.053	0.036	0.049	0.036
Host country risk	−0.099***	0.020	−0.106***	0.020	−0.115***	0.021	−0.105***	0.021
Trade ratio	0.052***	0.005	0.049***	0.005	0.052***	0.006	0.049***	0.006
Economic freedom	−2.344***	0.620	−2.516***	0.633	−1.926**	0.647	−1.622*	0.651
FDI legitimacy	1.725***	0.208	1.784***	0.212	1.625***	0.221	1.510***	0.223
ROA	2.898	2.064	2.761	2.065	2.794	2.065	2.844	2.064
R&D intensity	−30.397***	5.972	-31.282***	5.968	−32.510***	5.967	−31.680***	5.966
Marketing intensity	15.562†	8.454	16.086†	8.445	16.167†	8.444	16.096†	8.443
International experience	−9.890***	0.475	−7.698***	0.586	−7.785***	0.585	−7.735***	0.586
No. of parent firm employees	−1.594**	0.584	−1.630**	0.582	−1.689**	0.582	−1.695**	0.582

(continued)

Table 6.3 (continued)

Variable	*Model 1a*		*Model 2a*		*Model 3a*		*Model 4a*	
	Coefficient	*SE*	*Coefficient*	*SE*	*Coefficient*	*SE*	*Coefficient*	*SE*
No. of subsidiary employees	−1.888***	0.264	−1.757***	0.264	−1.727***	0.265	−1.758***	0.265
Subsidiary age	0.356***	0.033	0.415***	0.034	0.423***	0.034	0.418***	0.034
CD (B)			2.519***	0.434	0.943†	0.543	1.156*	0.546
Host country experience (C)			−2.119***	0.328	−2.257***	0.334	−2.269***	0.334
NEA (A)			−1.441***	0.416	−1.838***	0.426	−1.722***	0.427
A × B					−2.617***	0.519	−2.467***	0.520
A × C					0.665***	0.201	0.877***	0.207
B × C					−0.441†	0.258	0.182	0.300
A × B × C							1.213***	0.296
Wald χ^2	1271.73***		1366.23***		1409.66***		1426.68***	
Change in Wald χ^2			94.5***		43.43***		17.02**	

Notes [a]Dummies for industry and year are included in all models but not presented in the table. [b]N = 10,687 subsidiaries; 58,132 observations. [c]†p < 0.1; *p < 0.05; **p < 0.01; ***p < 0.001

Source Author's own creation

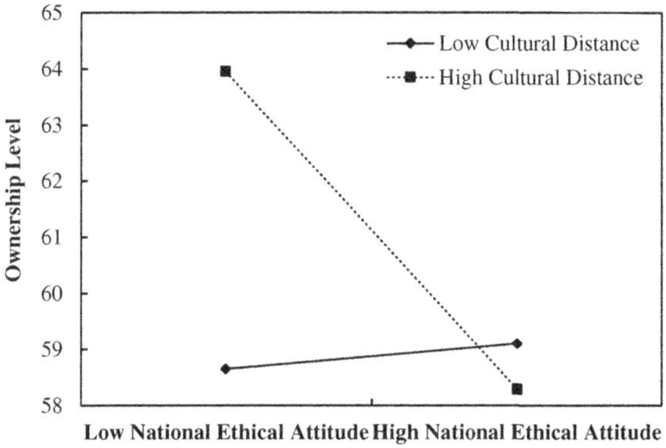

Fig. 6.1 The interaction effect between national ethical attitude and cultural distance (*Source* Author's own creation)

country experience is low. This hypothesis was tested by entering the three-way interaction term between NEA, CD, and parent firm host country experience in Model 4. The model fits well, as the model χ^2 values were significant at the $p < 0.001$ level. The three-way interaction term in Model 4 was significant at $p < 0.01$ level with the expected positive sign, supporting Hypothesis 4. The three-way interaction effect is shown in Figs. 6.2 and 6.3, which are respectively for the cases of low and high host country experience.

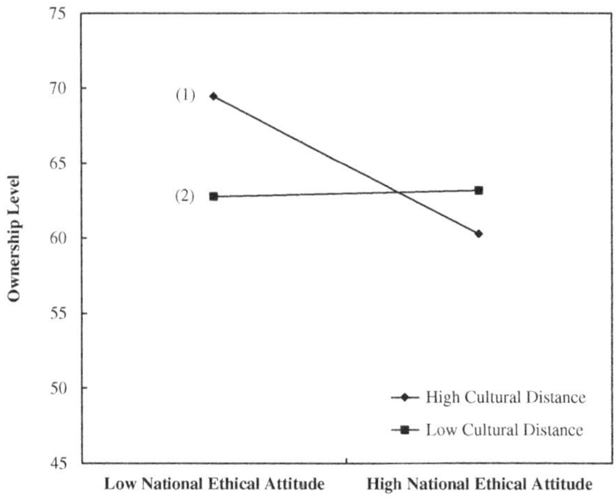

Fig. 6.2 The three-way interaction effect between national ethical attitude, cultural distance, and host country experience: Low host country experience (*Source* Author's own creation)

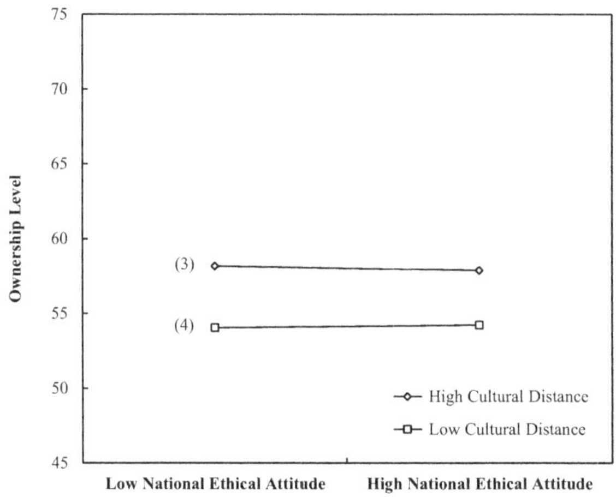

Fig. 6.3 The three-way interaction effect between national ethical attitude, cultural distance, and host country experience: High host country experience (*Source* Author's own creation)

NOTES

1. We refrain from testing both behavioral TCE and behavioral ROT sides in one study for lack of adequate measures for uncontrollable uncertainties across multiple host countries. Such uncertainties are often measured in perceptual terms using questionnaires regarding the unpredictability of demand, technology, or competition, among others (Leiblein 2003; Sutcliffe and Zaheer 1998). We chose to focus on the behavioral TCE side because it is the theme of the book. Nevertheless, all the relationships tested in this chapter are valid, except for Hypothesis 2, which is a 'hypothesis' on event regularity and by definition cannot be falsified (see Sect. 5.5).
2. Because opportunism is treated as an attitude and measured at the institutional level, ex ante differentiation of *potential* opportunists from *potential* non-opportunists implies that the behavior of economic agents (i.e., opportunism as a behavior) is not changed by observation and remains 'state unobservable'. As such, ex ante differentiation of opportunism as an attitude would not vitiate the explanatory power of TCE (Godfrey and Hill 1995). In other words, what matters is whether the behavior of economic agents is affected by observation, not whether it is observed ex ante or not. In fact, even if opportunism *as a behavior* were observable (and observed) ex ante, the explanatory power of TCE would still not be affected if such behavior had not been changed by observation. While Godfrey and Hill (1995) are concerned that if opportunism were observable ex ante, then comprehensive contingent contract could be specified, and there would exist little justification for hierarchy; comprehensive contingent contract will incur considerable transaction costs, and consequently hierarchy may still be preferred (cf. Endnote 6 below).
3. Dow (1987: 18) points out that 'in comparing costs across governance structures, it is essential that the relevant transaction be specified independently of the governance structure which is superimposed on it. Otherwise, the claim that "transaction X is organized under governance structure Y" would express not an empirical truth, but only a concealed tautology. If the attributes of a transaction do not remain invariant when one governance structure is replaced by another, the transaction costs involved are meaningless'. This is to say that transaction costs have to be specified ex ante.
4. Interestingly, bounded rationality is independent of the assumption of opportunism of economic agents in resource-based view (Gancarczyk 2016).
5. Broadly speaking, it can be argued that contextual factors such as social structure in place in advance of the transaction could influence firm

boundary and governance structures independent of uncertainty (e.g., Granovetter 1985; Huitink 2017).

6. Slater and Spencer (2000: 66) comment that 'were it not for cognitive limits, ubiquitous market contracting could continue'. But as explained in Endnote 2, hierarchy may still be preferred since market contracting may incur considerable costs.
7. In a disordinal interaction, the regression line that regresses Y onto the continuous predictor X for one group (or for a given level of the moderator, such as +1 SD) intersects with the corresponding regression line for the other group (or for a different level of the moderator, such as −1 SD). This is the case for Hypotheses 3 and 4, as shown in Figs. 6.1 and 6.2.
8. See Endnote 15 in Chapter 1.

References

Aiken, L. S., & West, S. G. (1991). *Multiple regression: Testing and interpreting interactions*. Newbury Park, CA: Sage.

Alchian, A. A., & Woodward, S. (1988). The firm is dead. *Journal of Economic Literature, 26*(1), 65–79.

Aldrich, H. E. (2015). Dimly through a fog. In A. Fayolle & P. Riot (Eds.), *Rethinking entrepreneurship* (pp. 12–27). London: Routledge.

Ambos, T. C., Cesinger, B., Eggers, F., & Kraus, S. (2020). How does deglobalization affect location decisions? *Global Strategy Journal, 10*(1), 210–236.

Arıkan, A. T. (2020). Opportunism is in the eye of the beholder. *Journal of Business Ethics, 161*, 573–589.

Beugelsdijk, S., Kostova, T., Kunst, V. E., Spadafora, E., & van Essen, M. (2018). Cultural distance and firm internationalization. *Journal of Management, 44*(1), 89–130.

Buckley, P. J., & Strange, R. (2011). The governance of the multinational enterprise. *Journal of Management Studies, 48*(2), 460–470.

Canabal, A., & White, G. O. (2008). Entry mode research. *International Business Review, 17*(3), 267–284.

Chaserant, C. (2003). Cooperation, contracts and social networks. *Journal of Management and Governance, 7*(2), 163–186.

Chen, H., & Hu, M. Y. (2002). An analysis of determinants of entry mode and its impact on performance. *International Business Review, 11*(2), 193–210.

Chiles, T. H., & McMackin, J. F. (1996). Integrating variable risk preferences, trust, and transaction cost economics. *Academy of Management Review, 21*(1), 73–99.

Coase, R. H. (1937). The nature of the firm. *Economica, 4*(16), 386–405.

David, R. J., & Han, S. (2004). A systematic assessment of the empirical support for transaction cost economics. *Strategic Management Journal, 25*(1), 39–58.

Dikova, D., & Brouthers, K. D. (2009). Establishment mode choice. In M. Kotabe & K. Helsen (Eds.), *SAGE Handbook of International Marketing* (pp. 218–237). London: Sage.

Dow, D., Baack, D., & Parente, R. (2019). The role of psychic distance in entry mode decisions. *Global Strategy Journal, 10*(2), 309–334.

Dow, G. K. (1987). The function of authority in transaction cost economics. *Journal of Economic Behavior & Organization, 8*(1), 13–38.

Downward, P., Finch, J. H., & Ramsay, J. (2002). Critical realism, empirical methods and inference. *Cambridge Journal of Economics, 26*(4), 481–500.

Dunning, J. H. (1998). Location and the multinational enterprise. *Journal of International Business Studies, 29*(1), 45–66.

Erramilli, M. K., & Rao, C. P. (1993). Service firms' international entry-mode choice. *Journal of Marketing, 57*(3), 19–38.

Fazio, R. H. (1990). Multiple processes by which attitudes guide behavior. *Advances in Experimental Social Psychology, 23*, 75–109.

Foss, N. J. (1996a). Knowledge-based approaches to the theory of the firm. *Organization Science, 7*(5), 470–476.

Foss, N. J. (1996b). More critical comments on knowledge-based theories of the firm. *Organization Science, 7*(5), 519–523.

Foss, N. J. (2003). The rhetorical dimensions of bounded rationality. In Rizzello S (Ed.), *Cognitive developments in economics* (pp. 158–176). London: Routledge.

Foss, N. J. (2004). Cognition and motivation in the theory of the firm. *Journal Des Economistes et Des Etudes Humaines, 14*(1), 79–100.

Foss, N. J., & Klein, P. G. (2010). Critiques of transaction cost economics. In P. G. Klein & M. Sykuta (Eds.), *The Elgar companion to transaction cost economics* (pp. 263–272). Northampton, MA: Edward Elgar.

Foss, N. J., & Weber, L. (2016a). Expand bounded rationality. *Academy of Management Review, 41*(4), 741–744.

Foss, N. J., & Weber, L. (2016b). Moving opportunism to the back seat. *Academy of Management Review, 41*(1), 61–79.

Franke, G. R., & Nadler, S. S. (2008). Culture, economic development, and national ethical attitudes. *Journal of Business Research, 61*(3), 254–264.

Gancarczyk, M. (2016). The integrated resource-based and transaction cost approach to the growth process of firms. *Journal of Organizational Change Management, 29*(7), 1189–1216.

Geyskens, I., Steenkamp, J. B. E. M., & Kumar, N. (2006). Make, buy, or ally. *Academy of Management Journal, 49*(3), 519–543.

Gigerenzer, G., & Selten, R. (2001). *Bounded rationality*. Cambridge, MA: MIT Press.

Godfrey, P. C., & Hill, C. W. L. (1995). The problem of unobservables in strategic management research. *Strategic Management Journal, 16*(7), 519–533.

Gomes-Casseres, B. (1989). Ownership structures of foreign subsidiaries. *Journal of Economic Behavior & Organization, 11*(1), 1–25.

Granovetter, M. (1985). Economic action and social structure. *American Journal of Sociology, 91*(3), 481–510.

Harms, R., & Schiele, H. (2012). Antecedents and consequences of effectuation and causation in the international new venture creation process. *Journal of International Entrepreneurship, 10*(2), 95–116.

Henisz, W. J., & Williamson, O. E. (1999). Comparative economic organization. *Business and Politics, 1*(3), 261–277.

Hill, C. W. L. (1990). Cooperation, opportunism, and the invisible hand. *Academy of Management Review, 15*(3), 500–513.

Hill, C. W. L., Hwang, P., & Kim, W. C. (1990). An eclectic theory of the choice of international entry mode. *Strategic Management Journal, 11*(2), 117–128.

Hodgson, G. M. (2004). Opportunism is not the only reason why firms exist. *Industrial and Corporate Change, 13*(2), 401–418.

Hodgson, G. M. (2010). Limits of transaction cost analysis. In P. G. Klein & M. Sykuta (Eds.), *The Elgar companion to transaction cost economics* (pp. 297–306). Northampton, MA: Edward Elgar.

Houston, D. A., & Fazio, R. H. (1989). Biased processing as a function of attitude accessibility. *Social Cognition, 7*(1), 51–66.

Huitink, Z. S. (2017). *Three essays on public procurement*. Dissertations - ALL. 698. https://surface.syr.edu/etd/698.

Hwang, S., & Satchell, S. E. (2010). How loss averse are investors in financial markets? *Journal of Banking & Finance, 34*(10), 2425–2438.

Jones, B. D. (1999). Bounded rationality. *Annual Review of Political Science, 2*(1), 297–321.

Jones, B. D. (2001). *Politics and the architecture of choice*. Chicago: University of Chicago Press.

Kahneman, D., Slovic, P., & Tversky, A. (1982). *Judgment under uncertainty*. New York: Cambridge University Press.

Kahneman, D., & Tversky, A. (1979). Prospect theory. *Econometrica, 47*(2), 263–291.

Kahneman, D., & Tversky, A. (1984). Choices, values, and frames. *American Psychologist, 39*(4), 341–350.

Ketokivi, M., & Mahoney, J. T. (2016). Transaction cost economics as a constructive stakeholder theory. *Academy of Management Learning & Education, 15*(1), 123–138.

Kirkman, B. L., Lowe, K. B., & Gibson, C. B. (2006). A quarter century of culture's consequences. *Journal of International Business Studies, 37*(3), 285–320.

Kogut, B., & Singh, H. (1988). The effect of national culture on the choice of entry mode. *Journal of International Business Studies, 19*(3), 411–432.

Kogut, B., & Zander, U. (1993). Knowledge of the firm and the evolutionary theory of the multinational corporation. *Journal of International Business Studies, 24*(4), 625–645.

Leiblein, M. J. (2003). The choice of organizational governance form and performance. *Journal of Management, 29*(6), 937–961.

Liang, K., & Zeger, S. (1986). Longitudinal data analysis using generalized linear models. *Biometrika, 73*(1), 13–22.

Love, J. H. (1995). Knowledge, market failure and the multinational enterprise. *Journal of International Business Studies, 26*(2), 399–407.

Love, J. H. (2005). On the opportunism-independent theory of the firm. *Cambridge Journal of Economics, 29*(3), 381–397.

Lubatkin, M., Lane, P., Collin, S., & Very, P. (2007). An embeddedness framing of governance and opportunism. *Journal of Organization Behavior, 28*(1), 43–58.

Luo, Y. (1999). Time-based experience and international expansion. *Journal of Management Studies, 36*(4), 505–534.

Luo, Y. (2007). An integrated anti-opportunism system in international exchange. *Journal of International Business Studies, 38*(6), 855–877.

Madhok, A. (1996). The organization of economic activity. *Organization Science, 7*(5), 577–590.

Magnusson, P., Baack, D. W., Zdravkovic, S., Staub, K. M., & Amine, L. S. (2008). Meta-analysis of cultural differences. *International Business Review, 17*(5), 520–532.

Mahajan, J. (1992). The overconfidence effect in marketing management predictions. *Journal of Marketing Research, 29*(3), 329–342.

Martynov, A., & Schepker, D. J. (2017). Risk preferences and asset ownership. *Managerial and Decision Economics, 38*(2), 125–143.

Meyer, K. E. (2001). Institutions, transaction costs, and entry mode choice in Eastern Europe. *Journal of International Business Studies, 32*(2), 357–367.

Meyer, K. E., Estrin, S., Bhaumik, S. K., & Peng, M. W. (2009). Institutions, resources, and entry strategies in emerging economies. *Strategic Management Journal, 30*(1), 61–80.

Morschett, D., Schramm-Klein, H., & Swoboda, B. (2010). Decades of research on market entry modes. *Journal of International Management, 16*(1), 60–77.

Nafziger, E. W. (2006). *Economic development*. Cambridge: Cambridge University Press.

Neuhaus, J. M., Kalbfleisch, J. D., & Hauck, W. W. (1991). A comparison of cluster-specific and population-averaged approaches for analyzing correlated binary data. *International Statistical Review, 59*(1), 25–35.

Nonaka, I., Toyama, R., & Nagata, A. (2000). A firm as a knowledge-creating entity. *Industrial and Corporate Change, 9*(1), 1–20.

Nooteboom, B. (2004). Governance and competence. *Cambridge Journal of Economics, 28*(4), 505–525.

O'Grady, S., & Lane, H. W. (1996). The psychic distance paradox. *Journal of International Business Studies, 27*(2), 309–333.

Peng, G. Z. (2009). *Multinational corporations' international experience and subsidiary performance: Learning, knowledge transfer, and dynamic capability perspectives* (Unpublished doctoral dissertation), Western University.

Peng, G. Z. (2012). FDI legitimacy and MNC subsidiary control: From legitimation to competition. *Journal of International Management, 18*(2), 115–131.

Peng, G. Z. (2018). *The Effects of opportunism and bounded rationality on MNC subsidiary ownership: Institutional and psychological perspectives*. AIBSEAR Conference Proceedings.

Peng, G. Z. (2021). *Subnational FDI legitimacy and MNC subsidiary location strategy: Organizational ecology and identity perspectives*. Xi'an, China: IACMR Conference.

Peng, G. Z., & Beamish, P. W. (2008). The effect of national corporate responsibility environment on Japanese foreign direct investment. *Journal of Business Ethics, 80*(4), 677–695.

Peng, G. Z., & Beamish, P. W. (2012). *The effect of national ethical environment on subsidiary ownership: Transaction cost and learning perspectives*. Academy of Management Annual Meeting, Boston, MA.

Peng, G. Z., & Beamish, P. W. (2014a). MNC subsidiary size and expatriate control. *Journal of World Business, 49*(1), 51–62.

Peng, G. Z., & Beamish, P. W. (2014b). The effect of host country long term orientation on subsidiary ownership and survival. *Asia Pacific Journal of Management, 31*(2), 423–453.

Peng, G. Z., & Beamish, P. W. (2017). Age dependence in MNC subsidiary mortality: the inverted S-curve hypothesis. In *Proceedings of the 2017 Academy of International Business Southeast Asia Regional Conference*.

Peng, G. Z., & Beamish, P. W. (2019). Subnational FDI legitimacy and foreign subsidiary survival. *Journal of International Management, 25*(3): Article 100662.

Pessali, H. F. (2006). The rhetoric of Oliver Williamson's transaction cost economics. *Journal of Institutional Economics, 2*(1), 45–65.

Popper, K. R. (1959). *The Logic of scientific discovery*. New York: Harper Zorch Books.

Richter, R. (2005). The new institutional economics. *European Business Organization Law Review, 6*(2), 161–200.
Rindfleisch, A., & Heide, J. B. (1997). Transaction cost analysis. *Journal of Marketing, 61*(4), 30–54.
Riordan, M. H., & Williamson, O. E. (1985). Asset specificity and economic organization. *International Journal of Industrial Organization, 3*(4), 365–378.
Sarasvathy, S. D. (2001). Causation and effectuation. *Academy of Management Review, 26*(2), 243–263.
Sarasvathy, S. D. (2008). *Effectuation: Elements of entrepreneurial expertise.* Cheltenham: Edward Elgar.
Sarasvathy, S. D., & Simon, H. A. (2000). *Effectuation, near-decomposability, and the creation and growth of entrepreneurial firms.* Paper presented at the first annual research policy technology entrepreneurship conference, University of Maryland.
Scott, W. R., & Davis, G. F. (2016). *Organizations and organizing.* New York: Routledge.
Shelanski, H. A., & Klein, P. G. (1995). Empirical research in transaction cost economics. *Journal of Law Economics and Organization, 11*(2), 335–361.
Simon, H. A. (1956). Rational choice and the structure of the environment. *Psychological Review, 63*(2), 129–138.
Simon, H. A. (1957). *Models of man.* New York: Wiley.
Simon, H. A. (1978). Rationality as process and as product of thought. *American Economic Review, 68*(2), 1–16.
Simon, H. A. (1991). Bounded rationality and organizational learning. *Organization Science, 2*(1), 125–134.
Slater, G., & Spencer, D. A. (2000). The uncertain foundations of transaction costs economics. *Journal of Economic Issues, 34*(1), 61–87.
Stoiko, M., Egan, T., & Duane, A. 2019. Entrepreneurial internationalization takes the effectuation turn. *SSRN* 3453813.
Sutcliffe, K. M., & Zaheer, A. (1998). Uncertainty in the transaction environment. *Strategic Management Journal, 19*(1), 1–23.
Thompson, J. D. (1967). *Organizations in action.* New York: McGraw-Hill.
Tihanyi, L., Griffith, D. A., & Russell, C. J. (2005). The effect of cultural distance on entry mode choice, international diversification, and MNE performance. *Journal of International Business Studies, 36*(3), 270–283.
Tsang, E. W. K. (2006). Behavioral assumptions and theory development. *Strategic Management Journal, 27*(11), 999–1011.
Turner, J. H. (2007). *Human emotions.* New York: Routledge.
Tversky, A., & Kahneman, D. (1981). The framing of decisions and the psychology of choice. *Science, 211*(4481), 453–458.

Verbeke, A. (2003). The evolutionary view of the MNE and the future of internalization theory. *Journal of International Business Studies, 34*(6), 498–504.

Verbeke, A., & Greidanus, N. S. (2009). The end of the opportunism vs. trust debate. *Journal of International Business Studies, 40*(9), 1471–1495.

Weaver, K. M., & Dickson, P. H. (1998). Outcome quality of small- to medium-sized enterprise-based alliances. *Journal of Business Venturing, 13*(6), 505–522.

Weber, L., & Mayer, K. (2014). Transaction cost economics and the cognitive perspective. *Academy of Management Review, 39*(3), 344–363.

Wilkinson, T. J., Peng, G. Z., Brouthers, L. E., & Beamish, P. W. (2008). The diminishing effect of cultural distance on subsidiary control. *Journal of International Management, 14*(2), 93–107.

Williamson, O. E. (1975). *Markets and hierarchies*. New York: Free Press.

Williamson, O. E. (1979). Transaction-cost economics. *Journal of Law and Economics, 22*(2), 233–261.

Williamson, O. E. (1985). *The economic institutions of capitalism*. New York: Free Press.

Williamson, O. E. (1998). Transaction cost economics. *De Economist, 146*(1), 23–58.

Yao, J., & Li, D. (2013). Bounded rationality as a source of loss aversion and optimism. *Journal of Economic Dynamics and Control, 37*(1), 18–31.

Zaheer, S., Schomaker, M. S., & Nachum, L. (2012). Distance without direction. *Journal of International Business Studies, 43*(1), 18–27.

Zhao, H., Luo, Y., & Suh, T. (2004). Transaction cost determinants and ownership-based entry mode choice. *Journal of International Business Studies, 35*(6), 524–544.

CHAPTER 7

Implications, Future Directions, and Conclusion

7.1 A Bird's-Eye View of the Concepts Used in the Book

Considering the many concepts used in this book, it is helpful to get a bird's-eye view of them to facilitate clearer presentation and understanding of this chapter. Since the major lacunas in the existing theories arise from conflating distinct strata in critical realism (CR), we map the various concepts into the three CR domains in Table 7.1, even though sometimes the fit is not perfect. Please note that the relationship between the three domains is hierarchical, not antithetical, and it is a conceptual error to conflate them (Archer 1995).

7.2 Theoretical Implications for Transaction Cost Economics

Adopting a critical realist (CR) position, this book aims to render transaction cost economic (TCE) behavioral by making it *genuinely* 'self-conscious about its behavioral assumptions' (Williamson 1985: 387). This is achieved by disaggregating the black box of the 'self' along the ontological depth of CR, center-staging the subject of human behavior (i.e., *manas*), and thus foregrounding psychological processes. Once the traditional TCE is freed out of the positivist straitjacket, it can have clear

G. Z. Peng, *Toward Behavioral Transaction Cost Economics*,
International Marketing and Management Research,
https://doi.org/10.1007/978-3-030-46878-1_7

Table 7.1 Mapping various concepts into critical realism domains

Chapter(s)	*Real domain*	*Actual domain*	*Empirical domain*
2	Critical realism	Pragmatism/constructivism	Positivism
2	Open system	Open system	Closed system
2, 4	Judgmental rationality	Fallibilist epistemology (epistemological relativism)	Fallibilist ontology (ontological realism)
2	Stratified ontology	Stratified ontology	Collapsed ontology
2	Generative mechanisms: • Mechanisms governing phenomena in open systems	Events: • Phenomena in open systems (may or may not be experienced)	Experiences: • Experienced phenomena in close system
2, 5	Competing mechanism: • Pre-commitment/risk aversion • Affordable loss/risk tolerance	Contingent conditions: • Uncertainty controllability • Cultural distance (CD)	Event regularities
2, 5, 7	Assumptional symmetry	→Assumptional symmetry	Assumptional asymmetry
2	Transfactual/transsituational/transphenomenal mechanisms	Situation-dependent propensities	Objectified probability
2, 7	Ontological unification	→Ontological unification	Derivational unification
2	Retroduction	Abduction	Deduction

Chapter(s)	*Real domain*	*Actual domain*	*Empirical domain*
2	Judgment	Effectuation + Actualization	Causation/prediction
2	Ontological uncertainty	Nonergodic uncertainty/change (subjectivized or psychologized)	Ergodic uncertainty/complexity (objectivized)
3	Values	Attitude	Behavior
3	Opportunism as value	Opportunism as attitude	Opportunism as behavior
3	Bounded rationality as value	Bounded rationality as attitude	Bounded rationality as behavior
3, 7	Etic	Dialectic (etic × emic)	Emic
4	Self	Mind	Brain
4	Volition	Emotion	Cognition
4	*Alaya* (The eighth consciousness)	*Manas* (The seventh consciousness)	Cognitive consciousness/cognition (The sixth consciousness)
1, 4, 7	Consciousness of self-consciousness	Self-conscious (self-consciousness)	Not self-conscious (Self-unconscious)
2, 3, 4	Dispositional	Propositional	Propositional

(continued)

Table 7.1 (continued)

Chapter(s)	*Real domain*	*Actual domain*	*Empirical domain*
4, 7	Meta-rationality/Judgmental rationality	Procedural rationality/Ecological rationality	Substantive rationality
4, 7	Entrepreneurial temperaments	Managerial services (*manas*-centric)	Resources (cognition-centric)
7	n.a.	Bounded rationality in the driver's seat	Opportunism in the driver's seat
1, 7	n.a.	Firm as an explanans	Firm as an explanandum
1, 4, 7	Storehouse of potentialized capabilities	Learning is paramount/capabilities are actualized	No learning

Chapter(s)	*Real domain*	*Actual domain*	*Empirical domain*
3, 4, 7	n.a.	• CD as part of mechanism (black box opened) • Creative inductive and assumption-symmetrical mechanisms with CD as a cognitive element susceptible to psychological biases • CD is objective and symmetrical, but emic differences at the two ends of CD can create uneven psychological perceptions about the same objective CD • CD as opportunity/the upside of CD	• CD as black box • Positivist/deductive relationship between CD and outcome variable • CD as a liability/the downside of CD
7	n.a.	Psychological market imperfection	Cognitive market imperfection
7	n.a.	→Blending internalization with externalization, specialization with diversification: • Country-specific advantages (internalized + externalized) • Subsidiary-specific advantages (internalized + externalized)	• **Exploitation of ex ante advantages** • Exploration of ex post new advantages

(continued)

Table 7.1 (continued)

Chapter(s)	*Real domain*	*Actual domain*	*Empirical domain*
7	(R) Relationship logics = **(I)** Internalization logic + (E) Externalization logic	**(L)** Location	**(O)** Ownership orientation • **Exploitation** • Exploration
5	**Prospect theory**	**Effectuation theory**	**Transaction cost economics (TCE)** Real options theory (ROT)
	↳	↓	↵
5, 7		**Behavioral TCE** (behavioral ROT) **Behavioral OLI** + behavioral OLE = Behavioral OLR **'Transaction value economics'**	

Source Author's own creation

generative mechanisms in the real domain and be integrated with effectuation theory in the actual domain of CR, and as a result, be turned into a behavioral theory. The behavioral approach adopted in this book has significant theoretical implications and contributions both for TCE in general and for international business in particular. We present them separately in Sects. 7.2 and 7.3, but with the understanding that they complement each other and the separation is only for convenience of discussion. Please note that there are quite a few of them because this book aspires to radically revise and overhaul the traditional TCE into a behavioral theory.

For TCE, this study shows that psychology has to be moved to the front seat in order to become more behaviorally realistic. This is consistent with the view that 'greater psychological realism will improve mainstream economics' (Rabin 2002: 657). However, in order to foreground psychology, the ontology of TCE has to be deepened and attention should be focused on the actual and real domains of CR. It is in the actual domain that firms can get out of the positivist pitfall, effectuate to cope with various uncertainties by actualizing various generative mechanisms in the real domain, and learn to adapt in a genuinely behavioral manner. The adoption of a CR worldview has the following implications and contributions to TCE for it to become behavioral.

1. A behavioral theory of the firm is a theory of human fallibility. It can be said that rationality is not compatible with a behavioral theory. In order for TCE to become behavioral, it must first be genuinely engaged with human fallibility and bounded rationality. For this to happen, TCE has to climb out of the empirical domain and embrace the actual domain. A behavioral theory cannot operate in the former wherein uncertainty is reduced to deterministic complexity (Liesch et al. 2011; Spender 2018), human epistemology is reduced to a non-necessity, and the human economic agent 'becomes a "zero"' (Foss 1994: 53). Under such circumstances, organizations have no room to 'behave'. It is in the actual domain that boundedly rational economic agents can 'behave' as a fallible decision-makers vis-à-vis perceived uncertainty based on procedural rationality/ecological rationality rather than substantive rationality (see Subsect. 4.5.1).

   The center-staging and prioritization of bounded rationality are of paramount significance for a behavioral theory. While it has been suggested that economic organization can be considered as arising from the need to 'economize on bounded rationality' or 'on mind as a scarce resource' (Williamson 1999: 1090), the collapsed ontology, the confusion of cognitive bounds with psychological rationalizing, and the conflation of the brain and the mind in traditional TCE prevented it from genuinely foregrounding bounded rationality. As such, TCE only did lip service to the central role of bounded rationality in its theorizing and empirical testing. In a broader sense, even Williamson' (1999) ceremonial adoption of bounded rationality has not been shared widely in economics. Simon (1979) had long pointed out that bounded rationality had limited impact on economics. Two decades later, Nobel laureate Reinhard Selten (1998) remarked that the situation had not changed much (Pessali 2006). Even within new institutional economics, of which TCE is a strand, objection to bounded rationality can be found: 'I do not think that bounded rationality is necessary for a theory of organizations', says Oliver Hart (1990: 700–701). On the contrary, this book suggests that bounded rationality has to be whole-heartedly accepted in a theory of the firm for it to be behaviorally realistic. Bounded rationality is downplayed by some (e.g., Hart 1990) exactly because traditional research in the broader new institutional economics has been done using equilibrium analysis instead of behavioral process analysis, as discussed in Chapter 1. In this book, the center-staging of bounded rationality was made possible after the conceptual separation of opportunism and bounded rationality, as discussed in Point 8 below. After the conceptual separation, we tested their separate and joint effects on subsidiary ownership, and the results shed light on an important debate in TCE and international business, which is concerned with the relative importance of bounded rationality and opportunism. We discuss this point in detail in Subsect. 7.3.1.

2. A behavioral theory is a theory of uncertainty rather than of opportunism as an abstract value. For TCE to become a behavioral theory, it has to shift its attention to uncertainty, which pervades managerial decision-making and is the true concern for behavioral theories (Argote and Greve 2007; Cyert and March 1963). It has long been suggested that the existence of uncertainty (and incomplete information) forms the foundation of behavioral analysis (Alchian 1950; Manne and Zywicki 2014). It is uncertainty

that *constrains* but 'does not destroy the basis of' (Alchian 1950: 221) firms' ability to predict and induces firms to effectuate. A theory that does not explicitly incorporate uncertainty would never be behaviorally realistic because it is impossible to understand how managers actually make decisions in real situations absent a clear conceptualization of uncertainty (Alvarez et al. 2018). Being a positivist theory of the firm which is stuck in the empirical domain, TCE fails to focus on uncertainty but instead has focused on complexity and information asymmetry (Alvarez et al. 2018; Spender 2018). By adopting CR, our behavioral TCE framework refocuses TCE's attention on uncertainty.

3. A behavioral theory is a *self-conscious* theory. The stratified, deep ontology of CR helped the opening up of the black box of the 'self' and the consequent disaggregation of the brain, the mind, and the self, which are located in the empirical, the actual, and the real domains, respectively. Only after such disaggregation can bounded rationality in TCE be treated as a process and an integral part of firm behavior. Thus, CR provides the ontological depth necessary for a self-conscious behavioral theory to unfold and operate. Our behavioral TCE contributes to make TCE 'more self-conscious about its behavioral assumptions' (Williamson 1985: 387).
4. The conceptual disaggregation of the self based on the eight-consciousness model, which is consistent with CR, made a significant contribution to modeling bounded rationality as a rationalizing process in which *manas* applies cognition in effectuation. While bounded rationality is regarded as a fundamental behavioral assumption across a wide spectrum of academic fields (Foss and Weber 2016b), how to model it remains a challenge. The conceptual separation of cognition and 'rationalizing' enable us to model bounded rationality as a process in a clear and sensible manner.
5. The conceptual separation of cognition from 'rationalizing' also enables us to find an easy measure for cognition or cognitive bounds, which contributes to the modeling of bounded rationality as process as mentioned above. While human cognitive bounds (processing capability, cortex, or the sixth consciousness) do exist, we have no way of measuring it in an accessible way even at today's scientific development. But this should not prevent us from modeling bounded rationality if we can find some measures for the changes in cognitive bounds or factors which affect them. Based

on the literature on socially extended cognition, we propose that CD fits the bill for such a measure, particularly considering that CD is an objective measure of cultural dissimilarity, as discussed in Subsect. 7.7.2.4.

Treating CD as a measure of cognitive bounds and applying it in the aforementioned *manas*-centric modeling is an extremely important insight this study provides, and it constitutes a significant contribution. While CD has been widely used in international business literature, it has seldom been explicitly viewed as a measure of cognitive bounds. This has significantly limited theoretical development and empirical testing along the line of bounded rationality, resulting in non-behavioral theories of the firm. In the empirical literature, CD is often inaccurately treated as a source of internal uncertainty and complexity (Beugelsdijk et al. 2018: 97), and its direct effect on governance structures was often *wrongly* treated as the main concern. This practice is in fact a result of the cognition-centric approach taken in the traditional TCE, which blindfolded TCE research by focusing solely on the tool used by *manas* rather than on *manas* itself and the external phenomena. It is also an etic only approach, ignoring the emic influence in the form of *manas*. To use a metaphor, a soldier should focus on spotting enemy activity on the ground using a military telescope rather than on the telescope itself, even though the quality of the telescope matters. This study suggests that a behavioral theory should be psychology-centric and focus how *manas* applies cognition ('the telescope') in coping with uncertainty ('the enemy') in a dynamic process, which can be modeled by the diminishing interaction effects of CD vis-à-vis various uncertainties (controllable ones vs uncontrollable ones). Such interaction effect reflects the diminishing constraining effects of cognitive bounds on governance structures with learning.

6. A behavioral theory also necessitates the consideration of social structures. Due to its shallow ontology, traditional TCE cannot consider social, cultural, and institutional contexts, such as social norms, values, uncertainties, and CD in a 'spatial' sense. As such, it is not genuinely committed to the management of uncertainties and cultural differences, thus failing to become behaviorally realistic. Our behavioral TCE, as a result of its deep ontology in CR, enables a dynamic view toward the interplay between social

structures (social contexts) and agency: Agency presupposes the existence of social structures and social structures can be dynamically affected by agency (Bhaskar 1986). Such social contexts are contingent conditions under which mechanism-expressing events (whether experienced or unexperienced by human agents) are generated. The consideration of such interplay and contingencies in a socio-institutional space is conducive to a behavioral theory of the firm.

7. The stratified ontology of CR also helps us to address the theoretical confusion surrounding TCE's opportunism and bounded rationality assumptions. Due to its positivist position, TCE lacked ontological depth to truly consider opportunism and bounded rationality in a behavioral way that necessitates an actual domain for these assumptions to operate. Traditional TCE conflated different CR domains and committed a conceptual error in its treatment of opportunism and bounded rationality (Archer 1995). As a result of its confused conceptualization of its most fundamental assumptions, TCE was not able to deal with them and the TCE literature has only invoked them in theorization. Such a conflation caused some prestigious scholars to believe that TCE has conflated 'opportunism as an attitude' and 'opportunism as a behavior' (Ghoshal and Moran 1996; Lubatkin et al. 2007; Verbeke and Greidanus 2009).

   By adopting CR and articulating the link between CR and the value-attitude-behavior (VAB) hierarchy, this study suggests that TCE in fact conflates values in the real domain with attitudes in the actual domain in its treatment of opportunism and bounded rationality. Because TCE is concerned with opportunism as an attitude or potential behavior rather than as a behavior which is a purely ex post phenomenon and cannot be observed until it has happened, bounded rationality and opportunism should be dealt with at the attitude level. Because attitudes are institutions (Busemeyer et al. 2020; North 1990) and because institutions operate in the actual domain (Leca and Naccache 2006), this study proposes that opportunism and bounded rationality be operationalized at an institutional level in order to render traditional TCE into a behavioral theory of organizational decision-making.

8. The adoption of an institutional approach to the operationalization of bounded rationality and opportunism as attitudes constitutes

a contribution to the TCE literature. It not only enables us to achieve the value-to-attitude shift but also turns TCE assumptions into variables and thus contributes to advance of TCE (Ketokivi and Mahoney 2016). The ability to measure the two variables as attitudes is conducive to the theoretical separation of the two TCE 'behavioral' assumptions and making them truly behavioral. It has been pointed out that TCE lacks institutional contextualization (Langlois 1989) and its opportunism and bounded rationality assumptions (i.e., as abstract values) are not amenable to measurement if not contextualized (e.g., Verbeke and Greidanus 2009). Due in part to measurement difficulty, TCE rhetorically conflates opportunism and bounded rationality with no intention to operationalize and model them (Foss 2003a; Pessali 2006). Our approach not only enables us to eliminate the conflation but also aids in the conceptual separation of them. A conceptually independent bounded rationality enables the conceptual separation of cognitive bounds and psychological rationalizing and the social expansion of cognitive bounds, thus facilitates the subsequent integration of TCE with prospect theory and organizational learning in order to transform TCE into a behavioral TCE.

After the conceptual and operational separation of opportunism and bounded rationality, we directly tested the opportunism and bounded rationality assumptions of TCE by using NEA and CD as proxies for opportunism and bounded rationality as attitudes, respectively. This is a significant contribution to the TCE since the two fundamental assumptions of TCE were only ***invoked*** but not tested in the literature, causing potentially inefficient subsidiary governance and leaving potentially significant residual variance in subsidiary ownership unexplained by failing to consider the variations in opportunistic propensity and bounded rationality between individuals and across cultures. In addition, our empirical results shed light on the relative importance of bounded rationality and opportunism, which has been a hot issue in TCE in general and in international business in particular. We discuss this point in detail in Subsect. 7.3.1 when we discuss the theoretical implications of our empirical findings in the settings of international business.

9. A behavioral theory is a theory of learning. Due to its focus on substantive rationality and deterministic complexity, traditional TCE is not able to link with learning in a behavioral sense. The

so-called learning in traditional TCE is in fact information acquisition at a cost. By being genuinely engaged with human fallibility and bounded rationality, our behavioral TCE framework genuinely opens up the possibility for firms to make initial biased decisions and then learn to reduce biases. In fact, the 'holy trinity' of CR (Bhaskar 2010; see Sect. 2.7) is conducive to organizational learning. While firms may be biased in the initial stage of effectuation due to fallible ontology and epistemology, the existence of judgmental rationality means that they will learn through interaction with social structure in the actual domain.

10. The foregrounding of bounded rationality and the consequent linking of it to learning also bring behavioral TCE close to an evolutionary theory of the firm (Nelson and Winter 1982), which builds upon Cyert and March's (1963) behavioralist notions (Foss 2003b; Williamson 1999). The 'organizational capabilities approach',[1] including the evolutionary theory of the firm (Foss 2003b; Williamson 1999), attaches significant importance to incomplete contracting and learning, both of which can be attributed to bounded rationality (Williamson 1999), particularly the adaptive aspect of it.

    This point needs to be understood by considering bounded rationality as an ecological rationality, as discussed in Subsect. 4.5.1. According to ecological rationality, decision procedures or heuristics are not irrational or rational per se; rather, their rationality is determined by the environment through their fit with the structure of the information in the environment under judgmental rationality. This is the view of the evolutionary theory of the firm, which regards organizational decision-making process as a set of interdependent routines that are adaptive to performance feedback (Nelson and Winter 1982). In other words, the evolutionary theory of the firm regards adaptation of an organization to its environment as the efficient exploitation of the structure of the information in the environment. Evolutionary pressures of the marketplace select firms most fit for survival, which are often those best at constraining their behavioral biases and thus more efficient in exploiting the environment (Manne and Zywicki 2014).

11. A behavioral TCE is a theory that centers on distance, and thus an internationalization-friendly theory. This is an important insight

into the relationships between TCE and some internationalization-related theories, such as the ownership-location-internalization (OLI)/eclectic paradigm, as we explain in Sects. 7.3 and 7.4. Particularly, *in international contexts*, the behavioral TCE largely becomes a *behavioral* OLI considering the central role of CD and other types of distance, which reflect cognitive bounds. In other words, the behavioral TCE and the OLI *enhanced with* psychological biases and Penrose learning (Penrose 1959) converge toward each other and become indistinguishable in international business settings. While the application of both traditional TCE and Hymer (1976)-type monopolistic advantage theory has been criticized for failing to distinguish between intra-country and international expansion (Penrose 1987), the establishment of our *behavioral* TCE makes this distinction less relevant since the intra-country application of the behavioral TCE differs from international application only in terms of types of distances. For example, technological distance may be a distance which can arise in a domestic setting and is not necessarily correlated with geographic distance in the OLI sense. Thus, the intra- and cross-country applications of the behavioral TCE are unified based on the concept of distance, which is a multidimensional concept, and the behavioral TCE subsumes the OLI and internalization theory. The focus should be on whether a certain type of distance challenges cognition and gives rise to biases rather than on whether it distinguishes between intra- and cross-country applications.

12. A behavioral theory of the firm is a theory of transaction value. The transaction value theory (Child et al. 2019; Peng and Beamish 2014; Zajac and Olsen 1993) reflects aspects of both TCE (or more accurately, effectuation-based TCE; see last paragraph in this point) and the resource-based view. The former focuses on cost minimization of governing a transaction while assuming that the revenue stream of a combination of assets will be constant across governance forms, while the latter emphasizes maximizing rents to the bundle of assets in a venture while essentially ignoring transaction cost differentials (Child et al. 2019). The transaction value perspective instead proposes that the real concern of a firm is joint value maximization while considering both cost and value. A governance structure having higher transaction costs can be justified if the added transaction costs increase revenues or values to a

greater degree by creating a unique asset bundle not available to a lower transaction cost approach; and likewise, lower rents might be accepted if they resulted from a much lower cost governance structure that provided a larger expected net value (Child et al. 2019).

The results in Figs. 6.2 and 6.3 vividly demonstrate the transaction value view. While it is generally suggested that in the long run economic agents approximate to rationality and the governance structure will converge on what is consistent with the economic logic of TCE for its clear efficiency-based logic (Buckley and Casson 2009; Narula et al. 2019; Williamson 1991), such a view suffers from several problems: (a) it treats rationality in a traditional economics sense as full rationality, as opposed to more behaviorally realistic ecological rationality; (b) it ignores that the purpose of MNC overseas activities is not merely to minimize transaction costs, but rather to maximize transaction values while not ignoring the cost side of value creation; and (c) the so-called efficiency logic has not been clearly explained about whether it refers to efficiency in reducing cost or creating value. If the former view is correct, then Line 1 in Fig. 6.2 should not have lowered and leveled into Line 3 in Fig. 6.3 since this leads to higher levels of transaction costs by ceding control through lowering ownership levels. Such behavior can only be explained by the transaction value perspective, according to which the MNC chooses higher transaction cost (low control) governance structure in order to increase revenues to an even greater degree by creating a unique asset bundle not available to a lower transaction cost (high control) governance structure. Such unique asset bundle often includes complementary resources of local business partners.

Considering that transaction costs are indeterminate since firms have to effectuate at their beginning stages and that our behavioral TCE implies a transaction value approach, a serious question can be raised about whether TCE was properly named. Indeed, we think that our behavioral TCE should in fact be more fittingly called '*transaction value economics*'. Nevertheless, we stick to the current book title because most scholars are currently domiciled in TCE (Williamson 2008). According to such transaction value economics, the aforementioned so-called clear efficiency-based logic of traditional TCE does not hold water and the supposed rational governance structure dictated by such a logic does not even exist and as such cannot be converged upon. Arguments based on such an untenable logic also unintentionally betrayed the fact that scholars are still trapped in positivism and they treat governance structure as a 'fixed' imaginary explanandum instead of an explanans (see Point 13 below). Our behavioral TCE instead proposes a value-enhancing logic and suggests that what the firm does with its governance structure is not to try to converge on a 'fixed' nonexistent target but to use it as a value-enhancing tool in a value-generating process based on a value-enhancing logic.

13. Consistent with the notion of the evolutionary theory of the firm and a focus on transaction value, the behavioral TCE approach treats the firm (or firm boundaries) as an explanans rather than as an explanandum (Foss 1997; Mäki 2004) or a black box (Pitelis 2007) as in traditional TCE. Point 12 above demonstrates exactly this advantage of behavioral TCE. This point is important since we are going to discuss the fundamental role of Penrose (1959) in internalization theory/the OLI paradigm in Sect. 7.3. Penrosean view of firm growth and the cause of firm growth are consistent with an evolutionary explanation (Foss 1997), which treats the firm as an explanans (Foss 1997), or 'a device for discovering possible uses for resources' (Foss and Grandori 2020: 588). In so doing, the explanandum black box of traditional TCE is opened up and firm boundaries become 'instruments for adaptation' that MNCs can exploit in order to increase their competitiveness and thus evolutionary success.
14. Last but not least, our behavioral approach is based on a clear conceptualization of the main concepts in the traditional TCE. Our behavioral TCE treats opportunism not as an assumption but as one of many potentially controllable uncertainties that MNCs face. It does not treat bounded rationality as an assumption but as a process. As mentioned in Chapter 1 and explained in Chapter 2, *controllable uncertainty* should be treated as an assumption in the traditional TCE, not opportunism. Williamson and the existing TCE literature have almost entirely missed this point. We consider this another major contribution to TCE.

7.3 Theoretical Implications for International Business

In Chapter 1, we hinted at the important implications that our behavior TCE approach holds for international business, considering that internalization theory, the dominant theoretical lens in international business, is believed to be TCE applied in the international business context (Rugman 1986; Verbeke and Greidanus 2009), and that the development of internalization theory parallels that of traditional TCE (Safarian 2003). We also mentioned that such implications could not be fully appreciated without first establishing the behavioral TCE. Now that the behavioral TCE has been fully presented in previous chapters and has been applied in an empirical example, time is ripe for us to discuss the links between the behavioral TCE and internalization theory and international business. We divide the discussion into three subsections. In Subsect. 7.3.1, we discuss the theoretical implications of the empirical findings obtained in Chapter 6 for an important debate in international business, i.e., whether bounded rationality or opportunism should be the management focus for MNCs (Foss and Weber 2016a; Kogut and Zander 1993; Lumineau and Verbeke 2016; Verbeke 2003; Williamson 1985). In this subsection, we also discuss the empirical implications of our approach considering the fact that the extant literature has not been clear about how to model bounded rationality. We suggest that a clear understanding of what CD measures and reflects is fundamental to the empirical modeling of bounded rationality. Additionally, we also include in this subsection some implications which are applicable to TCE in general. These are discussed here because we need to use our empirical findings to make these points clear.

Next, in Subsect. 7.3.2, we clarify the relationships among traditional TCE, internalization theory, and the OLI/eclectic paradigm (Narula et al. 2019), and point out some shortcomings that these theories share. After that, we suggest that our behavioral TCE is a broader framework which can subsume other theories. Subsequently, in Subsect. 7.3.3, we suggest that CR has the potential to contribute significantly to internalization theory and the OLI/eclectic paradigm by ontologizing the components of the OLI paradigm in a deeper ontology and by introducing non-positivist perceptual elements arising from distances into the positivist OLI paradigm and thus turning it into a *behavioral OLI paradigm*. In a CR framework, internalization theory and the

OLI/eclectic paradigm refer to the same process. We submit that the CR perspective holds promises for the rejuvenation and relegitimization of international business research (Poulis and Poulis 2018), which has shown signs of stagnation and decline (Buckley 2002; Delios 2017). These promises result from the recognition of psychological and perceptual aspects of internationalization, on which CR sheds new light.

7.3.1 What Should Be in the Driver's Seat: Bounded Rationality or Opportunism?

While the theoretical implications discussed in Sect. 7.2 are also applicable in international business settings, international business research has its peculiarities, such as the widely studied relationship between CD and governance structure and the debate between whether bounded rationality or opportunism should be the management focus for MNCs. The empirical findings in Chapter 6 shed light on both topics and make manifold contributions to international business literature and to how to model bounded rationality. We enumerate them below.

1. By conceptualizing CD as a measure of cognitive bounds, we answered the call by Aharoni et al. (2011) to test bounded rationality directly in international business settings. This has not been done in the existing literature. Though CD has been sometimes hinted at as a measure of bounded rationality, this notion has seldom been given actual application, largely due to the aggregation of the brain, the mind, and the self and the resulting failure to recognize CD as reflecting cognitive bounds, and the conflation of substantive rationality and procedural rationality. Even worse, some studies have treated CD as a measure for opportunism. Because bounded rationality and opportunism were conflated in TCE (Dietrich 1994; Pessali 2006), and because opportunism is generally not controlled for, there are conflicting findings about the effect of CD in the international business literature (see Subsect. 7.7.2). The use of NEA and CD as respective measures of opportunism and bounded rationality not only helps to clear the theoretical confusion with regard to what CD measures, but may also aid in the achievement of more conclusive findings about the effect of CD. This point becomes clearer in the next paragraph.

2. The joint effect of opportunism and bounded rationality after their theoretical separation further enhances our understanding of the effect of CD on subsidiary control. The results in Fig. 6.1 suggest that the predominant evidence in the literature about the positive relationship between CD and ownership levels is in fact a result of bounded rationality rather than opportunism. Bounded rationality, and psychological bounded rationality in particular, is most suitable at explaining the apparent irrationality in assuming dramatically higher ownership levels in countries with higher CD than in counties with lower CD for the same levels of NEA. Using opportunism alone would not only fail to explain this phenomenon but also lead to misaligned subsidiary governance. Figure 6.1 suggests that bounded rationality rather than opportunism should be the key governance challenge facing MNCs, as suggested by Verbeke (2003). We discuss this point in more detail in Contribution 6 below.
3. This study demonstrates that the foregrounding of psychological bounded rationality serves to make TCE a behavioral theory of organizational decision-making in international business. This is in accordance with hints in international business literature (e.g., Aharoni et al. 2011). Lumineau and Verbeke (2016: 739) suggest that 'giving more substance to the bounded rationality assumption can make the concept more actionable for researchers and practicing managers', and 'an extended bounded rationality concept could potentially contribute to extending the quality of TCE-based reasoning'. Even though TCE suggests that firms economize on transaction costs by aligning transaction characteristics with governance structures in a discriminating way, this economizing goal is often thwarted by psychological bounded rationality. While it was rightly pointed out that 'if economic organization is formidably complex, which it is, and if economic agents are subject to very real cognitive limits, which they are, then failures of alignment will occur routinely' (Williamson 1996: 311), TCE is not explicit about the severity of misaligned governance structures as a result of psychological biases because it considers only processing bounded rationality. Considering decision-making biases due to psychological bounded rationality would significantly increase the validity of ownership studies (Aharoni et al. 2011). [Note that explanation in this paragraph is only provided for argument's sake to be consistent

with international business literature. More accurate explanation can be developed based on Points 12 and 13 in Sect. 7.2. We refrain from repeating the arguments here, but would suggest one thing: the processing bounded rationality concept in the existing international business literature (e.g., Lumineau and Verbeke 2016) may not be conducive to the extension to include psychological bounded rationality; it is more convincing to do it the other way around by foregrounding psychology. After all, it is awkward to extend the 'servant' to include the 'master'].

Our results show that prospect theory may be a particularly useful perspective in studying the effect of psychological bounded rationality on subsidiary ownership. For example, our results in Figs. 6.2 and 6.3 show that, when lacking host country experience, MNCs irrationally overweigh the effect of opportunism when bounded rationality is high, and underweigh the same effect when bounded rationality is low (Line 1), as proposed by prospect theory. In Figs. 6.2 and 6.3, Line 1 and Line 3 would be more parallel to each other should there be no biases caused by psychological bounded rationality. While prospect theory has been suggested to be relevant to ownership research (Ramanathan et al. 1997), it has rarely been used. We hope this study can stimulate more research in this direction since considering decision-making biases would significantly increase the validity of ownership studies (Aharoni et al. 2011).

This study also points to a promising avenue of research using CD from a prospect theory perspective considering that CD contextualizes prospect theory. Because CD, as a measure of cognitive bounds, gives rise to various cognitive biases, how CD moderates prospect theory-based predictions in informing MNC ownership decision-making is of interest. Using CD as a measure of cognitive bounds also has the potential to foster continued interest in CD and further increase its explanatory power in international business research.

4. This study contributes to the TCE-based international business literature by linking bounded rationality to organizational learning, thus explicitly modeling bounded rationality as a process in international business settings, from which Williamson refrained (Foss 2003b). A conceptual focus on MNCs' ability to learn and thus to reduce decision bias due to bounded rationality adds dynamism to TCE (Verbeke and Greidanus 2009) and allows us to develop dynamic models of ownership adaptation (Aharoni et al. 2011). Bounded

rationality in TCE can be reduced by experiential learning, as the effect of CD diminished with organizational learning (Wilkinson et al. 2008). Our results show that firms can reduce their bounded rationality by learning and adapt their governance structures toward a more rational direction consistent with transaction value and ecological rationality arguments. This is in line with Simon's (1978) idea of 'rationality as process'. While it has been long pointed out that 'economics has largely been preoccupied with the results of [...] choice rather than the process of choice' and that it is 'essential to consider choice processes' (Simon 1978: 2), research progress along this line is slow in the TCE and international business literatures.

5. More specifically, our 'process' approach and empirical findings clarify TCE's '*remediableness criterion*', which holds that efficiency is a relative concept in that an existing governance structure is *presumed* to be efficient in the absence of feasible better alternatives (Williamson 1996, 1999). While the existing literature suggests that, due to bounded rationality, firms make inefficient choices which result in a non-equilibrium state and competitive pressures will force firms to adopt a more efficient governance mode and converge on equilibrium (Sampson 2004; Williamson 1985), TCE has not made it clear about on what basis the efficiency of governance structures should be determined. While TCE argues that the comparison of relative efficiency of different governance structures is based on transaction cost (Williamson 1999), this book suggests that the TCE view is incorrect and comparison of governance structures makes sense only when anchored externally to ecological rationality and transaction value in a behavioral process of organizational learning.

   The traditional TCE-based arguments have several fundamental difficulties or contradictions. First, if the criterion is to reduce transaction costs, then firms should gradually increase their ownership levels while biases are being reduced. This is because high control governance structures lead to reduced transaction costs. This is apparently not what our results show. Second, relatedly, a cost-based criterion also implies that the comparison of governance structures is internally focused and is not linked to the external environment, which provides performance feedback and thus ecological rationality. Third, even if external environment can be taken into account, due to the random nature thereof, 'equilibrium contracting' is still at the core of such analysis at each round of comparison. As such, the so-called remediableness criterion does not make much sense in terms of learning. Fourth, if we assume 'remediableness criterion', then it implies that it will result in non-equilibrium states in which transaction costs become indeterminate.

The above difficulties can be traced to Williamson (1985: 46), where he stated that '[e]conomizing on bounded rationality takes two forms. One concerns decision processes and the other involves governance structures'. However, TCE 'is principally concerned...with the economizing consequences of assigning transactions to governance structures in a discriminating way' (1985: 46). This is to say, 'Williamson is interested in making use of bounded rationality for the purpose of developing a theory of discriminating alignment rather than for the purposes of explaining [...] behavior' (Foss 2003b: 253). Nevertheless, if bounded rationalizing process is not explained, then the so-called assigning transactions to governance structures in a discriminating way is not achievable because it is devoid of a process.

Our empirical findings suggest that in order for the 'remediableness criterion' to become something that makes sense, the criterion has to be based on transaction value and ecological rationality. It has to be made explicit that the so-called dynamic models of ownership adaptation mentioned in Point 4 above are geared toward transaction value maximization instead of transaction cost minimization and the so-called rational direction is justified by ecological rationality and evolutionary fit instead of internal obsession with transaction cost reduction. Our approach helps to integrate both the results and the process of the decision-making process and thus deepens 'our understanding of the dynamics of rationality, and of the influences upon choice of [governance] structure within which it takes place' (Simon 1978: 3). Only after the shift in focus from transaction cost to transaction value has been made can learning be seriously taken into TCE so that governance structures can serve as 'instruments for adaptation' (Williamson 1999: 1101; Foss 2003a) rather than a goal in itself.

In short, TCE's 'remediableness criterion' suffers from a fundamental contradiction since the determination of governance structure efficiency has to be based on ecological rationality which necessitates a focus on transaction value and evolutionary fit instead of transaction cost alone. We return to this in Point 9 below. Our empirical findings supported the evolutionary view of the firm, not that of traditional TCE.

6. This study also offers insights into the debate about whether opportunism or bounded rationality is more relevant for MNC subsidiary governance decisions. In TCE, bounded rationality is regarded as a constraint facing economic agents, and the active control of opportunism becomes the key challenge subject to the bounded rationality constraint (Williamson 1975, 1985; Buckley and Chapman 1997). Others differ. Kogut and Zander (1993) dismiss the opportunism concept altogether and focus on MNCs' alleged, superior knowledge combination capabilities. Verbeke (2003) holds the middle ground, suggesting that the reduction of bounded rationality is the key governance challenge facing MNCs, and the control of opportunism, though important, is merely a constraint.

   Our results seem to support Verbeke's view. Contrary to commonly held TCE view, opportunism is not a major concern in most cases as can be seen from the three largely horizontal lines (Lines 2, 3, and 4) in Figs. 6.2 and 6.3. Opportunism is only perceived to be a concern when subsidiaries are located in culturally distance locales where bounded rationality is high and when the parent firms do not have host country experience. Under these circumstances, MNCs make irrational ownership decisions due to bounded rationality (Line 1). Once MNCs accumulate sufficient host country experience and thus become less boundedly rational, opportunism ceases to be a concern as the line becomes level (Line 3).

   Figs. 6.2 and 6.3 show that the reduction of bounded rationality is the key governance challenge facing MNCs regardless of situations. In addition, learning is especially effective in redressing the biases caused by psychological bounded rationality and bringing the biased initial ownership levels (Line 1) closer to the rational levels dictated by the environments based on ecological rationality (Line 3). These figures also show that learning can also reduce the effect of processing bounded rationality, as shown by the overall higher position of Lines 1 and 2 (low learning / host country experience) in comparison with Lines 3 and 4 (high learning / host country experience), respectively. Even when the threat of opportunism is reduced with increased experience as shown in Lines 3 and 4, bounded rationality still constitutes a challenge since there is a gap between the two lines, which reflect the tendency for MNCs to assume high ownership in culturally distant locales because low ownership levels will 'make large demands on cognitive competence' and thus are disfavored (Williamson 1985: 46). Thus, our results empirically corroborate calls to bring bounded rationality to the foreground (Foss and Weber 2016b; Lumineau and Verbeke 2016).

7. Our behavioral approach also serves in part to reconcile the conflicting views about the relationship between CD and subsidiary ownership. On the one hand, CD, as a measure of bounded rationality, can magnify the perceived threat of opportunism, which suggests that MNCs assume higher ownership in culturally distant countries. On the other hand, CD may also increase the need for local assets and knowledge, which encourages MNCs to lower ownership levels (Dow et al. 2019). It is difficult to discriminate between these two effects in the relationship between CD and ownership level if cross-sectional data are used.

   Adopting a longitudinal approach, our results suggest that the dual needs for control and complementary resources and capabilities in the CD-ownership relationship can be pleasingly teased out from a behavioral perspective. While the CD-ownership relationship reflects both needs, they cannot be discerned at one time point because they are always present simultaneously. Due to bounded rationality and the perceived threat of opportunism, the need for control using irrationally higher ownership levels may dominate the need for complementary resources and capabilities in countries with high CD if MNCs lack host country experience there; however, MNCs can focus on acquiring complementary resource and capabilities by reducing ownership levels if they have reduced their bounded rationality after accumulating sufficient host country experience. This implies MNCs adapt their ownership levels and are more likely to reduce their ownership levels based on rational economic considerations with decreasing bounded rationality. Here, again, 'rational' is in the sense of ecological rationality geared toward value creation and evolutionary fit rather than transaction cost minimization. This is in line with some scholars' observation that MNCs tend to start their subsidiaries with high control and subsequently share ownership after the subsidiaries are more established (e.g., Daniels et al. 1976: 403; Wilkinson et al. 2008).

8. Our behavioral approach further contributes to increasing the potential of TCE as 'an empirical success story' (Williamson 1999: 1092) by making opportunism and bounded rationality operational and empirically relevant and by taking a behavioral TCE or transaction value approach. After adopting an institutional approach to opportunism and bounded rationality, they become measurable a priori, thus enabling the generation of falsifiable hypotheses (Aldrich 2015). This is to say, our behavioral approach contributes to making TCE more scientific by increasing its falsifiability and testability (Popper 1959). We believe this is an important contribution since it opens up new avenues for TCE empirical literature. We suggest that future studies can explore falsifiable hypotheses involving the interaction effects between opportunism and bounded rationality as attitudes and other frequently used TCE variables, such as those suggested by Zhao et al. (2004) by introducing perceptual biases arising from CD.
9. Our empirical findings suggest that TCE suffers from another fundamental contradiction regarding whether it is based on equilibrium contracting. As explained in Point 2 of Sect. 1.5, TCE is thought to use 'equilibrium contracting' at its core of theorizing and assume rationality. Nevertheless, its 'remediableness criterion' implies that governance structures can only be determined on a non-equilibrium basis, resulting in inefficient choice of governance structures. If competitive pressures will force firms to adopt more efficient governance structures and converge on equilibrium (Sampson 2004; Williamson 1985), such equilibrium can only be reached based on transaction value and ecological rationality instead of transaction cost and rationality, as discussed in Point 5 above.

   This contradiction arises from that (1) TCE is not a dynamic model and cannot distinguish between the initial stages and the more mature stages of organizational evolution, through which the focus of organizational challenge shifts from transaction cost minimization to transaction value maximization. [here, we use the term 'transaction cost minimization' provisionally for argument's sake. In fact, the so-called minimization is misleading because transaction cost in traditional TCE is indeterminate since firms have to effectuate; cf. Point 12 of Sect. 7.2]; and that (2) at the initial stages organizations have to effectuate and effectuation is incompatible with an equilibrium mentality (Moroz and Hindle 2012).

To address this fundamental contradiction in traditional TCE, a process-based approach which can consider the shifting predominance of transaction costs and transaction values over time is necessary. Our behavioral TCE framework served the purpose.

7.3.2 Transaction Cost Economics and Internalization Theory/OLI Paradigm

Verbeke and Greidanus (2009: 1471–1472) and Rugman (1986) regard internalization theory as TCE thinking applied in the international business context, which relies heavily on Coase's (1937) original analysis of relative costs of internal vs external markets, and parallels to a large extent Williamson's (1975, 1985) development of TCE as a general theory of the firm (Safarian 2003). If so, the legitimacy of internalization theory can be challenged. For example, Penrose (1987) criticized both Coase-type (1937) and Hymer-type (1976) application to the theory of the MNC for failing to distinguish between intra-country and inter-country expansion. As such, the relationships between our behavioral TCE, the traditional TCE, and internalization theory/OLI paradigm need to be clarified for the sake of deliberating their individual legitimacy and merits in the theoretical space, particularly considering the rapid evolution of literature in the past decades. In order to facilitate understanding, we first present the major ideas of Subsects. 7.3.2 and 7.3.3 in Fig. 7.1 and Table 7.2.

7.3.2.1 Relationship Between Traditional TCE and Internalization Theory/OLI Paradigm

As a result of evolving theoretical development, internalization theory is not a monolithic body of knowledge but an amalgam of several 'streams', each of which appeals to the interests of an particular epistemic community (Narula et al. 2019). These streams include that of Buckley and Casson (1976), Hennart (1982), Rugman (1981), and Dunning (1977, 1988, 2000). Among them, the Buckley and Casson and Hennart streams and the initial Rugman (1981) stream rely heavily on traditional TCE, but the Rugman stream gradually built into it explicit considerations of resource characteristics in parallel to developments in the resource-based view, particularly the influence of Penrose (1959). Similar to the Rugman stream, the Dunning stream also merged TCE and Penrosean considerations, but it also brought in location considerations from the angle of neoclassical trade theory (Narula et al. 2019). Here, it is worth noting

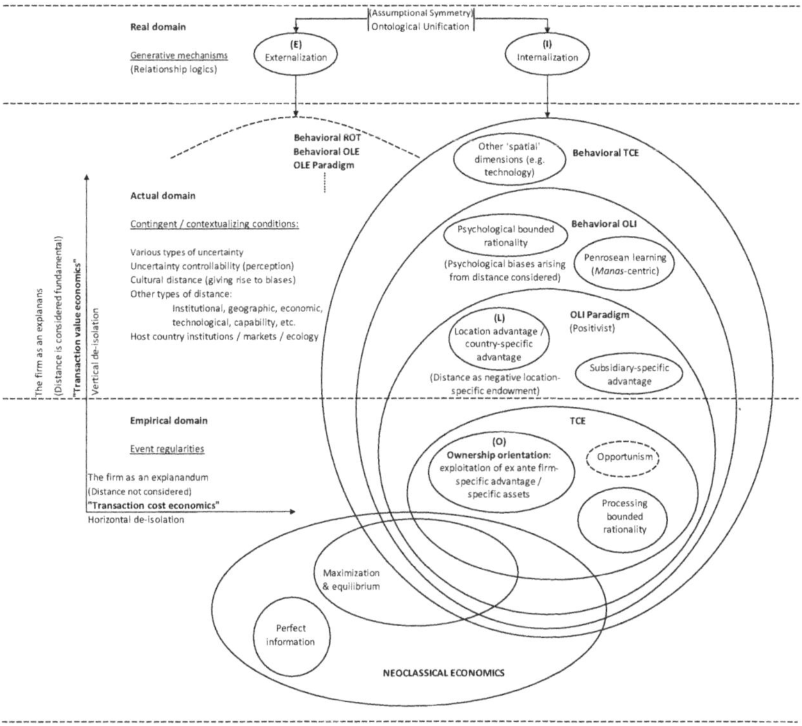

Fig. 7.1 Critical realism-based Venn diagram of relationships among theoretical perspectives (*Notes* [1] In order not to clutter the figure, we only present the behavioral TCE side of the assumption-symmetrical framework in full. Interested reader can easily complete the behavioral ROT side based on *symmetrical* definitions of relevant constructs (Foss and Hallberg 2014). [2] Penrosean learning (Penrose 1959) goes beyond the OLI paradigm by introducing a cognitive (extended to psychological in this book) dimension which is missing from the OLI (e.g., Pitelis 2011; Spender 1994). [3] Opportunism does not have a strong role in internalization theory (Lundan 2010; Verbeke and Greidanus 2009). The current book does not regard opportunism as a necessary assumption in TCE. [4] Behavioral TCE is broader in scope than behavioral OLI since the former can consider distances such as 'technological proximity' or 'distance in technology space' (e.g., Kim and Vonortas 2006), which may not necessarily be related to locations in a geographic sense. [5] For details regarding horizontal and vertical isolation and de-isolation in economic theorizing, reference is made to Mäki (2004). *Source* Author's creation based on modification of Rygh (2013) and other sources cited passim in this book)

Table 7.2 Ontologizing the OLI paradigm/internationalization theory in critical realism

Domain	*Real*	*Actual*	*Empirical*
Mechanisms (I) Internalization logic[1] + externalization logic = Relationship logics • Conscious of competing mechanisms (such as externalization)[2] • Conscious of assumptional symmetry (internalization vs externalization) • Judgmental rationality • Conscious of 'asset orchestration' (Pitelis and Teece 2018) • Etic	✓		
Events (L) Location • Exploration of ex post country-specific advantages/assets; subsidiary-specific advantages/assets • Psychological bounded rationality arising from cultural distance (biases considered) • Fully engaged with uncertainty and contexts • Value focus (transaction value) • Focus on Penrosean knowledge: endogenous knowledge/growth dynamic realized through managerial 'productive opportunity'—the dynamic interaction between internal resources and perceived external/market opportunity (Penrose 1959; Pitelis 2011) • Penrosean learning (Penrose 1959) introduces a cognitive (extended to psychological in this book) dimension which is missing from the OLI paradigm (e.g., Pitelis 2011; Spender 1994) • Decision processes that are 'locally embedded, relationally enacted, and iteratively unfolding' (Poulis and Poulis 2018: 525) • *Manas*-based (capability-centric)/dynamic[3] • Psychological market imperfection[4] • Location advantages have both inter-country and intra-country (location-specific) elements (Pitelis and Verbeke 2007). While the OLI paradigm treats inter-country elements such as cultural distance as negative location-specific endowments (Dunning 1980: 28; Buckley and Casson 1996), it is when they are not treated so that the Penrosean learning can be genuinely considered • Effectuation • Emic × Etic	✓	✓	

(continued)

Table 7.2 (continued)

Domain	*Real*	*Actual*	*Empirical*
Experiences **(O)** Ownership *orientation*: advantages, implying exploitation of ex ante advantages (specific assets in TCE)[(5)] • Firm-specific advantages/assets • Processing bounded rationality (biases not considered) • Not sufficiently engaged with uncertainty • Cost focus (transaction cost) • Focusing on exploiting ex ante internal knowledge and resources • Cognitive consciousness-based (resource-centric)/static[(3)] • Cognitive market imperfection[(4)] • Causation • Emic (Imposed etic/pseudo-etic)	✓	✓	✓

Notes

(1) The OLI components are essentially stated as generative mechanisms or conditions (Boddewyn and Iyer 1999)

(2) One of the weaknesses of the internalization theory/OLI paradigm is its inability to account for externalization (Pitelis and Teece 2018; Kedia and Mukherjee 2009)

(3) Capabilities are the firm's dynamic abilities to apply, learn and augment, and reconfigure knowledge and resources in a way geared toward transaction value rather than transaction cost

(4) Dunning (1981) and Dunning and Rugman (1985) distinguish between structural and cognitive market imperfections. The former arises where there are barriers to competition and rents are earned. Such imperfection may be created ***strategically*** (endogenously) by firms in order to exploit rents on their specific assets (Clegg 1987: 17; italic added). In the latter case, cognitive imperfections arises from information asymmetry and information cost (Dunning 1981). With cognitive imperfections, the firm circumvents exogenous or existing market imperfections (***missing*** or inefficient markets) by creating internal markets (Clegg 1987: 17; italic added). As discussed in detail in Chapter 4, structural and cognitive market imperfections should be respectively referred to as ***cognitive*** and ***psychological*** market imperfections in the context of this book. Please note that while traditional TCE ***invoked*** psychological market imperfection arguments, it was in fact based only on cognitive market imperfection due to its rational treatment of bounded rationality

(5) Asset specificity in TCE and ownership advantage in OLI paradigm are conceptually similar (Wulff 2016). Both of them are often measured using marketing intensity and R&D intensity

Source Author's creation based on Bhaskar (2008: 2)

that the fundamental insights from Penrose (1959) are that endogenous intra-firm knowledge generation through learning generates excess resources which can be put to profitable use and leads to firm growth. While both the Rugman and the Dunning streams are said to have incorporated Penrosean insights, it is doubtful whether this is true considering that both streams suffer from being positivist (Buckley and Casson 2003; Balasubramanyam 1994; Pitelis 2011; Poulis and Poulis 2018). Penrose emphasized the *subjective* element, whereby firm behavior results from an 'image' of the environment in the mind of managers (Boulding 1956), in contrast to much of the later resource-based literature (Clark and Blundel 2007). As such, it is more accurate to say that the two streams have incorporated resource considerations, but may still lack a genuine treatment of Penrosean insights by focusing on the psychological dimension in order to consider cognitive limitations (Pitelis 2011) and psychological biases.

Thus, the relationships among traditional TCE and internalization theory streams are in fact more complicated than what Rugman (1986), Safarian (2003), and Narula et al. (2019) suggested above. While there are still considerable similarities between TCE and internalization theories, it is too simplistic to consider the latter as the former applied in international business settings since how the traditional TCE can be 'applied' in international business has not been clearly articulated (e.g., is it applied in an emic or etic way?). Among the aforementioned streams, those of Buckley and Casson, Hennart, and Rugman are often referred to as internalization theories since they relied heavily on TCE, even though the Rugman stream took in resource considerations. While Narula et al. (2019) subsumed the OLI paradigm under internalization theory, oftentimes the OLI paradigm is treated as different from the rest of the streams, and there has been a long-run debate between Dunning and internalization scholars of other streams as to whether internalization or the OLI paradigm should be viewed as the core theory of international business (Eden and Dai 2010). In other words, it is not clear whether internalization theory should subsume the OLI paradigm or the other way around.

Despite the debate, it seems that the OLI/eclectic paradigm has become the *hegemonic* (Dörrenbächer and Geppert 2017), *preeminent* (Cantwell et al. 2010), *ascendant* (Narula et al. 2019), and dominant (Ferreira et al. 2011) framework in international business. The success of the paradigm can be attributed to several factors. First, it synthesizes the main elements of various explanations of MNC behavior, including internalization reasoning, and thus provides the most comprehensive theory of MNCs. According to this paradigm, MNC behavior is jointly determined by three advantages: *ownership advantages* (firm-specific advantage derived from a firm's own resources and capabilities that is not accessible for other firms, such as proprietary technology, trademarks, product differentiation, and reputation), *location advantages* (host country-specific advantage such as factor endowment and favorable institutions), and *internalization advantage* (arising from transaction cost reduction). Second, it appeals to audience, researchers, and practitioners alike, due to its intuitive *categories of factors* which explain MNC behavior. Third, even internalization scholars have been attempting to reconcile with the paradigm. If internalization theory and the OLI are reconcilable (e.g., Rugman 2010), even if not perfect, such reconcilability will prove a boon to the latter for its appealing features.

Nevertheless, the OLI has been confronted with challenges and difficulties. (1) internalization theory scholars argue that the O-component of the OLI paradigm is superfluous (Rygh 2013). Buckley (1988: 182) points out that 'if internalization is interpreted *dynamically*, the inclusion of ownership advantages is double counting' [italic added]. This criticism is based on the argument that internalizing provides the firm with an owner-specific advantage (Rygh 2013). More accurately, ownership advantages can be viewed as state variables in a dynamic process. Dunning and Lundan (2008: 102–103) agree with Buckley's point but argue that it is still conceptually useful to consider the OLI components separately. But if the OLI components are considered separately, then the question of 'what ownership advantages refer to' arises. In the original OLI framework, ownership advantages refer to firm-specific advantages that firms possessed prior to internalization (Eden and Dai 2010). But some scholars object to this view and argue that some firms might go abroad precisely for the purpose of acquiring potential firm-specific advantages (Mathews 2002). This was later acknowledged in the OLI (Rygh 2013). As such, OLI seems to struggle with how to define its O-component (Eden and Dai 2010). (2) the OLI paradigm is focused upon outward FDI rather than firm-level strategy (Rugman 2010). It also focuses on existing firm-specific assets and largely ignores capability contributions after an internalization decision is made, either through learning or from subsidiaries (Li 2007; Solberg and Askeland 2006). It is also a top-down approach which primarily focuses on headquarters control, transaction cost reduction, and the exploitation of ex ante advantages via internalization, rather than subsidiary capability development, transaction value enhancement, and the exploration of ex post new advantages via externalization or alliance (Li 2007; Solberg and Askeland 2006). (3) because the OLI components are considered separately, the linkage and interaction among the components and the resulting endogenous knowledge/growth dynamic have been given short shrift, and the importance of the MNC as a strategic actor is downplayed (Dunning

2001b; Pitelis 2011). In other words, the OLI model primarily focuses on the state of equilibrium rather than a dynamic process (Li 2007) and is thus not behavioral. It failed to see advantages as a dynamic process of endogenous knowledge generation and thus firm growth. While the OLI paradigm accepts that its components may be interdependent from a dynamic perspective (Dunning and Lundan 2008: 102–103) and 'the value of the eclectic paradigm has increased relative to the sum of its parts, with the contribution of each becoming increasingly interdependent of each other' (Dunning 2000: 167–168), how to make it more consistent with the Penrosean approach remains to be further pursued (Pitelis 2011). (4) relatedly, the relationship between Penrosean endogenous knowledge generation and the O-component is not reconciled. While Penrosean insights into endogenous growth are fundamental to internationalization, 'the Penrosean analysis alone is insufficient to explain firm-level growth' (Pitelis and Verbeke 2007: 143) and ownership advantages such as superior technological know-hows are indispensable to successful international growth. 'Excess' capabilities and the productive services made available through Penrosean learning cannot substitute for ownership advantages (Pitelis and Verbeke 2007: 143). But on the other hand, superior ownership advantages alone do not necessarily lead to optimal internationalization strategies and performance if the possession thereof is not geared toward transaction value, as discussed in Point 12 of Sect. 7.2.[2] The OLI paradigm juxtaposes various distinctive processes or sequential concepts as independent ones, thus blurring their causal links (Li 2007). Furthermore, treating them as independent also implies that the various types of distance and the psychological biases arising from these distances cannot be considered.

7.3.2.2 Distance Unifies Behavioral TCE and OLI Paradigm

Based on what we discussed above, it is clear that the relationships among traditional TCE, internalization theory, and the OLI paradigm are complicated and confusing, and all of them have difficulties incorporating Penrosean insights. We contend that the relationships can be better delineated and Penrosean insights can be better incorporated if the positivist tendency in international business literature is abandoned and a psychological dimension is added to the internalization theory and the OLI paradigm, like what we did in turning traditional TCE into the behavioral TCE. Similar ideas have been expressed in the literature. For example, Pitelis (2011) proposed the addition of a learning-based perspective to the OLI in order to introduce a cognitive (extended to psychological in this book) element which is missing from the OLI.

However, Pitelis was not explicit about the fundamental role of distance in giving rise to psychological biases. Since '[a] theory of MNE...needs to address the impact of distance on the internationalization process' (Pitelis & Verbeke 2007: 143), neglect of psychological biases arising from distance may have limited what Pitelis (2011) intended. We argue the various types of distance, whether correlated or uncorrelated with geographic distance, are the missing links among traditional TCE, internalization theory, and the OLI paradigm. It is also a missing link between these theories and Penrose (1959), which did not deal with locations and thus distances (Pitelis 2011). She only slightly and vaguely hinted at the relevance of 'distance' in the third edition of her 1959 book (Penrose 1995) by claiming that all theories of the MNC need to suitably adapt her ideas and account for the existence of national differences (Pitelis 2011).

Since distance affects cognitive bounds and gives rise to psychological biases, it adds a psychological dimension to the internalization theory and the OLI paradigm, and makes both behavioral. This point can be easily understood if we look back at how we theoretically built the behavioral TCE in this book, and we refrain from repeating the similar arguments for a behavioral internalization theory or behavioral OLI paradigm here. Instead, we explain how distances unify behavioral TCE with internalization theory and the OLI paradigm once they are rendered behavioral after the psychological dimension is taken into account (as shown in Fig. 7.1 and Table 7.2). The distances that we discuss here are correlated with geographic distance since we are concerned here with internationalization. But as to be discussed in Subsect. 7.3.2.3, our behavioral TCE is a broader framework capable of considering all distance types.

First, once distance and the psychological dimension are taken into account, internalization and the OLI paradigm become the same theory of an internationalization process in a dynamic behavioral way. They can also be subsumed under the behavioral TCE as shown in Fig. 7.1. In such a process, both the existing and potential to-be-acquired firm-specific advantages (both country specific and subsidiary specific) can be considered since ownership advantages and country- and/or subsidiary-specific advantages are now viewed as state variables in a dynamic process. In so doing, many concerns about the O-component of the OLI, such as its being superfluous (Rygh 2013) and double counting (Buckley 1988) and its unclear definition (Eden and Dai 2010), can be alleviated. A behavioral internalization theory will necessarily consider locations: It is in the actual domain of the CR that it can become behavioral and the actual domain largely consists of the international dimension for an MNC theory.

Second, the behavioral OLI paradigm reconciles the relationship between Penrosean endogenous knowledge generation and the O-advantages. In a behavioral theory, the two cannot be separated as they are integrated into the same process. The traditional OLI had not linked its components with distance and it adopted an O-advantage- or resource-centric approach where theorizing was conducted in a positivist manner. By foregrounding the importance of distance and by considering the psychological biases arising from distance, the Penrosean endogenous knowledge generation is center-staged, and such an approach is *manas*- or capability-centric, consistent with our behavioral TCE. One of the advantages of the *manas*-centric approach is that it does not ignore the O-component but will necessarily apply the O-component in the behavioral model. In essence, the Penrose effect is a manifestation of a *manas*-centric philosophy, which is naturally akin to organizational learning.

The Penrosean learning along a distance dimension is also consistent with Point 12 of Sect. 7.2. The consideration and exploitation of ownership advantages, location advantages, and subsidiary advantages must be tightly related to Penrosean learning in order to shift from a transaction cost focus to a transaction value focus. In the beginning stages of internationalization, MNCs may be more likely to have transaction cost focus for lack of *manas*-based managerial services and may focus their attention on existing ownership advantages (Vahlne and Johanson 2013). But as managers learn and accumulate excess managerial capabilities, they will be more likely to explore external location advantages and/or augment and develop subsidiary advantages even if such moves will incur higher transaction costs because they are now capable of generating values to a greater degree (Child et al. 2019).

Third, the distance dimension also implies that the traditional TCE logic of internalization is applied in a more contextualized, emic-etic interactive manner. In traditional internalization and OLI, the application of the internalization logic is implemented in a positivist, imposed etic way, and the OLI components are treated as separate categories of factors. While distance was mentioned in the OLI, it was 'treated as a negative location-specific endowment' or a *host country* determinant of FDI (Dunning 1980: 28; Buckley and Casson 1996; Vaccarini et al. 2017). By adopting a *manas*-centric approach and considering distance as a source of psychological biases, the OLI components are integrated in the actual domain of CR and the application of the internalization logic of TCE in international business can be done in an emic-etic dialectic manner. In so doing, the OLI components are not separate categories of factors, but aspects of a process. This opens up opportunities for Penrosean learning and the potential for benefiting from the upside of CD, as discussed in Subsect. 7.6.2.

7.3.2.3 Behavioral TCE Subsumes the OLI Paradigm

Considering the overlapping relationships among various theories as shown in Fig. 7.1, we conclude Subsect. 7.3.2 with a statement that our behavioral TCE subsumes internalization theory and the OLI paradigm, both their positivist version and behavioral version. This is because our behavioral TCE can consider other types of distances, in addition to those correlated with geographic distance or international settings. As we stated previously, a behavioral TCE is a theory that centers on distance, whether related to locations or not. The distance can exist in other 'spaces', such as technological space or capability space. As such, the legitimacy of our behavioral TCE is established in both intra-country and international settings.

7.3.3 Critical Realism Ontologizes OLI and Promises the Rebirth of International Business

The discussion in Subsect. 7.3.2 was based on the actual domain of CR, consistent with what we have done in the establishment of our behavioral TCE. Considering the dominance of the OLI paradigm in international business, we deem that it is important to ontologize the paradigm in CR to realize its full potential by opening up opportunities for it to become behavioral and to entertain competing mechanisms and symmetrical assumptions in the real domain (see Table 7.2). One of the weaknesses of the internalization theory/OLI paradigm is its inability to account for externalization (Pitelis and Teece 2018; Kedia and Mukherjee 2009).

Despite the fact that the OLI paradigm extends traditional TCE and has thus gained a hegemonic status in mainstream international business research (Dörrenbächer and Geppert 2017), it still suffers from symptoms of positivism (Geary and Aguzzoli 2016). In fact, we can say the same to the broader spectrum of international business theories (Poulis and Poulis 2018) and international management research (Jack et al. 2008). For example, Buckley and Casson (2003: 219) suggest that internalization theory 'was distinguished by its strongly positivist stance' and Balasubramanyam (1994: 84–85), in a review paper of several influential international business books, noted that 'in several articles Dunning elucidates the positivist nature of the theories of the [MNC]'. Pitelis and Teece (2018: 529) stated that internalization theories are ill-suited to address bounded rationality-related issues in a behavioral sense 'not least because of its adherence to a rational, positivist, choice-theoretic approach which treats the MNE as an automaton, and an intra-organizational conflict-free zone'. Pitelis (2011: 225) points out that '[e]xtant theories of the MNE are [...] are rather positivist, rationalist and static'. Even though it has been pointed out that 'ontology has been unreasonably sidelined for the sake of epistemological considerations' in international business and a call has been made for attention to 'an ontology that understands MNCs, their environment, or their decisions as emerging from processes that are locally embedded, relationally enacted, and iteratively unfolding' (Poulis and Poulis 2018: 525–526), the power of CR in helping achieve this ontological endeavor was not spelled out.

The limitations of such a positivist stance adopted in internalization theories have been discussed in many recent studies, such as Pitelis (2011) and Pitelis and Teece (2018). Some of these limitations have already been discussed in the previous subsections, and we do not repeat here, but would like to highlight some higher level limitations related to the needs for 'thicker' account of MNC internationalization, including: (1) the need for a better explanation of the choice between internalization and externalization (including offshoring and outsourcing). Over the past 25 years or so, externalization has grown steadily in significance, and it should be seriously integrated into international business theories; (2) the need for 'asset orchestration', which refers to 'the ability to combine selected technologies, individuals, and other resources in new products and processes regardless of location and across organizational boundaries' (Lessard et al. 2016: 214). The assets to be orchestrated can be outside or inside the firm (Lundan 2010), including firm-specific assets, country-specific assets, and subsidiary-specific assets. Some of these assets do not necessarily need to be internalized since firms could maintain control without the burden of ownership through externalization and network. As such, MNCs can internationalize by blending externalization with internalization and diversification with specialization (Pitelis and Teece 2018); and (3) uncertainty and bounded rationality are not well addressed in internalization theories because of their adherence to a positivist, rational, choice-theoretic approach (Pitelis and Teece 2018) and the tendency to treat OLI components as separate categories of factors rather than links of a value-creating process. In order for uncertainty and bounded rationality to be seriously addressed, attention should be paid to contexts within which internalization/externalization and other strategic choices take place and in which the resources and capabilities of MNCs are developed and leveraged (Pitelis and Teece 2018).

In order to address the above-mentioned limitations, we recommend that the internalization theory/OLI paradigm be ontologized in CR, as shown in Table 7.2 and Fig. 7.1. The link between OLI and critical realism comes natural since the OLI components are stated as conditions (Boddewyn and Iyer 1999; Pratten 2009; Rygh 2013), even though in a collapsed ontology where their causal links are blurred. The ontologically-hierarchized OLI offers the following benefits: (1) It contributes to deepen the ontology of the OLI paradigm/internalization theory and make it possible for the paradigm to be aware of alternative generative mechanisms such as externalization, and to allow for asset orchestration based on judgmental rationality in the choice between competing generative mechanisms. (2) A deeper ontology enables a shift away from treating various types of distance as negative location-specific endowments (Dunning 1980: 28; Buckley and Casson 1996) to treating them as inter-country elements (Pitelis and Verbeke 2007), which challenge cognition, give rise to psychological biases, and thus bring genuine behavioral consideration into the calculus of internationalization. (3) It will greatly facilitate the integration of Penrosean learning into internalization theories, which often claim the former as one of their important features (Narula et al. 2019). But, without a domain for the Penrosean effect to take place and without considering the subjective dimension, whether the internalization theories have incorporated Penrosean learning is a big question mark (Clark and Blundel 2007). It is in the actual domain of CR that the dynamics of psychological biases, judgmental rationality, and environmental selection mechanisms interact with each other and thus can be integrated into a behavioral process (Clark and Blundel 2007).[3] (4) It clarifies the aforementioned debate about relationship between internalization theory and the OLI paradigm regarding which should be the core theory of international business (Eden and Dai 2010). Table 7.2 suggests that the debate arises from a shallow ontology (Poulis and Poulis 2018) and positivism (Balasubramanyam 1994; Buckley and Casson 2003; Pitelis 2011) adopted in the mainstream international business literature. Once ontologized in a CR way, they converge and become the same behavioral theory of a dynamic internationalization process. (5) Similar to the case of traditional TCE, the deepening of ontology, particularly the considering of competing mechanisms in the real domain of CR, offers an opportunity to check the assumptional symmetry and to improve the definition of constructs in the OLI (see Sects. 2.12 and 5.5). Once competing mechanisms are considered (i.e., internalization vs externalization), then it becomes apparent that the definition of the O-component needs to be improved, as pointed out by Eden and Dai (2010) and Lundan (2010). Our assumption-symmetrical analysis shows that the term ownership advantage should be avoided because the construct is one-sided, implying the exploitation of ex ante advantages and precluding the possibility of exploring ex post new assets via alliances (Li 2007). A symmetrical term is preferred and we suggest the use of 'ownership orientation', which can accommodate both exploitation and exploration mentalities. As is well-known, a firm can benefit from assets without owning them by maintaining control through networks (Pfeffer and Salancik 1978; Pitelis and Teece 2018). Similarly, we also suggest that terms like country-specific advantages and subsidiary-specific advantages be used in an assumption-symmetrical sense, capable of being either internalized or externalized. (6) The opening up of the actual domain of CR and the placing of the L-component of the OLI therein also facilitate the proper consideration of uncertainty and bounded rationality after the abandonment of the positivist approach adopted in the original OLI (Pitelis and Teece 2018).

To conclude this subsection, we would comment about the potential of assumptional symmetry and ontological unification (Foss and Hallberg 2014) in advancing the OLI paradigm and internalization theories. While the need for considering externalization has been suggested in more recent literature (Kedia and Mukherjee 2009; Lundan 2010; Pitelis and Teece 2018; Li 2007), some of these literatures swung to the opposite end of the pendulum by focusing on externalization. The ontological unification along the ontological depth of CR was not achieved. For example, Kedia and Mukherjee (2009) proposed a disintegration–location–externalization framework, whereas Li (2007) suggested a linkage–leverage–learning framework (Li 2007). The former framework seems to struggle with coming up with a better term than disintegration since the meanings of disintegration and externalization may overlap; and both frameworks seem to have paid insufficient attention to ontological unification through symmetrical assumptions. While Lundan (2010: 57) suggests that 'internalization theory is as much a theory of externalization as it is of internalization' (Lundan 2010), such inflation of the meaning of the term 'internalization' to include that of its antonym is unbelievable to common sense. Since 'externalization and internalization do not bear on aspects of the object, but rather on the relationships and conflicts that are inherent in the object and that it maintains with other objects' (Schilton 2005: 537), and consistent with Point (5) in the previous paragraph, we wonder whether the unified framework in Fig. 7.1 can be referred to as the ownership-location-relationship (OLR) paradigm as an envelope for both the ownership-location-internalization (OLI) and the ownership-location-externalization (OLE) sides of the integrative framework shown in Fig. 7.1, which is ontologically unified and assumption-symmetrical. We discuss this point further in Subsect. 7.5.4 and in the fourth and fifth points of Subsect. 7.7.7.

Considering the multiple benefits that the CR perspective offers in ontologizing and extending the OLI paradigm, it is expected that, to certain degree, the behavioral OLI/OLR framework has the potential to rejuvenate international business research, which has been lamented as being 'running out of steam' (Buckley 2002) or even facing 'death' (Delios 2017) for some time.

7.4 The Potential of International Business Becoming the Base Camp for Behavioral TCE

While TCE is one of the dominant theoretical lenses in international business (Hennart 2010; Zhao et al. 2004), international business is not the dominant domain of TCE (Williamson 2005). While the underlying logic and analysis of TCE and internalization theories are 'characterized more by their similarity than any substantial differences' (Rugman 1986: 112; Verbeke and Greidanus 2009) and the development of internalization theories parallels to a large extent Williamson's (1975, 1985) development of TCE (Safarian 2003), internalization theorists are predominantly British-based whereas TCE theorists are American-based (Rugman 1986).

This book suggests that both camps can benefit from the adoption of a behavioral thinking, and the American-based TCE theorists can greatly improve their theoretical prospect by adding an international dimension in their theorization. We showed that the real significance of an international context has not been articulated in the extant TCE literature, and foresees that international business should become the base camp of *behavioral* TCE. This is largely because the international dimension provides TCE with an actual domain in the sense of CR, where organizations can effectuate in different social structures and contexts. The cross-context (David and Han 2004) variance will shift traditional TCE's attention from the internally-oriented comparison of alternative governance structures in one context to the externally-oriented consideration of cross-context social structures which could independently influence organizational boundaries (Huitink 2017). This book suggests that international business is a particularly rich ground for TCE research since the international business arena parallels the actual domain of CR in many ways (Leca and Naccache 2006), which we do not dwell upon here. Nevertheless, it is worth noting the following points.

First, CD is one of the most widely used constructs in international business (Zaheer et al. 2012; Zhao et al. 2004). As we discussed in Sect. 4.7, it is a construct of paramount importance to TCE because it relates to cognitive bounds. It is only when organizations venture out of their home terrains that their cognitive capacity is genuinely affected. As such, an international dimension is much desired to advance TCE. Nevertheless, despite its popularity, CD-based research has been dominated by a positivist approach (Burrell and Morgan 2017; Cheok 2016) and the fundamental role of CD in a behavioral theory of the firm has seldom been elucidated. This book adopts a CR approach to CD by considering biases arising from CD in the actual domain of CR, thus opening up opportunity for international business to become a main arena for a behavioral TCE.

Second, institutional theory is another dominant lens in international business, and the integration of traditional TCE and institutional theory has been proposed for long time (e.g., Brouthers 2002). It is a step away from the positivist mentality and toward a behavioral theory, considering that institutions are social structures operating in the actual domain, and they may or may not be experienced (Leca and Naccache 2006). In international business literature based on institutional theory, a frequently used institutional variable is institutional distance (Xu and Shenkar 2002) [we discuss the implications of this variable in Subsect. 7.7.4]. Considering cultures are institutions, institutional distance is also important to TCE. Since these distances occur only in cross-national contexts, international business should be a fundamental domain for TCE.

Despite the promising move to integrate TCE with institutional theory, the existing literature fails to bring TCE to the status of a behavioral theory since the integration itself has been done in a positivist way in a collapsed ontology without considering human fallibility. As such, CD and institutional distance were dealt with as positivist variables rather than social structures with ontological depths which contextualize psychological biases. Thus, the potential biases arising from perception of various social contexts and social structures due to cultural or institutional distances were not considered, resulting in a positivist consideration of the variation in social contexts and structures.

Nevertheless, this book suggests that the positivist integration can be converted into a behavioral integration in a CR framework after using CD and institutional distance as social contexts to account for human fallibility. After this, international business can be turned into a fertile ground for behavioral TCE research and it is foreseeable that international business should become the base camp of behavioral TCE.

Third, from an emic-etic perspective, TCE research has traditionally been done in an emic approach and in a positivist way based on 'native categories' or shared frames of references in a particular culture, often Western (Buckley and Chapman 1997; Buckley et al. 2014). When applied in international business, TCE is used in an imposed etic way wherein native categories are simply exported from the researchers' home culture (Berry 1990; Morris et al. 1999), and the relationship between market and hierarchy is defined in terms of an imposed etic relation (Stoltz 2018). This approach largely ignores the emic perspectives at the end of host countries and treats the transaction as given and unproblematic (Buckley and Chapman 1997; Martin 1993), and paid less attention to the potential interaction between home and host country perspectives. In addition, it also ignores the variation in emic perceptions of different home countries and how they may interact with etic constructs such as CD and other types of distance and the biases arising therefrom. While the international dimension opened a rather different cultural universe, and the question of 'native categories' at both ends of a transaction leaps to the fore (Buckley and Chapman 1997), the current TCE literature has not explored the potential international opportunities in terms of emic-etic interaction to the full extent.

7.5 Other Theoretical Implications

Since we used effectuation theory and prospect theory in developing the behavioral framework shown in Fig. 5.1, and since the framework is based on symmetrical assumptions, this book also has implications for the two theories and for the emerging literature on symmetrical assumption thinking and ontological unification. Since our focus is on behavioral TCE, we only briefly mention these implications below.

7.5.1 For Effectuation Theory

The CR-informed behavioral framework in Fig. 5.1 integrates effectuation theory in order to consider how firms effectuate when the ability to predict is constrained by and biases arise from CD which affects cognitive bounds. As such, this book has implications for effectuation theory. These implications can largely be summarized into two points: (1) Uncertainty controllability makes effectuation theory coherent (Sect. 2.10), and (2) CD contextualizes effectuation theory by enabling the consideration of both the constraints that CD places on the ability to predict and the psychological biases arising from CD (Sect. 4.8).

Due to its collapsed ontology and inattention to the hierarchical nature of CR domains, effectuation theory was not able to ontologically locate and coherently theorize its major concepts (i.e., pre-commitment, experimentation, affordable loss, and flexibility) and has paid insufficient attention to the deeper levels of generative mechanisms and structural and social contexts that generate the uncertainty that firms must manage (Kitching and Rouse 2020). Effectuation without sufficient attention to generative mechanisms and social structures is something out of context, and the potential contribution thereof may be discounted.

This book suggests two important ways through which theoretical and practical advancements can be made. One is the distinction between controllable and uncontrollable uncertainties and its role in 'coherentizing' and systemizing the major concepts in effectuation theory in various domains of CR, and the other is to use CD to contextualize effectuation by considering the constraints that CD places on the ability to predict and the psychological biases arising from CD. We draw attention to the fact that it is in the actual domain of CR that effectuation theory operates and psychological biases can be genuinely considered. As such, effectuation theory needs to become more ontology-conscious in order for theoretical advancements to occur. Future effectuation theory-based studies should focus on the implications of the perceptual and psychological aspects of uncertainty controllability and CD.

7.5.2 For Prospect Theory

While prospective theory is central to behavioral theories (Aharoni et al. 2011; Greve and Argote 2015) and conducive to the development of our behavioral TCE framework, the development process serves to cross-fertilize prospect theory as well. As mentioned in Chapter 5, even though prospect theory was developed in challenge to the neoclassical approach of expected utility and rational choice, it ironically overlaps with neoclassical model considerably, albeit with additional parameters, and prospect theory-based research has been carried out in a normative and deductive way (Berg and Gigerenzer 2010). By collapsing the real and the actual domains into the empirical domain, the prospect theory literature tends to focus on individual decision-making within a given context (Boettcher 1995) and assumes that problem frames are given (Bruch and Feinberg 2017), thus ignoring the role of environmental and social contexts which show considerable variations (Berg and Gigerenzer 2010), which may affect problem frames.

This study suggests that the aforementioned limitations with prospect theory literature can be overcome by deepening the ontology of and thus contextualizing prospect theory, and an international business context is particularly germane for such endeavors. Only through a more committed engagement with the actual domain of various cross-country social contexts can prospect theory regain its original abductive momentum toward a behavioral theory of decision-making under uncertainty which accounts for what people actually do.

In particular, we suggest that uncertainty controllability and CD can be used to contextualize and deepen the ontology of prospect theory. The former determines problem frames while the latter gives rise to biases in cross-country settings. While recent literature has started to pay attention to social and cultural contexts which affect individual and organizational risk behaviors across nations (Rieger et al. 2015), how the biases arising from CD interact with different cross-country risk behaviors has seldom been investigated. In a sense, studies on differences in risk preferences around the world (e.g., Rieger et al. 2015), while being a step forward, only serve to demonstrate the different impacts that different *individual country* settings can have on normative prospect theory research. This is a 'profile' approach (cf. Subsect. 7.7.2.3). The central role of psychological biases arising from CD in *cross-country* settings has not been spelled out. In order to make prospect theory more behavioral, the interaction effect between CD and cross-country risk differences over time should be the focus of future research.

Furthermore, the introduction of the concept of uncertainty controllability also helps prospect theory to pay more attention to how problem frames are determined in different social contexts and thus to realize its potential as an overarching grand theory because of its link to judgmental rationality, as we discussed in Chapter 5. Judgmental rationality suggests that 'there are some theoretical and methodological tools we can use in order to discriminate among theories regarding their ability to inform us about external reality' (Danermark et al. 2019: 10; Hu 2018). Prospect theory can be regarded as such a tool which helps us to determine the relative relevance of behavioral TCE and behavioral ROT. While the potential of prospect as an overarching grand theory has been suggested (e.g., Miller and Bamberger 2016), the reasons were not articulated.

In sum, the deep ontology and the international settings proposed in this book call for attention to the role of environment and context as explanatory variables that might condition what it means to make a good decision (Berg and Gigerenzer 2010). This will necessitate an emphasis on ecological rationality, which refers to decision-making strategies that exploit the structure of information in a given environment to arrive at efficacious decisions and judgments (Gigerenzer 2000). A focus on ecological rationality will induce prospect theory research to eschew the positivist tendency to generalize across all contexts and instead to focus on decision processes which fit with the environments where the theory is applied (Berg and Gigerenzer 2010). Such different environments are characterized by different levels of uncertainty controllability and CD, which provide ground for applying prospect theory in a truly behavioral way.

7.5.3 For Penrose's (1959) Theory of the Growth of the Firm

Our *manas*-centric approach also has implications for Penrose's (1959) *Theory of the Growth of the Firm*. While the importance of Penrosean learning has been recognized and scholars are said to have incorporated it into internalization theory/OLI paradigm, the incorporation has been carried out in a cognition-centric, positivist way. The fundamental link between various types of distance and Penrosean learning and the concomitant critical role of psychological biases arising from distances has not been brought into awareness and used to inform Penrose (1959).

In a sense, the lack of attention to distance can be said to be a weakness of Penrose (1959). While Penrose (1987) criticized both traditional TCE and Hymer (1976)-type monopolistic advantage theory for failing to distinguish between intra-country and international expansions, Penrose (1959) did not deal with locations and thus distances either (Pitelis 2011). Throughout her early writings, Penrose considered MNCs as the natural outcome of the very pressures for growth (Pitelis 2009). While the differences between national and international firms were acknowledged, she believed that 'the differences are not such as to require a theoretical distinction between the two types of organizations, only a recognition that national boundaries make an empirical difference to their opportunities and costs' (Penrose 1987: 563). Only until 1996 did she change her idea a little by saying that '[i]nternational borders make enough difference to justify separate treatment of international firms. The differences arise from the additional obstacles (or advantages) relating to culture, language and similar considerations' (Penrose 1996: 1720). Nevertheless, what Penrose (1996) suggested was a paraphrasing of Dunning (1980), which treated cross-country differences as negative/positive endowments. Consequently, the Penrosean theory applied in international settings is still cognition-centric rather than *manas*-centric, making it a positivist theory rather than a behavioral one. It implicitly assumes that managers qua managers can apply excess resources to a given set of opportunities and change their world and future (Arend et al. 2016). She had not articulated the need for emic-etic interaction based on psychological biases arising from distances, be it cultural or other types.

As discussed in Chapter 4 passim (Sect. 4.10 in particular), various types of distance are fundamental factors which affect cognitive bounds, constrain managerial productive services, and thus limit the rate of firm growth. Since the fundamental role of distances has not been spelled out, the Penrose effect in international settings pays insufficient attention to psychological biases and human fallibility, thus failing to become a behavioral theory (Joseph and Wilson 2018; Pitelis 2007). This book showed that in order for Penrosean learning to become behavioral, the black box of managers' minds has to be opened up and the cognitive bounds and *manas* have to be separated in reasoning in order for the Penrosean effect to get out of the cognition 'box'. Only after such conceptual separation can various psychological biases arising from constrained cognitive bounds due to various types of distance be seriously considered to inform Penrose (1959). Real Penrosean effect is *manas*-centric and is fundamentally related to the reduction of psychological biases. It can be said that the Penrose effect is a manifestation of *manas* itself.

In short, this book provided the missing link in Penrose (1959) and made the Penrose effect *manas*-centric or behavioral by breaking its cognition 'box' and thus allowing for the consideration of psychological biases arising from distances. In the resulting 'behavioral theory of the growth of the firm', *manas* applies cognition, the bounds of which are constrained by various types of distance. The difference between our behavioral version and the original Penrosean version of the theory of the growth of the firm primarily lies in that distances are fundamental for the former but inessential in the theorizing of the latter (Pitelis 2011). While it has been suggested that all theories of the MNC need to suitably adapt ideas in Penrose (1959) and account for the existence of national differences (Penrose 1995; Pitelis 2011), the national differences referred to here are etic differences rather than dialectic emic-etic interactions which are conducive to behavioral considerations and allow for psychological biases. The behavioral theory of the growth of the firm also foregrounds *manas*-centric managerial services rather than excess resources. This further strengthens Penrose's view that, strictly speaking, it is managerial services[4] rather than resources that are the 'inputs' in the firm production process and are thus fundamental to firm growth (Mahoney 2004). Once Penrose's theory of the growth of the firm is rendered behavioral by the introduction of the fundamental role of distances, it is not necessary to differentiate and to justify a theoretical distinction between national and international firms since various types of cross-country distances can be subsumed under the umbrella term 'distance'. In intra-country settings, firm growth in Penrose (1959) can be viewed as an 'added distance' (cf. Hutzschenreuter et al. 2011) in some 'spatial' dimensions, such as technological space, and customer space.[5]

To conclude this subsection, we would suggest that the fundamental role of various types of distance for Penrose's (1959) Theory of the Growth of the Firm, as mentioned in Sect. 4.10 and this subsection, implies that distance-enhanced Penrose effect will have even bigger impact on the theory of the MNC and international business scholarship. While Penrose (1959) has been a canonical reference in international business, its main domains of applications are resource-, knowledge-, and (dynamic) capabilities-based approaches to business strategy (Pitelis 2009). While Penrosean learning is said to have been integrated with Rugman and the Dunning streams of internalization theory, as discussed in Sect. 7.3, the reality is that it has been considered in a positivist way in which distance is considered as a negative endowment (Dunning 1980: 28; Buckley and Casson 1996). The fundamental role of distances in affecting cognitive bounds and constraining the production of managerial services has been given short shrift. After the disaggregation of cognition and *manas* and by treating (cultural) distance as reflecting cognitive bounds and giving rise to psychological biases, we expect that international business can become another main domain for Penrosean research.

7.5.4 Implications for Symmetrical Assumption Thinking and Explanatory Unification

Since TCE assumes only *controllable* uncertainty and equivocates about *uncontrollable* uncertainty, it suffers from assumptional asymmetry and lacks 'ontological unification' (Foss and Hallberg 2014), which suggests that, to the extent that phenomena share basic characteristics, research should aim at 'redescribing apparently independent and diverse phenomena as manifestations (outcomes, phases, forms, aspects) of one and the same small number of entities, powers, and processes' (Mäki 2001: 498). Our CR-informed aesthetically symmetrical framework in Fig. 5.1 centers on the concept of uncertainty controllability, which symmetrically accounts for both controllable and uncontrollable uncertainties. This book shows that CR, due to its ontological depth and particular awareness of competing generative mechanisms, can act as an '*enabler*' of symmetrical assumption thinking and ontological unification (see Sect. 5.5). Our framework shown in Fig. 5.1 can serve as an exemplar example of what Foss and Hallberg (2014) propose, particularly considering that TCE is incapable of considering competing assumptions for its collapsed ontology in a closed system. Such attention to assumptional symmetry and ontological unification merits particular explanation in the case of the OLI paradigm, which involves a large number of parameters (belonging to the respective categories of the O-, L-, and I-components) to describe the internationalization dynamics but still faces challenges such as its inability to consider externalization (see Subsect. 7.3.3).

7.5.4.1 *Explanatory Unification: Derivational Unification vs. Ontological Unification*

Explanatory unification refers to 'the urge to "explain much by little"', and serves as an ideal of theorizing not only in the social sciences, most notably in economics, but also in natural sciences (Mäki 2001: 488). Two major variants can be distinguished: 'derivational unification' and 'ontological unification' (Mäki 2001). The former is a logical unification, which is brought about 'when more and more statements within a discipline become derivable from the same set of axioms, or when the same set of statements becomes derivable from a smaller set of axioms' (Mäki 1990: 331). It is called derivational unification since it concerns 'derivational efficiency' (Mäki 2001: 494): Explanation is a matter of reducing the number of logically independent lawlike sentences (Friedman 1974: 15–16), or a matter of 'deriving large classes of explanandum sentences from a parsimonious set of theoretical sentences or inference patterns' (Kuorikoski and Lehtinen 2010: 348). Thus, in derivational unification, explanations are basically understood as 'derivations from premises to conclusions, where the conclusions give the explananda and the premises give the explanantia' (Mäki 2001: 494). In contrast, ontological unification involves 'redescribing apparently independent and diverse phenomena as manifestations (outcomes, phases, forms, aspects) of one and the same small number of entities, powers, and processes' (Mäki 2001: 498), or causal mechanisms in CR (Lehtinen 2012). Here, the independent explanandum phenomena are only *apparently* independent but are in fact unified by being dependent on the same underlying generative mechanisms (Lehtinen 2012; Mäki 2001). Thus, ontological unification results in 'integral efficiency'.

Mäki (2001: 499) contrasted 'derivational unification' and 'ontological unification' (see Table 7.3). Derivational as opposed to ontological unification gives priority to lawlike sentences instead of generative mechanism; derivation and inference instead of representation and reference; imposition instead of discovery; or in sum, 'unification as formal constraint' instead of 'unification as factual discovery'. Mäki (2009a: 363) argues that derivational unification has value only if it is accompanied by ontological unification since it 'is based on the derivational capacities of theories [which] are regarded as logical formulae, possibly devoid of truth-value'. The latter should thus serve as a constraint for the former (Kuorikoski and

Table 7.3 Explanatory unification: Derivational unification vs ontological unification

Derivational unification	*Ontological unification*	*Subsection#*
• Positivism	• Critical realism	7.5.4.1
• Closed system (Mäki 2009b)	• Open system (Mäki 2009b)	
• Lawlike sentences (Friedman 1974)	• Generative mechanisms (Mäki 2009b)	7.5.4.1
• Derivation and inference	• Representation and reference	7.5.4.1
• 'Unification as formal constraint' (Mäki 2009a)	• 'Unification as factual discovery' (Mäki 2009a)	7.5.4.1
• 'The law of abstraction' (Zeki 2001): bounded rationality as a limitation	• 'The law of constancy' (Zeki 2001): bounded rationality as a capability	3.4.2
• 'Derivational efficiency' (Mäki 2001)	• Integral efficiency	
• Assumptional asymmetry	• Assumptional symmetry	7.5.4.1
• Testing the prediction of assumptions (Mariyani-Squire 2017)	• Testing the assumptions (Mariyani-Squire 2017)	
In the context with regard to different approaches to cultural distance (CD)		
• Cognition-centric approach trapped in the black box of CD	• *Manas*-centric approach outside the black box of CD	7.7.2.1 and 7.7.3
• Used in models where the firm is an explanandum	• Used in models where the firm is an explanans	7.7.2.1 and 7.7.3
• Propositions/relationships between CD and outcome variables are already assumed to exist in a deductive and constrained manner, possibly devoid of truth-value (Mäki 2009a)	• CD is relegated to the role of cognitive bounds, which is open to different causal mechanisms and thus different propositions/relationships.	7.7.2.1 and 7.7.3
• Given the constrained propositions/relationships, research moves from propositions to assumptions to look for assumptions that would justify such propositions, or moves from propositions to contextual factors to look for those factors which potentially moderate the propositions in a positivist way	• Moves from CD to the phenomena of concern, with open assumptions	7.7.2.1 and 7.7.3

(continued)

Table 7.3 (continued)

Derivational unification	*Ontological unification*	*Subsection#*
• CD is treated as a black box; psychological biases arising from CD cannot be considered	• Psychological biases arising from CD can be considered in the process of *manas* applying cognition	7.7.2.1 and 7.7.3
• Contextual intelligence (Tung and Verbeke 2010)	• Ontological intelligence	7.7.2.1 and 7.7.3
• Self-unconscious	• Self-conscious	7.7.2.1 and 7.7.3
In the context with regard to theory formalization (Adner et al. 2009)		
• Verbal theorizing	• Theory formalization	7.7.8
• Moves backward from propositions to assumptions, looking for assumptions that would justify such propositions	• Goes from assumptions to propositions/can lead to counterintuitive and surprising propositions that might follow from a set of assumptions	7.7.8
• An apparent limitation to this approach is that one cannot find the unexpected	• Tends to yield new insights into the management phenomena of concern and leads to theoretical advancement	7.7.8
• Verbal theorizing leads researchers to treat assumptions in an ad hoc and partial way	• Formal theorizing allows scholars to consider assumptions in a systematic and comprehensive manner	7.7.8
• Focuses on the justification of propositions by using ad hoc assumptions	• Focuses on the examination of the assumptions themselves	7.7.8
In the context with regard to OLI paradigms vs OLR paradigm (or traditional TCE vs Behavioral TCE/ROT)		
• Focuses on explananda or scope expansion, whereby new kinds of phenomena are explained in terms of the same explanatory principles (Mäki 2004, 2009b)	• Focuses on explanantia or causal penetration (articulation), whereby black boxes are opened so as to reveal deeper causal mechanisms responsible for the phenomena to be explained (Mäki 2004, 2009b)	

(continued)

Table 7.3 (continued)

Derivational unification	*Ontological unification*	*Subsection#*
• OLI is concerned with derivational efficiency: – Categorizing factors into the O-, L-, and I-components reflects its effort to reduce the number of axioms into inference patterns – The numerous explanatory variables identified by the paradigm reflect its efficiency in 'deriving large classes of explanandum sentences from a parsimonious set of theoretical sentences or inference patterns' (Kuorikoski and Lehtinen 2010: 348)	• OLR focuses on integral efficiency: – Symmetrical definitions of constructs and mechanisms – Symmetrical thinking implies that both the OLI and the OLE side of the OLR, which are seemingly independent in a positivist constrained system, are 'manifestations … of one and the same small number of [causal mechanisms]' (Mäki 2001: 498; Lehtinen 2012). – In order to achieve ontological unification, an ontological depth is indispensable, and deep ontology facilitates the linking of the O-, L-, and I-components into a process, which further increases integral efficiency	7.3.3 and 7.5.4.2
• Positivist derivational unification becomes formal constraint (Mäki 2009a): – Assumptional asymmetry (of both constructs and mechanisms) – Cannot consider externalization – O-, L-, and I-components tend to be treated separately, preventing linkage and interactions among them	• Critical realist ontological unification facilitate mechanism discovery (Mäki 2009a): – Assumptional symmetry (of both constructs and mechanism) – Can consider both externalization and internalization – Facilitates the linking of the O-, L-, and I-components into a process, thus conducive to mechanism discovery (such as Penrosean learning)	7.3.3 and 7.5.4.2
• Focuses on tractability and formal rigor: theoretical isolation leads to inability to consider additional causal mechanisms (Mäki 2004, 2009b)	• Pays attention to ontological conviction, which is conducive to considering 'rival and complementary isolations' (Mäki 2009b)	

(continued)

Table 7.3 (continued)

Derivational unification	*Ontological unification*	*Subsection#*
• Cognition-centric approach to CD, which is used in a positivist deductive way as a negative location-specific endowment, preventing Penrose effect from realizing its full potential	• *Manas-centric* approach to CD, capable of considering psychological biases arising from CD and thus conducive to the integration of Penrosean learning	7.3.3 and 7.5.4.2

Source Author's own summary based on the views expressed passim in this book, Adner et al. (2009), Friedman (1974), Foss and Hallberg (2014), Mäki (2001, 2009a, b), among others

Lehtinen 2010: 347). As such, the two should not be viewed as an either-or choice, but be integrated in a similar way to that between positivism and CR, as discussed passim in this book, particularly in Chapter 2.

We have previously discussed the potential for CR framework to contribute to assumptional symmetry and ontological unification (Foss and Hallberg 2014). This is consistent with the fact that critical realists share many of the fundamental tenets in Mäki's emphasis on finding causal mechanisms (Lehtinen 2012). In order to achieve assumptional symmetry and ontological unification, an ontological depth is indispensable. As pointed out in Subsect. 3.4.2, the distinction between derivational unification and ontological unification reflects one of the recurring theme in multiple streams of literature. As such, in Table 7.3 we also include: (1) the contrast between the OLI paradigm and the OLR paradigm which combines the OLI and OLE sides, as was discussed in Subsects. 7.3.3 and 7.5.4.2; (2) the contrast between the cognition-centric and *manas*-centric approaches to CD, which is to be discussed in Subsects. 7.7.2.1 and 7.7.3; and (3) the contrast between verbal theorizing and theory formalization, which will be discussed in Sect. 7.7.8. As shown in Table 7.3, much of the confusion and debate in various streams of literature can be traced back to the fundamental tension between the needs for derivational vs ontological unification.

7.5.4.2 Explanatory Unification and the OLI Paradigm

Explanatory unification is particularly germane to the OLI paradigm which faces challenges in terms of both derivational unification and ontological unification. On the derivational front, it involves a large number of parameters (belonging to the respective categories of the O-, L-, and I-components) to describe the internationalization dynamics, and 'it has been claimed that the explanatory variables identified by the paradigm are so numerous that its predictive value is almost zero' (Dunning 2001a: 177). However, this criticism may have missed the point that it reflects exactly what the OLI paradigm is intended for, that is, a focus on explananda and derivational efficiency. Dunning's effort in categorizing factors into the O-, L-, and I-components reflects a desire to reduce the number of axioms into a small number of generic inference patterns, and the numerous explanatory variables identified by the paradigm reflect its efficiency in 'deriving large classes of explanandum sentences from a parsimonious set of theoretical sentences or inference patterns' (Kuorikoski and Lehtinen 2010: 348). Both are conducive to derivational unification and efficiency as described by Friedman (1974), Kuorikoski and Lehtinen (2010), and Mäki (1990, 2001). Indeed, the original aim of the OLI paradigm was to 'offer a holistic framework by which it was possible to identify and evaluate the significance of the factors influencing both the initial act of foreign production by enterprises and the growth of such production' (Dunning 1988: 1). While such an aim was later toned down a bit in Dunning (2001a: 177), which stated that 'the purpose of the eclectic paradigm is not to offer a full explanation of all kinds of international production but rather to point to a methodology and to a generic set of variables which contain the ingredients necessary for any satisfactory explanation of particular types of foreign value-added activity', the focus of the paradigm is still on explananda or scope expansion, whereby new kinds of international business phenomena are explained in terms of the same explanatory principles (Mäki 2004, 2009b).

Nevertheless, such a focus on derivational unification has its limitations. Positivist derivational unification tends to become formal constraint (Mäki 2009a). Its theoretical isolation leads to inability to consider additional causal mechanisms, such as externalization, as a result of assumptional asymmetry (Mäki 2004, 2009b). This is because derivational unification takes partial assumptions as given and focuses on testing the predictions of assumptions rather than assumptions themselves (Mariyani-Squire 2017). Since 'empirical data characteristically manifest a multiplicity of causal influences, while a theoretical model typically isolates just one or a few causal mechanisms' (Mäki 2009b), the low predictive value of the OLI paradigm (Dunning 2001a) should not be a surprise because of its inability to consider externalization. To increase predictive power, a theory has to revise some of its isolations (Mäki 2004) in order to allow for hybrid explanations which consider the complex nature of economic reality and the fact that multiple generative mechanisms may be simultaneously at work (Hodgson 1998).[6] In other words, focus should be shifted to ontological unification in a deeper ontology of CR where competing mechanisms can be considered. This study suggests that the OLI paradigm described only one side of MNC behavior based on one generative mechanism, i.e., internalization logic. Since MNC behavior is subject to multiple mechanisms at the same time, the predictive power of a model like the OLI is limited since it isolated only one mechanism (i.e., internalization logic). In order to increase its predictive power, it has to be de-isolated and then re-isolated to consider more mechanisms, such as the OLE side of the proposed OLR, as discussed in Subsect. 7.3.3. Foss and Hallberg (2014) suggest that attention to assumptional symmetry may serve as an effective tool in identifying more causal mechanisms.

This study vividly demonstrated the role of CR in facilitating the consideration of assumptional symmetry and ontological unification (Foss and Hallberg 2014), which emphasize on finding causal mechanisms (Lehtinen 2012). In order to find these mechanisms, attention should be paid to the real domain of CR where different generative mechanisms are 'domiciled'. Thus, it is in the real domain that better causal articulation and penetration can be achieved and theory be advanced (Foss and Hallberg 2014, 2017; Mäki 2004, 2009b).

7.6 Practical Implications

Our findings have practical relevance for MNC managers. We discuss them in two subsections below. The first subsection is about implications for management focus and world view, and the second subsection covers those for performance, learning, and competitiveness.

7.6.1 Implications for Management Focus

This book suggests that the most important thing for managers is the need for them (or the firm) to be self-conscious and adopt a deep ontology thinking. Only when managers are self-conscious can they come out of the black box of the firm and treat the firm in a behavioral way as an explanans and use firms as 'instruments for adaptation' in value creation and competitiveness enhancement. In order to reduce repetition, we list some specific practical implications in Table 7.4, which contrast the normative implications based on traditional TCE and our behavioral TCE. The explanations for these implications can be found passim in this chapter.

The theoretical development and empirical findings in this book clearly recommend the adoption of the management focus profile on the right column of the table in accordance with the behavioral approach. The findings showing that firms behave in a manner consistent with the behavioral TCE-based management focus profile also serve to downplay TCE's negative view of managerial motives and behavior. This makes the relationship

Table 7.4 Comparing normative implications of traditional TCE and behavioral TCE

Traditional TCE	*Behavioral TCE*
Self-unconscious	Self-conscious
Firm (or firm boundaries) as an explanandum • The economic agent is in the black box of the firm	Firm (or firm boundaries) as an explanans, or 'instruments for adaptation' used by self-conscious economic agent • For this view to work, the economic agent has to be self-consciously outside of the black box of the firm
Management focus: • Opportunism • Substantive rationality • Transaction cost • Static • Internal orientation (Wright et al. 1991)	Management focus: • Bounded rationality (the reduction of) • Ecological rationality • Transaction value • Dynamic • External orientation (Wright et al. 1991)
View toward bounded rationality: • As a learning constraint • 'The law of abstraction' (Zeki 2001; cf. Subsect. 3.4.2)	View toward bounded rationality: • As a learning enabler: 'bounded rationality can be seen as an adaptive capacity instead than as a limitation' (Novarese 2009) • 'The law of constancy' (Zeki 2001; cf. Subsect. 3.4.2)
View toward CD: • Negative • CD as liability • CD hinders learning (exploitation)	View toward CD: • Positive • CD as asset • CD promotes learning (exploration)
View toward the relationship between culture and CD: • Emic | Etic	View toward the relationship between culture and CD: • Dialectic (Emic × Etic)

Source Author's own creation

between behavioral TCE and management theory and the relationship between management scholars and managers less acrimonious and more congruent (Donaldson 1990).

7.6.2 *Implications for Performance, Learning, and Competitiveness*

The theory building and empirical findings in this book also have practical implications for MNC performance, learning, and competitiveness, particularly with regard to CD. At a higher level, our findings also have implications for national and/or industry competition policy.[7] We discuss these in turn below, even though they are related to each other in a sense.

1. An important insight provided in this book is that psychological biases arising from CD coexist with and are proportional to CD (cf. Turner 2007), and there are competing types of biases coexisting along the range of CD where their strengths change in opposite directions (see Sect. 4.11). This suggests that human agents, by nature, cannot objectively perceive CD most of times, and there will be a 'distance divergence' between objective CD and perceived CD (Azar and Drogendijk 2019). Despite much research on CD, little attention has been paid to such divergence as a result of managers' perceptual biases arising from CD and its performance implications. Azar and Drogendijk (2019) showed that the larger the distance divergence, the lower the performance; and that over-estimation and under-estimation of CD do not have differential effects on firm performance. Their findings match neatly with our theoretical framework, and we explain why below.

According to Sect. 4.11, when CD is at low levels, assimilation biases dominate. Under such circumstances, MNC managers will tend to underestimate CD. In contract, when CD is at high levels, contrast biases prevail. Under such circumstances, managers will tend to overestimate CD. Because both over-estimation and under-estimation are divergences from objective CD, and because over-estimation and under-estimation of CD do not have differential effects on firm performance (Azar and Drogendijk 2019), the performance of MNCs will be low at both low and high levels of CD. In other words, the relationship between CD and MNC performance will be inverted U-shaped.

The inverted U-shaped relationship has significant practical implications. It serves to warn MNC managers against their tendency to overestimate their perceived CD at high objective CD levels and the tendency to underestimate their perceived CD at low objective CD levels. These tendencies have negative performance implications, as this book suggests.

2. Williamson (1999) rightly pointed out that the cognitive assumption out of which the organizational capabilities approach (i.e., competence-based approach) works is that of bounded rationality, which ascribes great importance to learning. However, due to the rational treatment of bounded rationality in traditional TCE, learning cannot be considered (Slater and Spencer 2000). The behavioral TCE framework in international business settings genuinely opens up opportunities to incorporate learning into TCE.

Particularly, the insights provided in this book suggest that some common views based on traditional TCE need to be reversed. For example, Williamson (1999: 1090) states that TCE 'holds that economizing on transaction costs is the 'main case'—which is not to say the only case. The attributes of human actors are centrally implicated. Thus one productive way to think about economic organization is as a means by which to economize on bounded rationality and mitigate the hazards that accrue to opportunism. Cognitive specialization, within and between firms, is a means by which to economize on mind as a scarce resource' (Williamson 1999: 1090). Consistent with the theoretical implication discussed in Subsect. 7.3.1, this book suggests that transaction cost economization cannot be the main concern in our behavioral TCE if human limitations are genuinely 'centrally implicated'. Instead, cognitive economization should be the main concern.

As such, this book draws the attention of MNC managers away from transaction cost economization toward a focus on organizational learning, which is of the main concern in international settings. Related to Subsect. 7.3.1, another practical implication is that a refocus on bounded rationality as an attitude in the actual domain of CR will enable MNCs to shift their attention to the learning-enabling and capability-enhancing aspect of bounded rationality (Novarese 2009). This point is particularly relevant in international business settings where CD and some other distance measures in fact reflect important dimensions of the social structures in the actual domain of CR. In the mentality of traditional TCE, bounded rationality is treated as an abstract value, which tends to lead the economic agent to shut down his mental processes and learning, and thus is viewed as a limitation (Novarese 2009). In our behavioral framework, bounded rationality is treated as an attitude, and thus, it is situational and has to be contextualized or subject to varied or changing situations in order for it to be manifested, identified, and understood. It is a prerequisite for learning since context recognition is a tool or a step of procedural rationality which activates learning. As such, bounded rationality as an attitude can be seen as an adaptive capacity rather than as a limitation (Novarese 2009). MNCs that are more aware of the learning benefit of bounded rationality in the actual domain will have competitive advantage over those that are less aware of this benefit.

In terms of the emic-etic interaction discussed in Sect. 3.3, our behavioral TCE framework is conducive to organizational learning because it is in the actual domain of CR that the full psychological process of internationalization can be captured by considering both emic and etic views. In the process of forming new mental models, organizations tend to adopt an emic perspective and promote a more positive perspective on CD as a result of the need to make sense of a host culture's internal logic (Stahl and Tung 2015). Emic sense-making often reports more rationality and structure in the host cultures (Woodside et al. 2005), and as a result, such an intimate understanding of host cultures will likely lead to improved learning and organizational performance.

3. Indeed, our behavioral TCE approach renders it closer to the 'organizational capabilities approach', including the evolutionary theory of the firm, which emphasizes ecological rationality (Gigerenzer 2000; Nelson and Winter 1982) and localized experiential knowledge that explains firm heterogeneity and thus competitive advantage (Foss 2003b; Hodgson 1998). This point is easy to understand in terms of CD as cognitive bounds and the biases arising from it. Due to CD, organizations have to effectuate in markets which pose bounded rationality challenges and such effectuation is prone to biases. As such, there will be a 'distance divergence' between objective CD and perceived CD (Azar and Drogendijk 2019), and such divergence will be dependent on the levels of CD, as just explained.

> Due to such divergences, organizational performance will be negatively affected (Azar and Drogendijk 2019). Since human agents, by nature, cannot objectively perceive CD (Azar and Drogendijk 2019), negative performance implications should be the norm than exception.

Assuming firm heterogeneity in learning, the existence of 'distance divergence' between objective CD and perceived CD implies that learning firms that reduce their psychological biases faster will be more competitive and have better performance since they are more efficient in exploiting the structure of information in a given environment to arrive at efficacious decisions and judgments (Gigerenzer 2000; Vaccarini et al. 2017). Evolutionary pressures of the marketplace select firms most fit for survival, which are often those that best at constraining their behavioral biases (Manne and Zywicki 2014), accurately forecasting the effects of uncertainty on their operations, and therefore devising better strategies (Fisch 2008). The speed in reducing psychological biases thus has significant implications for firm competitiveness. It is also expected that, over the long term, the observed governance structures will gravitate toward what is required by the objective environment with diminishing biases based on ecological rationality (Lo 2017; Narula et al. 2019).

It is based on the above explanation that we can further expound the 'upside of cultural distance' (Morosini et al. 1998; Stahl and Tung 2015), namely CD as an opportunity for competitive advantage. CD can be a source of competitive advantage because it reflects bounded rationality. When pursuing business opportunities, all organizations are faced with a 'frontier problem', which is characterized by various uncertainties at the boundary of the firm. Depending on the internalizability of these uncertainties, some are to be internalized, while others to remain outside of the firm. Uncertainties present both threats and opportunities in the same process, but individuals tend to sense more threats than opportunities due to psychological biases arising from cognitive limitations. The initial defensive reaction to uncertainties has its merits to avoid danger. However, once the danger is believed not to be present with initial learning, it is now up to the 'self' of the organization to switch from psychological to cognitive mode (Lo 2005), and learn and adapt toward more ecologically rational direction (Lo 2017).

This is when we need to take a positive view of CD or bounded rationality, since it offers an opportunity for firm heterogeneity in cultural intelligence. While CD per se may not be a direct competitive advantage, it can offer opportunities for competitive advantages in terms of ecological rationality vis-à-vis competitors in devising more efficacious strategies that better exploit the environmental information structure (Gigerenzer 2000). It becomes someone's competitive advantage because it is everyone's liability in the first place. While CD has traditionally been regarded as a liability, the recent emergent view is that it is a source of learning and innovation (Maseland et al. 2018; Stahl and Tung 2015; Stahl et al. 2017). To liken internationalization to 100 m dash, the former view applies when runners are at the starting blocks, while the latter view operates when runners are sprinting. Internationalization is a race that has to be run. As such, CD has to be viewed as a source of competitive advantage in order to win the race.

In a deeper sense, the upside of CD is related to the organizational routines and the need for an emic-etic interaction perspective in augmenting organizational routines in host countries. In international arena, an MNC cannot rely solely on the exploitation of its existing routines as is for competitive advantage, but have to either adapt existing routines or develop new ones based on organizational learning. CD reflects differences in the repertoires of activities and in routines between the home and host countries and can thus be considered as a source of competitive advantage and learning (Morosini 1998; Morosini et al. 1998). And similar to the arguments we used in Point 2 above, an emic-etic interaction perspective is necessary for such competitive advantages to realize in the actual domain of CR and our behavioral TCE framework is conducive to the development of competitive advantages.

4. At a higher level, our findings also have practical implications for national and/or industry competition policy. One of the major concerns of competition policy is the understanding of the effects of competition on consumer welfare and economic efficiency. However, industrial organization theory and standard neoclassical economics, which are the primary sources of economic advice and analysis that competition authorities consult, often offer different recommendations from those based on TCE (Holland 2019; Williamson 1985). For example, in deliberating cases about vertical restraints, what the former models may consider as anti-competitive exploitation of market power may be considered as efficiency-enhancing firm responses to the need to economize on

transaction costs based on the latter model. Relatedly, certain market structures may be the cumulative and aggregate outcome of transaction cost economizing behavior by firms rather than the result of the exercise of market power (Holland 2019). Williamson (1985) discussed these points in detail in Chapter 14 of his book. Nevertheless, the conflicting opinions based on industrial organization and TCE are difficult to reconcile in a traditional way, because the firm in the mainstream economics has often been treated as a 'black box' (Augier 2013; Coase 1991). Even though traditional TCE tried to open up the black box a bit, it achieved little because it is not genuinely behavioral. Deliberation of national and/or industry competition policy should not be based on cost considerations only but also on value creation potentials.

By using a longitudinal data and modeling bounded rationality in a behavioral way, this study opened up the black box, and the dynamic firm boundary adaptation in the form of MNC subsidiary ownership over time shows that MNC tends to reduce their ownership levels as predicted by our *behavioral* TCE (i.e., transaction value) framework. This is a very insightful finding, which suggests that firm behavior is not focused on exercising market power but on enhancing efficiency. This finding is also consistent with the Penrosean (1959) view that, while monopoly power could lead to short-term success, only the building of 'relatively impregnable bases' was important for the long-run success of firms (Pitelis 2004). Competition authorities' heavy reliance on standard neoclassical economics and industrial organization theory may be largely attributed to the 'black box' approach to the firm through which no fine-grained insights can be gained. In order to better inform policy, the black box of the firm has to be opened up and temporally studied in a behavioral way.

Because the efficiency of the economic system depends to a very considerable extent on how firms in it conduct their affairs (Coase 1991), and because our findings suggest that firms are value-oriented while not ignoring efficiency, then, assuming their consistency in behavior, they will aim for other types of economic value added and increase efficiency as well, such as higher levels of output and service, improved quality of products, lower prices, and increased rates of innovation (Holland 2019). Thus, strategies by firms to reduce transaction costs and increase transaction values will ultimately lead to economic efficiency and consumer welfare at a higher level. As such, the findings in this study suggest that competition authorities need to lean more toward behavioral TCE or 'transaction value economics' for future advice.

7.7 Future Research Directions

While this study contributed to theory and practice by building a behavioral TCE and applying it in an empirical example, it still leaves much to be desired. In this section, we suggest some future research directions, particularly considering the existence of quite a few long-standing unresolved paradoxes and unanswered questions. We think that these new research avenues hold promises to considerably advance our understanding of some important international business issues, thanks to our ontologically more coherent behavioral theoretical framework. Please note that, among many of our suggestions, we spend considerable space discussing the resolution of the 'cultural distance paradox' considering its vital importance in international business.

7.7.1 *Resolving the 'Uncertainty Paradox'*

In TCE and international business literature, it has long been noticed that there have been contradictory theoretical arguments and inconsistent and contradictory empirical results about the relationship between uncertainty and governance decision (such as vertical integration, ownership levels, and entry mode) (Shenkar 2001; Slangen and van Tulder 2009; Zhao et al. 2004; Sutcliffe and Zaheer 1998), which presents researchers with an '*uncertainty paradox*'. As pointed out by Mahoney (1992) and Sutcliffe and Zaheer (1998), such inconsistent theoretical arguments and contradictory empirical results can in part be attributed to the different types of uncertainty and variety of measures. As such, it is necessary to have a clear understanding of various types of uncertainty in order to resolve the 'paradox'.

The assumption-symmetrical, *manas*-centric behavioral framework shown in Fig. 5.1 can contribute to a more conclusive and coherent understanding of the effect of various types of uncertainties on governance decisions. Based on the concept of uncertainty controllability and the framing effects which are affected by controllability, our framework provides a comprehensive view toward how to cope with uncertainty in a *manas*-centric, controllability-differentiated manner which can consider various biases arising from cognitive bounds vis-a-vis uncertainty controllability. We suggest that TCE is better suited for considering controllable uncertainties while ROT for uncontrollable uncertainties (cf. Ahsan and Musteen 2011). While the integration of TCE and ROT has been suggested (Barney and Lee 2000; Chi and McGuire 1996; Folta 1998; Leiblein 2003; Sanchez 2003), our framework goes a step further by considering behavioral TCE and behavioral ROT, which uses prospect theory as the integrative mechanism and considers the effects of behavioral biases. It is hoped that the uncertainty paradox will disappear once more fine-grained conceptualization of uncertainty is adopted and the ontology of uncertainty is deepened to allow for the competing generative mechanisms which are activated by different types of uncertainties. Future research thus should carry out empirical tests for various types of uncertainties (De Weck et al. 2007; Miller 1992; Miller and Lessard 2001) according to their controllability and the corresponding behavioral TCE and/or behavioral ROT arguments. For this purpose, the framework presented in Fig. 5.1 should be used as a guide.

In addition, the lack of attention to the *manas*-centric dynamic interaction between uncertainty and cognitive bounds over time may have also contributed to the uncertainty paradox. Traditional TCE is inherently a static framework based on 'equilibrium contracting' or 'comparative static equilibration' at its core and as a result, could not genuinely account for the dynamic iteration and the accompanying learning as well as a behavioral TCE could in a deeper ontological context. As Fig. 5.1 suggests, the statistical power of using traditional TCE to detect the effect of controllable uncertainty could have been compromised for its usual cross-sectional setup in a collapsed ontology, which is incapable of considering time and thus learning. Future studies should employ longitudinal methodology to increase statistical power and doing so would contribute to the resolution of the uncertainty paradox.

The same is true for the behavioral ROT side of the framework in Fig. 5.1. The potential biases arising from cognitive bounds have seldom been incorporated into real options models (Chi et al. 2019), with a few exceptions (Leiblein et al. 2017; Posen et al. 2018; Trigeorgis 2014). The integration of psychological biases into real options theory has been considered as 'an emerging line of research' in international business (Chi et al. 2019). Considering what we discussed above about the significant influence that the biases arising from cognitive bounds play on the effect of controllable uncertainty, we suggest that future studies should explicitly consider how biases arising from cognitive bounds affect the effects of uncontrollable uncertainty using longitudinal methods.

In sum, the uncertainty paradox has to be resolved by simultaneously considering competing generative mechanisms which are activated by different types of uncertainty. For scholars to embrace such an assumption-symmetrical thinking, they have to shift their mentality from being cognition-centric to being *manas*-centric. The reasons for the importance of this shift can be found in Subsects. 7.7.2.1, 7.7.3 and 7.7.8 regarding the theoretical and empirical implications of reasoning direction.

7.7.2 Resolving the 'Cultural Distance Paradox': Black Box vs. Mechanism

Another future direction is to resolve the so-called *cultural distance paradox*, which refers to the contradictory empirical evidence about the relationship between CD and subsidiary ownership / entry mode (Brouthers and Brouthers 2001). In the past two decades, multiple meta-review papers have consistently reaffirmed the inconclusiveness of this relationship (e.g., Beugelsdijk et al. 2018; Harzing and Pudelko 2016; Kirkman et al. 2006; Magnusson et al. 2008; Morschett et al. 2010; Reus and Rottig 2009; Shenkar 2001; Tihanyi et al. 2005; Zhao et al. 2004). Kirkman et al. (2006: 302) stated that 'the most glaring need…is to explain the conflicting findings regarding the effects of cultural distance on various organizational decisions such as entry mode choice' (Kirkman et al. 2006: 302). Harzing and Pudelko (2016: 25) reached the conclusion that 'cultural distance (or any other type of distance) has very little explanatory value' and recommended the need to distance ourselves from the distance concept. Based on these reviews, Ambos and Håkanson (2014: 1) commented that 'it is unclear what this large stream of papers has collectively accomplished'. Some scholars even surmised that 'cultural distance is not central to transaction cost economics' (e.g., Dikova and Brouthers 2009).

Ambos and Håkanson (2014), based on literature, suggested a number of reasons for the aforementioned inconclusiveness, including insufficient attention to asymmetries and directionalities in CD, the use of CD as a numeric quantification as employed in physics, and the 'reification' of CD whereby scholars come to take CD for granted and, by largely ignoring the rationale and assumptions that underpinned it originally, fail to derive useful insights (Lane et al. 2006). Among these reasons, the reification of CD is the most apparent. According to Ambos and Håkanson (2014) and Stahl and Tung (2015), despite CD being a widely used variable, it is often only 'ritually' cited or used as a control with little or no attempt to interpret and discuss its statistical (non-)significance in the results. Only a handful of studies used CD as their main construct, albeit with an increasing trend. However, even such studies may have suffered from simplistic replications of the original arguments and failed to make progress toward a better understanding of how CD matters (Maseland et al. 2018).

The rationale underpinning CD was based on the need to measure the degrees of dissimilarity in the study of internationalization process by 'Uppsala School' scholars (e.g., Johanson and Vahlne 1977), a concept which can be traced to Beckerman's (1956) concept of 'psychic distance'. The introduction of the concept of CD is to emphasize the fact that international business is affected not only by physical or geographic distance but also by the cost of collecting and interpreting information required to effect international transactions (Ambos and Håkanson 2014). This seems to suggest that CD should not be treated in a similar way to physical distance in the form of a numeric quantification as employed in physics, maybe in part due to concerns about the asymmetries and directionalities in CD. However, this book provided several new insights into the inconclusiveness of the relationship between CD and entry mode. We discuss them in turn.

7.7.2.1 It Is Erroneous to Focus on the Direct Effects of Cultural Distance

The majority of existing studies studied the main effect of CD on various organizational decisions (e.g., Beugelsdijk et al. 2018; Kirkman et al. 2006). Nevertheless, as suggested by our behavioral framework in Fig. 5.1, CD is only part of cognition, and it is *erroneous* to expect a direct effect on governance structures because it can have entirely different predictions according to uncertainty controllability. The arguments in support of a positive relationship between CD and governance structure based on TCE can be readily used to support a negative relationship based on ROT. As such, instead of distinguishing between physical and cultural distances and blaming the inattention to asymmetries and directionalities in CD, we suggest that a more productive way of resolving the 'cultural distance paradox' lies in the recognition of CD as a measure of cognitive bounds and the consequent shift of focus from CD itself to the mechanisms through which CD is applied in interpreting environment in the internationalization process. Instead of focusing on the main effects of CD, future research should study the interaction effects between CD and various other variables.

The erroneous assumption about a direct and unambiguous causal linkage between CD and managerial choice or other outcome variables has been hinted at in some studies (e.g., Tihanyi et al. 2005; Tung and Verbeke 2010). These studies suggest that greater attention to the context—or 'contextual intelligence'—and processes can help us better appreciate how contexts affect specific outcomes arising from CD (Tung and Verbeke 2010). This is to say that more research attention should be placed on the interaction effects of CD and other contextual or process variables. Meta-analyses indeed show that the direct effect of CD failed to receive statistical support, but the moderation effects yielded important insights. The moderators include country of investment, industry type, MNC origin, sample time frame, and measurement instrument used (Tihanyi et al. 2005).

Nevertheless, there is a significant difference between the view in this book and the view in the literature (e.g., Tung and Verbeke 2010), even though they both call for attention to the interaction effect between CD and other contextual or process variables. Despite the suggested attention to 'contextual intelligence' in the existing literature, the intended focus is still on CD, albeit greater attention is called for on contextual factors. The suggestion is still cognition-centric, positivist, and non-behavioral and, hence, less likely to consider psychological biases that arise from CD. In order to realize the full explanatory power of CD, the approach expressed in this book is a self-conscious, emotion-, or psychology-centric one, which relegates CD as reflecting cognitive bounds and treats it as a 'tool' used by *manas* in perceiving and interpreting external environment. The approach is thus truly behavioral, capable of accounting for psychological biases arising from CD. The 'cultural distance paradox' is a symptom of a cognition-centric view and cannot be resolved without an emotion-centric turn (cf. Panksepp 2004). We discuss this further in Subsect. 7.7.3.

The arguments in the previous paragraph parallel that of the distinction between derivational unification and ontological unification (see Subsect. 7.5.4.1), and the third point in Subsect. 7.7.8, concerning the importance of *reasoning direction* in theory advancement and knowledge discovery. When the focus is on CD, scholars move from contextual factors to justify the relationship between CD and an outcome variable. Such a relationship is already assumed to exist in a deductive manner. Under such circumstances, CD is assumed to be fixed, and, as such, psychological biases arising from CD cannot be considered. In other words, the black box of CD is not of concern. On the contrary, the approach adopted in this book is *manas*-centric and focuses on external phenomena, and it moves from CD to the phenomena of concern. Under such circumstances, CD is relegated to the role of cognitive bounds and thus psychological biases arising from CD can be considered in the process of *manas* applying cognition. This is to say, a *manas*-centric approach opens up the black box of CD.

Once the importance of a *manas*-centric, behavioral approach is understood, two things follow: (1) Scholars can go ahead with studying various interaction effects between CD and different types of uncertainty, which are fundamental contextual factors. Because a behavioral approach is also inherently dynamic, such interaction effects should be studied in a longitudinal way. Otherwise, the benefits of the psychology-centric approach cannot be realized. (2) It becomes irrelevant to study the main effect of CD since it can have totally opposite directions depending on the types of uncertainty. It is erroneous to assume the existence of a direct causal link between CD and some outcome variables, as hinted in Tihanyi et al. (2005) and Tung and Verbeke (2010). The relationships between CD and outcome variables in the traditional TCE framework are tested in an assumption-omitted way as a result of assumptional asymmetry and as a result, offer little value to managers' practical decision-making. Even worse, MNC managers may have been misinformed by such assumption-omitted reasoning and made wrong decisions due to inattention to competing decision-making mechanisms. This book refocuses attention on mechanisms. The resolution of the 'cultural distance paradox' should not be based on the study of how contextual factors contextualize CD in a positivist, deductive manner but should rely on a creative, inductive approach, whereby the black box of CD is opened up and the reasoning direction goes from CD to various contextual factors. The resolution should not aim to confirm the main effects between CD and some outcome variables but instead to elucidate the mechanisms through which CD affects managerial decisions in different ways. In doing so, CD can be used in non-superficial ways and attention can be paid to the mechanisms which are at play in the influence of CD (Zaheer et al. 2012). Since this approach is outside the black box of CD and capable of considering generative mechanisms, it is more concerned with competing causal mechanisms in a deeper ontology—or 'ontological intelligence'—rather than 'contextual intelligence' as suggested by Tung and Verbeke (2010).

As for the distinction between physical and cultural distances, we think the distinction is of less importance. As mentioned in Sects. 4.7 and 4.1, various types of distance operate in a similar way and cause similar biases (Trout 2007; Zaheer et al. 2012). The arguments supporting the relationships between CD and some common outcome variables can often be extended to other types of distances such as temporal, institutional, and geographic distance (e.g., Gooris and Peeters 2014; Peng and Beamish 2014; Peng and Camp 2015). We discuss this point in Subsects. 7.7.3 and 7.7.4.

7.7.2.2 Studying the Effect of Cultural Distance on Ownership Level Rather Than Mode

No matter whether the resolution of the 'cultural distance paradox' is approached through a traditional positivist way or a behavioral way, greater variation in outcome variables and longitudinal data is desirable to increase the statistical power of explanatory models. While behavioral TCE, or even traditional TCE (David and Han 2004),[8] can and should be applied across time, the TCE literature in general and the entry mode literature in international business focus on the binary comparison of governance structure or entry modes by estimating logistic models, rather than the study of ownership levels over time using longitudinal regression methods (Beugelsdijk et al. 2018: 98). Among various binary comparisons, the most frequently examined choice is between joint ventures (JVs) and wholly owned subsidiaries (WOSs), which are ownership-based modes (Brouthers and Hennart 2007). Ownership level strategy is 'commonly subsumed under the broader topic of entry mode strategy' (Delios and Beamish 1999: 915; Peng and Beamish 2019; Zhao et al. 2004), reflecting the frequency of entry mode studies over that of ownership levels. While the benefits of longitudinal methods have been acknowledged, the examination of longitudinal data is often only mentioned as one item on the wish list (David and Han 2004; Geyskens et al. 2006).

Comparing mode instead of ownership levels has multiple disadvantages. First, it is a bad practice in terms of statistics since it means the categorization or aggregation of a continuous range of ownership data into arbitrarily assigned groups (Taylor et al. 2006). Second, many entry mode studies focus on a limited set of modes and examine choice among them. This raises the questions of whether choice sets are complete and whether the constraints placed on choice sets have forced scholars to investigate only part of a potentially broader question (Shaver 2013). Third, related to the previous point, entry mode is a multidimensional concept, and Brouthers and Hennart (2007) identified 16 different mode types that have been used in the literature. The most commonly studied choice is that between JVs and WOSs, which are ownership modes. Other dimensions include green field vs. acquisition (establishment mode) and contracts vs. equity. But as pointed out by Brouthers and Hennart (2007: 397), there is unfortunately no consensus as the precise relationship among contracts, JVs and WOSs, on the one hand, and among these three modes and entry through green fields or acquisitions. Fourth, longitudinally, the ownership adjustment over time is often not through mode switch but through level adjustment within a specific mode. This is because entry modes, once established, are difficult to change (Pedersen et al. 2002). Under such circumstances, mode comparison does not reflect organizational dynamics since they are too coarse-grained. Fifth, cross-culturally, the categorical nature of the comparison between JVs and WOSs disregards the fact that CD reflects not a dichotomous distinction of same vs different but the whole gamut of country options, providing a yardstick by which many alternatives can be measured and compared (Zaheer et al. 2012).

Considering these disadvantages, we call for longitudinal studies on ownership levels rather than entry mode comparisons, particularly between JVs and WOSs. A behavioral theory is a temporally dynamic theory, and as such, the models for it should also reflect the dynamic nature using longitudinal data on outcome variables which show detectable variation. That said, we do not deny the need for more entry mode studies (Hennart and Slangen 2015). Our suggestion is that some fundamental questions about entry mode research, such as 'What determines the evolution of operations resulting from suboptimal mode choices?' and 'How is the entry decision process structured?' (Hennart and Slangen 2015: 120), may be answered far more precisely by studying ownership levels than entry modes. We think that our suggestions may increase the chance that the 'cultural distance paradox' be resolved and a fuller understanding be gained about the role of CD in organizational decision-making process. Once this paradox is resolved, subsequent studies can then focus on teasing out more nuanced insights into the precise relationship among various entry modes along different dimensions.

7.7.2.3 Precise Conceptualization of Cultural Distance

For the resolution of the 'cultural distance paradox', it is also paramount to have a clear conceptualization of CD itself. In the existing literature, there are two related confusions surrounding the concept.

1. The first confusion is about what CD measures and does not measure. In a recent comprehensive review paper of CD and firm internationalization, it is said that most studies view 'cultural distance as a source of uncertainty, complexity, and additional costs' (Beugelsdijk et al. 2018: 97). This conflated statement largely summarized how CD is used in the international business literature: It is used in an ambiguous way and treated as a black box, without considering the mechanisms through which CD operates. When incorrectly used as a source of uncertainty, CD has been used widely as a measure for both external (uncontrollable) and internal (or more accurately, partner or controllable) uncertainties, which theoretically can have opposite effects (Peng 2012; Shenkar 2001; Slangen and van Tulder 2009; Zhao et al. 2004), as explained in Chapter 5. As such, the existing literature is confused about what CD measures. This book suggests that CD measures neither controllable nor uncontrollable uncertainties, but instead reflects cognitive bounds. We believe that our clear conceptualization of CD will facilitate the resolution of the 'cultural distance paradox'.
2. The second source of confusion is the tendency to conflate cultural profiles (cultural dimensions) or other contextual factors with distance—the so-called 'distance-profile conflation' (Maseland et al. 2018). This tendency is widespread, and its occurrence is not limited to published works but also often appears in peer review comments based on the author's own experience. However, cultural dimensions/cultural profiles and CD are two fundamentally different concepts (e.g., Drogendijk and Holm 2012; Maseland et al. 2018; Peng and Beamish 2014; Shenkar et al. 2008) and measure two different constructs: Cultural dimensions (cultural profiles) measure culture itself (Hofstede 1991; Shenkar et al. 2008) in an emic way,

while CD measures cultural dissimilarity in an etic way and reflects cognitive bounds.

The current study suggests that distance and profiles (contexts) should be clearly distinguished but not separated in order to adopt a *manas*-centered behavioral approach, in which distance reflects cognitive bounds and cultural profiles embody contexts, and their dialectic (emic × etic) interaction elucidates the explanatory power of CD. In other words, the relationship between CD and host country contexts is not an 'either-or' question focusing on parts but a 'both' question focusing on mechanisms through which CD operates. When separated from contexts, CD has little explanatory power (Harzing and Pudelko 2016), but when clearly distinguished from and placed in contexts, CD becomes an integral part of a behavioral process and can offer additional explanatory power which was unaccounted for by the traditional TCE.

Considering the low explanatory power of CD per se, a 'paradigm shift' is called for to move 'away from the—admittedly conceptually highly seductive—distance concept' and instead focus 'first and foremost on context' (Harzing and Pudelko 2016: 26). It is also concluded that 'the explanatory power of distance is highly limited once home and host country contexts are accounted for, and that any significant effects of cultural distance on entry mode choice might simply be caused by inadequate sampling' (Harzing and Pudelko 2016: 1). This book suggests that the Harzing and Pudelko (2016)'s approach is a good example of the 'either-or' mentality focusing on parts but losing sight of the mechanisms through which CD operates. It moved away from a partial, CD-centric view, but went to the other extreme by embracing a context-centric view, which is still partial. In terms of the emic/etic distinction discussed in Sect. 3.3, what they propose is a shift from an etic perspective to an emic one, instead of the adoption of a dialectic perspective that we call for, in which the emic perspective complements and interacts with the etic perspective (e.g., Buckley et al. 2014). We hope that the framework shown in Fig. 5.1 will help scholars to overcome the 'distance-profile conflation' and resolve the 'cultural distance paradox'. The explanatory power of CD does not lie in its main effect but rather in its interaction effects with various contextual factors in a process manner using longitudinal data.

7.7.2.4 Cultural Distance Is a Symmetrical Construct: Empirical Implications

An important criticism toward the CD measure commonly used in international business is its assumption of symmetry, as brilliantly argued by Shenkar (2001, 2012), and followed by many others (e.g., Ambos and Håkanson 2014; Kirkman et al. 2006; Tung and Verbeke 2010; Zaheer et al. 2012). This study, on the contrary, suggests that the CD construct and its measures based on Kogut and Singh (1988) should be regarded as symmetrical since it is a measure of cognitive bounds. Recent research supports our view. For example, Vaccarini et al. (2017) and Azar and Drogendijk (2019) suggest that the CD measure is a measure of *objective* CD, which is different from perceived CD. If CD is objective, then it should be considered as a symmetrical concept, and research focus should be placed on how managers or other economic agents perceive the objective CD differently according to their country of origin. Another argument which supports our view is the fact that CD and its Kogut and Singh (1988) measure were based on etic research (Hofstede 1991; Zhu and Bargiela-Chiappini 2013). If a concept is based on cultural universals and its measurement is based on etic cultural dimensions, it should be symmetrical because the etic perspective aims to identify cultural components with equivalent meanings across cultures (Berry 1990; Morris et al. 1999). By definition, 'etic statements are verified when independent observers [i.e. analysts] using similar operations agree [with one another]....' (Harris 2001: 575). As such, CD is an objective concept derived from cultural universals underlying social structures (Schwartz 1992).

In a sense, Shenkar (2001, 2012)'s view reflected the conflation of cognition with psychology and the treatment of CD as a black box rather than a process-friendly construct. The confusion arose from a CD-centric approach where psychology was not placed in the driver's seat. Recent developments, such as the works by Vaccarini et al. (2017) and Azar and Drogendijk (2019), are consistent with the view expressed in this book and have potential to open up the black box of CD and point to an important avenue of future research. Interestingly, distorted perceptions about objective distances is not limited to CD. For example, researchers have long documented the discrepancies between perceived and objective geographic distance (e.g., Tversky 1992, 2003)

In terms of the emic-etic distinction, the concerns about CD's symmetrical assumption result from the conflation of emic and etic perspectives.

From the perspective of the emic-etic distinction, CD is etic (universal) but psychological biases are emic or cultural specific (e.g., Rieger et al. 2015). Emic differences at the two ends of CD can create uneven psychological perceptions about the same objective CD. As such, in order to shed more light on the different views about the (a)symmetry of CD, future research should use data on MNCs from more home countries in order to have more variations in cultural emics. The etic and emic perspectives have to be integrated to consider CD as a process-friendly construct.

7.7.2.5 Meta-Reviews on the Interaction Rather Than Main Effects of Cultural Distance

Among the numerous meta-reviews on the relationship between CD and subsidiary ownership / entry mode (e.g., Beugelsdijk et al. 2018; Harzing and Pudelko 2016; Kirkman et al. 2006; Magnusson et al. 2008; Morschett et al. 2010; Reus and Rottig 2009; Shenkar 2001; Tihanyi et al. 2005; Zhao et al. 2004), none is specially dedicated to the review of interaction effects of CD. Even though sometimes such interaction effects are included in the reviews, the variables which interact with CD are categorical, such as country of investment, industry type, MNC origin, sample time frame, and measurement instrument used (Tihanyi et al. 2005).

This book suggests that more insights can be gained from future meta-reviews on the interaction effects of CD, considering that it is erroneous to expect a direct effect of CD on governance structures. While scholars may have not been consciously aware of the importance of a paradigm shift that we recommended above, they may have tested various interaction effects between CD and some explanatory variables based on some other theoretical justifications. We hope such existing empirical evidence, once recast into our *manas*-centric perspective, can shed some unintended new light.

7.7.2.6 Resolving the 'Cultural Distance Paradox' of Performance

While this book applied the behavioral TCE to the study of MNC subsidiary ownership, its explanatory power is not limited to ownership and entry mode research. Even though TCE is a theory of firm mainly concerned with organizational boundary, the theorizing at the core is based on supposed efficiency (or value in the case of our behavioral TCE) which has performance implications, for both MNC parent firms and their subsidiaries. Magnusson et al. (2008) concluded in their meta-analytic review paper that, overall, 'the results for the cultural differences—performance relationship are highly similar to those for entry strategy'. We suggest that future research can similarly aspire to resolve the 'cultural distance paradox' of performance (Wang and Schaan 2008).

There are multiple review papers on the CD-performance link (e.g., Beugelsdijk et al. 2018; Magnusson et al. 2008; Reus and Rottig 2009; Tihanyi et al. 2005). The relationship is believed to be a *slightly* negative one, as shown in Magnusson et al. (2008), Reus and Rottig (2009), and Tihanyi et al. (2005). But the relationship may differ according to whether it is for the whole MNC or subsidiaries. For example, Beugelsdijk et al. (2018) found that CD has a negative effect on subsidiary performance but no effect on the performance of the whole MNC. Considering that the meta-analytic findings are based on the aggregation of both positive and negative relationships and that the negative relationship is a weak one, the CD-performance link is not conclusive and presents a 'cultural distance paradox' of performance (Wang and Schaan 2008).

To resolve the paradox, Wang and Schaan (2008) proposed an inverted U-shaped relationship, based on the argument of the existence of two competing effects (disruptive and synergistic effects) at play at different levels of CD. This study can enhance their theoretical arguments by providing deeper insights based on managerial perceptions and competing biases, consistent with new development in international business research (Azar and Drogendijk 2019).

7.7.3 CD Is Dead, Long Live CD: A Call for a Paradigm Shift from Distance to Biases

Due to the long-standing inconclusiveness of empirical findings on the relationships between CD and some common outcome variables, the validity of CD has been challenged by many scholars, among whom Kirkman et al. (2006), Shenkar (2001, 2012), and Tung and Verbeke (2010) may be noteworthy for their systematic critiques. For example, Tung and Verbeke (2010), revisiting and augmenting Shenkar's (2001) seminal analysis, presented 10 common assumptions characteristic of much applied empirical work on CD measures and dimensions. It is believed that the conceptualization of CD as objective, fixed, homogenous, symmetrical, and linear is flawed and not particularly useful in its current state (Shenkar 2001; Zaheer et al. 2012). This diagnosis seems to have been backed up by the empirical side. As pointed out by Ambos and

Håkanson (2014), in spite of CD being a widely used variable, it is most of the time only ritually cited or used as a control variable. In addition, it is not clear what has been accomplished in the large literature of papers on CD. While it is an overstatement to say that CD is dead, we can at least say that the research progress is stagnant.

Nevertheless, this book suggests that the stagnation of theoretical and empirical advancement related to CD can largely be attributed to the self-*un*conscious, CD-centric, positivist approach adopted in the current literature, which ignores the emics. In such an approach, while CD is *rightly* regarded as 'a rational, objective and quantifiable gauge' in the etic sense (Shenkar 2012: 15), the more 'messier' but interesting emic-etic interactions are eschewed.

This study calls for a paradigm shift. We call for a self-conscious, *manas*-centric approach to CD which opens up the black box of CD and treats CD as cognitive bounds giving rise to various levels of biases. In this *manas*-centric approach, CD as 'a rational, objective and quantifiable gauge' (Shenkar 2012: 15) is not a shortcoming but becomes a merit, because it is characteristic of cognitive bounds. As discussed in Subsect. 7.7.2.4, CD is meant to be a conceptually symmetrical concept, contrary to what some scholars have argued (e.g., Shenkar 2001, 2012). As a result, our *manas*-centric approach reaffirms the intrinsic values of CD for its considerable appeal[9] that have made it a well-entrenched construct (Zaheer et al. 2012).

Once a self-conscious angle is taken, the black box of CD is opened up and psychological biases arising from CD can be considered. In so doing, CD is not treated as a positivist variable but as a dimension of social structures which give rise to psychological biases. Consequently, numerous research avenues are unlocked. Here, we suggest a few: (1) the examination of how CD contextualizes prospect theory; (2) the examination of how CD contextualizes effectuation theory; (3) the examination of how CD interacts with cultural dimensions or cultural profiles to gain more insights into and resolve the 'distance-profile conflation' (Maseland et al. 2018) in the spirit of emic-etic interaction. Interested readers can similarly come up with their own research questions so long as they do not treat CD as a positivist variable but appreciate the importance of CD as a dimension of social structures wherein biases can arise and learning can take place. These research questions will be embodied in three-way interactions with a temporal dimension to consider learning. While the need to consider contextual factors has been suggested, our approach to CD is new in the sense that 'everything of importance has been said before by someone who did not discover the importance of it' (Augier 2013).

In sum, by considering CD not merely as a rational and objective gauge but also as a source of biases for *manas*, our *manas*-centric approach considers the subjective and perceptual side of CD (Chapman et al. 2008; Zaheer et al. 2012). CD not only serves as a parsimonious quantitative measure of cognitive bounds but also facilitates the contextualization of the socially complex MNC behavior in an ontological deeper and wider actual domain of CR. In so doing, CD is used as a springboard rather than a crutch (Maseland et al. 2018). We predict that there will be a new surge of studies adopting our proposed psychology-centric perspective. CD thus has the potential to rejuvenate 'a mature field' of international business (Poulis and Poulis 2018). Considering this, we can reasonably declare, 'long live cultural distance!'

7.7.4 Exploring Other Distance Measures

As expressed by Zaheer et al. (2012: 19): 'international management is the management of distance'. Similarly, Pitelis and Verbeke (2007: 143) noted that a 'theory of MNE growth…needs to address the impact of distance on the internationalization process'. Nevertheless, there are numerous other distance measures in addition to CD. These include institutional distance (Xu and Shenkar 2002), geographic distance (Peng and Beamish 2014), temporal distance (Peng and Camp 2015), economic distance (Ghemawat 2001), and psychic distance (Håkanson and Ambos 2010), to name a few. Since various types of distance operate in a similar way and cause similar biases (Trout 2007; Zaheer et al. 2012), and since the arguments supporting the relationships between CD and some common outcome variables can often be extended to other types of distances such as temporal, institutional, and geographic distance (e.g., Gooris and Peeters 2014; Peng and Beamish 2014), future studies should consider more types of distance in a similar way to our behavioral approach which considers the biases arising from these distances. Considering more types of distance implies the widening and broadening of social and institutional width and depth in the actual domain of CR, which has the potential to further our understanding of MNC social life, its cultural and institutional embedding, and its interactional patterns. It has been called for that 'when possible use more than one distance measure' (Ambos and Håkanson 2014: 5; Tung and Verbeke 2010).

Again, this book suggests that the incorporation of various distance measures should be done in a psychology-centric way in order to eschew the aforementioned traps in which CD has traditionally fallen. The current status seems to suggest that these various other distance measures are being treated in a similar way to the conventional treatment of CD. In other words, instead of focusing on the biases arising from these distance measures, attention is concentrated on them per se and on their interrelationships. For example, Håkanson and Ambos (2010) studied the relationship between geographic distance and psychic distance and found that the former predicts the latter. Similarly, Dastidar and Zaheer (2010: 2) found that 'geographic distance overwhelms cultural and institutional distance in explaining the need for knowledge to mitigate information asymmetry'. Berry et al. (2010) showed that many of these distances are highly correlated. Summarizing these findings, Zaheer et al. (2012: 20) commented that 'such objective, lower-order distance constructs such as time, space and perhaps even language and religion may in fact provide more powerful tools of investigation than complex higher-order distance constructs whose multidimensionality has been reduced', and that it is difficult to untangle their individual effects if they are included in the same analysis.

But as discussed in previous subsections, it may again be erroneous to focus on these distance measures per se because they may behave in a similar way to that of CD, being neutral concepts and capable of yielding opposite predictions according to uncertainty controllability. Hence, comparing relative predictive power of various distance measures in their main effects is a meaningless and futile endeavor. As suggested in Subsect. 7.7.3, the research focus should be addressed to the subjective side of these distances and the potential biases arising therefrom, and sufficient attention should be paid to the mechanisms through which these distances operate. Along with these arguments, we suggest that more productive strategy to use these distance measures would be to focus on the *different* levels of psychological biases arising from different distance measures. Instead of studying the relationships among and relative predominance of the main effects of various distance measures (e.g., Håkanson and Ambos 2010; Dastidar and Zaheer 2010), future study can compare the different levels of psychological biases arising from different distance measures in the interaction effects between these distance measures and contextual factors which activate competing mechanisms. For example, we surmise that, in today's global environment, geographic distance may give rise to lower levels of psychological biases than cultural and institutional distances, even though geographic distance dominates or overwhelms other types of distance in their main effects without considering psychological biases. Future studies should validate these suggestions.

In sum, this book concurs with the comment by Zaheer et al. (2012: 19) that 'international management is the management of distance'. Additionally, this book casts new light on this interesting comment. Considering that cultural distance reflects cognitive bounds, and that different distances operate in a similar way and cause similar biases (Trout 2007; Zaheer et al. 2012), we suggest that it can be more accurately said that international business is the management of psychological biases arising from various distances.

7.7.5 Exploring Other Controllable Uncertainties

In Chapter 2, we proposed the term 'controllable uncertainty' instead of other terms such as opportunism. The existing TCE literature predominantly focuses on partner uncertainty or opportunism, which is only one of a broad set of uncertainties which are considered controllable. Future studies should pay more attention to other types of controllable uncertainties. For example, Cuypers and Martin (2010) studied capability uncertainty and scope uncertainty. As we discussed in Chapter 2 and other places, too much focus on opportunism blindfolded research about the importance of other important uncertainties.

7.7.6 Use Uncertainty Controllability as a Continuous Variable

As mentioned in Chapter 1 and explained in Chapter 2, Williamson and the existing TCE literature have almost entirely missed the point that TCE actually assumes *controllable* uncertainty. In Chapters 2 and 5, we explained that TCE is not well suited to the study of uncontrollable uncertainties, for which (behavioral) ROT is the applicable theory. In Fig. 5.1, for demonstration purpose, we treated uncertainty controllability as a dichotomous 'yes/no' variable. In the empirical application in Chapter 6, we assumed that opportunism, as one type of uncertainty, is controllable. This was due to the archival data and single uncertainty type (partner uncertainty or opportunism) setting, which does not allow us to ask firms in our sample to rate their perceived uncertainty controllability in a more graduated and fine-grained manner.

Nevertheless, uncertainty controllability is apparently a continuous, or at least ordinal, variable according to the uncertainty perception literature (De Weck et al. 2007; Miller and Lessard 2001). Treating uncertainty controllability as a dichotomous variable, while a welcome step for its being based on perception, disregards the variations in perceptions of uncertainty controllability across nations and uncertainty types and between economic agents. For the former case, research shows that risk preference and uncertainty avoidance propensity are subject to considerable cross-national variation (e.g., Hofstede 1991; Rieger et al. 2015), and such difference will interact with the perception of controllability of different types of uncertainty. For the latter, due to firm heterogeneity, controllable uncertainty for one firm may be perceived as uncontrollable by another firm and vice versa, depending on many factors, such as firm size, subsidiary size, and experience. Future studies should use questionnaires to consider uncertainty controllability in more detail. Additionally, the interaction effects between uncertainty controllability and other contextual factors and transaction attributes (such as asset specificity) may also yield more valuable insights.

7.7.7 *Are TCE Relationships Merely Empirical Regularities and/or Self-fulfilling Prophecy?*

In consideration of so many 'uncertain' empirical findings waiting for resolution, it may be reasonable to put forward a more general research direction, that is, to radically examine whether the majority of TCE-based empirical findings are actually empirical event regularities based on partial assumptions and self-fulfilling prophecies (cf. Ghoshal and Moran 1996). This is because TCE empirical literature (e.g., Macher and Richman 2008; David and Han 2004) has been dominated by assumption-omitted testing using reduced models, and empirical findings so derived are subjected to *indefinite* number of alternative explanations (Bunge 1997; Tsang 2006). While event regularities can be obtained in a closed system which TCE assumes, due to its omission of consideration of generative mechanisms, such event regularities do not offer much of the most needed insights into the mechanisms which affect decision-making. Such regularities may simply be spurious correlations or may reflect the existence of a third variable which simultaneously impacts the dependent and independent variables in the event regularity relationship (Lawson 2003). Critical realism rejects the notion of causality as event regularity in favor of causality as generative powers. Critical realism also considers that the major concern of a theory is to explain the mechanism rather than merely to predict event regularities.

Based on the arguments leading to Hypothesis 2 in Chapter 6, which is a reconceptualization of the relationship between CD and ownership level, we suspect that the majority of TCE empirical findings may in fact reflect similar event regularities devoid of mechanisms. Such findings may also similarly be the aggregate effects of multiple competing mechanisms contingent upon different types of uncertainties and depending on the relative numbers of serious investors and 'gamblers', among others. The positivist approach adopted in traditional TCE prevented it from looking beyond opportunism-based explanations.

In order to advance empirical TCE literature, attention should be paid to the relationship between asset specificity and governance structure, because asset specificity is the most frequently numerically operationalized one among various TCE concepts (e.g., Buckley and Chapman 2002; Joskow 1988; Whinston 2003). Asset specificity is also a multifaceted concept characterized by complex definitional features which are reflected in an inconsistent and rather ad hoc operationalization of the construct (De Vita et al. 2011). We suggest that this relationship should be put under more mechanism-informed testing in several intertwined ways.

First, the focus should be on various potentially mechanism-informed interaction effects between asset specificity and other contextual variables. Similar to the arguments leading to Hypothesis 2, it may be misguided to study the main effect of asset specificity considering that such effect may similarly be contingent on uncertainty types or degree of uncertainty controllability. The main effect, even if empirically supported using assumption-omitted reduced models, is not much informative because it offers no insights into the mechanisms or routes through which asset specificity affects governance decision-making.

Second, the relationship needs to be tested using competing hypotheses, which is an effective way to deliberate the relative merits of alternative theories (Losee 2005; Miller and Tsang 2011). It is an effective way because considering only one theory in hypothesis development not only shuts off the vision of researchers in theorizing but also prevents scholars from reporting insignificant or opposite relationships which are of the same, if not more, value for theory advancement. 'Analysis of competing hypotheses' also helps researchers overcome or reduce cognitive biases (Heuer 1999). While sometimes implemented (e.g., Poppo and Zenger 1998), it generally has been considered 'atypical' and been under-utilized by researchers in spite of its potential in advancing theory (Pleggenkuhle-Miles and Peng 2009).

The consideration of alternative theories is particularly relevant to the relationship between specific assets and governance structures and their consequent performance implications, considering the many dimensions of asset specificity (De Vita et al. 2011). There has been an increasing interest in studying the role of specific asset in organizational boundary decision from different theoretical perspectives other than TCE, such as the resource-based view and relational exchange theory (De Vita et al. 2011).

Third, the relationship can be tested by considering competing mechanisms in the same model using various relevant interaction effects. While it is difficult to do so in a closed system using reduced models and with the conflation of various types of uncertainty, our proposed conceptual separation and individual measurement of opportunism and bounded rationality and the classification of uncertainty based on controllability make it possible to consider competing mechanism in the same model. Particularly, the international dimension of this book means that there are variations in some common TCE variables such as opportunism (partner uncertainty), uncertainty, and cognitive bounds, thus opening up opportunities to test alternative mechanisms based on alternative theories in the same model using multiple interaction effects. The interaction effects between bounded rationality (cognitive bounds) and various types of uncertainty will likely aid in teasing out different causal mechanisms.

Fourth, and ideally, the relationship needs to be dealt with in a behavioral way and longitudinally, as our framework in Fig. 5.1 shows. Behavioral TCE will, perforce, induce scholars to consider generative mechanisms and use structural models. Traditional TCE's static equilibrium assumption-omitted modeling does not allow the testing of alternative theories due to its inability to consider alternative generative mechanisms in an equilibrium setting (cf. Poppo and Zenger 1998). In reality, however, firm boundary may reflect more of a relationship than a transaction, more of a repeated-game of self-enforcing relational contracts than a deterministic equilibrium outcome. Under such situations, specific assets can be argued for non-integration since they make it possible to design relational contracts with higher-powered incentives (Kvaløy 2007; cf. Subsect. 7.5.4).

Fifth, the previous point may be even more germane considering that the specific assets considered in traditional TCE are largely existing, internal, and one-sided ones. However, asset specificity can also be two-sided or reciprocal (Artz 1999; De Vita et al. 2010; Héritier et al. 2009; Kvaløy 2007; Thauer 2014), such as non-transferable investments made by both parties, which are geared toward the consideration of future asset growth and performance instead of only governance. The notion of reciprocal investments and their beneficial effects had been suggested by Williamson (1983, 1996) himself (De Vita et al. 2011). Firms focused on growth opportunities are more likely to choose low integration governance structures (Cotei and Farhat 2017). An additional asset feature to consider is whether they are enduring or not (Poppo and Zenger 1998). Governance structure will differ according to these features of specific assets. The majority of literature in the traditional TCE has not been based on more fine-grained conceptualization of specific assets and their implications in terms of internalization vs. externalization (cf. Subsect. 7.5.4).

In sum, we call for more critical examination of TCE relationships because the positivist assumption-omitted settings in the literature may have significantly hindered theory development and advancement (Tsang 2006). By assuming controllable uncertainty, TCE's predictive power and 'success story' (Macher and Richman 2008; Williamson 1999) may reflect only a tautology as a result of its positivist philosophy.[10] While such tautological analysis does have its merits, it is not a good idea to 'have the empirical cart before the theoretical horse' (Williamson 2008: 254). Because predictions based on positivist reasoning can often be justified from alternative theoretical perspectives and because the realism of assumptions and the importance of underlying mechanisms were brushed aside, limits need to be placed on the normative implications of positivist theories. As Hodgson comments, '[a] faulty explanation would be likely to lead to faults in corporate strategy and in the design of governance structures' (Hodgson 2004: 404).

7.7.8 *The Formalization of Transaction Cost Economics*

Finally, TCE would benefit considerably from future efforts to formalize its theoretical foundation (Macher and Richman 2008), since TCE continues to suffer from a lack of rigorous mathematical foundation as noted first by Joskow (1988).[11] Williamson concurred that a 'continuing challenge to transaction cost economics is to move beyond semiformal analysis of a reduced-form kind to do fully-formal analysis' (1998: 50) since TCE has been preoccupied with the question 'What's going on here?', as opposed to the imperative 'This is the law here' (Williamson 1993: 38). There are several principal advantages of a more formal approach to theory building.

First, formalization will force scholars to increase the precision in their definitions of key concepts and consequently reduce definitional ambiguities (Adner et al. 2009; Asmussen and Foss 2014; Buckley and Hashai 2009; Macher and Richman 2008). In the formalization process, implicit assumptions have to be brought to the surface and made explicit. As pointed out by Adner et al. (2009), whereas an assumption or a proposition can often be stated in verbal theorizing (the natural language approach commonly adopted in management research) without being even fully understood, formal languages require that they be understood deeply. Traditional TCE suffers exactly from the former. As discussed in Chapter 2, despite the extensive size of TCE theoretical and empirical literature, the basic assumptions and concepts in TCE (opportunism, uncertainty, and bounded rationality) have been seriously conflated with no questions asked. The role of controllable uncertainty or uncertainty controllability as an assumption has *never* been spelled out in the literature. We hope that our propositions aimed at increasing definitional precision, as discussed in Chapter 2, can help scholars in future endeavors in formalizing TCE or our behavioral TCE.

Second, theory formalization can help researchers to more easily and accurately test theoretical propositions (Adner et al. 2009). Hypotheses can be refined and tested with more precision as a result of reduced ambiguity surrounding the meaning of and, hence, the more accurate measurement of key concepts (Adner et al. 2009; Macher and Richman 2008).

Third, maybe more importantly, theory formalization can help researchers identify unanticipated implications of the assumptions of a theory, and thus leads to theoretical advancement (Adner et al. 2009). This point can particularly be elucidated from the perspectives of assumptional symmetry and explanatory unification (Foss and Hallberg 2014; Mäki 2001). As pointed out by Adner et al. (2009), most verbal theorizing exercises involve recognizing a relationship between two variables and then trying to identify a set of assumptions that would lead to such a relationship. In such exercises, one moves backward from propositions to assumptions which justify the propositions. An apparent limitation on this approach is that one cannot find the unexpected. On the contrary, theory formalization goes from assumptions to propositions and, hence, can lead to counterintuitive and surprising propositions that might follow from a set of assumptions. In other words, verbal theorizing leads researchers to treat assumptions in an ad hoc and partial way, whereas formal theorizing allows scholars to consider assumptions in a systematic and comprehensive manner. The focus of the former is the justification of propositions by using ad hoc assumptions, while that of the latter is first of all the examination of the assumptions themselves. The former parallels derivational unification, whereas the latter parallels ontological unification. Since symmetrical assumption thinking is a systematic and comprehensive approach to assumptions, and 'an important scientific and methodological principle that promotes generally accepted characteristics of good theory' (Foss and Hallberg 2014: 911), it can be considered as an effective tool in theory formalization, which tends to yield new insights into the management phenomena of concern and leads to theoretical advancement (Foss and Hallberg 2014, 2017).

Figure 5.1 vividly demonstrated the theory-advancing potential of theory formalization based on assumptional symmetry. While traditional TCE empirical literature largely used verbal theorizing and went from propositions to assumptions, which are not clearly defined and used in an ad hoc manner, our behavioral framework moves from a clear and precise definition of key concepts and a symmetrical analysis of assumptions toward more formalized development of hypotheses. And as a result of this exercise, new insights into more precise definitions of key concepts and their relationships with governance structures are obtained. While it is beyond the author's expertise to mathematically formalize the behavioral framework in Fig. 5.1, it is hoped that scholars who are mathematically equipped will be able to formalize it in the future.

7.8 Conclusion

This book is an outcome of an academic journey of organizational 'self-enquiry', in which the organizational 'self' is examined in a critical realist framework by disaggregating cognitive bounds ('the brain'), rationalizing ('the mind') and the self, and ontologically hierarchizing them in their respective empirical, actual, and real domains. It shows that a behavioral theory of the firm should first of all be a theory of organizational 'self', which has ontological intelligence or an awareness of its deep ontology wherein the organizational 'self' can utilize the firm as an explanans in order to enhance its value creation and evolutionary fit. Otherwise, the black box of the firm cannot be opened and the firm could not be treated as an explanans but as an explanandum, which prevents the firm from engaging with psychological biases (bounded rationality) and evolutionary considerations as well as results in a systematic array of theoretical and empirical deficiencies.

The book shows that many of the confusions and debates in international business, and in management research in general, arise from an 'inside the box' thinking due to shallow ontology, which drives research toward 'derivational unification' and an internal focus on costs. This can be attributed to the fact that 'the international management field seems to have engaged in a continuous disavowal of epistemic reflexivity and a critical trajectory for theory development' (Jack et al. 2008). When the organizational self is not disaggregated, it is impossible to consider the much needed epistemic reflexivity.

This book recommends that firms shift to an 'outside the box' thinking, in order for them to gear toward 'ontological unification' and an external focus on value creation and evolutionary fit. But for the black box of organizational self to be opened, organizations need an ontological 'landing place' *substrating* the firm. We suggest that critical realism can provide such ontological landing in the form of an actual domain. It is in the actual domain of critical realism that psychological processes can be foregrounded and MNCs can shift their attention to the learning-enabling and capability-enhancing aspect of bounded rationality and focus on transaction value and evolutionary fit based on ecological rationality. It is also in the actual domain that the firm can be used as an explanans, and governance structures can be used as instruments for adaptation in a behavioral process in which firms effectuate, learn, and adjust toward more ecologically rational directions in a market of uncertainty. This book highlights the fundamental role of various types of distances in making bounded rationality theoretically and empirically relevant to behavioral theories.

In conclusion, a behavioral TCE should be a self-conscious theory which uses the firm as an explanans in order to cope with environmental uncertainties in the actual domain by activating various (competing) generative mechanisms in the real domain of critical realism. Such a theory is in fact a theory geared toward transaction value and evolutionary fit, and should be more fittingly referred to as 'transaction value economics'. In order to make TCE self-conscious, this book introduced the eight-consciousness model of the mind into the traditional TCE and opened up the black box of the theory of the firm. This book showed that a behavioral TCE, or more broadly, a behavioral theory of the firm, is just a theory of the mind writ large.

Notes

1. It is shorthand for a group of approaches to the organization and behavior of the firm that lie in-between strategic management and economics, including 'evolutionary theory of the firm', 'competence-based', 'dynamic capabilities', and 'resource-based' approaches (Foss 2003b).
2. This is a criticism of the resource-based view at large. For example, Spender (1994: 354) pointed out that '[r]esource-based theory has paid little attention to the *construction* and *management* of the [resource] bundle' (italic added). Penrose (1959) distinguished between resources and services. The former can be defined independently of their use (etic), while the latter are capabilities unique to each individual firm (emic).
3. Penrose (1959: 41) stated that "'expectations' and not 'objective facts' are the immediate determinants of a firm's behaviour, although there may be a relationship between expectations and 'facts' – indeed there must be if action is to be successful … In the last analysis the 'environment' rejects or confirms the soundness of the judgements about it, but the relevant environment is not an objective fact discoverable before the event".
4. Please note here that Penrosean managerial services are cognition-based and positivist, which assumes that managers qua managers can apply excess resources to a given set of opportunities without biases, while our approach in this book made such services *manas*-centric and more consistent with a behavioral theory approach.
5. Penrosean firm growth suggests that boundedly rational managers make decisions that lead to path-dependent exploitation of the current bundle of resources and knowledge into *adjacent* activities (Gancarczyk 2016). As such, a sense of distance is implied.
6. Note that critical realists accept that how we perceive the world is highly dependent on pre-existing explanations of reality, even if those explanations are partial or unrealistic (Lam 2010; Mir and Watson 2001).
7. We thank the series editor for suggesting a reference which points to this.
8. See Note 12 in Chapter 1 and Point 2 in Sect. 1.5 regarding the 'equilibrium contracting' and the remediability or remediableness criterion in

traditional TCE. Even though longitudinal data can be used in models based on either behavioral TCE or traditional TCE, longitudinal analysis in the latter case can at best be regarded as pseudo-longitudinal analysis. This is for several reasons. First, such analysis is concerned with the comparison of governance forms (David and Han 2004) as a result of *random* external environmental change (as mentioned in Subsect. 7.3.1). Second, 'equilibrium contracting' is still at the core of such analysis at each round of comparison. Third, systematic behavioral effect is not considered. As such, the seemingly dynamic analysis using longitudinal data based on traditional TCE is not behavioral in nature.

9. These advantages include its strong convergent validity based on Hofstede's scores (Magnusson et al. 2008) and stability over time (Beugelsdijk et al. 2015).
10. This should not be taken as a criticism of TCE in particular. To be tautological is the first criterion of a positive theory, as pointed by Milton Friedman in his classic 1953 essay (Johnsen 1995). Williamson (2008: 253–254) specifically pledged his allegiance to the positivist tradition and called 'would-be theories, in economics and throughout social sciences...to stand up and be counted – by making predictions and inviting empirical tests'.
11. While the 'property rights theory of the firm' (Grossman and Hart 1986; Hart 1995; Hart and Moore 1990) has been widely regarded as a formalization of TCE (Salanié 1997), it 'suppresses ex post governance issues by making two very strong assumptions: ex post payoffs are common knowledge and renegotiation to achieve the efficient ex post outcome is costless. Not only is common knowledge of payoffs a very strong assumption...but the idea of costless bargaining over complex contractual impasses is gratuitous' (Williamson 2002: 32). TCE is mainly concerned with the ex post stage of contract where maladaptation problems arise (Williamson 2002).

References

Adner, R., Polos, L., Ryall, M., & Sorenson, O. (2009). The case for formal theory. *Academy of Management Review, 34*(2), 201–208.

Aharoni, Y., Tihanyi, L., & Connelly, B. L. (2011). Managerial decision-making in international business. *Journal of World Business, 46*(2), 135–142.

Ahsan, M., & Musteen, M. (2011). Multinational enterprises' entry mode strategies and uncertainty. *International Journal of Management Reviews, 13*(4), 376–392.

Alchian, A. A. (1950). Uncertainty, evolution, and economic theory. *Journal of Political Economy, 58*(3), 211–221.

Aldrich, H. E. (2015). Dimly through a fog. In A. Fayolle & P. Riot (Eds.), *Rethinking entrepreneurship* (pp. 12–27). London: Routledge.

Alvarez, S. A., Afuah, A., & Gibson, C. (2018). Should management theories take uncertainty seriously? *Academy of Management Review, 43*(2), 69–72.

Ambos, B., & Håkanson, L. (2014). The concept of distance in international management research. *Journal of International Management, 20*(1), 1–7.

Archer, M. S. (1995). *Realist social theory: The morphogenetic approach.* Cambridge: Cambridge University Press.

Arend, R. J., Sarooghi, H., & Burkemper, A. C. (2016). Effectuation, not being pragmatic or process theorizing, remains ineffectual. *Academy of Management Review, 41*(3), 549–556.

Argote, L., & Greve, H. R. (2007). A behavioral theory of the firm—40 years and counting. *Organization Science, 18*(3), 337–349.

Artz, K. W. (1999). Buyer-supplier performance. *British Journal of Management, 10*(2), 113–126.

Asmussen, C. G., & Foss, N. J. (2014). Competitive advantage and the existence of the multinational corporation. *Global Strategy Journal, 4*(1), 49–54.

Augier, M. (2013). Behavioral theory of the firm. *M@n@gement, 16*(5): 636–652.

Azar, G., & Drogendijk, R. (2019). Ex-post performance implications of divergence of managers' perceptions of 'distance' from 'reality' in international business. *Management International Review, 59*(1), 67–92.

Balasubramanyam, V. N. (1994). The transnational corporation. *Business History, 36*(2), 83–89.

Barney, J. B., & Lee, W. (2000). Multiple considerations in making governance choices. In N. J. Foss & V. Mahnke (Eds.), *Competence, governance, and entrepreneurship* (pp. 304–317). Oxford: Oxford University Press.

Beckerman, W. (1956). Distance and the pattern of intra-European trade. *Review of Economics and Statistics, 38*(1), 31–40.

Berg, N., & Gigerenzer, G. (2010). As-if behavioral economics: Neoclassical economics in disguise? *History of Economic Ideas, 18*(1), 133–165.

Berry, H., Guillen, M., & Zhou, N. (2010). An institutional approach to cross-national distance. *Journal of International Business Studies, 41*(9), 1460–1480.

Berry, J. W. (1990). Imposed etics, emics, derived etics: Their conceptual and operational status in cross-cultural psychology. In T. N. Headland, K. L. Pike, & M. Harris (Eds.), *Emics and etics: The insider/outsider debate* (pp. 28–47). Newbury Park, CA: Sage.

Beugelsdijk, S., Maseland, R., & van Hoorn, A. (2015). Are scores on Hofstede's dimensions of national culture stable over time? *Global Strategy Journal, 5*(3), 223–240.

Beugelsdijk, S., Kostova, T., Kunst, V. E., Spadafora, E., & van Essen, M. (2018). Cultural distance and firm internationalization. *Journal of Management, 44*(1), 89–130.
Bhaskar, R. (1986). *Scientific realism and human emancipation*. London: Routledge.
Bhaskar, R. (2008). *A realist theory of science*. London: Routledge.
Bhaskar, R. (2010). Contexts of interdisciplinarity. In R. Bhaskar, C. Frank, K. G. Høyer, P. Naess, & J. Parker (Eds.), *Interdisciplinarity and climate change* (pp. 15–38). London: Routledge.
Boddewyn, J. J., & Iyer, G. (1999). International-business research: Beyond déjà vu. *Management International Review, 39*(2), 161–184.
Boettcher, W. A. (1995). Context, methods, numbers, and words. *Journal of Conflict Resolution, 39*(3), 561–583.
Boulding, K. E. (1956). *The image: Knowledge in life and society*. Ann Arbor: University of Michigan Press.
Brouthers, K. D. (2002). Institutional, cultural and transaction cost influences on entry mode choice and performance. *Journal of International Business Studies, 33*(2), 203–221.
Brouthers, K. D., & Brouthers, L. E. (2001). Explaining the national cultural distance paradox. *Journal of International Business Studies, 32*(1), 177–189.
Brouthers, K. D., & Hennart, J. F. (2007). Boundaries of the firm: Insights from international entry mode research. *Journal of Management, 33*(3), 395–425.
Bruch, E., & Feinberg, F. (2017). Decision-making processes in social contexts. *Annual Review of Sociology, 43*, 207–227.
Buckley, P. J. (1988). The limits of explanation: Testing the internalization theory of the multinational enterprise. *Journal of International Business Studies, 19*(2), 181–193.
Buckley, P. J. (2002). Is the international business research agenda running out of steam? *Journal of International Business Studies, 33*(2), 365–373.
Buckley, P. J., & Casson, M. (1976). *The future of the multinational enterprise* (Vol. 1). London: Macmillan.
Buckley, P. J., & Casson, M. (1996). An economic model of international joint venture strategy. *Journal of International Business Studies, 27*(5), 849–876.
Buckley, P. J., & Casson, M. (2003). The future of the multinational enterprise in retrospect and in prospect. *Journal of International Business Studies, 34*(2), 219–222.
Buckley, P. J., & Casson, M. (2009). The internalization theory of the multinational enterprise. *Journal of International Business Studies, 40*(9), 1563–1580.
Buckley, P. J., & Chapman, M. (1997). The use of native categories in management research. *British Journal of Management, 8*(4), 283–299.

Buckley, P. J., & Chapman, M. (2002). Transactions costs and uncertainty: Theory and practice. In S. C. Dow & J. Hillard (Eds.), *Post Keynesian Econometrics, Microeconomics and the Theory of the Firm* (pp. 44–59). Cheltenham, UK: Edward Elgar.

Buckley, P. J., & Hashai, N. (2009). Formalizing internationalization in the eclectic paradigm. *Journal of International Business Studies, 40*(1), 58–70.

Buckley, P. J., Chapman, M., Clegg, J., & Gajewska-De, Mattos H. (2014). A linguistic and philosophical analysis of emic and etic and their use in international business research. *Management International Review, 54*(3), 307–324.

Bunge, M. (1997). Mechanism and explanation. *Philosophy of the Social Sciences, 27*(4), 410–465.

Burrell, G., & Morgan, G. (2017). *Sociological paradigms and organizational analysis*. New York, NY: Routledge.

Busemeyer, M. R., Abrassart, A., Nezi, S., & Nezi, R. (2020). Beyond positive and negative. *British Journal of Political Science*, 1–26.

Cantwell, J. A., Dunning, J. H., & Lundan, S. M. (2010). An evolutionary approach to understanding international business activity. *Journal of International Business Studies, 41*(4), 567–586.

Chapman, M., Gajewska-De Mattos, H., Clegg, J., & Buckley, P. J. (2008). Close neighbours and distant friends—Perceptions of cultural distance. *International Business Review, 17*(3), 217–234.

Cheok, J. B. C. (2016). *'Friction' in cross-cultural service interactions*. (Doctoral dissertation). Victoria University.

Chi, T., Li, J., Trigeorgis, L. G., & Tsekrekos, A. E. (2019). Real options theory in international business. *Journal of International Business Studies, 50*(4), 525–553.

Chi, T., & McGuire, D. J. (1996). Collaborative ventures and value of learning. *Journal of International Business Studies, 27*(2), 285–307.

Child, J., Faulkner, D., Tallman, S., & Hsieh, L. (2019). *Cooperative strategy: Managing alliances and networks*. Oxford: Oxford University Press.

Clark, P., & Blundel, R. (2007). Penrose, critical realism and the evolution of business knowledge. *Management & Organizational History, 2*(1), 45–62.

Clegg, J. (1987). *Multinational enterprise and world competition*. London: Macmillan.

Coase, R. H. (1937). The nature of the firm. *Economica, 4*(16), 386–405.

Coase, R. H. (1991). *The institutional structure of production*. Nobel Prize Lecture. https://www.nobelprize.org/prizes/economic-sciences/1991/coase/lecture/. Accessed 21 May 2020.

Cotei, C., & Farhat, J. (2017). The leasing decisions of startup firms. *Review of Pacific Basin Financial Markets and Policies, 20*(04), 1750022.

Cuypers, I. R. P., & Martin, X. (2010). What makes and what does not make a real option? *Journal of International Business Studies, 41*(1), 47–69.

Cyert, R. M., & March, J. G. (1963). *A behavioral theory of the firm*. Oxford: Blackwell.

Daniels, J. D., Ogram, E. W., & Radebaugh, L. H. (1976). *International business: Environments and operations*. Reading, MA: Addison-Wesley.

Dastidar, P., & Zaheer, S. (2010). *Dealing with information asymmetry in cross-border acquisitions*. Best Paper Proceedings, Academy of Management Annual Meeting, Montreal, Canada.

David, R. J., & Han, S. (2004). A systematic assessment of the empirical support for transaction cost economics. *Strategic Management Journal, 25*(1), 39–58.

De Vita, G., Tekaya, A., & Wang, C. L. (2010). Asset specificity's impact on outsourcing relationship performance. *Journal of Business Research, 63*(7), 657–666.

De Vita, G., Tekaya, A., & Wang, C. L. (2011). The many faces of asset specificity: A critical review of key theoretical perspectives. *International Journal of Management Reviews, 13*(4), 329–348.

De Weck, O., Eckert, C. M., & Clarkson, P. J. (2007). A classification of uncertainty for early product and system design. In *Proceedings of ICED 2007*.

Delios, A. (2017). The death and rebirth (?) of international business research. *Journal of Management Studies, 54*(3), 391–397.

Delios, A., & Beamish, P. W. (1999). Ownership strategy of Japanese firms. *Strategic Management Journal, 20*(10), 915–933.

Danermark, B., Ekström, M., & Karlsson, J. C. (2019). *Explaining society: Critical realism in the social sciences*. London: Routledge.

Dikova, D., & Brouthers, K. D. (2009). Establishment mode choice. In M. Kotabe & K. Helsen (Eds.), *Sage Handbook of International Marketing* (pp. 218–237). London: Sage.

Dietrich, M. (1994). *Transaction cost economics and beyond*. London: Routledge.

Donaldson, L. (1990). The ethereal hand. *Academy of Management Review, 15*(3), 369–381.

Dörrenbächer, C., & Geppert, M. (2017). Multinational corporations and organization theory: An introduction to post-millennium perspectives. In C. Dörrenbächer & M. Geppert (Eds.), *Multinational corporations and organization theory* (pp. 3–42). Emerald: Bingley.

Dow, D., Baack, D., & Parente, R. (2019). The role of psychic distance in entry mode decisions. *Global Strategy Journal, 10*(2), 309–334.

Drogendijk, R., & Holm, U. (2012). Cultural distance or cultural positions? *International Business Review, 21*(3), 383–396.

Dunning, J. H. (1977). Trade, location of economic activity and the MNE: A search for an eclectic approach. In P.-O. Hesselborn, B. Ohlin, & P. M.

Wijkman (Eds.), *The international allocation of economic activity* (pp. 395–418). London: Palgrave Macmillan.
Dunning, J. H. (1980). Toward an eclectic theory of international production. *Journal of International Business Studies, 11*(1), 9–31.
Dunning, J. H. (1981). *International production and the multinational enterprise*. London: Allen & Unwin.
Dunning, J. H. (1988). The eclectic paradigm of international production. *Journal of International Business Studies, 19*(1), 1–31.
Dunning, J. H. (2000). The eclectic paradigm as an envelope for economic and business theories of MNE activity. *International Business Review, 9*(2), 163–190.
Dunning, J. H. (2001a). The eclectic (OLI) paradigm of international production. *International Journal of the Economics of Business, 8*(2), 173–190.
Dunning, J. H. (2001b). The key literature on IB activities: 1996–2000. In A. C. Rugman & T. L. Brewer (Eds.), *Oxford handbook of international business* (pp. 33–68). Oxford: Oxford University Press.
Dunning, J. H., & Lundan, S. M. (2008). *Multinational enterprises and the global economy*. Cheltenham, UK: Edward Elgar.
Dunning, J. H., & Rugman, A. H. (1985). The influence of Hymer's dissertation on the theory of foreign direct investment. *American Economic Review, 75*(2), 228–232.
Eden, L., & Dai, L. (2010). Rethinking the O in Dunning's OLI/eclectic paradigm. *Multinational Business Review, 18*(2), 13–34.
Ferreira, M. P., Pinto, C., Serra, F., & Filipe, L. (2011). John Dunning's influence in international business/strategy research. *Journal of Strategic Management Education, 7*(2), 1–24.
Fisch, J. H. (2008). Investment in new foreign subsidiaries under receding perception of uncertainty. *Journal of International Business Studies, 39*(3), 370–386.
Folta, T. B. (1998). Governance and uncertainty. *Strategic Management Journal, 19*(11), 1007–1028.
Foss, N. J. (1994). The two Coasian traditions. *Review of Political Economy, 6*(1), 37–61.
Foss, N. J. (1997). Evolutionary and contractual theories of the firm: How do they relate? *Rivista Internazionale Di Scienze Sociali, 105*(3), 309–337.
Foss, N. J. (2003a). The rhetorical dimensions of bounded rationality. In S. Rizzello (Ed.), *Cognitive developments in economics* (pp. 158–176). London: Routledge.
Foss, N. J. (2003b). Bounded rationality in the economics of organization. *Journal of Economic Psychology, 24*(2), 245–264.

Foss, N. J., & Grandori, A. (2020). Entrepreneurship and the firm. *Industrial and Corporate Change, 29*(3), 581–598.
Foss, N. J., & Hallberg, N. L. (2014). How symmetrical assumptions advance strategic management research. *Strategic Management Journal, 35*(6), 903–913.
Foss, N. J., & Hallberg, N. L. (2017). Changing assumptions and progressive change in theories of strategic organization. *Strategic Organization, 15*(3), 410–422.
Foss, N. J., & Weber, L. (2016a). Expand bounded rationality. *Academy of Management Review, 41*(4), 741–744.
Foss, N. J., & Weber, L. (2016b). Moving opportunism to the back seat. *Academy of Management Review, 41*(1), 61–79.
Friedman, M. (1974). Explanation and scientific understanding. *Journal of Philosophy, 71*(1), 5–19.
Gancarczyk, M. (2016). The integrated resource-based and transaction cost approach to the growth process of firms. *Journal of Organizational Change Management, 29*(7), 1189–1216.
Geary, J., & Aguzzoli, R. (2016). Miners, politics and institutional caryatids. *Journal of International Business Studies, 47*(8), 968–996.
Geyskens, I., Steenkamp, J. B. E. M., & Kumar, N. (2006). Make, buy, or ally. *Academy of Management Journal, 49*(3), 519–543.
Ghemawat, P. (2001). Distance still matters. *Harvard Business Review, 79*(8), 137–147.
Ghoshal, S., & Moran, P. (1996). Bad for practice. *Academy of Management Review, 21*(1), 13–47.
Gigerenzer, G. (2000). *Adaptive thinking: Rationality in the real world*. Oxford: Oxford University Press.
Gooris, J., & Peeters, C. (2014). Home-host country distance in offshore governance choices. *Journal of International Management, 20*(1), 73–86.
Greve, H. R., & Argote, L. (2015). Behavioral theories of organization. In J. D. Wright (Ed.), *International encyclopedia of the social & behavioral sciences* (pp. 481–486). Amsterdam: Elsevier.
Grossman, S. J., & Hart, O. D. (1986). The costs and benefits of ownership. *Journal of Political Economy, 94*(4), 691–719.
Håkanson, L., & Ambos, B. (2010). The antecedents of psychic distance. *Journal of International Management, 16*(3), 195–210.
Harris, M. (2001). *The rise of anthropological theory: A history of theories of culture*. London: AltaMira.
Hart, O. D. (1990). Is "bounded rationality" an important element of a theory of institutions? *Journal of Institutional and Theoretical Economics, 146*(4), 696–702.

Hart, O. D. (1995). *Firms, contracts and financial structure*. New York: Oxford University Press.
Hart, O. D., & Moore, J. (1990). Property rights and the nature of the firm. *Journal of Political Economy, 98*(6), 1119–1158.
Harzing, A. W., & Pudelko, M. (2016). Do we need to distance ourselves from the distance concept? *Management International Review, 56*(1), 1–34.
Hennart, J. F. (1982). *A theory of multinational enterprise*. Ann Arbor, MI: University of Michigan Press.
Hennart, J. F. (2010). Transaction cost theory and international business. *Journal of Retailing, 86*(3), 257–269.
Hennart, J. F., & Slangen, A. H. (2015). Yes, we really do need more entry mode studies! *Journal of International Business Studies, 46*(1), 114–122.
Héritier, A., Müller-Debus, A. K., & Thauer, C. R. (2009). The firm as an inspector: A transaction cost explanation of private ordering. *Business and Politics, 11*(4), 1–32.
Heuer, R. J. (1999). *Psychology of intelligence analysis*. Washington, DC: CIA.
Hodgson, G. M. (1998). Evolutionary and competence-based theories of the firm. *Journal of Economic Studies, 25*(1), 25–56.
Hodgson, G. M. (2004). Opportunism is not the only reason why firms exist. *Industrial and Corporate Change, 13*(2), 401–418.
Hofstede, G. (1991). *Cultures and organizations: Software of the mind*. London: McGraw-Hill.
Holland, M. (2019). *Transaction cost economics: Applications to competition policy in South Africa*. Paper Presented at the Fifth Annual Conference on Competition Law, Economics and Policy, University of Johannesburg.
Hu, X. (2018). Methodological implications of critical realism for entrepreneurship research. *Journal of Critical Realism, 17*(2), 118–139.
Huitink, Z. S. (2017). *Three essays on public procurement* (Dissertations—ALL. 698). https://surface.syr.edu/etd/698.
Hutzschenreuter, T., Voll, J. C., & Verbeke, A. (2011). The impact of added cultural distance and cultural diversity on international expansion patterns: A Penrosean perspective. *Journal of Management Studies, 48*(2), 305–329.
Hymer, S. H. (1976). *The international operations of national firms: A study of foreign direct investment*. Cambridge, MA: MIT Press.
Jack, G. A., Calás, M. B., Nkomo, S. M., & Peltonen, T. (2008). Critique and international management: An uneasy relationship? *Academy of Management Review, 33*(4), 870–884.
Johanson, J., & Vahlne, J. E. (1977). The internationalization process of the firm. *Journal of International Business Studies, 8*(1), 23–32.
Johnsen, D. B. (1995). The Quasi-rent structure of corporate enterprise: A transaction cost theory. *Emory Law Journal, 44*(4), 1277–1356.

Joseph, J., & Wilson, A. J. (2018). The growth of the firm: An attention-based view. *Strategic Management Journal, 39*(6), 1779–1800.

Joskow, P. L. (1988). Asset specificity and the structure of vertical relationships. *Journal of Law Economics and Organization, 4*(1), 95–117.

Kedia, B. L., & Mukherjee, D. (2009). Understanding offshoring: A research framework based on disintegration, location and externalization advantages. *Journal of World Business, 44*(3), 250–261.

Ketokivi, M., & Mahoney, J. T. (2016). Transaction cost economics as a constructive stakeholder theory. *Academy of Management Learning & Education, 15*(1), 123–138.

Kim, Y., & Vonortas, N. S. (2006). Technology licensing partners. *Journal of Economics and Business, 58*(4), 273–289.

Kirkman, B. L., Lowe, K. B., & Gibson, C. B. (2006). A quarter century of culture's consequences. *Journal of International Business Studies, 37*(3), 285–320.

Kitching, J., & Rouse, J. (2020). Contesting effectuation theory. *International Small Business Journal, 38*(6), 515–535.

Kogut, B., & Singh, H. (1988). The effect of national culture on the choice of entry mode. *Journal of International Business Studies, 19*(3), 411–432.

Kogut, B., & Zander, U. (1993). Knowledge of the firm and the evolutionary theory of the multinational corporation. *Journal of International Business Studies, 24*(4), 625–645.

Kuorikoski, J., & Lehtinen, A. (2010). Economics imperialism and solution concepts in political science. *Philosophy of the Social Sciences, 40*(3), 347–374.

Kvaløy, O. (2007). Asset specificity and vertical integration. *Scandinavian Journal of Economics, 109*(3), 551–572.

Lam, S. (2010). What kind of assumptions need to be realistic and how to test them: A response to Tsang (2006). *Strategic Management Journal, 31*(6), 679–687.

Lane, P. J., Koka, B. R., & Pathak, S. (2006). The reification of absorptive capacity: A critical review and rejuvenation of the construct. *Academy of Management Review, 31*(4), 833–863.

Langlois, R. N. (1989). Rationality, institutions, and explanation. In R. N. Langlois (Ed.), *Economics as a process* (pp. 225–255). Cambridge: Cambridge University Press.

Lawson, T. (2003). *Reorienting economics*. London: Routledge.

Leca, B., & Naccache, P. (2006). A critical realist approach to institutional entrepreneurship. *Organization, 13*(5), 627–651.

Lehtinen, A. (2012). Uskali Mäki's realist philosophy of economics. In A. Lehtinen, J. Kuorikoski, & P. Ylikoski (Eds.), *Economics for real: Uskali Mäki and the place of truth in economics* (pp. 1–40). New York: Routledge.

Leiblein, M. J. (2003). The choice of organizational governance form and performance. *Journal of Management, 29*(6), 937–961.
Leiblein, M. J., Chen, J. S., & Posen, H. E. (2017). Resource allocation in strategic factor markets. *Journal of Management, 43*(8), 2588–2608.
Lessard, D., Teece, D. J., & Leih, S. (2016). The dynamic capabilities of meta-multinationals. *Global Strategy Journal, 6*(3), 211–224.
Li, P. P. (2007). Toward an integrated theory of multinational evolution. *Journal of International Management, 13*(3), 296–318.
Liesch, P. W., Welch, L. S., & Buckley, P. J. (2011). Risk and uncertainty in internationalization and international entrepreneurship studies. *Management International Review, 51*(6), 851–873.
Lo, A. W. (2005). Reconciling efficient markets with behavioral finance: The adaptive markets hypothesis. *Journal of Investment Consulting, 7*(2), 21–44.
Lo, A. W. (2017). *Adaptive markets: Financial evolution at the speed of thought*. Princeton: Princeton University Press.
Losee, J. (2005). *Theories on the scrap heap*. Pittsburgh, PA: University of Pittsburgh Press.
Lubatkin, M., Lane, P., Collin, S., & Very, P. (2007). An embeddedness framing of governance and opportunism: Towards a cross-nationally accommodating theory of agency. *Journal of Organization Behavior, 28*(1), 43–58.
Lumineau, F., & Verbeke, A. (2016). Let's give opportunism the proper back seat. *Academy of Management Review, 41*(4), 739–741.
Lundan, S. M. (2010). What are ownership advantages? *Multinational Business Review, 18*(2), 51–69.
Macher, J. T., & Richman, B. D. (2008). Transaction cost economics. *Business and Politics, 10*(1), Article 1.
Magnusson, P., Baack, D. W., Zdravkovic, S., Staub, K. M., & Amine, L. S. (2008). Meta-analysis of cultural differences. *International Business Review, 17*(5), 520–532.
Mahoney, J. T. (1992). The choice of organizational form. *Strategic Management Journal, 13*(8), 559–584.
Mahoney, J. T. (2004). *Economic foundations of strategy*. London: Sage.
Mäki, U. (1990). Scientific realism and Austrian explanation. *Review of Political Economy, 2*(3), 310–344.
Mäki, U. (2001). Explanatory unification: Double and doubtful. *Philosophy of the Social Sciences, 31*(4), 488–506.
Mäki, U. (2004). Theoretical isolation and explanatory progress: Transaction cost economics and the dynamics of dispute. *Cambridge Journal of Economics, 28*(3), 319–346.
Mäki, U. (2009a). Economics imperialism: Concept and constraints. *Philosophy of the Social Sciences, 39*(3), 351–380.

Mäki, U. (2009b). Realistic realism about unrealistic models. In H. Kincaid & D. Ross (Eds.), *Oxford handbook of the philosophy of economics* (pp. 68–98). Oxford: Oxford University Press.

Manne, G. A., & Zywicki, T. J. (2014). Uncertainty, evolution and behavioral economic theory. *Journal of Law, Economics & Policy, 10*(3), 555–580.

Martin, R. (1993). The new behaviorism: A critique of economics and organization. *Human Relations, 46*(9), 1085–1101.

Mariyani-Squire, E. (2017). Critical reflections on a realist interpretation of Friedman's 'methodology of positive economics'. *Journal of Economic Methodology, 24*(1), 69–89.

Maseland, R., Dow, D., & Steel, P. (2018). The Kogut and Singh national cultural distance index: Time to start using it as a springboard rather than a crutch. *Journal of International Business Studies, 49*(9), 1154–1166.

Mathews, J. A. (2002). Competitive advantages of the latecomer firm: A resource-based account of industrial catch-up strategies. *Asia Pacific Journal of Management, 19*(4), 467–488.

Miller, C. C., & Bamberger, P. (2016). Exploring emergent and poorly understood phenomena in the strangest of places. *Academy of Management Discoveries, 2*(4), 313–319.

Miller, K. D. (1992). A framework for integrated risk management in international business. *Journal of International Business Studies, 23*(2), 311–331.

Miller, K. D., & Tsang, E. W. (2011). Testing management theories: Critical realist philosophy and research methods. *Strategic Management Journal, 32*(2), 139–158.

Miller, R., & Lessard, D. R. (2001). *The strategic management of large engineering projects*. Cambridge, MA: MIT Press.

Mir, R., & Watson, A. (2001). Critical realism and constructivism in strategy research. *Strategic Management Journal, 22*(12), 1169–1173.

Morosini, P. (1998). *Managing cultural differences: Effective strategy and execution across cultures in global corporate Alliances*. Oxford: Pergamon.

Morosini, P., Shane, S., & Singh, H. (1998). National cultural distance and cross-border acquisition performance. *Journal of International Business Studies, 29*(1), 137–158.

Moroz, P. W., & Hindle, K. (2012). Entrepreneurship as a process: Toward harmonizing multiple perspectives. *Entrepreneurship Theory and Practice, 36*(4), 781–818.

Morris, M. W., Leung, K., Ames, D., & Lickel, B. (1999). Views from inside and outside: Integrating emic and etic insights about culture and justice judgment. *Academy of Management Review, 24*(4), 781–796.

Morschett, D., Schramm-Klein, H., & Swoboda, B. (2010). Decades of research on market entry modes: What do we really know about external antecedents of entry mode choice? *Journal of International Management, 16*(1), 60–77.

Narula, R., Asmussen, C. G., Chi, T., & Kundu, S. K. (2019). Applying and advancing internalization theory. *Journal of International Business Studies, 50*(8), 1231–1252.

Nelson, R. R., & Winter, S. G. (1982). *An evolutionary theory of economic change*. Cambridge, MA: Belknap Press of Harvard University Press.

North, D. C. (1990). *Institutions, institutional change, and economic performance*. New York: Cambridge University Press.

Novarese, M. (2009). *Is bounded rationality a capacity, enabling learning?* (EERI Research Paper Series [No. 12/2009]).

Panksepp, J. (2003). An archaeology of mind: The ancestral sources of human feelings. *Soundings: An Interdisciplinary Journal, 86*(1/2), 41–69.

Panksepp, J. (2004). *Affective neuroscience: The foundations of human and animal emotions*. New York: Oxford University Press.

Pedersen, T., Petersen, B., & Benito, G. R. (2002). Change of foreign operation method: Impetus and switching costs. *International Business Review, 11*(3), 325–345.

Peng, G. Z. (2012). FDI legitimacy and MNC subsidiary control: From legitimation to competition. *Journal of International Management, 18*(2), 115–131.

Peng, G. Z., & Beamish, P. W. (2014). The effect of host country long term orientation on subsidiary ownership and survival. *Asia Pacific Journal of Management, 31*(2), 423–453.

Peng, G. Z., & Beamish, P. W. (2019). Subnational FDI legitimacy and foreign subsidiary survival. *Journal of International Management, 25*(3), Article 100662.

Peng, G. Z., & Camp, R. D. (2015). Temporal distance and subsidiary control. *Academy of Management Proceedings, 2015*(1): Article 11840.

Penrose, E. T. (1959). *The theory of the growth of the firm*. Oxford: Oxford University Press.

Penrose, E. T. (1987). Multinational corporations. In J. Eatwell, P. Newman, & M. Milgate (Eds.), *The new Palgrave: A dictionary of economics* (pp. 562–564). London: Macmillan.

Penrose, E. T. (1995). *The theory of the growth of the firm* (3rd ed.). Oxford: Oxford University Press.

Penrose, E. T. (1996). Growth of the firm and networking. In M. Warner (Ed.), *International encyclopaedia of business and management* (pp. 1716–1724). London: Routledge.

Pessali, H. F. (2006). The rhetoric of Oliver Williamson's transaction cost economics. *Journal of Institutional Economics, 2*(1), 45–65.

Pfeffer, J., & Salancik, G. (1978). *The external control of organizations*. New York: Harper & Row.

Pitelis, C. N. (2004). Edith Penrose and the resource-based view of (international) business strategy. *International Business Review, 13*(4), 523–532.

Pitelis, C. N. (2007). A behavioral resource-based view of the firm: The synergy of Cyert and March (1963) and Penrose (1959). *Organization Science, 18*(3), 478–490.

Pitelis, C. N. (2009). Introduction: 'Edith Penrose's 'the theory of the growth of the firm' fifty years later. In E. Penrose (Ed.), *The theory of the growth of the firm* (4th ed., ix–xlvii). Oxford: Oxford University Press.

Pitelis, C. N. (2011). A knowledge: Learning-based perspective on foreign direct investment and the multinational enterprise. In P. Nijkamp & I. Siedschlag (Eds.), *Innovation, growth and competitiveness* (pp. 221–234). Berlin: Springer.

Pitelis, C. N., & Teece, D. J. (2018). The new MNE: 'Orchestration' theory as envelope of 'internalisation' theory. *Management International Review, 58*(4), 523–539.

Pitelis, C. N., & Verbeke, A. (2007). Edith Penrose and the future of the multinational enterprise. *Management International Review, 47*(2), 139–149.

Pleggenkuhle-Miles, E. G., & Peng, M. W. (2009). Embracing debates to advance global strategy research. In D. D. Bergh & D. J. Ketchen (Ed.), *Research methodology in strategy and management* (Vol. 5, pp. 301–318). Bingley: Emerald.

Popper, K. R. (1959). *The Logic of scientific discovery.* New York, NY: Harper Zorch Books.

Poppo, L., & Zenger, T. (1998). Testing alternative theories of the firm. *Strategic Management Journal, 19*(9), 853–877.

Posen, H. E., Leiblein, M. J., & Chen, J. S. (2018). Toward a behavioral theory of real options. *Strategic Management Journal, 39*(4), 1112–1138.

Poulis, K., & Poulis, E. (2018). International business as disciplinary tautology: An ontological perspective. *Academy of Management Perspectives, 32*(4), 517–531.

Pratten, S. (2009). Critical realism and causality: Tracing the Aristotelian legacy. *Journal for the Theory of Social Behaviour, 39*(2), 189–218.

Rabin, M. (2002). A perspective on psychology and economics. *European Economic Review, 46*(4/5), 657–685.

Ramanathan, K., Seth, A., & Thomas, H. (1997). Explaining joint ventures. In P. Beamish & J. Killing (Eds.), *Competitive strategies: North American perspectives* (pp. 51–85). San Francisco, CA: New Lexington.

Reus, T. H., & Rottig, D. (2009). Meta-analyses of international joint venture performance determinants. *Management International Review, 49*(5), 607–640.

Rieger, M. O., Wang, M., & Hens, T. (2015). Risk preferences around the world. *Management Science, 61*(3), 637–648.

Rugman, A. M. (1981). *Inside the multinationals: The economics of internal markets*. New York: Columbia University Press.
Rugman, A. M. (1986). New theories of the multinational enterprise: An assessment of internalization theory. *Bulletin of Economic Research, 38*(2), 101–118.
Rugman, A. M. (2010). Reconciling internalization theory and the eclectic paradigm. *Multinational Business Review, 18*(2), 1–12.
Rygh, A. (2013). Inherited philosophy of science? Economics and international business research. In T. M. Devinney, T. Pedersen, & L. Tihanyi (Eds.), *Advances in international management* (Vol. 26, pp. 91–125). Bingley, UK: Emerald.
Safarian, A. E. (2003). Internalization and the MNE: A note on the spread of ideas. *Journal of International Business Studies, 34*(2), 116–124.
Salanié, B. (1997). *The economics of contracts: A primer*. Cambridge, MA: MIT Press.
Sampson, R. C. (2004). The cost of misaligned governance in R&D alliances. *Journal of Law Economics and Organization, 20*(2), 484–526.
Sanchez, R. (2003). Integrating transaction costs theory and real options theory. *Managerial and Decision Economics, 24*(4), 267–282.
Schilton, D. (2005). Externalization-internalization. In A. de Mijolla (Ed.), *International dictionary of psychoanalysis* (p. 537). Detroit: Macmillan Reference USA.
Schwartz, S. H. (1992). Universals in the content and structure of values. In M. P. Zanna (Ed.), *Advances in experimental social psychology* (Vol. 25, pp. 1–65). Orlando, FL: Academic Press.
Selten, R. (1998). Features of experimentally observed bounded rationality. *European Economic Review, 42*(3–5), 413–436.
Shaver, J. M. (2013). Do we really need more entry mode studies? *Journal of International Business Studies, 44*(1), 23–27.
Shenkar, O. (2001). Cultural distance revisited: Towards a more rigorous conceptualization and measurement of cultural differences. *Journal of International Business Studies, 32*(3), 519–535.
Shenkar, O. (2012). Beyond cultural distance. *Journal of International Business Studies, 43*(1), 12–17.
Shenkar, O., Luo, Y., & Yeheskel, O. (2008). From 'distance' to 'friction'. *Academy of Management Review, 33*(4), 905–923.
Simon, H. A. (1978). Rationality as process and as product of thought. *American Economic Review, 68*(2), 1–16.
Simon, H. A. (1979). Rational decision making in business organizations. *American Economic Review, 69*(4), 493–513.
Slangen, A. H. L., & van Tulder, R. J. M. (2009). Cultural distance, political risk, or governance quality? *International Business Review, 18*(3), 276–291.

Slater, G., & Spencer, D. A. (2000). The uncertain foundations of transaction costs economics. *Journal of Economic Issues, 34*(1), 61–87.

Solberg, C. A., & Askeland, V. (2006). The relevance of internationalization theories: A contingency framework. In F. M. Fai & E. J. Morgan (Eds.), *Managerial issues in international business* (pp. 9–32). London: Palgrave Macmillan.

Spender, J. C. (1994). Organizational knowledge, collective practice and Penrose rents. *International Business Review, 3*(4), 353–367.

Spender, J. C. (2018). Managing—According to Williamson, or to Coase? *Kindai Management Review, 6*, 13–34.

Stahl, G. K., Miska, C., Lee, H.-J., & De Luque, M. S. (2017). The upside of cultural differences. *Cross Cultural and Strategic Management, 24*(1), 2–12.

Stahl, G. K., & Tung, R. L. (2015). Towards a more balanced treatment of culture in international business studies. *Journal of International Business Studies, 46*(4), 391–414.

Stoltz, D. S. (2018). Relations and relationships. *American Sociologist, 49*(1), 64–79.

Sutcliffe, K. M., & Zaheer, A. (1998). Uncertainty in the transaction environment. *Strategic Management Journal, 19*(1), 1–23.

Taylor, A. B., West, S. G., & Aiken, L. S. (2006). Loss of power in logistic, ordinal logistic, and probit regression when an outcome variable is coarsely categorized. *Educational and Psychological Measurement, 66*(2), 228–239.

Thauer, C. R. (2014). Goodness comes from within: Intra-organizational dynamics of corporate social responsibility. *Business and Society, 53*(4), 483–516.

Tihanyi, L., Griffith, D. A., & Russell, C. J. (2005). The effect of cultural distance on entry mode choice, international diversification, and MNE performance: A meta-analysis. *Journal of International Business Studies, 36*(3), 270–283.

Trigeorgis, L. (2014). *Real options with bounded rationality* (Working Paper).

Trout, J. D. (2007). The psychology of discounting. *Public Affairs Quarterly, 21*(2), 201–220.

Tsang, E. W. K. (2006). Behavioral assumptions and theory development. *Strategic Management Journal, 27*(11), 999–1011.

Tung, R. L., & Verbeke, A. (2010). Beyond Hofstede and GLOBE: Improving the quality of cross-cultural research. *Journal of International Business Studies, 41*(8), 1259–1274.

Turner, J. H. (2007). *Human emotions*. New York: Routledge.

Tversky, B. (1992). Distortions in cognitive maps. *Geoforum, 23*(2), 131–138.

Tversky, B. (2003). Structures of mental spaces: How people think about space. *Environment and Behavior, 35*(1), 66–80.

Vaccarini, K., Spigarelli, F., Tavoletti, E., & Lattemann, C. (2017). *Cultural distance in international ventures*. Cham: Springer.
Vahlne, J. E., & Johanson, J. (2013). The Uppsala model on evolution of the multinational business enterprise. *International Marketing Review, 30*(3), 189–210.
Verbeke, A. (2003). The evolutionary view of the MNE and the future of internalization theory. *Journal of International Business Studies, 34*(6), 498–504.
Verbeke, A., & Greidanus, N. S. (2009). The end of the opportunism vs. trust debate. *Journal of International Business Studies, 40*(9), 1471–1495.
Wang, H., & Schaan, J. L. (2008). How much distance do we need? Revisiting the 'national cultural distance paradox'. *Management International Review, 48*(3), 263–278.
Whinston, M. D. (2003). On the transaction cost determinants of vertical integration. *Journal of Law Economics and Organization, 19*(1), 1–23.
Wilkinson, T. J., Peng, G. Z., Brouthers, L. E., & Beamish, P. W. (2008). The diminishing effect of cultural distance on subsidiary control. *Journal of International Management, 14*(2), 93–107.
Williamson, O. E. (1975). *Markets and hierarchies*. New York: Free Press.
Williamson, O. E. (1983). Credible commitments: Using hostages to support exchange. *American Economic Review, 73*(4), 519–540.
Williamson, O. E. (1985). *The economic institutions of capitalism*. New York: Free Press.
Williamson, O. E. (1991). Comparative economic organization. *Administrative Science Quarterly, 36*(4), 269–296.
Williamson, O. E. (1993). The evolving science of organization. *Journal of Institutional and Theoretical Economics, 149*(1), 36–63.
Williamson, O. E. (1996). *The mechanisms of governance*. Oxford: Oxford University Press.
Williamson, O. E. (1998). Transaction cost economics: How it works; where it is headed. *De Economist, 146*(1), 23–58.
Williamson, O. E. (1999). Strategy research: Governance and competence perspectives. *Strategic Management Journal, 20*(12), 1087–1108.
Williamson, O. E. (2002). *The lens of contract: Applications to economic development and reform* (Working Paper for Forum 2). The Institutional Economics Approach to Aid Effectiveness.
Williamson, O. E. (2005). Transaction cost economics and business administration. *Scandinavian Journal of Management, 21*(1), 19–40.
Williamson, O. E. (2008). Friedman (1953) and the theory of the firm. In U. Mäki (Ed.), *The Methodology of Positive Economics* (pp. 241–256). Cambridge: Cambridge University Press.

Woodside, A. G., Pattinson, H. M., & Miller, K. E. (2005). Advancing hermeneutic research for interpreting interfirm new product development. *Journal of Business & Industrial Marketing, 20*(7), 364–379.

Wright, P., Kroll, M., Chan, P., & Hamel, K. (1991). Strategic profiles and performance. *Journal of the Academy of Marketing Science, 19*(3), 245–254.

Wulff, J. N. (2016). A systematic assessment of empirical research on foreign entry mode. *European Journal of Marketing, 50*(5/6), 942–972.

Xu, D., & Shenkar, O. (2002). Institutional distance and the multinational enterprise. *Academy of Management Review, 27*(4), 608–618.

Zaheer, S., Schomaker, M. S., & Nachum, L. (2012). Distance without direction: Restoring credibility to a much-loved construct. *Journal of International Business Studies, 43*(1), 18–27.

Zajac, E. J., & Olsen, C. P. (1993). From transaction cost to transactional value analysis. *Journal of Management Studies, 30*(1), 131–145.

Zeki, S. (2001). Artistic creativity and the brain. *Science, 293*(5527), 51–52.

Zhao, H., Luo, Y., & Suh, T. (2004). Transaction cost determinants and ownership-based entry mode choice. *Journal of International Business Studies, 35*(6), 524–544.

Zhu, Y., & Bargiela-Chiappini, F. (2013). Balancing emic and etic. *Academy of Management Learning & Education, 12*(3), 380–395.

Index

G. Z. Peng, *Toward Behavioral Transaction Cost Economics*, International Marketing and Management Research, https://doi.org/10.1007/978-3-030-46878-1

F

G

R

The manufacturer's authorised representative in the EU is Springer Nature Customer Service Centre GmbH, Europaplatz 3, 69115 Heidelberg, Germany. If you have any concerns regarding our products, please contact ProductSafety@springernature.com

Printed and bound by CPI Group (UK) Ltd, Croydon, CR0 4YY
30/09/2026
02225461-0019